Catholicism in Rhode Island

Catholicism in Rhode Island
and the
Diocese of Providence

1780-1886

by
Robert W. Hayman

Diocese of Providence
1982

This book is dedicated to the bishops, priests, religious and laity
whose lives and works are recounted in these pages.

List of Illustrations

Following page 170

Contents

              McFARLAND, 1858-1872
              The Diocese Awaits a New Bishop   145
              The Pastoral Task   148
              Rhode Island Catholics and the Civil War   149
              Renewed Attempts to Remove Constitutional Res-
                trictions   154
              Renewed Growth in Rhode Island   158
              The Incorporation of the Diocese in Connecticut
                and Rhode Island   177
              Recruitment of Clergy and Funding their Educa-
                tion   179
              Ministry to Canadian and German Catholics   180
              The Missionary Church   185
              Popular Devotions, Organizations and Causes   186
              Social Concerns of the Bishop and his Clergy   188
              The Division of the Diocese   191

Chapter V   THE EPISCOPATE OF BISHOP THOMAS F.
              HENDRICKEN, 1872-1886
              Thomas F. Hendricken—First Bishop of the Provi-
                dence Diocese   197
              The Pastoral Task and the Panic of 1873   201
              First Expansion of the Diocese Under Bishop Hen-
                dricken   207
              Ministry to the French Canadians   229
              Ministry to the Portuguese   242
              Ministry to the Germans, Italians and Black Cathol-
                ics   244
              Second Expansion of the Diocese under Bishop
                Hendricken   248
              New Educational and Social Agencies   256
              Problems Involving Priests and Pastoral Care   262
              The Church and Social Concerns   280
              Anti-Catholicism in the 1870s and 1880s   292
              The Struggle for Political Rights   299
              Catholic Awareness of a Unique Heritage   304
              A New Cathedral   305
              Bishop Hendricken in Retrospect   311

              BIBLIOGRAPHY   317

              INDEX   331

Preface

While Rhode Island inherited from Roger Williams an ideal that civil government accord all religious views equal respect, there was to be in reality a wide gap between the convictions of Williams and the prejudices of later Rhode Islanders. Confronted with the reality of Catholics living among them, native Rhode Islanders in time came to emphasize the differences between the natives and foreigners, not only in religious views, but also in customs, political traditions and later in language. Therefore, it is important to place the history of Catholicism in Rhode Island against the background of political, social, and economic developments within the state which both affected Catholics and were affected by them.

A significant factor in the formation of the character of the Catholic Church in Rhode Island was the diverse backgrounds of the Catholic immigrants, particularly that of the first sizable wave of immigrants, the Irish. As would all immigrants, the Irish recreated in America the religious practices and parochial traditions they knew in Ireland. Until the 1870s Irish ecclesiastical traditions and Irish clergy dominated the Catholic Church in Rhode Island.

When Irish immigration to Rhode Island slowed in the 1860s, Rhode Island employers found a new and closer source of labor for their mills among the *habitants* of French Canada. The French Canadians brought their own religious customs and traditions bound up as they believed with their French language. Many Irish clergymen in whose parishes the Canadians first settled found themselves unable to overcome the clash of traditions and consequently failed to effectively minister to their needs. The demands of Canadians for churches and priests of their own created profound tensions within the new Diocese of Providence. A climax was reached when the French Canadians of Notre Dame parish, Fall River attempted to force Bishop Thomas F. Hendricken to give them a French Canadian pastor. The question raised by the Canadians regarding their right to have a priest of their nationality presented grave problems not only to the bishop of Providence but carried with it important implications for the Catholic church in the United States as a whole.

Ultimately the history of Catholicism in Rhode Island and the Diocese of Providence is a history of individual people. Because of the scarcity of documents and the demands of space, it is by necessity a history of the leaders of the Catholic community, of the bishops and priests who shared their ministry. However, wherever possible, attention is paid to the many religious sisters and brothers, as well as laymen and women, without whose labor, zeal, cooperation and financial sacrifices the work of spiritual and temporal building up of the Church would have been impossible.

This study ends with the death of Bishop Thomas F. Hendricken in 1886. It was not the fact of the bishop's death alone that dictated ending the narrative at this point. Rather it was the conviction that by the decade of the 1880s the Catholic church in Rhode Island had become an integral part of the social, economic, and political fabric of the state. The sons of first generation Irish immigrants were beginning to win elective state-wide office and serve in increasing numbers in the state legislature. Foreign-born citizens had finally won the right to vote on an equal basis with native-born. The collective wealth of the Catholic community had grown to the point where they could erect a magnificent cathedral in Providence and at the same time support an ever increasing number of parish churches and schools. These successes did not mean that resistance to Catholic influence in the state had ended; it had merely retreated to other strongholds. In the decades ahead the major challenges to and difficulties of Catholicism would not come from without but from within.

Many people have played important roles in the production of this history. The initiative for this study and its early support came from Bishop Daniel P. Reilly during the time he was vicar general of the Diocese of Providence. Bishop Louis E. Gelineau and Bishop Kenneth A. Angell have continued to strongly support the project begun by Bishop Reilly. Dr. Patrick T. Conley has offered many valuable criticisms and insights as have many of my colleagues at Providence College and the Seminary of Our Lady of Providence. Dr. Conley's and Matthew J. Smith's *Catholicism in Rhode Island: The Formative Era,* which the Diocese of Providence published in 1976, is intended to complement this more detailed history.

Over the years this work has been in progress, many people have assisted its research and preparation. The staffs of the Providence Public Library's Microfilm Reading Room and the Rhode Island Historical Society Library were of particular help as were the staff of the University of Notre Dame Archives. Mr. Joseph Cichon and later Miss Elizabeth E. McDeed at the Providence Diocesan Archives as well as chancery officials and the archivists at the Boston and Hartford Chancery Offices also extended both courtesy and aid. While I am grateful for the help of many in typing the manuscript, Mrs. Angelina Marran deserves special thanks for her work in preparing the final drafts of the work. Finally, I wish to acknowledge the help I received from Mr. Paul Campbell who prepared the manuscript for the printer and guided this work through the process of printing. As always any responsibility for errors in this work is mine alone.

Robert W. Hayman
November 1, 1982

Chapter I

The Appearance of Catholicism in Rhode Island

French Troops in Rhode Island During the Revolution

The citizens of Newport gazed uneasily at the ships riding at anchor in the harbor. It was the eleventh of July 1780. At the mastheads of the ships flew the lillies of France. Seven months before, the last of the British troops that had occupied Newport for over two years had left. Now another army was preparing to disembark. Prejudice against the French and against Catholicism was part of the New England legacy. The Tory press could be counted on to take a certain satisfaction in the prospect of the landing of a French army in New England since, as they told their readers, it would mean the establishment of French government, customs and religion.[1]

At noon of that fateful day the Count de Rochambeau, the commander of the French land forces, came ashore with his aides. No one welcomed him. The streets were deserted and only a few sad and frightened faces peered at the Frenchmen from darkened windows. The French had been expected for two months. When news of their arrival off the Rhode Island coast was received in Providence, General William Heath, whom Washington had sent to Providence in June to prepare for their arrival, set off at once for Newport, but light winds delayed his arrival until midnight. Rochambeau stayed on shore that first night in a Newport hotel. The next morning General Heath and the town officials called on Rochambeau and made arrangements for landing his troops.

The French commander informed his visitors that his King, Louis XVI, had instructed him to commence operations under the command of General Washington and to consolidate the French

---

[1]For a sampling of Tory press statements, cf. DeB. Randolph Keim, *Rochambeau* (Washington: Government Printing Office, 1907), pp. 308, 320.

Army with the Army of the United Colonies. Rochambeau worked out with them the details of quartering his troops, adding that his troops would maintain themselves in good discipline, and that they would pay for what they used in cash. This was good news to a community that had so recently endured an army of occupation. These morning meetings were successful in allaying Newport apprehensions. General Heath would write to Washington the same day that "the inhabitants appear disposed to treat our allies with much respect. The town is to be illuminated this evening, by a vote of the inhabitants. For myself, I am charmed with the officers."[2]

French troops spent almost a year in Rhode Island in private homes in Newport, and town officials provided quarters for officers in Newport and Providence. Almost one third of the French soldiers and sailors were suffering from scurvy when the fleet arrived off Rhode Island. Four hundred of these men came to be quartered in what is now known as University Hall in Providence and an equal number convalesced in the old Colony House and in several churches in Newport "without there being any evidence of dissatisfaction from the inhabitants, regardless of sect." The healthy were sent into the barracks that the American troops had built on Poppasquash Neck at Bristol.[3]

From its beginnings as a colony Rhode Island had acquired a notorious reputation among New England Puritans for tolerating a wide variety of political and religious opinions that were abhorrent to its more orthodox neighbors.[4] In the 1760s James Otis, in the midst of a political argument, fumed at the cosmopolitanism of Newport. "Such," he wrote of Newport, "is the little, dirty, drinking, drabbling, contaminated knot of thieves, beggars, and transports . . . collected from the four winds of the earth, and made up

[2]John R. Stevens, "The French in Rhode Island:" An address delivered in Newport in 1897, pp. 11-12; Jean-Edmond Wellen, *Rochambeau, Father and Son, A Life of the Marshal de Rochambeau and The Journal of the Vicomte de Rochambeau* (New York: Henry Holt & Co., 1936), pp. 204-05; Howard C. Rice, Jr. and Anne S. K. Brown, ed., *The American Campaigns of Rochambeau's Army, 1780, 1781, 1782, 1783,* Vol. I: *The Journals of Clermont-Crevecoeur, Verger and Berthier* (Jointly Printed, Providence: Brown University Press and Princeton: Princeton University Press, 1972), pp. 17-28, 123-26.

[3]Marquis de Chastelleux, *Travels in North America in the Years 1780, 1781 and 1782,* ed. by Howard C. Rice, Jr. (Chapel Hill: University of North Carolina Press, 1963), I, 249. On July 4, 1926 the Ancient Order of Hibernians unveiled a tablet in the old Colony House in Newport that reads in part, "The south room of this building was used from 1780-1781 by the Catholic Chaplains of the French allies quartered in Newport under Rochambeau, de Ternay and de Dillon for the preservation of the Blessed Sacrament for the sick and dying and for the celebration of the holy sacrifice of the Mass."

[4]Carl Bridenbaugh, *Fat Mutton and Liberty of Conscience: Society in Rhode Island, 1626-1690* (New York: Atheneum, 1976), pp. 3-8.

of Turks, Jews and other infidels, with a few renegado *(sic)* Christians and Catholics."[5] For many Rhode Islanders the arrival of the French fleet marked the first time that they encountered Catholics in large numbers or witnessed any Catholic ceremonies.[6] Each major French ship and regiment probably had its own chaplain. At least one priest, the Abbe de Glesnon, who had been assigned chaplain to the hospital, was quartered in Newport itself.

The sudden death from a fever of Admiral de Ternay, the commander of the French fleet, and the funeral that followed created a lasting memory in the mind of one citizen of Newport, Thomas Hornsby, who claimed to be an eyewitness. The admiral's body was carried from Washington Street to Trinity churchyard and the coffin was preceded by twelve priests who chanted the burial service at the grave. Years later Hornsby recalled that the people of Newport were deeply impressed by the scene and reflected that Catholicism was "not the vain thing which their education had taught them to believe."[7]

In June 1781, all but five hundred of the French troops left Newport and Providence and headed south, and by September the last of them were gone. The troops returned briefly to Rhode Island in the middle of November on their way to Boston to embark for home. Some of the French soldiers seemed to have carried with them pleasant memories of America. An officer in the French army, the Comte de Segur, writing of the last stage of the march, noted that he was obliged to "keep night and day a strict watch. The desire of happiness which liberty presented to the soldiers, had created in many of them a desire of quitting their colors and of remaining in America. In several corps, therefore, the desertion was considerable."[8]

America's successful defense of her liberties made men more conscious of the liberties of their fellow citizens. Many of the former

---

[5]Quoted in Moses Coit Tyler, *The Literary History of the American Revolution, 1763-1783*, (New York: T. T. Putnam, Sons, 1897), I, 18.

[6]Both Catholic laymen and priests had lived in or visited Rhode Island in the years before the arrival of the French forces. Patrick T. Conley and Matthew J. Smith, *Catholicism in Rhode Island: The Formative Era* (Providence: The Diocese of Providence, 1976), pp. 4-7.

[7]Edward M. Stone, *Our French Allies* (Providence: The Providence Press Company, 1884), pp. 347-50. There are printed lists of French officers' lodgings in the Newport Historical Society. The Abbe de Glesnon, the Almoner of the Army, is listed as staying at the Widow Brayton's, 348 Spring Street.

[8]Comte de Segur, quoted in Charles Carroll, *Rhode Island: Three Centuries of Democracy* (New York: Lewis Historical Publishing Company, Inc., 1932), I, 346. Some eighteen of Rochambeau's former officers later joined the Newport Lodge of Masons in October 1790; Stone, *Our French Allies*, p. 529.

colonies in framing their state constitutions eliminated or modified
the political penalties against Roman Catholics written into their
colonial charters. Rhode Island's position regarding religious liberties was unique in the entire British Empire. From Roger Williams,
who established his home in a valley he called Providence in 1636,
the citizens of the colony and state of Rhode Island and Providence
Plantations inherited a strong tradition of freedom of conscience.
Williams's convictions as to the proper relation of church and state
were written into the colony's charter approved by Charles II in
1663 which granted the inhabitants of the colony "full liberty in
religious concernments."[9] In 1719, Rhode Island officials seem to
have made a concession to the anti-Catholic sentiment aroused by
the Jacobite efforts of 1715-1716 to bring the Catholic Pretender to
the English throne. It was probably in 1719 that the compilers of the
Digest of Rhode Island Laws and Acts inserted into the *Digest* a provision
that read:

> All Men *Professing Christianity,* and of Competent Estates, and of Civil
> Conversation, who acknowledge, and are Obedient to the Civil Magis-
> trate, though of different Judgments in Religious Affairs *(Roman Catholics
> only excepted)* shall be admitted Free-men, And shall have Liberty to Choose
> and be Chosen Officers in the Colony both Military and Civil.[10] (Italics
> mine)

This act was allegedly passed in the March 1663 session of the
General Assembly. Its enactment then or at any time prior to 1719
is possible but highly improbable.[11]

This discrimination clause was finally removed from the *Digest*
on February 24, 1783. The act that accomplished the removal, however, not only failed to recognize the spurious nature of the disabling "statute," it also neglected to define the civil status of those
professing the Jewish faith. The presence of the French in Rhode
Island, their stay in the homes of many of the most prominent men
of the state and the admirable discipline of the troops perhaps
provided some of the force that moved the Rhode Island General

---

[9]For Roger Williams's view on the individual's conscience and the state cf. Ed-
mund S. Morgan, *Roger Williams: The Church and the State* (New York: Harcourt, Brace
& World, 1967).

[10]"Laws and Acts, Made from the First Settlement of Her Majesties Colony of
Rhode Island and Providence Plantations" (1719), Rhode Island State Archives,
p. 3.

[11]The disabling clause has been the object of several studies. Patrick T. Conley,
"Rhode Island Constitutional Development 1636-1841: Prologue to the Dorr Rebellion," (unpublished doctoral dissertation, University of Notre Dame, 1970),
pp. 22-24 is the most recent and is perhaps definitive.

Assembly to remove the disabling clause that was inconsistent with Rhode Island's traditions.[12] Rhode Islanders in the nineteenth century developed a true pride in their political and religious convictions. According to what in time would be called the Roger Williams doctrine, the thoughtful and principled social and political leaders of the state espoused the belief that their legislature should not recognize religious differences and should treat all religious denominations with equal justice.[13]

Catholic Residents in Rhode Island

The names of the earliest Catholic residents of Rhode Island are long since forgotten. That there were a small number of Catholics in the state after the Revolution is recorded because several of them took advantage of the fact that a French priest, who called himself the Abbe de la Poteries, passed through Providence in December 1789. The small group asked the French cleric to celebrate Mass for them on December 8th, the Feast of the Immaculate Conception.[14] The abbe's real name was Claude Florent Bouchard. He was perhaps the same Abbe la Poteries who served as chaplain aboard the *Neptune* when she called at Newport during the Revolution. When the *Neptune* was in Boston in 1788, the abbe deserted the French navy. Through the good offices of a French merchant in Boston, who was ignorant of the abbe's past and was anxious to have Catholic services in Boston, the priest soon established himself as pastor of a small congregation in Boston late in 1788. The Abbe la Poteries's personal conduct and his administration of his parish became in time a matter of public scandal. In less than a year, Fr. John Carroll, then the Apostolic Prefect of the American Mission, learned of la Poteries's past, and he felt obliged to suspend the abbe's faculties. To avoid the consequences that his suspension might bring, la Poteries tried to challenge the authority of Fr. Carroll. His plan failed and in July 1789, the French priest left Boston

---

[12]John Russell Bartlett, ed., *Records of the Colony of Rhode Island and Providence Plantations* (Providence: A. Crawford Greene, 1856-1865), IX, 674-75; Samuel Greene Arnold, *History of the State of Rhode Island and Providence Plantations* (New York: D. Appleton & Co., 1874), III, 497 suggests that increasing numbers of French Catholic residents in the state caused the statute to have a practical bearing and thus prompted the repeal of the disabling clause.

[13]*Providence Journal*, February 11, 1854.

[14]*Providence Gazette*, December 12, 1789; Franklin B. Dexter, ed., *The Literary Diary of Ezra Stiles, D.D., L.L.D., President of Yale College* (New York: Charles Scribner's Sons, 1901), III, 375-76.

first for New York and later for Quebec. Not finding employment
in Quebec he decided to return to Boston seemingly by way of New
York. When he stopped in Providence he carried in his baggage a
pamphlet attacking the Jesuits in general, and Fr. Carroll, who was
a former Jesuit.[15]

Rhode Island does not seem to have hosted another Catholic
priest until early February 1791, when Fr. John Thayer baptized a
Negro boy, Joseph Deane, in Newport.[16] Fr. Thayer was a New
England-born Yale graduate, who became a convert to Catholicism
during the course of an extended trip to Europe. After several years
of study, he was ordained a priest in Europe and returned to America in December 1789 determined to be a missionary to his New
England compatriots. Fr. Thayer again baptized in Newport on
October 28th of that year when he stopped there on his way to a
diocesan synod in Baltimore. This time he baptized the daughter of
a French officer from Santo Domingo.[17]

Newport's ties with the colonies of the French West Indies
flowed from its trading connection and from the city's fame as a
summer refuge from the heat and fevers of the islands. There seems
also to have been a small number of residents of French descent
living in Newport, since the unsuccessful attempt to establish a
French Huguenot colony in East Greenwich. Their numbers were
augmented when in July 1793 free mulattoes of the island of Santo
Domingo joined with Negro slaves of the French planters in a revolt
against the cruelty and injustice of the ruling classes. The National
Assembly in Paris had passed a decree giving the free mulattoes
many privileges commensurate with their wealth and education.
The whites refused to accept the decree. When French naval officers
attempted to resolve the social difficulties on the island by force,
trouble erupted. In the violence and destruction that followed an
estimated five thousand men, women, and children were killed. The

---

[15]Robert H. Lord, John E. Sexton and Edward T. Harrington, *History of the Archdiocese of Boston in the Various Stages of Its Development, 1604 to 1943* (New York: Sheed
& Ward, 1944), I, 340, 375-411. Hereafter referred to as Lord, Sexton and Harrington, *History of the Archdiocese of Boston.*

[16]Holy Cross, Boston, "Baptismal Register." In the 1790s Catholic priests in England and the United States were addressed formally as "Rev. Mr." It was not until
the 1850s that "Father" came into general usage as a form of address for secular
priests. Because of the familiarity of Father, I have chosen to use it in the text from
the very beginning.

[17]*Ibid.* These entries of Fr. Thayer are in the form of a letter sent by him to Boston
to attest to the fact that the baptism had been performed. Such a statement was
signed by the parents and godparents of the child. It is at least possible that there
were other baptisms in this and later years that were not recorded in the "Baptismal
Register" in Boston. Some of the subsequent notices recorded in Boston were
received after the baptisms were performed.

more fortunate whites escaped on board the ships in the harbor. Most were able to bring with them nothing but the clothes they were wearing.[18] In October the vessel *Providence* brought about fifty refugees to Rhode Island where others from the islands either awaited them or joined them soon afterwards.[19] Most of the exiles, as they were called, were without means of support. Their numbers were such as to prompt the Rhode Island General Assembly in October to pass a resolution requiring the state to defray expenses incurred by the towns in caring for the exiles. In February 1794 the General Assembly voted almost £ 171 for the support of French exiles in Providence and allocated £ 246 to the town of Newport for the same purpose while limiting the aid to exiles from the island of Santo Domingo. The assembly continued to appropriate money in decreasing amounts through October 27, 1795.[20]

At least one young gentleman tried to put his education to work for him when he advertised his services as a dancing instructor.[21] Many of those who initially came to Rhode Island went elsewhere in search of a livelihood. There is no conclusive evidence as to whether the number of French Catholic exiles in Rhode Island, when added to the number of Catholics already here, were enough to attract the ministration of a priest. However, when Father Thayer returned from a short stay in the South, he did receive Bishop Carroll's permission to work in the New England area but not in Boston or in its environs. He is reported to have gone to New York in early April 1796 to assist in that city and "to make missionary journeys into Rhode Island and Connecticut." Possibly, he did not wish to discontinue a work already begun in those states.[22]

It is not until July 2, 1798, that there is another recorded visit of a priest to Rhode Island. Again it was the Rev. Thayer who was on his way south, this time to a new assignment in Kentucky. On this occasion Thayer baptized two girls, one of whom was the daughter of Don Josef Wiseman, who had served as Spanish vice-consul to the port of Newport since 1795. The next day, the priest delivered "a Federal discourse" in the Court House at six o'clock. The day after his address Fr. Thayer again baptized, this time the daughter of the French vice-consul in Newport, Louis Arcambal.[23] The great political issue of the day was the growing strain in the relationship be-

[18]*Providence Gazette,* July 13, 20, 23, 27, 1793.

[19]*Ibid.*, October 12, 1793.

[20]Rhode Island, *Acts and Resolves,* October, 1793; February, May, June, October, 1794.

[21]*Newport Mercury,* November 5, 1793.

[22]Lord, Sexton and Harrington, *History of the Archdiocese of Boston,* I, 514-16.

[23]Holy Cross, Boston, "Baptismal Register;" *Newport Mercury,* July 3, 1798.

tween the United States and the new revolutionary government in
France. Few public speakers had kind words for the French, especially the Federalists in New England. Fr. Thayer was an exception.
Two months earlier, he had delivered a sermon in Boston in which
he had spoken with compassion for the French nation.[24]

In June 1798 Congress passed a Naturalization Act which
changed the period of residence required for admission to full citizenship from five to fourteen years. On the twenty-fifth of that
month, the Federalist controlled Congress passed a more drastic
measure to use against their Republican opponents. The Alien Act
authorized the president to order the deportation of any foreigner
considered dangerous. The act was a political maneuver by the
Federalists designed to cut off an increasingly important source of
Republican strength. It was aimed not just at the French immigrants
from the West Indies but at English, German, French and Irish
refugees from Europe as well. Many of these newcomers, especially
among the Irish and French, had extensive political experience, and
they soon added their criticism of the Adams administration to that
of the Democratic-Republicans.[25]

On July 10th there appeared in the *Newport Mercury* a notice
written in French addressed to the refugees from Santo Domingo.
The notice informed any who wished to return home to France to
go to the French consulate to obtain the necessary documents.[26] In
the increasingly hostile political climate, many of the French of
Newport appear to have followed the same pattern as their fellow
exiles in Boston and Newburyport and left during 1798 and 1799.[27]

Shortly after Fr. Thayer departed for Kentucky, another priest,
Rev. John S. Tisserant, a priest of the Diocese of Bourges in France
and a refugee from the anti-Catholicism of the French Revolution,
took up residence in Wethersfield, Connecticut. Fr. Tisserant was in
Newport to baptize the son of Jean and Catherine Gibert on August
14, 1802. The boy's parents, the records note, had come to Newport
in 1795 from Guadelupe. Just over a year later, in November 1803,
the Catholics of Newport received an unscheduled visit from Bishop
Carroll himself. The bishop was on his way south after a month's visit
in Boston where he had gone to dedicate the new church of the Holy

[24]Lord, Sexton and Harrington, *History of the Archdiocese of Boston,* I, 543.
[25]James M. Smith, *Freedom's Fetters* (New York: Cornell University Press, 1956), pp.
22-25, 50-62.
[26]*Newport Mercury,* July 10, 1798.
[27]Lord, Sexton and Harrington, *History of the Archdiocese of Boston,* I, 552. It is quite
possible that the unfriendly political climate worked to divert Irish and French
Catholics from immigrating to the United States.

Cross. While his ship was windbound in Newport harbor, he took the opportunity to go ashore to visit the Catholic colony there. The family of Joseph Mehe of Martinique availed themselves of the bishop's visit to have their two young sons baptized.

Father Tisserant perhaps made other visits to Newport. The existing records of his activity are, like those of Fr. Thayer, in the form of letters he sent to Boston to testify to the fact that baptism had taken place. There could have been others that were not re-corded in Boston. Besides the stop in 1802, the only other recorded visit Fr. Tisserant made to Newport was in June 1804 when he again baptized in the Gibert family.[28]

When Fr. Tisserant left New England for New Jersey, care of the southern mission was added to the responsibility of the priests who made their headquarters in Boston. In September 1805 Fr. Francis Matignon journeyed to Newport and made the first of his recorded visits to that community. Fr. Matignon was another refu-gee from the revolution in France who had left France in 1792 and arrived in Boston in August to take charge of the parish in that city. Together with his former pupil, Fr. John Cheverus who joined him in Boston on October 3, 1796, Matignon was successful in restoring harmony to the factionalized church in Boston. By 1802 the two priests had succeeded in building a new church to replace the small building the congregation had hired to use as a church. It was Fr. Matignon who made annual visits to Rhode Island, generally in the fall of the year, from 1805 to 1811.[29]

In 1808 Rome acted on Bishop Carroll's request to divide his diocese by erecting two additional dioceses. Fr. Matignon had twice refused even to consider accepting the office of bishop and had suggested Fr. Cheverus's name instead. As a result, Fr. John Cheve-rus became the first bishop of the Diocese of Boston which was to include all of New England and a total of three priests. Because of the difficulties in arranging for the consecration of the newly ap-pointed bishops, Bishop Cheverus was not consecrated until Nov-ember 1, 1810.[30]

---

[28]Fr. Austin Dowling in William Byrne, *et al.*, *History of the Catholic Church in the New England States* (Boston: The Hurd & Everts Co., 1899), I, 429 says that the Giberts moved to Brooklyn shortly after this date. Mr. Audinet, another name that appears in the "Register," was a refugee from Guadelupe and Nicholas Gibert's father-in-law. He died shortly after this date. Mr. Wiseman died in 1805 and was buried in Trinity Church yard in "the common ground" in the south west corner. His wife and family also moved from Newport that year.

[29]Holy Cross, Boston, "Baptismal Register."

[30]Lord, Sexton and Harrington, *History of the Archdiocese of Boston*, I, 632-39.

The Coming of Irish Catholics to Rhode Island

In the years immediately after the American Revolution, Rhode Island encountered many of the same economic and social difficulties as did the other states in the Union. Between 1790 and 1800 considerable numbers of people moved out of Rhode Island in search of better economic and farming conditions in the West. Newport, the leading commercial town before the Revolution, was slow in recovering after the British occupation and wartime disruption of its commerce. In contrast, Providence, which in colonial times took second place to Newport, experienced a boom in shipbuilding and its merchants, freed from the rivalry of Newport, reached out for world commerce.[31]

Between 1800 and 1820 the economic pace in Rhode Island quickened, a fact that is reflected in the increase in the state's population from 69,122 in 1800 to 77,031 in 1810. Some of the increase, of course, can be ascribed to a slowing down of the movement of people out of the state. The appearance of Irish names in baptismal registers in 1806, however, suggests that part of the increase in population was due to immigration into the state. Irish had been coming to Rhode Island since colonial times.[32] It is only in 1806 that there is any evidence that sizable numbers of Irish Catholics settled here. The discovery of what was regarded as a potentially rich coal seam in Portsmouth in 1809 opened up job opportunies for laborers.[33] In 1811 Fr. Matignon notes that he stopped at the coal pits in Portsmouth and baptized a child in the Kassedy family.[34]

In 1791 the firm of Almy and Brown began to machine produce commercially satisfactory cotton yarn in Samuel Slater's cotton mill in the village of Pawtucket. When the demand for cloth increased as a result of Jefferson's embargo in 1807, men with weaving skills found commercial employment on looms set up in cellars or on the first floors of their homes or in weaving sheds such as those set up in the mills of the cotton spinners.[35] The manufacture of woolen

---

[31]Kurt B. Mayer, *Economic Development and Population Growth in Rhode Island* (Providence: Brown University Press, 1953), pp. 23–26.

[32]Thomas Hamilton Murray, "The Irish Vanguard in Rhode Island," *Journal of the American Irish Historical Society,* IV (1904), 108-33.

[33]*Providence Gazette,* January 7, 1809. Strip mining was first employed at Portsmouth. Later a deep shaft would be sunk to mine the coal.

[34]Holy Cross, Boston, "Baptismal Register."

[35]Caroline F. Ware, *Early New England Cotton Manufacture* (Boston and New York: Houghton Mifflin, 1931), pp. 19-59.

cloth began in 1804 in South Kingstown and in Providence in 1812 when the Providence Woolen Manufacturing Company attempted a large scale operation. Textile production alone did not account for Providence's prosperity, but the rise of the mills was indicative of a change in investment practice from commercial ventures to manufacturing. In the early 1800s, Providence and its environs were alive with activity and the city was well on its way to establishing itself as the most important city in the state.[36]

While these developments in Rhode Island were creating business opportunities, abortive revolutions in Ireland in 1798 and 1803 ended others. The Act of Union passed by the British Parliament in 1800 shifted the seat of Irish government to London. Many of the Irish gentry followed the government to London, taking with them the market for Irish manufactures. In search of opportunities denied them at home, the small farmer-weavers of the north of Ireland together with shopkeepers, carpenters, printers, glassblowers, smiths, millwrights and other artisans began to emigrate to America.[37]

Some of these Irish immigrants, among whom were a proportionate number of Catholics, settled in New England where they initially found economic conditions better than those they had left behind. However, in the second decade of the nineteenth century the economies of American port towns were hard hit by President Jefferson's embargo. Boston's economic stagnation forced its residents to look for work elsewhere and made Bishop Cheverus's first years in Boston difficult ones. Dependent as they were on their people for financial support, the bishop and Fr. Matignon cheerfully endured the resulting poverty.[38] In contrast to Boston's declining Catholic population, the Catholic population of Providence was growing. In addition to a few French families Fr. Matignon continued to visit up to 1813 whenever he visited the state, the records contain an increasing number of Irish names.

After Easter 1814 an elderly Irish priest, Rev. Matthew O'Brien, who had temporarily taken over charge of the church at Salem, Massachusetts, journeyed to New York to raise funds for the building of a church in Salem. From New York Fr. O'Brien wrote a letter

---

[36]John C. Pease and John M. Niles, *A Gazetteer of the States of Connecticut and Rhode Island* (Hartford: Printed and published by William S. March, 1819); Peter J. Coleman, *The Transformation of Rhode Island, 1790-1860* (Providence: Brown University Press, 1963), pp. 71-107.

[37]Oscar Handlin, *Boston's Immigrants: A Study in Acculturation* (New York: Atheneum, 1968), pp. 31-33, and notes.

[38]Lord, Sexton and Harrington, *History of the Archdiocese of Boston*, I, 642-44.

to Bishop Carroll detailing the progress of the church in Providence:

> A building at Providence has been rented and formed into a church by a few Catholics who are there. A mere grain of mustard seed only eighteen months ago is now rapidly starting up, and, watered as it has been by the amiable and laborious Bishop, will soon become a tree.[39]

The building Fr. O'Brien mentions was an old wooden schoolhouse on the north side of Sheldon Street near Benefit that was rented in 1813 and later moved to another lot.[40]

During these years Bishop Cheverus seems to have visited Providence once a month. The "Baptismal Register" of Holy Cross, Boston shows that the bishop was in Providence at least three times in 1813 and was there again in early January 1814. Only five baptisms and confirmations are noted in the records for 1813, an increase of at least two over the previous year. The small number of baptisms together with the fact the community was large enough to rent a building suggests that the congregation in Providence was largely made up of unmarried Catholic men. Although the Irish preferred to emigrate in family units, Irish artisans, who probably made up the bulk of the Providence Catholic community, regularly came to the United States as individuals.[41]

By 1814, the Irish population of Providence seems to have grown to the point where they comprised a small but noticeable part of the town's population. During the invasion scare that followed the appearance of a British fleet off the Rhode Island coast, the citizens of the town volunteered in groups to work with pick and shovel on the forts defending Providence. On October 9, the *Providence Gazette,* in outlining the work schedule for the week, noted that "Thursday next is the day the Irish of the town and vicinity have

---

[39]Father O'Brien to Archbishop Carroll, May 15, 1814, Baltimore Archdiocesan Chancery Archives.

[40]The chapel in Providence is mentioned by Fr. John Corry in a letter to Judge Staples. Rev. John Corry to William R. Staples, January 10, 1843, Rhode Island Manuscripts, X, 120, Rhode Island Historical Society.

[41]The only family mentioned in the baptismal records before 1813 and still in Providence when the first directory was published in 1824 was Andrew Dillon whose occupation is given as that of tailor. Other names in the 1824 *Providence Directory* who might be the same people as those whose names appear in sacramental records list their occupations as laborer, weaver, gardener, truckman, and possibly the owner of a music store. One of the better books on this early Irish immigration is William F. Adams, *Ireland and Irish Immigration to the New World From 1815 to the Famine* (New Haven: Yale University Press, 1932). Although Adams's study does not cover Irish immigration to America prior to 1815, his observations seem to be valid for this early period as well.

volunteered to assist in a body in preparing the old fort on Fox Point."[42]

No use was made of these defenses and on February 12, 1815 word reached Providence that peace had been declared. Ships that had been idle for months quickly made ready for sea and business in the rest of the town and state responded to take advantage of the opportunities offered by peace. Although escaping the ravages of war, nature dealt the state a far more devastating blow on September 23, 1815 when the state was swept by a storm of hurricane proportions. In the two hours the wind blew at full force, the Providence waterfront was extensively damaged; bridges were destroyed, buildings blown down and ships sunk or were stranded by a tide that rose to twelve feet above the spring tide mark. The loss of life was small but one-fourth of the town's total property evaluation was estimated to have been destroyed. Among the buildings leveled in the gale was the chapel used by the Catholics for Mass.[43]

Providence, though stunned by the disaster, rallied to rebuild its bridges and improve and extend its waterfront. While certain segments of Providence's commercial life prospered, the combination of a post-war slump, the dumping of British goods on the American market after the peace, and the collapse of the western currency ruined many cotton and woolen producers. A brief period of prosperity followed the enactment of a protective tariff on woolen and cotton goods, but it was short-lived. Bankruptcies overtook mercantile and shipping interests; factories and workshops closed, men lost their jobs and moved away in search of work.[44] The economic slump and instability of the immigrant job market is reflected from May 1815 by the declining number of Rhode Island visits of priests from Boston. They dropped to an annual visit in the spring and perhaps one in the fall. Occasionally Bishop Cheverus would pass through the state on other business as he did in December 1817 to take a steamboat to New York on his way to the consecration of Ambrose Marechal as Archbishop of Baltimore. On his way back he spent the early part of January in Providence. The next month, in a report to the Roman office of the Propagation of the Faith, the

---

[42]Byrne, *Catholic Church in the New England States*, I, 357. The bulk of the Irish population would continue to be made up of older Protestant immigrants rather than new waves of mixed Catholic-Protestant immigrants.

[43]Welcome Arnold Greene, *et al.*, *The Providence Plantations for Two Hundred and Fifty Years* (Providence: J. A. & R. A. Reid, 1886), pp. 72-73.

[44]Walter R. Danforth, "Pictures of Providence in the Past, 1790-1820: The Reminiscences of Walter R. Danforth," ed. by Clarkson A. Collins, 3rd, *Rhode Island History*, X (January-October 1951), 1-13, 45-60, 80-96, 119-29, XI (January-April 1952), 17-29, 50-63; Coleman, *The Transformation of Rhode Island*, pp. 88-89 and notes.

bishop wrote that "in Rhode Island, Connecticut, New Hampshire and Vermont, there is no Catholic church or chapel; there are almost no Catholics and consequently not even one priest."[45]

In 1819 there were two recorded baptisms in Rhode Island, however, surviving documents do not record another baptism in the state until June 6, 1825. In 1820 the Catholic population of the town of Providence seems to have shrunk to seven people. For the next few years Mass was celebrated in private homes, in the old police station, and in a building on the corner of Richmond and Pine Streets.[46]

On May 1, 1817, Bishop Cheverus baptized a child in the McLean family in Bristol. The mother of the boy, a native of France, requested that the child be called Napoleon. Still deploring what that name meant to his beloved country and Church, the bishop persuaded the parents to substitute the name Nicholas. As was his custom, the bishop gave a brief talk before and after administering the sacrament. Among his listeners was Alexander Viets Griswold, the Protestant Episcopal bishop of the Eastern District. After the ceremony Bishop Griswold stayed to talk with Bishop Cheverus. Three days later on Sunday, May 4th, Bishop Cheverus offered Mass for the workers of a coal pit three miles from Bristol, and that afternoon he returned to Bristol to preach in the court house. Sometime after his encounter at the McLean home, Bishop Griswold sent invitations by his seminarians to Bishop Cheverus offering the use of the St. Michael's Episcopal Church on Hope St. for his preaching. Bishop Cheverus seems to have accepted the invitation. However, after two successive talks, the objections of some in the town caused the bishop to forego a third talk.[47]

Bishop Cheverus's burdens and responsibilities were increased in 1818 when his friend Fr. Matignon fell ill in June and died the following September. Fr. Matignon's death was both a personal and pastoral loss to the bishop. Bishop Cheverus made the traditional visit to Rhode Island in May 1819. It was on this visit that the bishop first baptized in Pawtucket, suggesting a shift in concentration of Catholics from Providence to the then rising mill town at the falls

[45]Bishop Cheverus to Cardinal Litta, February 7, 1817, Boston Chancery Archives, hereafter cited as BChA.

[46]Greene, *The Providence Plantations,* p. 155; Edwin M. Snow, (comp.), *Census of the City of Providence taken in July, 1855 . . . Giving an account of Previous Ennumerations of the Population of Providence* (Providence: 1856), pp. 73-74 notes that there were thirty-nine aliens living in Providence.

[47]Annabelle M. Melville, *Jean Lefebvre de Cheverus 1768-1836* (Milwaukee: The Bruce Publishing Company, 1958), pp. 188-221; Lord, Sexton and Harrington, *History of the Archdiocese of Boston,* I, 703-704.

of the Blackstone River. The bishop made a familiar stop on his visit
when he journeyed to Bristol to baptize another child in the McLean
family.[48]

Whether Bishop Cheverus and his fellow priests were able to
embark on more frequent visits to the few Catholics residing in
Rhode Island can only be conjecture. There probably were other
times when they came to celebrate the Eucharist or to perform other
of their pastoral tasks. But it is doubtful that there were many more
visits than those noted above. While the Catholic population of the
Boston diocese grew from a total of 720 Catholics in 1810 to almost
three thousand in 1820 and would increase to seven thousand in
1830, the rate of increase was small when compared to that of the
dioceses of Baltimore, Philadelphia, and New York where Irish immigration was responsible for a large increase in the Catholic population.[49]

Bishop Cheverus would not see the growth of the diocese he
had labored so hard to nurture. Since the death of Fr. Matignon, he
seems to have considered the idea of returning to France. After
much hesitation Cheverus consented to his nomination to the Diocese of Mantauban in southern France. With great sadness Boston
said good-bye to its bishop on September 26, 1822. Bishop Cheverus's personal choice for his successor in Boston fell on Rev. William Taylor who had served in the Boston diocese since 1821, and
as vicar general since 1822. However, from a list of men sent to
Rome by the bishops of the United States, the Holy See decided to
appoint a Jesuit, Fr. Benedict J. Fenwick, as second bishop of Boston.

The product of an old Maryland Catholic family, Benedict Fenwick was educated at Georgetown and studied for a time at St.
Mary's Seminary in Baltimore. When the Jesuit order was reorganized in 1805, Fenwick was among those who asked to join. After
pastoral years in New York and Charlestown and administrative
work as president of Georgetown College, he received notice in July
1825 of his nomination to the bishopric of Boston. On November
1, 1825, he was consecrated the second bishop of Boston.

The condition of the Boston diocese in 1825 was not a happy
one. The Church in New England was so small and weak that Bishop
DuBourg of Louisiana twice suggested to Rome the advisability of
uniting the sees of Boston and New York.[50] In the entire diocese in

[48]Holy Cross, Boston, "Baptismal Register."
[49]Bishop Fenwick to Propaganda Fide, April 24, 1831, BChA.
[50]Lord, Sexton and Harrington, *History of the Archdiocese of Boston,* II, 30.

1825 there were, apart from the cathedral in Boston, only eight small churches and only three priests to assist the bishop in his ministry to some seven thousand Catholics. With only a young Irish priest, Rev. Patrick Byrne to assist him in caring for the large and growing cathedral congregation, Bishop Fenwick confined himself as Bishop Cheverus and Fr. Taylor had done earlier, to sending Fr. Byrne to the outlying districts for occasional brief visits.[51]

The First Catholic Churches and Mission Stations

While Boston was awaiting and welcoming its new bishop, important changes were occurring in Rhode Island. The economic life of the state was shaking off the effects of the depression that followed the decline of trade caused by the new American tariff acts. In 1824 the Federal government began to reconstruct Fort Adams in Newport. Together with the coal pits in Portsmouth which were fitfully worked, the two projects created job opportunities for men with strong backs and particular skills. Manufacturers in the Blackstone Valley and along the Blackstone Canal were increasing production in old mills and taking advantage of the water sources created for the canals to build new factories.[52] Some employers, at least, readily welcomed the Irishmen who came to fill the new jobs since they were often willing to work for less money than native workmen.

The promise of what was for the Irish better paying jobs in America was not the only reason the Irish left their ancestral homes. They were also driven out by the threat or the reality of the loss of their jobs or their livelihoods. The decline of Irish manufactures, which began with the Act of Union, was speeded in 1821 by the removal of protective duties on English goods entering Ireland. The once flourishing woolen and cotton trades withered in the face of competition of English machine made goods and Irish workmen's reluctance to accept change. The decline of Irish industries coincided with the dislocation of its agriculture due to the drive to consolidate many small farms. The number of Irish leaving their homeland grew noticeably in the years after the Napoleonic wars. Temporarily checked by the American business depression in 1819 and various other factors, the year 1827 saw the numbers of immi-

---

[51]Lord, Sexton and Harrington, *History of the Archdiocese of Boston,* II, 30-31.
[52]Coleman, *The Transformation of Rhode Island,* pp. 90-107.

grants again begin to swell. The Irish immigrants of this period continued to be drawn mainly from the small landholders and artisan classes, for agricultural laborers were usually too poor to pay the cost of passage. Although the Protestant counties of the north continued to send out large numbers of immigrants, the tendency to emigrate in the late 1820s and into the 1830s began to spread among the Catholics of Munster and Leinster. New England received a smaller number of Irish immigrants than did the rest of the Country. But the bulk of immigrants arriving in New England during this period were Irish, prompting Marcus L. Hansen to speak of their coming as "the second colonization of New England."[53]

When in January 1827, Fr. Patrick Byrne stopped in Newport on one of his infrequent visits, he was surprised to find a greater number of Catholics than he had anticipated. About one hundred and fifty people received the sacraments in Newport and about twenty or thirty at the coal pits in Portsmouth.[54] Nine months later James Lenox of Pawtucket called on bishop Fenwick to inform him that "the number of Catholics in and near that village has considerably increased and amounts now to two or three hundred souls, who are very anxious to have a small church erected for their convenience."[55]

The bishop's promise to visit the people of Pawtucket in a week or two went unfulfilled when he was suddenly called to the deathbed of his brother Enoch in Maryland. At the beginning of the next year the Catholics of Pawtucket and Providence joined in requesting a priest and offered to build a small church in one or the other of those towns. In December 1827 Bishop Fenwick ordained three men to the priesthood, and on January 2, 1828 he accepted the services of a young man, Rev. Robert D. Woodley. Woodley was a Virginian who had graduated with distinction from Georgetown in 1825 the last year of Bishop Fenwick's presidency and who had prepared for the priesthood under Bishop England in Charleston. The bishop commissioned him on January 4th to go to Rhode Island to investigate the feasibility of founding a church there.[56] When Fr. Woodley returned three weeks later, his report to the bishop in Boston was so optimistic that Fenwick sent him back on

[53]Adams, *Ireland and Irish Immigration,* pp. 158-206; Marcus L. Hansen, "The Second Colonization of New England," *New England Quarterly,* II (October 1929), 539-60.
[54]Bishop Fenwick, "Memoranda," February 2, 1827, BChA. Hereafter referred to as "Memoranda."
[55]*Ibid.* October 31, 1827.
[56]*Ibid.* January 2, 4, 1828.

a permanent assignment to minister to the people in Pawtucket, Providence, Newport and the Massachusetts towns of New Bedford and Taunton, although he was "to spend most of his time at Pawtucket and Providence where a Catholic church was to be erected in the course of next spring."[57]

In the first few weeks of his new assignment Fr. Woodley visited and baptized in Providence and Pawtucket. In late February he went on to Newport where he wrote to Bishop Fenwick that "there was a school house in a central location in the town capable of holding four or five hundred people, then being offered for sale. The price for both the building and the lot was eleven hundred dollars and the owner was willing to allow five years to pay it with interest."[58] The building, situated on Barney Street, belonged to Eleazer Trevett who had conducted an academy there until Newport's newly established free school system reduced his profits. More recently it had been used as a meeting place for a tribe of the Tammany Society of Newport. With Fr. Woodley's assurance that the Catholics in Newport would be able to pay it within the five year period, the bishop gave his consent to the purchase. After repairing the building, setting up an altar and installing pews, Fr. Woodley celebrated the first Mass there on April 6, 1828.[59] At the end of October 1828, Bishop Fenwick came to Newport and said Mass in the new chapel. He was disappointed with the size of the lot and the condition of the building. The bishop understood that Fr. Woodley, young and perhaps gullible, had acted out of concern for finding a suitable place to say Mass, but felt that a better building could have been purchased with the $1,100. Later he urged the young priest to remedy the situation by purchasing an adjacent lot in order to gain adequate room and footage on the street.[60]

Although Newport was the site of the first Catholic church established by Fr. Woodley, his main concern in these first years was still with Providence and Pawtucket. On coming to Rhode Island, Fr. Woodley established his residence in Providence at 81 Benefit Street. On August 1st he reported to the bishop that he had rented Mechanics Hall, which was on the upper floor of the building opposite the market in Providence, as a place to say Mass on Sundays.[61]

Providence was the largest town in the mission district. By 1830

[57]*Ibid.*, January 10; February 6, 1828.
[58]*Ibid.*, March 7, 1828.
[59]*Ibid.*, April 12, 1828; *Newport Mercury,* April 12, 1828; Byrne, *Catholic Church in the New England States,* I, 358.
[60]"Memoranda," November 1, 1828.
[61]*Ibid.*, August 1, 1828.

its population had increased to 16,836, a gain of about 4,000 inhabitants over the census figure of 1820.[62] To the north of Providence,
the village of Pawtucket was divided into two parts by the Blackstone
River which at this time formed the state line between Rhode Island
and Massachusetts. The inhabitants of the place probably numbered only some two thousand but Fr. Woodley found the largest
number of Catholics there rather than in Providence. By summer
1828, Fr. Woodley would be dividing his time between the four
hundred or so Catholics in Providence and Pawtucket and the approximately two hundred in Newport.[63] He visited each place every
other week and once every two months he went to New Bedford.
There were, in addition, about eighty Catholics in the growing
manufacturing town of Taunton and a smaller group in nearby Fall
River who were also Fr. Woodley's responsibility. In September
1828, Fr. Woodley's responsibilities were further increased when
his mission was extended to include Hartford and with it the state
of Connecticut. Fortunately, his service in Connecticut lasted less
than a year.[64] It is a tribute to Fr. Woodley's zeal that he attempted
to visit his scattered parishioners at regular intervals in addition to
visiting every group of Catholics brought to his attention at least
once.[65]

    In the same month that Fr. Woodley reported renting Mechan-
ics Hall, a prominent Pawtucket iron manufacturer and inventor,
David Wilkinson, offered Bishop Fenwick a large lot in that town as
a site for a church. The lot was then in the south part of the village
near the Providence and Pawtucket turnpike.[66] Since Pawtucket at
the moment had more Catholic residents than Providence, the decision was made to build a church there first, and the bishop asked
the Catholics in Providence to assist in the task. One day in September after he said Mass in Providence, the bishop, in the company of

---

[62]Snow, *Providence Census,* pp. 73–74.

[63]Massena Goodrich, *Historical Sketch of the Town of Pawtucket* (Pawtucket: Nickerson, Sibley & Co., 1876), p. 184, notes that "whilst attending to the Pawtucket
mission Fr. Woodley resided at the old house beyond the toll-gate known as the
Carpenter House." It is possible that Fr. Woodley moved out there so he would be
convenient to both towns.

[64]*Providence Patriot,* October 22, 1828; Lord, Sexton and Harrington, *History of the
Archdiocese of Boston,* II, 86, 94-98.

[65]Until 1870 a priest could only offer one Mass each day. After 1870 the Congregation of the Propaganda of the Faith granted American priests permission to binate,
i.e., to offer two Masses on a Sunday and holy days of obligation when pastoral need
demanded it.

[66]"Memoranda," August 30, 1828. The text of the deed, dated August 27, 1828,
is printed in John H. McKenna, *The Centenary Story of Old St. Mary's, Pawtucket, R. I.,
1829-1929* (Providence: Providence Visitor Press, 1929), pp. 12-15.

Fr. Woodley and the deacon, Mr. Tyler, went out to Pawtucket to see the lot. Quite pleased with the location, the bishop urged Fr. Woodley to make a collection as speedily as possible in order to carry out Wilkinson's plan.[67]

The Catholics of both towns appealed to their fellow citizens for help in building their church.[68] The Catholic priests, however, had not established their credit in the community and the banks would not lend them money. They had a sympathetic supporter in William Simons, editor of the *Providence Patriot,* who in reporting Mr. Wilkinson's gift suggested that some of the wealthy men of Providence might offer some encouragement to efforts to build a church in Providence as well.[69] Appeals to their fellow citizens went unheeded and the bulk of the twelve hundred dollars that the church was to cost was raised by the Catholics of the two towns, by their friends in Boston, and by means of a loan from the bishop. Since his priests were mostly young men with little experience, the bishop himself frequently drew the plans for their churches and instructed them in the manner of securing bids and watching specifications.

Mr. Wilkinson's generosity and the support of William Simons was typical of the attitude of business leaders of Rhode Island in the 1820s. When on September 14, 1828, Bishop Fenwick visited Providence to offer Mass, he was pleased to note that the congregation on that Sunday included several Protestants.[70] In these years before the anti-Catholic riots in Boston and Charlestown, the bishop had great hope that sizable numbers of Protestants would "come over" once the faith of the Catholic church was fairly presented. His long and frequent journeys in the close quarters of stagecoach and steamship brought him into contact with many Protestants whom he found to be receptive and open, although most seemed uninformed of the Catholic religion. A good part of the bishop's favorable impression by his traveling companions was probably due to their acceptance of his engaging character.[71]

Work on the new church in Pawtucket began during the last week of April 1829, with the hope it would be completed by Pentecost.[72] Construction of the church was well along but still unfinished when Bishop Fenwick got his first look at it. In November 1829, the

[67]"Memoranda," September 15, 1828.
[68]*Providence Patriot,* October 22, 1828.
[69]*Ibid.,* September 3, 1828.
[70]"Memoranda," September 14, 1828.
[71]Byrne, *Catholic Church in the New England States,* I, 360.
[72]*Providence Patriot,* April 29, 1829; "Memoranda," April 30, 1829.

bishop together with Bishop Rosati of St. Louis and two other travelers, Fathers Blanc and Jeanjean, had taken the steamer from New York on their way back from the Provincial Council in Baltimore and had landed in Providence at ten in the morning. The four men boarded the stage for Boston at Market Square but it broke down before it left the town. The four of them walked to Pawtucket along the turnpike and while the stage was repaired and reached the town before the stage overtook them. There the bishop had a chance to inspect the new church which he thought looked well, "a neat wooden building painted white with green doors and venetian blinds."[73] On Christmas Day 1829, Fr. Woodley dedicated the church under the title of St. Mary's.

The joy of the people of Pawtucket that year was dampened by the industrial depression that had settled on the town. Money, which was already scarce in 1828, all but disappeared the following year when the Farmers' and Merchants' Bank in Pawtucket failed, involving merchants and manufacturers in heavy losses. The cause of the depression was not wholly financial but was also due to an over supply of goods and evolving technology. The effects, however, on the people of Pawtucket were the same, loss of their jobs.[74]

As a result of the depression Fr. Woodley was unable to pay the second installment on his contract for the building of the church. The carpenters who built the church asked the bishop on January 30, 1830 to meet the obligations and threatened to attach the church. In March, Fr. Woodley turned to the Irish Charitable Society in Boston for a loan of four hundred dollars at a high rate of interest. As surety, he had to deed the church in trust to the Society. On July 7, 1830, the treasurer of the Irish Society demanded the return of the money and the bishop had to refund it out of his money.[75]

During the construction of the church in Pawtucket, the Catholics of Providence seem to have done what they could to help. The Providence Catholic community continued to worship together in Mechanics Hall. They hoped that once the Pawtucket church was finished they would have one of their own in Providence. It was probably with this idea in mind that Fr. Woodley, in June 1830, bought a lot on Pearl Street in the southwestern part of town.[76] In the same month he petitioned the General Assembly in his name

---

[73]"Memoranda," November 11, 1829.
[74]Coleman, *The Transformation of Rhode Island,* pp. 103, 196.
[75]"Memoranda," January 23, 1830; March 24, 1830; July 7, 1830.
[76]Providence Registry of Deeds, June 8, 1830, Book 59, p. 75, Providence City Hall.

and in the name of the Roman Catholic Congregation of Providence
for a grant of a lottery to raise the sum of ten thousand dollars to
erect a church. His petition arrived in the legislature at a time of
general reaction to a grant of lotteries to anyone for any purpose.
On January 12, 1831, the House of Representatives voted over-
whelmingly against the petition.[77]

In spite of the setback in his plans for a church in Providence
and financial trials in Pawtucket, the first two years that Fr. Woodley
spent in Rhode Island were, on the whole, successful ones for him
and the church. He somehow managed to visit his scattered parishioners at regular intervals and his "Baptismal Register" records the
fact that he was the first priest to offer Mass in many Rhode Island
communities including several villages in the town of Smithfield and
what would in 1867 become the town of Woonsocket.

In 1814 or 1815, Francois Proulx had moved his family from
St. Ours in the Canadian Province of Quebec to Woonsocket Hill
where he worked on the farm of Mr. Arnold. Over the next twenty
years several other French Canadian families settled in the area, but
they were not all Catholics and those who were, found the services
offered by the Irish priests as foreign as those offered by the Protestant ministers.[78] The community which prompted Fr. Woodley to
travel to Woonsocket were not the Canadians but Irish laborers who
settled in Woonsocket where manufacturing had already made its
appearance after the opening of the Blackstone Canal in 1826.

The register of the Cathedral in Boston notes that Fr. Byrne,
when he was in Rhode Island in 1826, officiated at "Smithfield, on
the Canals" which might have been Woonsocket or a labor camp
near the town. Among the Irish laborers who first settled in Woonsocket was a young man by the name of Michael Reddy. Reddy had
arrived in the United States from Ireland in 1824 when he was about
twenty-three. After working for a time in Boston, he grew dissatisfied with his surroundings and walked from Boston to Providence by way of Woonsocket. He worked awhile in Providence
before securing work on a canal construction crew. On settling in
Woonsocket, Reddy found lodging with another Irishman named
Patrick Mullen on what was known as "the island," a portion of land
that ran from South Main Street to the Blackstone River. Soon after
Fr. Woodley came to Rhode Island, Reddy invited him to Woonsocket. Fr. Woodley visited the town on Sunday, October 12, 1828,

---

[77]Petitions Not Granted, June-October 1830. Rhode Island State Archives; Carroll, *Rhode Island,* I, 420-21.

[78]Marie Louise Bonier, *Débuts de la Colonie Franco-Américaine de Woonsocket, Rhode
Island* (Framingham, MA: Lakeview Press, 1920), pp. 79-80, 110-12, 222, 252-56.

which is probably the date on which he celebrated Mass in the home of Walter Allen, a liberal Quaker. Allen's home was in Union Village and was later known as the Osborne House. The congregation at this first Mass consisted of ten persons, all of them Irishmen who seemed to have been well off, since the ten of them gave Fr. Woodley a purse of $50.[79] In January, Fr. Woodley visited Woonsocket again when he baptized three children of the same family in Woonsocket Falls.[80] The village's Catholic population grew slowly in the following years. There were only thirty Catholics in Woonsocket Falls when Mass was next known to have been said there in 1834.[81] Other areas receiving visits from Fr. Woodley were the Cumberland coal mines and Cranston, a town immediately south of Providence.

Early Confrontations and Growth

As Catholic priests moved about in Rhode Island society, native Rhode Islanders adjusted to their presence. Americans at this time called the priest, "the old priest," even if he was a young man. Pictures of the early clergy show them dressed like ministers in somber-colored clothes, frequently brown, with a cravat. Avoidance of distinctive garb resulted in part from the desire of clergy not to draw attention to themselves and suffer the taunts and insults of hostile Protestants. Nevertheless, priests such as Fr. Woodley felt free enough to carry on debates in the public press and through the medium of pamphlets. On August 11, 1830, the Rev. Thomas H. Skinner of Philadelphia issued an appeal in Rev. Mr. Wilson's church in Providence for financial help in establishing Sunday schools in the Mississippi Valley. Fr. Woodley objected to Skinner's ideas and voiced his objections in a series of four published tracts addressed to the clergymen of Providence.[82]

Ironically, most of Fr. Woodley's troubles came not from the Protestants but from his fellow Catholics. The people who made up the earliest Catholic communities in Providence and Pawtucket

---

[79]James W. Smyth, *History of the Catholic Church in Woonsocket and Vicinity from the Celebration of the First Mass in 1828 to the Present Time* (Woonsocket: 1903), pp. 53–57.

[80]SS. Peter and Paul, Providence, R. I., "Baptismal Register."

[81]The development of the Catholic community in Woonsocket is perhaps typical of other towns. The congregation was made up chiefly of laborers who went there for work and only settled down after holding several jobs. It was only after settling down that their families joined them.

[82]*Providence Patriot,* August 11, 18, 1830; Arthur E. Wilson, *Paddy Wilson's Meeting House in Providence Plantations, 1791-1839* (Boston: The Pilgrim Press, 1950), pp. 210-22.

came from the north of Ireland.[83] Most of the Irish immigrants were a rural people who could find work only in cities. Strangers in a new land, the immigrants tended to gather in neighborhoods where other Irish, who had come a few years earlier, had established themselves. Each family tried to live near friends and relatives from the same village. The men helped the newcomer find work on the same construction gang or in the same mill where they worked.[84]

Fr. Woodley, being a "native," (i.e. American-born), appears to have had little success in dealing with his "foreign" parishioners. His struggle to pay the debt of the church in Pawtucket in the face of the fact that many of the people there were drifting away in search of work only added to his burden. The lot on Pearl Street had to be mortgaged November 15th for a loan of thirty-five dollars, and shortly afterwards, it was sold.[85]

On November 3, 1830, when Bishop Fenwick was about to leave on an extended visit to northern New England, he sent Fr. John Corry, a priest whom he had ordained only a few weeks before, to assist Fr. Woodley in his work. Fr. Corry, a native of Ireland, had come to the United States as a boy and had just recently completed his studies at Mt. St. Mary's College, Emmitsburg. The two men divided the ministry between them. Fr. Corry took charge of Pawtucket and Taunton while Fr. Woodley retained responsibility for Providence, Newport and Fall River (a settlement then partly in Massachusetts and partly in the town of Tiverton, Rhode Island).

There is no certainty as to what happened next. Bishop Fenwick's "Memoranda" noted only that there was some "ferment" to the disparagement of Fr. Woodley. About November 30th, the Vicar General, Fr. O'Flaherty, in charge of the diocese in the absence of the bishop, asked Fr. Woodley to return to Boston and release his ministry to Fr. Corry. On his return in late December, Bishop Fenwick confirmed Fr. O'Flaherty's action.[86] Five months later Fr. Woodley left the Diocese of Boston to enter the Jesuit order. He later returned to Maryland, there to complete a long and fruitfull career in the service of Christ.

[83]Byrne, *Catholic Church in the New England States,*, I, 357, states merely that the early immigrants came from the north; George Potter, *To the Golden Door: The Story of the Irish in Ireland and America* (Boston: Little, Brown and Co., 1966), p. 180, is more specific. He writes that the early Irish in Providence were cloth printers from Donegal. Neither author offers information as to his sources.

[84]William V. Shannon, *The American Irish* (New York: The Macmillan Company, 1969), p. 34.

[85]*Providence Registry of Deeds,* Book 59, p. 219 and Book 60, p. 177, Providence City Hall.

[86]"Memoranda," December 22, 29, 1830 supply what little data we have as to the reasons for Fr. Woodley's recall; Rev. John Corry to William R. Staples, January 10, 1843, RI Mss, X, 120, RIHS.

Fr. Corry was not only young but energetic and a great organizer. In time he would prove also to be partisan, unbending and self-reliant. Fr. Corry's energies first found an outlet in response to the wishes of a small group of Catholics in Taunton, who in June 1830, petitioned the bishop for permission to build a church.[87] Fr. Corry had just begun his work in Taunton in addition to serving the Catholics in Pawtucket when Fr. O'Flaherty gave him complete charge of the mission territory. The bishop at that time considered Taunton the central point of the mission, and it was there that Fr. Corry resided.[88] Bishop Fenwick first advised the Catholics of Taunton to purchase a building for Mass, but in the end, they built one. On October 28, 1832, Bishop Fenwick dedicated the newly completed church of St. Mary's.[89]

Even before the dedication of the church in Taunton, the Catholics in Providence had begun to lay plans for a church of their own. In spite of the fact that Fr. Corry easily arranged with the civil authority of the town to give Catholics the use of the "Old Town House" on the corner of Towne and College Streets, purchase of property for a church proved more difficult.[90] When word that the Catholics were looking for a site to build a church became known, property owners in the Irish neighborhood in the western section of Providence resolved not to sell an inch of their property to the Catholics. Fr. Corry left the matter of the purchase of a church site in the hands of Francis Hye, a trader by occupation and one of two naturalized Catholic Irishmen living in Providence.

On January 17, 1832, Hye arranged to purchase from Isaac Matthewson a parcel of land on High Street which was centrally located for the Catholics of Providence and large enough to afford room for a church and rectory. Hye, however, did not reveal why he wanted the land. After the deed was drawn and the deal closed, Hye finally revealed to Matthewson the reason for his purchase of the land: "If you wait two or three years you will see a Catholic church on it." The next day Matthewson offered to repurchase the land for one hundred dollars more than he had received. When Hye refused that offer, Matthewson gradually increased it to five hundred dollars more than the original purchase price. Hye talked the matter over with his fellow Catholics. They decided to let Fr. Corry settle it after he had a chance to view the site. It took Fr. Corry only

---

[87]"Memoranda," June 29, 1830.
[88]Bishop Fenwick to Prefect, Congregation of the Propaganda, Rome, April 24, 1831, BChA.
[89]"Memoranda," June 19, 1831; October 28, 1832.
[90]Rev. John Corry to William R. Staples, January 10, 1843, RI Mss, X, 120, RIHS.

a few moments to see that in a few years there would be no such place in Providence for a church as the one Hye had purchased. He advised Mr. Hye to refuse the offer, and he did.[91]

Shortly after the dedication of the new church in Taunton, Bishop Fenwick decided to divide Fr. Corry's widely scattered mission. The bishop transferred Fr. Peter Conolly, another young priest ordained the same day as Fr. Corry, to the pastorate of Providence, Pawtucket and Canton in Massachusetts. Fr. Corry was to retain Taunton, where he was living, as well as Newport and Fall River.[92]

Fr. Corry was not long in his new assignment when he embarked again on a building project. As a first step towards replacing the remodeled schoolhouse in Newport purchased by Fr. Woodley, Fr. Corry purchased an additional piece of property adjacent to the two lots bought previously. He hoped to begin construction on the new church in the summer of 1833, and for that purpose he asked the bishop to give him plans for the church.[93]

Construction on the new church progressed slowly and it was not until August 20, 1837 that Bishop Fenwick finally dedicated the church under the title of St. Joseph's. The bishop arrived in Newport the night before the dedication on the steamer that ran between Providence and New York. Fr. Corry met him at the dock and the two men stayed at Townsend's Hotel at the foot of Pelham Street. The bishop found the church "agreeably situated and sufficiently well finished." It was a large Gothic frame church, sixty-five by forty feet, with a gallery at the end and large enough to accommodate almost eight hundred people. To raise funds for the church and keep "Protestant blackguards" of the town from rushing in and occupying the best seats to the exclusion of the Catholics, Fr. Corry charged a one dollar admission fee at the dedication services. It was a hot day and a long one because the bishop confirmed in the afternoon.[94] With the Newport church dedicated, the bishop felt it was time to solve difficulties that had developed in Providence after he removed that city from Fr. Corry's care.

Fr. Peter Conolly, who had succeeded Fr. Corry in Providence, was a young, exceptionally tall Ulsterman with considerable energy

[91]Interview with Mary Hye, daughter of Francis Hye, *Weekly Visitor,* May 12, 1878; Isaac Matthewson to Francis Hye, January 17, 1832; Francis Hye to Bishop Fenwick, March 13, 1832; *Providence Registry of Deeds,* Book 61, pp. 234 and 258, Providence City Hall; "Memoranda," March 26, 1832.
[92]"Memoranda," November 16, 1832.
[93]*Ibid.,* February 22; April 8, 24, 1833; Byrne, *Catholic Church in the New England States,* I, 429-30.
[94]"Memoranda," August 19, 20, 1837.

but of independent temperament. His first assignment after ordination was to minister to the Catholics of New Bedford and Cape Cod. Some of his people at Sandwich complained to the bishop of the rarity of Fr. Conolly's visits and of the difficulty they had in getting acquainted with him. To relieve tension, the bishop transferred him to Providence. In January 1833, Fr. Conolly optimistically informed the bishop that he would shortly raise, from among the Catholics of the town, sufficient money to pay off the remainder due on the lot Mr. Hye had purchased. His expectations were premature.[95]

A month after his report to the bishop, he and other members of the Providence community got involved in an argument with an outspoken "foreigner," as he called himself, who had been raised a Catholic and had come to question his faith or, perhaps more specifically, the place of the Irish-American clergy in the church. His views on religion had caused some scandal within the Irish community. In an attempt to defend his reputation he published a notice or a "card" in the *Manufacturers' and Farmers' Journal* and the *Providence Journal* informing the Catholic community that if the false stories stopped, he would forgive and forget. Fr. Conolly responded to the first "card" from the pulpit by calling the writer "an infidel, a liar, and a vagabond," accusations which prompted two more cards. In both these cards the writer disputed such things as the necessity of confession, the place of the Papacy in the Church and the veneration of the Blessed Virgin.[96]

In April 1833, Fr. Conolly arranged to have Fr. O'Flaherty give a Sunday evening lecture in the Town House explaining and defending the Catholic faith. Both Fr. O'Flaherty and the bishop often gave such lectures in the Boston cathedral. The three hour lecture was frequently interrupted by a group of young men seated in one of the galleries and by another group outside the hall who threw stones at the building's windows. One rock shattered the glass over Fr. O'Flaherty's head. Several members of the audience, among them Mr. Thomas F. Carpenter, a prominent Providence attorney, succeeded in quelling the disturbance before any serious damage resulted. *The Manufacturers' and Farmers' Journal,* in reporting the incident, asked the reverend gentleman to understand the kind of persons who threw the rocks and "not, in consequence of their proceedings, carry away any impressions unfavorable to the manners and liberality of our citizens."[97]

[95]*Ibid.,* January 21, 1833.
[96]*Manufacturers' and Farmers' Journal,* January 31 and February 7, 1833. The third card is found in the *Providence Journal,* February 16, 1833.
[97]*Manufacturers' and Farmers' Journal,* April 22, 1833; *Weekly Visitor,* May 17, 1878.

The following month, on the 12th, the bishop himself was in Rhode Island to administer confirmation. He took the new railroad as far as Canton, which was as far as it was open, and came by stage from there. Finding Fr. Conolly sick in bed and unable to get up for Sunday services, the bishop himself assumed the duties of the day. He offered Mass at ten and confirmed only five adults because the children were not prepared. During the day he officiated in the chapel that was connected with Fr. Conolly's house. After Vespers in the afternoon, the bishop assembled the male portion of the congregation in another part of the house and urged the building of a church. The bishop noted in his diary that the Catholic population of Providence at that time was about two hundred and fifty souls.[98]

On April 30, 1834, Bishop Fenwick transferred Fr. Conolly to Lowell and assigned Fr. Constantine Lee to take charge of the mission in Providence and Pawtucket. Fr. Lee had come into the Boston diocese in 1833 with high recommendations from the vicar apostolic of Edinburgh. Educated at Rome and a Doctor of Theology, he was a talented, eloquent, and pious man, a "polished Irish gentleman," and was thirty-seven when assigned to Providence.[99]

On August 11, 1834, the hopes entertained by Bishop Fenwick and his clergy for the "coming over" of the Protestants once they knew the truth of the Catholic faith died in the attack of a Boston mob on the Ursuline Convent in Charlestown. The Providence newspapers published a rather objective account of the incident taken from the Boston papers and labeled it a disgrace.[100] No echoes of violence rumbled through Providence or other Rhode Island cities. A number of Newport's citizens wrote Bishop Fenwick inviting him to relocate the Ursuline Convent in their city. The idea received public support from two Rhode Island papers, the *Newport Republican* and the *Republican Herald*.[101]

In the same year as the attack on the Boston convent, an attempt was made in the Rhode Island legislature to pass a bill regulating religious corporations. Since the property of the two Catholic churches was held as personal property in the name of the bishop of Boston or of Fr. Woodley, the proposed law would not have had an effect on Rhode Island's Catholics. There is also no evidence of anti-Catholic feeling connected with the statute, enacted in 1835,

---

98"Memoranda," May 11, 12, 1833. The bishop's estimates tend to be low.
99"Memoranda," April 30, 1834; *Boston Pilot*, June 18, 1834.
100*Manufacturers' and Farmers' Journal*, August 14, 1834; *Republican Herald*, August 16, 1834; *Providence Journal*, August 14, 1834.
101*Republican Herald*, November 1, 1834.

that made all religious and educational property taxable unless it was held under a charter from the state legislature, and which affected and restricted the amount of realty a church could hold. This statute affected many religious denominations, not just Catholics.[102] When Fr. Corry was leaving Newport in 1837, he wrote the Rev. Mr. Ross, a fellow Newport clergyman, a letter in which he praised the spirit of toleration shown by the citizens of Newport. "Our church," he says, "stood for two years with its windows unprotected by blinds and during that time not one pane of glass was broken."[103] The slow growth of the Catholic church in Rhode Island continued with at least the traditional toleration the leaders of Rhode Island society had accorded other religious groups and in which they had developed a true pride.

Fr. Constantine Lee took up his residence in a large house Fr. Conolly had bought near a popular tavern, the Halfway House, on the turnpike between Providence and Pawtucket. It had some land attached which Fr. Lee farmed himself. Fr. Lee called the place O'Connellsville.[104]

Fr. Lee managed to pay the balance of money due on the Providence lot, and on December 31, 1834, he informed the bishop he would begin construction there early the next spring. In the meantime he rented Tin Top Congregational Church at the corner of Pine and Richmond streets for one year for Sunday services at a rent of one hundred and fifty dollars.[105] The building was built in 1807 and abandoned in 1827 when the rift between the Congregationalists of the Beneficent Congregational Church was healed. In May 1835, Fr. Lee arranged to purchase the building for twenty-three hundred dollars. A final agreement, however, was not reached and within a few weeks, the owners rented the building to a showman for a circus. The showman simply "tumbled out" the Catholics' church fixtures. For two months after that Fr. Lee said Mass in the house of John Devlin on 2 Union Street before he obtained permission to again say Mass in the Town House.[106] Later that same year, on September 16th, Fr. Lee asked for an assistant citing the number of places in and around Providence he had to visit. The bishop was

---

[102]Coleman, *Transformation of Rhode Island*, p. 145, suggests that the Regulating Bill of 1834 would have caused serious difficulties for the Catholic Church if the bill passed and sees the bill as a significant manifestation of religious animosity. For a list of Religious Corporations, 1770-1834, see *Republican Herald*, September 20, 1834. For the law of 1835, see *Manufacturers' and Farmers' Journal*, January 19, 1835.
[103]Byrne, *Catholic Church in the New England States*, I, 366.
[104]*Boston Pilot*, June 18, 1834.
[105]"Memoranda," December 31, 1834.
[106]*Providence Visitor*, June 14, 1916.

able to meet his request and sent Fr. Michael Lynch to Providence.[107]

The increase of the Catholic population of Providence coincided with the completion of the rail line from Boston and the construction of its terminus at India Point. In 1831, the Massachusetts legislature had chartered a company to build a railroad from Boston to the Rhode Island line in Pawtucket or Seekonk. As the road approached completion, businessmen in Rhode Island saw that if the state were to benefit from the line, the line had to be continued across the Seekonk River into the city. The Boston and Providence Railroad and Transportation Company was organized and in 1835 the line, with its new terminus at India Point, was completed. Here one could get a steamer for New York. Spurred on by the prospects of profit from the railroads, businessmen built other lines to connect Providence with cities of the other states in New England, the first of which was a line that ran from Providence to Stonington, Connecticut.[108]

Irishmen made up a large part of the labor force on these projects. Most of the men had left their families behind in Ireland to seek work on the railroads. Men from one of Ireland's counties would secure employment and often enough would immediately raise a ban against the employment of Irishmen of another county. Life for these men was a hard experience, and only by banding together did the individual have some protection against exploitation. It was quite common in those days for laborers to remain where they were when the line was completed, either "squatting" on vacant land, or buying or renting land where it was cheapest. Many of the laborers who built the rail line towards Providence had emigrated from Cork and Kerry in the south of Ireland. Many of them settled in Fox Point, a section of Providence on the lower east side of the river.[109]

The third Providence neighborhood where a large number of Catholics settled in the 1830s was in the north end in what is now called Smith Hill and Randall's Square. In 1831 Philip Allen established the Allen Print Works on Thurbers Lane. As early as 1835 he introduced machines to print cloth instead of wooden blocks used up to that time. As others had before him, Allen turned to Ireland for skilled cloth workers needed to operate his new machines. Most of the two hundred and fifty men he employed emigrated from

[107]"Memoranda," September 16, 1835.
[108]Coleman, *The Transformation of Rhode Island*, pp. 174-76.
[109]Byrne, *Catholic Church in the New England States*, I, 361-62; Thomas E. Ryan, *Burrillville, R. I. and the Catholic Church: A Historical Sketch* (Providence: n.d.), p. 91.

Ireland, and most of them settled in the vicinity of the mill.[110]

In the seven years between 1832 and 1839 the Catholic population of Providence increased from about two hundred to a total population of 1,696. No other city in New England, save Boston, witnessed such a rapid increase at that time.[111] The growth of the Catholic community in Providence brought new tensions. Bishop Fenwick wrote succinctly in his "Memoranda" on December 18, 1835: "The Bishop writes letters to Providence, There is trouble there." The same short notation appears again on April 6, 1836. The word "trouble" in the bishop's "Memoranda" usually referred to disagreements within a congregation, either between factions or between the people and their pastor. In the case of Providence it might well have been both. It is at least possible that the cause of division was a dispute over the site for a church in Providence.

In July 1836, men of the parish finished digging out a foundation hole on the lot on High Street. Masons then began work on an eighty by forty foot foundation. Lack of funds brought the project to a stop the following October with the stone walls half finished, the floor laid, and a debt on the parish of over one thousand dollars.

The money was owed to the masons and carpenters working on the church because, like the church in Pawtucket, no bank would loan the money for construction. The bishop came to Providence on the new railroad on October 22nd, covering the distance from Boston in two and one-half hours. Fr. Lee met him at the depot, and they went out to his house on the Pawtucket turnpike where Fr. Patrick McNamee, Fr. Lynch's replacement, awaited them. On Sunday, the bishop said Mass in the chapel in the house where twenty-three people assisted. Afterward they went to the Town House in Providence for Sunday services. Here, Fr. Lee offered the Mass for a large group of Catholics and non-Catholics. After administering confirmation in the church in Pawtucket, the bishop returned to Fr. Lee's house to meet the committee in charge of building the new church. The bishop stressed the need for proper collection of funds

---

[110]"Memoranda," February 5, 1842; William Harold Munro, *Memorial Encyclopedia of the State of Rhode Island* (New York: The American Historical Society, 1916), pp. 410-11.

[111]Rev. John Corry to William R. Staples, January 10, 1843, RI Mss, X, 120, RIHS. "Memoranda," November 4, 1838, January 4, 1840; James Fitton, *Sketches of the Establishment of the Catholic Church in New England* (Boston: Patrick Donahue, 1877), p. 225. Fitton gives the figures gathered in the census taken by the Hibernian Orphans Society in December 1839: Adult population, 1,087; children of four years of age and under, 217; children between four and ten years, 273; between ten and seventeen, 119.

in order to meet the debt and appointed twenty collectors to take
on the work.[112]

In January 1837, Fr. Lee went south on a collecting tour, leaving Fr. McNamee in charge. Building operations continued in Fr.
Lee's absence. On the 25th of January, Fr. Corry brought news to
the bishop from Providence that the men working on the church
there had attached the building for $250 due according to their
contract to the carpenters and $1,100 due to the masons. The
workers threatened to sell the lot if the debt was not paid. Not
wishing to lose such valuable property and with it, he felt, the hope
of building a church in Providence, the bishop himself arranged to
have the debt secured. Fr. Lee's efforts in the south met with some
success, for in February, he was able to send $500 from Philadelphia
to be put towards the payment of the debt.[113]

Within a week of Fr. Lee's return home on March 20th, Fr.
McNamee was in Boston bearing "bad news." The exact nature of
the news is not recorded. But from succeeding events it would seem
that the "bad news" was another divisive rift within the Catholic
community in Providence. The situation grew worse during Bishop
Fenwick's absence from the diocese at a Provincial Council in Baltimore from April 6th to May 14th. He was not back in Boston but
a few days when he made a change in personnel in that mission. On
May 18th he sent Rev. Michael Mills, a Dublin priest who had just
recently requested service in the diocese, to assist in attending the
Providence congregation. That same day the bishop told Fr. Lee to
suspend building operations of his church.[114] The difficult financial
situation in Providence was made impossible when news arrived in
Boston that the banks throughout the country were suspending
specie payments. The overheated and immature American economy
was in the process of readjusting itself. 1837 would be a depression
year for the entire country, but it would prove especially severe in
Providence and other manufacturing towns.

The change in personnel did not prove to be the answer to the
problems in Providence. Fr. Lee was unable to quiet his unruly
parishioners, and at last Bishop Fenwick's patience with Fr. Lee
gave way when a new chorus of complaints against the Providence
pastor reached him. To complicate matters, serious friction erupted
between Fr. McNamee and Fr. Lee after Fr. Lee's servant sued Fr.
McNamee for slander. On the day after Fr. McNamee appeared in

[112]"Memoranda," October 22, 24, 1836.
[113]*Ibid.,* January 25; February 22, 1837.
[114]*"Ibid.,"* March 29; May 18, 1837.

court in Providence, Bishop Fenwick withdrew Fr. Lee's faculties at Providence, leaving the newly arrived Fr. Mills in charge of the parish.[115]

By June, Fr. McNamee succeeded in extricating himself from the slander suit, and a short time later Bishop Fenwick directed him to go to Benedicta, Maine. Fr. McNamee declined the assignment and asked for his *exeat* which the bishop gave him.[116] Fr. Lee was assigned to the church in Pawtucket. Bishop Fenwick's troubles with Providence, however, were not over yet. He was back but a few days from an extended trip when he received news from Providence that the new church was again threatened by the congregation's inability to pay its debts. For the second time, the bishop himself undertook to arrange payment.[117]

The bishop's concern for the Providence church did not ease as the months progressed. On August 10th, he asked Fr. Corry to make some inquiries concerning the state of church property in Providence and on other unspecified matters. Fr. Mills's arrival in Boston the next day might have given the bishop the opportunity to talk over the situation with him personally. On the 19th of August, the bishop passed through Providence to take the steamboat for Newport and the dedication of the new church there. While in Newport, the bishop probably talked with Fr. Corry about the possibility of transferring him to Providence, if he did not actually tell him of the change.[118]

More bad news of troubles in the congregations in Lowell and Providence awaited Bishop Fenwick when he returned to Boston. The bishop began to realize that disputes such as those which disturbed Lowell and Providence were endemic among Irish congregations. But in both these cases he felt that the time had come for action. The day after he received news of further disputes in Providence, both Fathers Corry and Lee arrived in Boston, and Fr. Mills left his Providence assignment for New York, not to return. The bishop sent Fr. Corry to Providence in place of Fr. Mills and a few days later assigned Fr. Lee to administer to the Newport and Pawtucket parishes.[119]

Reaction from the congregation in Providence was not long in

---

[115] "*Ibid.,*" May 26, 27, 31, 1837.
[116] *Ibid.,* June 13, 17, 1837.
[117] *Ibid.,* August 8, 1837.
[118] *Ibid.,* August 10, 11, 19, 20, 1837. Fr. Corry, on the flyleaf of the "Baptismal Register" of SS. Peter and Paul, says he took charge of the parish on the 20th of August.
[119] *Ibid.,* August 23, 24, 26, 1837.

coming. A delegation of parishioners called on the bishop on August 29th. Coincidently a twelve man delegation from Lowell on a similar mission had left the bishop's office just a short time earlier. Both delegations found the bishop unwilling to reinstate the priests he had dismissed. Bishop Fenwick followed his actions a few days later with a letter to the Catholics of Providence stating his position in reference to Fr. Mills.[120]

Fr. Corry seems to have quite literally "taken charge of the parish." His restless energy provided the impetus to move construction of the church forward again at the end of September. A visitor to Providence reported to the bishop on November 13th that the church had just received its roof. On December 10, 1837, the second Sunday of Advent, Fr. Corry celebrated the first Mass in the still uncompleted church.[121]

With Fr. Corry's coming to Providence the divisions within the Catholic population were quieted but not healed. Among the Irish of the city, who made up almost the entire congregation, there were certain men who were not reluctant to challenge Fr. Corry for leadership of the congregation. Among those whom Fr. Corry would later identify on the flyleaf of his "Baptismal Register" as the leaders of the opposition were John McCarthy, James McCarthy and Hugh Duffy. John McCarthy was a calico printer who lived on Thurbers Lane near Philip Allen's Calico Print Work. He later became manager of the plant. McCarthy is singled out by Fr. Corry as one "who did all he could to create a schism." James McCarthy, a designer who lived at 331 North Main Street, and Hugh Duffy, a bleacher who lived on Charles Street, were also active leaders in Irish societies and other groups in the community.

Fr. Corry's responsibilities were increased in February 1838 when Bishop Fenwick again adjusted the pastoral charges of his priests. Fr. Lee was assigned to take charge of New Bedford in addition to Newport and to surrender charge of the Pawtucket church to Fr. Corry.[122] Like Fr. Woodley, Fr. Corry went to visit his parishioners wherever they clustered together.

The Catholic communities in southern New England administered by Fr. Corry resembled those in Ireland with which many of the immigrant clergy and people were well acquainted. George Potter again is a valuable guide. He notes that

---

[120]*Ibid.*, August 27, 31, 1837.
[121]SS. Peter and Paul, Providence, "Baptismal Register."
[122]"Memoranda," February 16, 1838.

the Irish were accustomed to travel by horse or foot for miles to attend services on Sunday, but this was out of the question for Catholics who lived in remote villages. Twice a year, starting Easter and Christmas, a priest traveled on regular schedule to the outlying bounds of the parish on what was called stations, to hear confessions and give Communion. There he also collected the parish dues—a shilling or two from a man and wife. In the absence of the services of a priest regularly, the people kept their relationship with the Church by a public saying of the Rosary each Sunday, and it was the common custom of households to close each evening with the Rosary.[123]

The same practices continued in America.

Fr. Corry was the first priest to record a baptism in the town of Warwick, which then encompassed the present town of West Warwick with its villages of Crompton and Riverpoint. Irishmen had begun moving into the Pawtuxet valley as early as 1834, when Michael Carroll, his wife and his brother Edward, emigrants from Ballybay, County Monaghan, secured work in the Green and Pike Bleachery at Clyde and settled nearby. These three were soon followed by their friends and neighbors, and within a few years a sizable community of Irish had grown up in the valley. Most of them came from the same town, Ballybay, but there were a few representatives from County Roscommon. In 1838 Michael Carroll is thought to have brought the first Catholic priest to the valley to celebrate Mass in Carroll's home at Birch Hill. Until 1844, if the young men and women in the area wished to attend Mass on Sunday, they walked the nine miles to the new church in Providence.[124] Although there are no similar details, it appears that another group of Irish Catholics began to cluster around the Sprague Print Works in Cranston village. By the early 1840s several hundred Irishmen were employed in the Sprague works.

During 1838 work on the interior of the new church in Providence went slowly. On October 25th, Fr. Corry journeyed to Boston to inform the bishop that his church was nearly complete and arrange a date for its dedication. Early on the morning of November 4, 1838, Bishop Fenwick celebrated Mass in the church. At ten o'clock, accompanied by Fathers Corry and Wiley, he returned through the rain to the church for the ceremony of dedication. Some three hundred people gathered in the church, each having

---

[123]Potter, *To the Golden Door,* pp. 82-83, 357-58.

[124]"From Ireland's Flax Fields to Pawtuxet Valley Pines." *The Evening Tribune,* March 5, 1911. The author of the article records it was Fr. James Fitton who said the Mass in Carroll's house, but Fitton, in his *Sketches,* does not mention the incident nor does the date of the Mass correspond with a time when Fr. Fitton was known to be in the area.

paid one dollar for a ticket. Fr. Corry had again sold tickets as a way of avoiding disturbances caused by "idle and disorderly Protestants" and reducing the nearly $5,000 debt burdened on the church. After the bishop dedicated the new church to God under the patronage of St. Peter and St. Paul, Fr. Corry celebrated Mass and assisted the bishop in administering confirmation. Later that day Bishop Fenwick returned again to celebrate Vespers.[125]

The church, dedicated after so much effort and struggle, was by today's standards a small, but impressive structure built of slate stone covered with cement. Its total cost was approximately $12,-000, a considerable sum for a fifteen hundred member congregation that was largely made up of the "laboring class of people." The bell tower of the church was still unfinished when the church was dedicated, and the parish lacked a bell. This deficiency was remedied the following month when Philip Allen donated a Spanish bell to the parish. Fr. Corry publicly thanked Allen in a letter published in the *Republican Herald.* [126]

Conflict Within the Church and Rebellion in the State

The rapid increase in Irish Catholic population in Rhode Island in the 1830s contributed to a heightening of tensions within the political community of the state and personal conflicts within the Catholic community in Providence. The Irish in Providence settled together in distinct neighborhoods that were close to the places where they worked. Fr. Corry encouraged his parishioners to buy homes and settle in the area around the church in order to defend church property or perhaps so that he might more easily maintain an influence over them. Whatever the reasons, in 1840, he bought the lot adjacent to the church and sold it in parcels to his parishioners. Probably many of the first Catholics of Providence lived in the long, low, one-storied houses, in rented rooms in older buildings or in small, three room cottages like that which the next pastor would build near the church. Fr. Corry himself lodged with some of his parishioners. His address, in 1838, was listed as 128 Broad Street.[127]

Most men of the parish held jobs either as laborers, mill work-

---

[125]"Memoranda," November 4, 1838; *Republican Herald,* November 7, 1838.
[126]*Republican Herald,* January 12, 1839.
[127]Byrne, *Catholic Church in the New England States,* I, 362-63, 394.

ers with various degrees of skill, or shopkeepers.[128] Philip Allen
alone employed over two hundred Irishmen in his print works.[129]
Young women of the Irish community would often work as domes-
tics in the homes of the well-to-do. Prior to 1840, an Irish woman
in the mills, was a rare sight. After that date an increasing number
of Irish, both men and women, began finding employment in the
new manufacturing enterprises springing up all over New England.
The large influx of Irish immigrants allowed employers to pay mill
operatives lower wages because of the abundance of laborers. However, the specter of the Irishman as a job competitor with the Rhode
Island native proved less a cause for antagonism than the specter
of the Irish Catholic as a potential voter.[130]

Few Irish immigrants became actively involved in the political
and social issues that agitated America. Rather, they concerned
themselves with the political and social problems of their homeland.
As early as 1827 the Irish of Providence had formed the Hibernian
Relief Society to raise funds to aid in Daniel O'Connell's fight for
Catholic emancipation in Ireland. The society was revived in the
early 1830s as the Society of the Friends of Ireland which, as early
as 1835, gathered the Irish together on March 17th to celebrate St.
Patrick's day.[131]

Members of the group were also prominent among the officers
of the Hibernian Orphans Society that was founded early in 1839.
One of the first activities of this society was to appoint a committee
of its members to take a detailed census of Catholics in Providence
to determine the number of children in the city.[132]

In the early part of July 1840, Fr. Corry asked Bishop Fenwick
for a short leave because of ill health. Only eight days after the
bishop made a note of Fr. Corry's request, he recorded the cryptic
phrase, "Great trouble in Providence."[133] The "trouble" was ignited by Fr. Corry's refusal to allow members of the Hibernian
Orphans Society to use school rooms in the basement of SS. Peter
and Paul's for their monthly meeting. Henry Duff, who was active

[128]Among the occupations listed in the Providence *Directory* after the names of
Irish Catholics were block printer, bleacher, dyer, laborers, mason, tailor and dry
goods merchant.

[129]"Memoranda," February 7, 1842.

[130]Ware, *Early New England Cotton Manufacture,* pp. 229-35; James L. Marsis,
"Agrarian Politics in Rhode Island, 1800-1860." *Rhode Island History,* XXXIV (February 1975), 13-21.

[131]Lord, Sexton and Harrington, *History of the Archdiocese of Boston,* II, 349; *Republican Herald,* March 20, 23, 1839.

[132]Henry J. Duff to Thomas Wilson Dorr, November 11, 1841, Dorr Papers, A 949,
John Hay Library, Brown University.

[133]"Memoranda," July 8, 16, 1840.

in the society, mentions the incident in a public letter written several years later. He says simply that "a serious quarrel took place between Rev. John Corry and a part of his flock." Duff declined to judge Fr. Corry's action at the time. He stated that since the circumstances of the case were familiar to all, it was sufficient to state the fact "that one-half of his congregation disliked him and he returned their indifference with a cordial hatred." It seems that in Duff's mind, at least, the heart of the division in Providence lay with Fr. Corry's attempt to establish his complete moral authority over the Catholic community. The quarrel that came to the surface that July between Fr. Corry and his parishioners colored all activities of the Catholic community in Providence for the next four years.[134]

On the first Sunday of October 1840, Fr. Corry organized a Catholic Temperance Society. Temperance was a popular cause in Providence and there were at least two other temperance societies in the city when Fr. Corry organized his.[135] The members of the society pledged not to use "ardent spirits, strong beer, or porter, nor wine or cider where they are offered for sale." Although the society was reputed to have enrolled between thirteen hundred and fourteen hundred members among the growing Irish community, Duff, McCarthy and the other dissidents were not among its members.[136]

Fr. Corry's pastoral responsibilities were lightened in January 1841, when Bishop Fenwick transferred Rev. William Fennelly from St. Mary's church in the Charlestown section of Boston to the pastoral charge of St. Mary's in Pawtucket. Pawtucket, like Providence, was experiencing a significant increase in population with the arrival of new immigrants drawn by the rapid expansion of New England's manufacturing centers. Bishop Fenwick felt the time was right to make Pawtucket a separate mission with its own pastor, and he gave Fr. Fennelly charge of Woonsocket as well.[137]

On January 23, 1841, Irish patriotism precipitated a chain of events that would have great repercussions for the church in Providence. When in the early 1840s, Daniel O'Connell launched a campaign in Ireland to repeal the legislative union between England and Ireland, a committee of the Boston Repeal Association named

        [134]Henry J. Duff, "Repeal in the City of Providence as It is," *Evening Chronicle*, September 12, 13, 14, 15, 1843. Duff's letter appeared under the title of an advertisement in four installments.
        [135]Joseph Brennan, *Social Conditions in Industrial Rhode Island: 1820-1860* (Washington: Catholic University of America, 1940), pp. 82-87.
        [136]*Providence Directory*, 1841, p. 206.
        [137]"Memoranda," January 13, 19, 1841.

ten citizens of Providence to set about organizing a repeal association in Providence. The Providence committee's call for an organizational meeting brought upwards of four hundred persons to
Washington Hall on February 6, 1841. Out of the meeting emerged
the Providence Repeal Organization of the Friends of Ireland. Patrick O'Connell was elected president and Hugh Duff secretary.

In Duff's version of the events that followed, Fr. Corry objected
to the fact that his parishioners would join an organization led by
individuals whom he found obnoxious and denounced some of
them from the altar.[138] To counter the influence of O'Connell and
Duff, Fr. Corry, the following week, proposed to the temperance
society, which met at SS. Peter and Paul, that it expand its concerns
to embrace the cause of repeal. The society accepted their pastor's
suggestion and formed a second repeal organization, the Providence Temperance and Moral Reform Repeal Association, with
Thomas Cosgrove and John Bennis among its officers. Conscious
that a divided movement would work against the success of the
repeal movement, the leaders of the Friends of Ireland Society
unsuccessfully attempted to effect a union between the two associations at a meeting on February 20th. Each side accused the other
of acting out of motives of "vanity" and "wild ambition for celeb-
rity." In the end, the Friends of Ireland conceded the field to the
rival association.[139] Whether one event is related to the other, there
is no evidence, but four days after the failure of the meeting to effect
a union between the two groups, John McCarthy wrote to Bishop
Fenwick broaching the possibility of building a second Catholic
church in the city.[140]

There definitely was a practical need for a second church in
Providence. The increase in the Catholic population of the city in
the two years since SS. Peter and Paul was dedicated was such that
there simply was no room to accommodate the faithful in one
church. The Catholic population of the city had increased by "one
half at least" between January 1839 and November 1841.[141] Faced
with a considerable debt on the existing church, Fr. Corry was
compelled to oppose any division of his parish in the immediate
future, especially one which would deprive him of some of the

---

[138]Duff, *Evening Chronicle,* September 12, 1843.

[139]*Republican Herald,* February 24; March 13, 1841.

[140]A reference to McCarthy's letter is given in the bishop's reply to McCarthy, a
copy of which is found in a parish diary kept by the first pastor of St. Patrick's parish,
Providence. The diary will be referred to hereafter as "St. Patrick's Records," St.
Patrick's, Providence.

[141]Duff to Dorr, November 11, 1841, Dorr Papers, A949, Hay Library, Brown
University.

wealthier members of the northern section of his parish. Later that year, on November 3, 1841, Fr. Corry himself bought land on the corner of Broadway and Barton streets for use as a burying ground and the site of a church he felt would be needed in that area in the course of the next two or three years to meet the needs of a growing Catholic population in Olneyville.[142]

The bishop, in his reply to McCarthy on March 5th, gave his full consent to the project provided that McCarthy and his fellow petitioners follow the decrees of the American bishops regarding the deeding of the property. He informed McCarthy in the letter that rather than have the priest in Pawtucket serve the proposed church, he would rather appoint a separate priest to the new parish when the time was appropriate.[143]

The movement to build the new church got underway at a meeting of Catholics favorable to the project on March 13th in Washington Hall. Those who attended this first meeting were primarily people who lived in the northern part of the city and in the adjacent town of North Providence, and who wanted a church close to their homes and places of occupation. The meeting elected a church committee with the familiar names of John McCarthy and Patrick O'Connell as president and secretary. Those at the meeting also voted to ask the bishop to send a priest whom the group could recognize as their pastor, and at a later meeting, appointed a committee of three to present their petition to the bishop.[144]

Finding a site for the new church required compromise with the original hopes of the group. A site on Benefit Street, north of the Baptist church, was the preferred location, but the cost of land in that locality was such that the committee charged with the task of finding a site chose one on Fletcher's Hill or Smith Hill, as it was later known, which though not centralized, was readily accessible.[145] On April 15, 1841, the committee reported on their work to Bishop Fenwick and received his promise to come to look over the site. True to his word, the bishop arrived in Providence on April 19th and was met by Mr. McCarthy and the other members of the committee. The bishop approved the site and its $2,000 purchase price. After viewing the lot, the group went out to the village of Pawtucket to call on Fr. Fennelly. Fr. Fennelly agreed to take charge of the new

[142]Rev. John Corry to William R. Staples, January 10, 1843, RI Mss, X, 120, RIHS; Land deed, Jeremiah Baggott to Rev. John Corry, November 23, 1841, Providence Diocesan Chancery Archives, hereafter cited PChA.
[143]"St. Patrick's Records," p. 1.
[144]Ibid., p. 3.
[145]Ibid., pp. 10-11.

parish and to superintend the building of the new church. With
matters settled, the bishop returned to the station to catch the train
for Boston.[146] Evidently Fr. Corry was not consulted in any matters
concerning the new parish.

Through the medium of frequent meetings and committee action, the people of the north end collected funds, decided on a plan
for the church, collected bids, selected a contractor and hired a man
to superintend the actual construction of the church. On Tuesday,
July 13, 1841, Bishop Fenwick, assisted by five of his clergy including Fathers Fennelly and Corry and joined by a crowd of Catholics
and Protestants, laid the cornerstone under the invocation of St.
Patrick.[147]

Funds were raised by a door to door canvass of the parish,
through pledges and through the assistance of a committee of
women who took on the task of collecting from the women of the
parish, who most likely worked as maids or performed some other
domestic service. Other revenue came in through pew rentals and
weekly collections. Although the people of the north end were perhaps better off materially than the congregation who built the first
church in Providence, they were unable to raise the entire amount
needed for construction of the church by subscription alone. A
meeting of the parishioners empowered the building committee
with the authority to borrow from $3,000 to $5,000 for three years
at interest. The source of the loan is not noted.[148]

On August 23, 1841, Bishop Fenwick again noted in his diary,
"Bad news from Providence." Again there is no echo in other
sources as to what the trouble was. The repeal association of which
Fr. Corry was the moving force had launched a campaign to raise
funds, but the results were only moderately successful. Perhaps the
Friends of Ireland complained about the amount collected and the
way it was passed on to Ireland, as they would later.[149] After September 1841 both groups allowed agitation on behalf of repeal to
lapse for two years.

Fr. Fennelly's place in Pawtucket was taken temporarily by Fr.
Dennis Ryan, one of the older priests of the diocese whose previous
assignment had been in Whitefield, Maine. On August 30th Fr.
Ryan was able to report to the bishop that, under the circumstances,
things were going well in Providence and the new church was pro-

---

[146]"Memoranda," April 15, 19, 1841.
[147]"St. Patrick's Records," p. 18; "Memoranda," July 13, 1841.
[148]"St. Patrick's Records," pp. 12, 14; William Wiley to William R. Staples, January 9, 1843, RI Mss, X, 120, RIHS.
[149]Duff, *Evening Chronicle,* September 13, 1843.

gressing. Although the contract called for completion of the church in November, the building was still unfinished when on Christmas day, 1841, Fr. Ryan celebrated Mass in the church for the first time.

During the second week of January, the bishop transferred Fr. Ryan to Taunton and Taunton's pastor, Fr. William Wiley moved to Providence. Fr. Wiley's parishioners were disturbed about his transfer, and Fr. Ryan met with a protest on his arrival.[150] Fr. Wiley was a convert who spent his early years in an orphan asylum in New York. After being apprenticed to a farmer in upstate New York, he was befriended by an Irishman who introduced him to the Catholic faith. In time Wiley sought out Bishop Cheverus in Boston, where he received instruction and baptism in 1820. Lacking any schooling, yet wishing to become a priest, he eventually acquired an academic background and came to study in the seminary Bishop Fenwick maintained in his house. Ordained on December 23, 1827, he was an experienced and successful priest in whom the bishop had confidence when sent to Providence.[151] Fr. Wiley took possession of his charge on January 15, 1842. He quickly discovered that defective materials and workmanship were going into the building. Working closely with the building committee, he halted work on the defective part of the building and received an award of approximately $1,000 from arbitrators set up to handle the congregation's dispute with the builders. The original contract was paid off, and in March another firm of carpenters was engaged to finish the building.[152]

On January 26th the bishop came to Providence to bless the new bell purchased largely with a $300 contribution given by Philip Allen.[153] Bishop Fenwick returned again on Sunday, February 5th, this time to offer Mass and, in the evening, attend a concert of sacred music which Fr. Wiley arranged to help pay for the furnishings of the as yet unfinished altar and vestry. Eleven hundred people, who paid fifty cents each, filled the church and, to the bishop's mind, enjoyed the concert. On Monday the bishop visited Allen's calico print works with its steam driven machinery and paid a call on its owner to thank him for his generosity.[154]

Later that week, on his visit to Providence on February 11th, the bishop appointed Rev. Patrick O'Beirne to assist Fr. Corry at SS. Peter and Paul. The size of the Catholic population of Providence justified another priest being assigned to the parish. The

---

[150]"Memoranda," January 12, 17, 1842.
[151]Lord, Sexton and Harrington, *History of the Archdiocese of Boston,* II, 43-44.
[152]"St. Patrick's Records," January 15, 1842.
[153]"Memoranda," January 26, 1842.
[154]*Ibid.,* February 5, 6, 1842.

timing of Fr. O'Beirne's appointment grew out of the disagree-
ment Fr. O'Beirne had with his fellow priest, Fr. O'Flaherty, in St.
Mary's in the north end of Boston. The dispute between the two
priests led to a bitter division in the parish that saw parishioners
arrayed on the side of their favorite. Fr. O'Beirne asked for a
change of assignment, and his transfer to Fr. Corry's parish was
the result.[155] Fr. O'Beirne was not there over two weeks before
Bishop Fenwick received an "insolent letter from a meeting of
Catholics in SS. Peter and Paul complaining of his sending Fr.
O'Beirne, of his having formed two congregations, and of drawing
the lines of division between them." Because of the letter, the
bishop withdrew Fr. O'Beirne and informed the parishioners in a
return letter, that they would soon hear from him as to when he
might also remove Fr. Corry.[156]

One can only surmise the nature of the relationship between Fr.
Corry and his bishop. Corry's name rarely appears in Bishop Fenwick's "Memoranda" as having visited Boston after the division of
his parish. When, in early March, Bishop Fenwick went to New York
to see Bishop Hughes, he stopped in Providence on March 6th, said
Mass in St. Patrick's and in the afternoon took tea at John
McCarthy's. The next day the bishop went out to Pawtucket where
the revival of business had caused the population to increase rapidly. Previously, on February 15th, the bishop had appointed Rev.
William Ivers to be Pawtucket's pastor and to take charge of Woonsocket as well. The bishop spent an hour with him and recorded his
satisfaction at Fr. Ivers's apparent enthusiasm for his new position.
Taking the afternoon steamer to Newport, the Boston prelate spent
the next two days with Fr. O'Reilly before leaving for New York.
Again, there is no mention of Fr. Corry.[157]

The tension within the Catholic community in Rhode Island
was overshadowed during the next few months by the threat of civil
war within the state over demands for extension of the suffrage.[158]
During the course of the agitation for constitutional reform the
previous year, defenders of the status quo, such as the editor of the
Providence Journal Henry B. Anthony, attempted to arouse the fears

[155]Lord, Sexton and Harrington, *History of the Archdiocese of Boston,* II, 304.
[156]"Memoranda," February 24, 1842.
[157]*Ibid.*, March 6-9, 1842.
[158]Patrick T. Conley, *Democracy in Decline: Rhode Island's Constitutional Development, 1776-1841* (Providence: Rhode Island Historical Society, 1977); George M. Denni-son, *The Dorr War: Republicanism on Trial, 1831-1861* (Lexington: The University Press of Kentucky, 1976); Marvin E. Gettleman, *The Dorr Rebellion: A Study in American Radicalism, 1833-1849* (New York: Random House, 1973); Conley and Smith, *Catholicism in Rhode Island,* pp. 39-52.

and prejudices of Rhode Islanders by raising the specter of the state falling under the control of a growing population of naturalized Catholic citizens.[159] Once in control, the writers argued, the Catholics could be expected to seek special privileges such as public support of parochial schools. They frequently cited the political situation in New York, where such claims were then being made, as an example of what might happen in Rhode Island.[160] Like most appeals to prejudice, the *Journal's* "facts" as to the number of naturalized citizens lacked a basis in reality.[161] While some among the Irishmen of Rhode Island did support or cooperate with Thomas Dorr and other leaders of the suffrage movement, most of them, like Henry J. Duff, stopped short of taking up arms with the Dorrites. At least one member of the Irish community likened the attitude of those supporting limited suffrage to English rulers in Ireland and found that he could live with the situation in Rhode Island just as he had lived with the same situation in Ireland.[162]

The two priests in Providence, regarded by all as being politically neutral, did their best to dissuade their parishioners from joining Dorr's forces. They succeeded for the most part. To the relief of the *Journal,* the Irish did not participate in the "clambake" at which the supporters of Dorr gathered soon after the dispersal of his forces. The newspaper noted that whenever Fr. Corry was asked about attending the affair, he invariably advised taking no part in the proceedings.[163] Fr. Austin Dowling records that Mr. Allen, who was Dorr's uncle, approached Fr. Wiley suggesting the use of St. Patrick's church as a barracks. The request, if ever made, was not granted.[164]

Among the prisoners rounded up after the dispersal of Dorr's troops there were at least three men who identified themselves as Irishmen. Two of them were residents of Providence and one of them, David M. Hamilton, was possibly the same man whose name appears on the list of the building committee of St. Patrick's but who was later replaced when he failed to be an active member.[165]

[159]Joseph T. McNulty, "The Journal, Nativism and Suffrage" (unpublished seminar paper prepared for Dr. Patrick T. Conley, Providence College, 1965).
[160]*Manufacturers' and Farmers' Journal,* January 3, 4, 13, 1842.
[161]*Republican Herald,* March 12, 1842.
[162]*Boston Pilot,* June 17, 1843. Henry J. Duff was a native of Ireland who spent twenty-seven years in New England, twenty of them in Providence where he took up residence in 1833. In 1853 he moved to California. See also Thomas Wilson Dorr to Pres. Franklin Pierce, March 5, 1853, Dorr correspondence, Vol. 14, Hay Library, Brown University.
[163]*Providence Journal,* August 31, 1842.
[164]Byrne, *Catholic Church in the New England States,* I, 367.
[165]*Evening Chronicle,* July 11, 13, 1842.

The civil tension created a dilemma for Fr. Wiley. At Bishop Fenwick's request, Fr. Wiley had gone to New York during the first part of June to ask Bishop John Hughes to preach at the dedication of the new church. Bishop Hughes consented, and the dedication was scheduled for the first Sunday of July. Because of the threat of violence, caused by Dorr's forces, Governor Samuel King had placed the state under martial law. Fr. Wiley was faced with the decision of postponing the dedication ceremony or risking trouble with an already tense community by bringing together a large number of foreigners. Perhaps to forestall trouble and to allay fears, Fr. Wiley, in announcing the details of the ceremony in a notice published in the papers, offered an explanation for the timing of the ceremony. He informed the people of the state that the arrangements had been made long before and maintained that he could not postpone the event without considerable disappointment and inconvenience.[166]

The church was full but not crowded when Bishops Fenwick and Hughes together with the clergy who gathered for the occasion solemnly blessed and dedicated the church under the patronage of St. Patrick. The church, smaller than SS. Peter and Paul, was built in gothic style of slate stone at a cost of $15,000 for the structure alone. On the day of the dedication Bishop Fenwick celebrated the first Pontifical Mass sung in Providence.[167]

The growth of the two Providence parishes by 1842 was readily apparent when Bishop Fenwick again came to Providence in October to celebrate the sacrament of Confirmation. The bishop confirmed 128 adults and children in St. Patrick's in the morning and in the afternoon confirmed 230 in SS. Peter and Paul. The month before, during the Jubilee proclaimed by Gregory XIV, thirteen hundred people received the Eucharist in SS. Peter and Paul and seven hundred in St. Patrick's. The older parish then was almost twice as large as the new one.[168]

The bitter feelings between the two Catholic factions in Providence that had remained quiet for almost two years flared again in June 1843. The dispute arose in a meeting in the Town House on June 12th, during which Fr. Corry's group allegedly violated the spirit of an agreement, aimed at uniting the repeal movement in Providence.[169] The incident served both to weaken the repeal

---

[166]*Providence Journal*, June 28, 1842.
[167]"St. Patrick's Records," July 3, 1842, pp. 21-22; "Memoranda," July 3, 1842.
[168]"St. Patrick's Records," p. 24, Fr. Wiley in 1843 estimated the parish's population at about eight or nine hundred adults; "Memoranda," October 22, 23, 1842.
[169]*Evening Chronicle*, June 13; September 14, 1843; *Boston Pilot*, June 17, 1843.

movement and increase the antipathy of many against Fr. Corry.[170] Finally in early September, Bishop Fenwick removed Fr. Corry from his charge at SS. Peter and Paul and on September 9th the bishop sent a priest from Boston to say Mass in the parish on Sunday.[171]

Fr. Corry's removal brought the dissension among Catholics in the city to the surface. The first part of Henry Duff's letter, giving his version of the cause of the conflict, appeared in the *Evening Chronicle* on the 12th. On the 15th a seven-man committee of supporters of Fr. Corry headed by John Bennis met with Bishop Fenwick to protest Fr. Corry's removal. Bennis had barely begun his statement when the bishop asked him to identify himself. When Bennis told the bishop who he was, the bishop ordered the group out of the room declaring that "he would receive no communication from a man who had already by his foul and intemperate language made himself too well known." The bishop accused Bennis of having used every opportunity to light the fire of discord in the parish.[172]

The situation in the parish apparently grew more serious during the bishop's absence from Boston on a trip to Hartford and Cabotville in Connecticut. Fr. Corry's opponents in the city were quick to take the side of the bishop and expressed their opinion in such language that the editor of the *Chronicle* refused to publish a letter from one of them except as an advertisement.[173]

Sometime during this period a thirteen-man committee of laymen seized possession of the church's books, keys and other property and assumed so insolent an attitude that they were apparently threatened with interdict. Throughout the conflict a priest from Boston continued to say Mass each Sunday in the church.[174] On October 15th, Fr. James Fitton confronted the congregation at the end of the Mass. As he recalled the incident later, he spoke of the propriety of obedience to authority, of the sad consequences of lay interference with church affairs that did not concern them, and that the cause of the strife and contention was the result of man's neglecting his own, to attend to his neighbor's business. He ended by asking the congregation to accept him as their pastor and to return the keys, account books and all else belonging to the church. All those willing to accept these conditions were asked to rise. When the congregation complied, Fr. Fitton gave his blessing "for each

[170]*Boston Pilot,* August 12, 1843.
[171]"Memoranda," September 8, 9, 1843.
[172]*Ibid.,* September 15, 1843.
[173]*Evening Chronicle,* September 19, 1843.
[174]"Memoranda," September 9, 16; October 9, 1843.

to retire quietly, and take their dinner in peace and comfort."[175]

The bishop sent one of his priests to Providence on October 21st to examine Fr. Corry's accounts before he gave him his *exeat* from the diocese. Evidently all was in order. Fr. Corry later labored for five years in the frontier diocese of Little Rock, Arkansas before returning east and serving as pastor in Greenbush, later Rensselaer, New York where he died in 1866.[176]

Fr. Fitton did not follow his predecessor's practice of lodging with his parishioners and established his own residence on Pond Street. The new pastor was a classmate of Fr. Wiley. Born in Boston, Fr. Fitton was the first candidate for the priesthood accepted by the newly arrived Bishop Fenwick. Before he came to Providence Fr. Fitton had served in the missions of Connecticut and central Massachusetts. His work through the years would build his reputation of having been the greatest missionary priest in the history of the Diocese of Boston.[177]

Fr. Fitton was not long in his post when he and Fr. Wiley moved to heal the dissension in the city. On November 16, 1843, the two priests founded the Catholic Temperance Confraternity with themselves as the only officers and presumably embracing all in the city who wanted to join. At least in Fr. Wiley's mind there was great need for such a society whose members would abstain from all drink. He says in his parish diary that "the vice of intemperance, increasing to an alarming degree among us, seems to render the measure absolutely necessary."[178] This new society differed from the one established by Fr. Corry in that the members vowed to abstain from drinking totally, not just from consuming it in public places.

There is an interesting note in Bishop Fenwick's "Memoranda" for November 29, 1843, that reveals a light side of the character of the bishop and some of the hazards of traveling in those days. The bishop left Boston for Providence just when it began to snow. When he reached Providence he found to his great astonishment and disappointment that there was no hackney cab or other transportation available. It was already dark and he first thought of spending the night in a tavern rather than walk the two miles through the snow to Fr. Wiley's house on State Street. But remembering that he had told Fr. Wiley that he would preach for him on the next day, which was Thanksgiving Day, the bishop set out into the storm. His intention wavered more than once during the long walk through the

[175]James Fitton, *Sketches,* pp. 228-29.
[176]Lord, Sexton and Harrington, *History of the Archdiocese of Boston,* II, 285.
[177]*Ibid.,* II, 43-44.
[178]"St. Patrick's Records," November 19, 1843, pp. 29-30.

snow. Sliding and slipping and at one point being barked at by a couple of dogs, he succeeded in reaching his destination. After celebrating Mass the next day the bishop accompanied by Fathers Wiley and Fitton went out to the eight acre plot of land that had recently been purchased and deeded to the bishop as a burial ground for the Catholics of Providence. The land was on Douglas Avenue opposite Bailey Street, a ten minute walk from St. Patrick's. Evidently Fathers Wiley and Fitton thought that the lot Fr. Corry had purchased in 1841 was unsuitable or unavailable due to the circumstances of Fr. Corry's leaving the diocese.

In March 1844, another important step was taken in healing the division within the Catholic community of Providence. First at SS. Peter and Paul, and then at St. Patrick's the two priests working together conducted a week-long retreat that met with success far beyond their expectations. To Fr. Wiley, the retreat produced immense spiritual good and restored peace and harmony among the divided flock. "Hundreds who had neglected their religious duties for many years were led back to God, scandals repaired, dissension healed and almost complete reunion affected between congregations."[179]

Similar progress was being made elsewhere in Rhode Island. In August 1837, Bishop Fenwick had assigned Fr. Constantine Lee to Pawtucket, then added Newport as well. At the end of 1837, the bishop gave the Pawtucket mission to Fr. Corry and assigned New Bedford, Sandwich and Wareham to Fr. Lee's pastoral charge. Education and piety made little impression on the laborers who were his parishioners. In spite of the fact he had four missions to draw on for support, Fr. Lee found it impossible to support himself. He withdrew from the diocese early in 1839 and after a stay in Illinois, moved to Canada where he at last found a successful and fruitful ministry.[180]

Fr. Lee's successor on the mission circuit in the Newport area was Fr. James O'Reilly who seems to have made Newport his usual residence. The affairs of the church there proceeded smoothly for a few years. Although the days of Newport's prosperity as a summer resort were still in the future, Newport then, as now, was an attractive place to spend the summer, especially to people who lived in the warm southern climates. In August 1841, Bishop Fenwick visited the city and stayed with Mrs. Robert Goodloe Harper, a daugh-

[179]*Ibid.*, March 10, 1844, p. 31.
[180]"Memoranda," August 26, 1837; Lord, Sexton and Harrington, *History of the Archdiocese of Boston,* II, 164-65.

ter of Charles Carroll, of Carrolton. The bishop noted that Vespers that Sunday were sung "by some southern ladies."[181]

At this time the mainstay of the economy of the Catholic community in Newport was the construction work on Fort Adams. In 1837, the year the new church of St. Joseph was dedicated, the bishop noted that there were about two hundred Catholics in the town, and five hundred were employed on the works at Fort Adams.[182] In 1842, five years after the dedication of the church, construction on the post was halted. With Newport's economy in a state of decline the laborers had no choice but to look for work elsewhere. The scattering of his congregation left Fr. O'Reilly with an income from the Newport community of $80 a year, and he received little support from his other mission stations.

When Fr. O'Reilly attempted to collect money owed for pew rent by having his sexton keep the defaulters out of the church, some of his parishioners took him to court. The case was tried in the Court of Common Pleas, but the justices could not agree on a verdict. Perhaps it was Fr. O'Reilly's personality or approach that lay at the heart of his financial difficulties as the people in Newport were generous in contributing to other causes. A repeal meeting in Newport on August 3, 1843, raised $70 for the cause and drew support from native Irishmen, some prominent members of the Newport community and ladies and gentlemen from the South.[183]

Fr. O'Reilly continued to live in Newport until November 1843, when the bishop ordered him to reside, for economy's sake, with the priest in Fall River.[184] Most likely he continued to visit Newport as well as his other missions until he succeeded in having himself transferred to Boston in March 1844.

Economic problems also affected the manufacturing towns of Rhode Island. When Woonsocket was a mission station of Fr. Fitton's circuit out of Worcester in 1834, he was able to gather together only thirty Catholics for Mass. At that time Mass was said in private homes. In 1841 the number of Catholics in Woonsocket and nearby Massachusetts communities of Blackstone and Waterford had increased to the point that the owner of the Woonsocket Tavern allowed the Catholics to use the hall in the tavern for Mass.[185]

In Pawtucket, Fr. William Ivers, a former professor of French, Moral Philosophy and Mathematics, found time to engage his pen

[181]"Memoranda," August 1, 1841.
[182]*Ibid.*, August 19, 1837.
[183]*The Boston Pilot*, August 12, 1843.
[184]"Memoranda," December 4, 1843.
[185]Smyth, *Catholic Church in Woonsocket*, pp. 61-62, 65.

in defense of the Catholic position on the Bible against the attacks
of Protestant ministers in New York and Providence.[186] Besides
Pawtucket and Woonsocket, the other large concentration of Catholics that attracted the separate pastoral attention of the priests in
Rhode Island was in the Pawtuxet Valley where soon after he arrived
in his new assignment in Providence, Fr. Fitton began to pay a
monthly visit.[187]

In 1843 the Catholics of Rhode Island witnessed the beginnings of two important movements in the Church. In May a Catholic
newspaper, the *Providence Catholic Layman,* appeared for two diminu-
tive numbers and failed for lack of support.[188] The second movement, the establishment of a Catholic school in Providence, would
prove a success. There were two school-rooms in the basement of
SS. Peter and Paul, which at this time were used for catechetical
instruction on Sundays and for meetings. The people of St. Patrick's
felt the need for similar facilities for the one hundred to one hundred and fifty children who assembled each Sunday for religious
instructions given by Fr. Wiley and "subordinate teachers."[189] The
parish built a school that measured thirty-six by twenty-four feet at
a cost of $500 and completed it in November 1843. At first the
school enrolled only girls, for the boys had to work during the
day.[190]

The growth of the Catholic population of Rhode Island paralleled that of New England as a whole. By the beginning of 1843 the
Diocese of Boston had a Catholic population of over sixty-eight
thousand people. Given the demands of the diocese on its aging
bishop, it was only a matter of time before the diocese would have
to be divided. During the Fifth Provincial Council in Baltimore in
May 1843, Bishop Fenwick presented a proposal for the division of
his diocese. He suggested that the four northern New England
states remain under the Diocese of Boston and the two southern
New England states, Connecticut and Rhode Island, with a joint
Catholic population of some ten thousand, be placed under a new
Diocese of Hartford. While Hartford was closer to the geographical
center of the proposed diocese, Providence had a much larger Catholic population. The fathers of the council accepted the proposal
and submitted it to Rome along with Bishop Fenwick's recommen-

[186]McKenna, *The Centenary Story of Old St. Mary's,* p. 31.
[187]Fitton, *Sketches,* p. 231.
[188]*Boston Pilot,* May 6, 1843; Byrne, *Catholic Church in the New England States,* II, 392.
[189]Rev. William Wiley to William R. Staples, January 9, 1843, RI Mss, X, 120,
RIHS.
[190]"St. Patrick's Records," November 19, 1843, pp. 30, 36.

dation that the first bishop of the new diocese be his good friend,
Fr. William Tyler.[191] On November 28, 1843, Pope Gregory XVI
formally accepted the recommendations of the American bishops.[192]

---

[191]Lord, Sexton and Harrington, *History of the Archdiocese of Boston,* II, 292-94.
[192]Donald C. Shearer, *Pontificia Americana: A Documentary History of the Catholic
Church in the United States, 1784-1884* (Washington: Catholic University of America
Press, 1933), pp. 218-20.

Chapter II

The Episcopate of Bishop William Tyler

William Tyler—the Man, the Priest and the Bishop

William Tyler received episcopal ordination in Baltimore from the hands of his own ordinary, Bishop Fenwick, and two fellow bishops on March 17, 1844. After concluding his affairs in Boston, the new bishop, accompanied by Bishop Fenwick, journeyed to Hartford by train and boat on April 12th. The pastor of Holy Trinity church in Hartford, Rev. John Brady, was their host and guide on their arrival in Hartford. On Sunday, April 14, 1844, Fr. Brady celebrated Mass and Bishop Fenwick preached at the ceremony of installation of Bishop Tyler in his new diocese. Bishop Fenwick took the occasion to eulogize his fellow priest and long time friend.[1]

The new bishop was thirty-eight years old when ordained for the Hartford diocese. Born in Derby, Vermont on June 5, 1806, his family moved in his early youth to Claremont, New Hampshire. His father was a respectable and well-to-do farmer. His mother was a daughter of Rev. Daniel Barber and sister of Rev. Virgil Barber, who were noted Congregational ministers in New England until they entered the Catholic Church and eventually were ordained priests. A year or so after her father and brother entered the Catholic Church, Mrs. Tyler followed their example together with her husband, her three sons and four daughters.[2]

William was about fifteen years old when he became a Catholic. His uncle had opened a school at Claremont and young William became his first student in the classics. Determined to follow Christ as a priest, the young man went to Boston in August 1826, to live

---

[1]"Memoranda," April 12-14, 1844.

[2]*The Metropolitan Catholic Almanac,* 1850, pp. 216-17; Lucius I. Barber, "The First Bishop of Hartford—William Tyler, D.D., A Short Genealogical Sketch of His Family," *The Catholic Standard,* May 8, 1880, first published in the *Connecticut Catholic.* Dr. Barber was a cousin of Bishop Tyler.

with Bishop Fenwick and continue his studies under the bishop's direction. His fellow students in the bishop's household included James Fitton and William Wiley. Two days after his twenty-first birthday in June 1827, he began the study of dogmatic theology. On May 3, 1829, Bishop Fenwick ordained the young man a priest.[3]

Most of Fr. Tyler's priesthood, except for a year's missionary duty at the Catholic settlement of Aroostook, Maine, was spent in the cathedral parish in Boston. He was Bishop Fenwick's frequent companion and eventually his vicar-general. His good friend, John Fitzpatrick, in later years recalled his impressions of Fr. Tyler as a young priest and later as bishop: "His talents were not brilliant nor was his learning extensive, though quite sufficient. But he possessed great moderation of character, sound judgment, uncommon prudence and much firmness." He gave not one hour "to idleness nor vain amusements or visits. He was methodical in the distribution of his time . . . Zeal for the glory of God and the salvation of souls, true humility, total indifference to popular favor and applause, and a perfect spirit of poverty, were his peculiar virtues." It is little wonder that Bishop Fenwick would advance his name to be bishop of the new diocese, although the departure of his good friend was probably quite a personal loss.[4]

Fr. Tyler's own estimate of his fitness for the vocation of bishop was not as strong. The Papal Bulls establishing the new diocese and the formal approval of Fr. Tyler as its first bishop arrived in Boston on February 13, 1844. On the 21st, Fr. Tyler, along with John Fitzpatrick who was elected at the same time as co-adjutor Bishop of Boston, left the city for Frederick, Maryland, to make a retreat before ordination. His fellow priest, Fr. Fitton, recalls in his memoirs that Fr. Tyler accepted ordination as bishop only because of his great respect for Bishop Fenwick whom he revered as a father, and because of a formal decision of Fr. Francis Dzierozinski, S.J. Provincial of the Maryland Province, under whose direction he made his retreat. Fr. Tyler's reluctance is also mentioned by his fellow retreatant, Bishop Fitzpatrick.[5]

Within a few months of his taking charge of the new diocese, it became obvious to Bishop Tyler that Providence rather than

---

[3]Richard H. Clarke, *Lives of the Deceased Bishops of the Catholic Church in the United States* (Published by the author: 1887-1889), II, 272-83; James H. O'Donnell, "Diocese of Hartford," in Byrne, *Catholic Church in the New England States*, II, 122-25; "Memoranda," May 3, 1829.

[4]Bishop John Fitzpatrick's "Diary," cited in Byrne, *Catholic Church in the New England States*, II, 133.

[5]Fitton, *Sketches*, pp. 235-36.

Hartford would be the better place for his episcopal residence. While Hartford counted 13,000 inhabitants, from 500 to 600 of whom were adult Catholics, Providence had a population of 23,000, of whom over 2,000 were Catholics. It also provided better opportunities for an episcopal residence. After first talking the matter over with Bishop Fenwick, Bishop Tyler came to Providence on the first Sunday of July 1844, and announced to the parishioners of SS. Peter and Paul his intention of taking up residence there.[6] There were certain disadvantages in selecting that church as a cathedral. It was built on so narrow a piece of ground that neighboring land-owners could easily block the windows if they cared to build. Secondly, there were stables on both sides of the church which the bishop noted were very offensive in warm weather. Numerous reports of fires in the neighborhood added to the undesirability of the location of the church. In spite of these problems Bishop Tyler selected SS. Peter and Paul because it was larger than St. Patrick's and because it was free of debt.[7]

Just behind the church, there was a small, one story, three room, wooden building which Fr. Fitton had built as a rectory. The size of the building was irrelevant to Fr. Fitton, for he says, his work lay principally in the church basement. It was this house that now became Bishop Tyler's episcopal residence.[8]

The move from Hartford to Providence required more than just the support of Bishop Fenwick. When his fellow bishops assembled in Baltimore for the Sixth Provincial Council in May 1846, Bishop Tyler asked them to petition Rome either to officially grant permission for the change of residence or to make Providence the name of the diocese. The bishops agreed to Tyler's request and they sent the petition on to Rome. A year later the Holy See granted permission for the change of residence but declined to change the original title of the diocese.[9]

While the process of getting official permission went forward, Bishop Tyler began the task of organizing the new diocese. In a letter dated February 24, 1845, he lamented that his diocese was poor and destitute of everything and that he, on assuming his new post, was overwhelmed with the sad prospect before him.[10] The task

---

[6]*Boston Pilot,* July 6, 1844.

[7]Bishop Tyler to the Society for the Propagation of the Faith, Paris, February 24, 1845, Archives, Society for the Propagation of the Faith, Paris. Hereafter cited SPFA.

[8]Fitton, *Sketches,* p. 233.

[9]Schearer, *Pontificia Americana,* p. 243.

[10]Bishop Tyler to the Society for the Propagation of the Faith, Paris, February 24, 1845, SPFA.

confronting him would have taxed the strength of a man in good health which Bishop Tyler was not.

About the time of his appointment as bishop, Tyler had caught a severe cold which either caused or aggravated a lung disease. Some time toward the end of the year the bishop asked Dr. Edward P. Le Prohon, a young doctor from Montreal, to call on him. The doctor described his patient as being a thin, bespeckled man about six feet tall, with "a well featured countenance, sweet and calm, and delicate white skin" and of "lymphatic temperament." The entire external appearance of the bishop showed symptoms of "latent consumption."[11]

The bishop was concerned to maintain his health in view of the task of organizing the new diocese. Dr. Le Prohon warned his patient to find another residence because his quarters were damp and he ran the risk of being affected by bad weather.[12] The change of residence did not take place until March 1846, after the bishop was confined for several weeks to his bed with an attack of typhoid fever. His new home was an old frame building on the corner of Fenner and Pond Streets. It was only a short distance away from other buildings, but the sun could make its way into the house, and it was safe against dampness. Fr. Austin Dowling recorded the memory of one time when the bishop was sick in bed, which, because of the smallness of the place, was so near the door that he could hear people asking for him. The woman who kept his house would try to keep people out when Tyler was sick, but frequently enough the bishop would, especially if they were children, invite them in to tell him their complaints.[13]

Bishop Tyler looked on the money he received from his people as a contribution to the Church. He was most reluctant to use the little money he received for purposes not intimately connected with "religion." As a result, he dispensed with anything not immediately useful. He had no carriage and traveled within the city on foot. His house had only the most necessary articles of furniture and was without carpeting. His table was common and his meals plain. His silverware was a gift from a lady in Boston.[14] The bishop's cousin would observe that "in all that the bishop said and did there was an earnestness and sincerity which gave a charm to his character. He was

[11]Edward P. Le Prohon, "Memorial to the Rt. Rev. William Tyler, First Bishop of Hartford, Connecticut," translated by Rev. J. M. Toohey from the original French, *American Catholic Historical Researches,* XXII (1895), 3-4.

[12]*Ibid.,* pp. 4-5.

[13]Byrne, *Catholic Church in the New England States,* I, 370.

[14]Le Prohon, "Memorial," p. 5.

genial without levity. He was mild and amiable but firm as a rock."[15]

On his arrival in Rhode Island Bishop Tyler found that in
addition to the three priests in Connecticut, he had only four other
priests to assist him in his ministry to the approximately ten thousand Catholics in Connecticut and Rhode Island. Besides Fathers
Wiley and Fitton in Providence and Fr. Ivers in Pawtucket, Fr. James
O'Reilly served two dioceses in ministering to the parishes at Newport and New Bedford. Within weeks of the bishop's arrival in July
1844, Fr. Ivers in Pawtucket, a contentious and seemingly restless
man, left the diocese and by 1847 was working in Louisiana. To
supply the needs of his people, Bishop Tyler assumed parochial
duties in SS. Peter and Paul while Fr. Fitton again resumed a roving
ministry.[16]

Bishop Tyler was not an accomplished preacher, although
some thought him eloquent.[17] He wrote out most of his important
sermons and a few on the commandments, invalid marriages, and
education together with various announcements, have survived to
give witness to some of his pastoral concerns and problems. However, Bishop Tyler's most eloquent sermon was his own life. Dr. Le
Prohon's "Memorial" reflects the deep admiration of the people of
Providence for a priest who was constantly at their service. Although
titular head of the diocese, he worked as hard in ministering to the
individual spiritual needs of his people as any of the young priests
who gained their first pastoral experience in the cathedral parish.
He could be found on foot often out of breath carrying an umbrella
to protect himself from rain or snow, visiting the sick and the poor.
He heard their confessions and was approachable even by those
most ashamed of their sins. Every Monday at his residence Tyler
distributed bread and other food and occasionally a little money to
those in need. He considered this duty as the most important of his
mission and inseparable from the responsibility of bishop. The
bishop solemnized his parishioners' marriages, baptized their children, and attended the sick until the last year of his life.[18]

There were those who had their disagreements with the bishop.
Tyler was a strict temperance man and like many others attacked the

[15]Barber, "A Short Genealogical Sketch," *The Catholic Standard,* May 8, 1880.
[16]*Sadlier's Catholic Almanac,* 1844, pp. 90-91; Fr. William Ivers to Bishop Anthony
Blanc, New Orleans, Louisiana, March 30, 1847, Archives, University of Notre Dame.
Hereafter cited UNDA.
[17]*Boston Pilot,* June 14, 1845.
[18]Le Prohon, "Memorial," p. 7. The cathedral "Baptismal Register" has a note
in Tyler's hand noting that he baptized a baby he found in a washtub in the rear of
the church. Later he found that the baby's mother had married an Irish Protestant
who deserted her, forcing the mother to give up the baby.

problem of drink both by calling on his people to swear off liquor
and attacking those who sold it. These sellers of whiskey and beer
were, in Le Prohon's words echoing the bishop's, "genuine robbers
of the purses of their fellow citizens and destroyers of their nationality and their families." Some of the men the bishop singled out for
criticism were among the better off of his parishioners. He assured
them he would rather depend on the small contributions of his poor
parishioners than the large sums earned from the sale of adulterated
and intoxicating liquors.[19]

The Early Priests of the Diocese of Hartford

Bishop Tyler's own efforts and the labors of his few fellow
priests were hardly adequate to supply the needs of the widely
scattered Catholic population. One of the bishop's first concerns
was to increase the number of clergy administering to the growing
needs of his diocese. During his tenure as bishop, he ordained two
young men who were native Americans and converts to Catholicism.
Edward Putnam, a New Hampshire man, was ordained on Trinity
Sunday, June 1845, and James Gibson, a young Bostonian, was
ordained June 8, 1848.[20] Bishop Tyler also accepted into his diocese
one priest whose doctor had advised him to seek a more healthful
climate and at least three priests, ordained in Ireland, who applied
to him for admission into the Hartford diocese. While these Irish
priests helped to fill the great need of the new diocese for clergy,
Bishop Tyler was aware of their limitations. All of them would
become involved in confrontations with their bishop in future years.
During the first months of his administration Bishop Tyler
turned to what would prove the most fruitful source of priests for
the diocese, the missionary college of All Hallows, Drumcondra,
Dublin. Rev. John Hand, a Vincentian Father, who conceived the
idea of founding a college to train young Irishmen for the foreign
missions, had opened the college on November 1, 1842. Bishop
Tyler saw an account of it in the Dublin *Directory* and on August 15,
1844, wrote Fr. Hand to request him to assign two young men to
his diocese. "This diocese," he wrote "has a peculiar claim upon
you, in as much as all the Catholics here are Irish, with very few
exceptions." In the same letter he asked Fr. Hand to send seven or

[19]Le Prohon, "Memorial," p. 5.
[20]Byrne, *Catholic Church in the New England States,* I, 369; *Providence Visitor,* January
11, 1892.

eight circulars describing the college. The Providence prelate was considering a collection in the different congregations of the diocese in order to raise funds to support the young men in All Hallows.[21]

After Fr. Hand replied that he had appointed two young men to the diocese, Bishop Tyler wrote of the qualities he looked for in his priests, "I hope these young men will make pious and disinterested priests . . . if so they will do much here for the salvation of souls, but religion has already suffered much in this country from priests who were destitute of the proper spirit. . . . It is not great learning that is required in priests on the mission here so much as solid piety, a spirit of poverty and sincere zeal for the salvation of souls."[22]

The two young men appointed by Fr. Hand—Michael O'Neil and Peter Taaffe—arrived in Providence in October 1847. O'Neil was already ordained a priest when he came, but Taaffe's ordination was delayed in spite of the fact that Bishop Tyler had given a dispensation of eighteen months from the canonical age of twenty-five for ordination to the priesthood. Needing priests badly at this time, Bishop Tyler soon assigned Fr. O'Neil to the mission in Waterbury, Connecticut and accompanied the young priest to his new assignment. Taaffe was ordained on December 21, 1847 and stayed to assist the bishop at the cathedral. Shortly after Taaffe's ordination Bishop Tyler wrote the priests of All Hallows that he was well pleased with these young clergymen. Taaffe himself, still quite immature, was not pleased with his fellow countrymen. "The greatest bar to the distress of the Irish Priest here," he wrote, "is the scandalous conduct of his own countrymen."[23]

On May 21, 1848, Fr. Taaffe became ill and later delirious. In his delirium he became so violent that on June 3rd the bishop was obliged to send him to the Insane Hospital. In a few days he improved a bit, and his brother came from New York to take him home. Later Taaffe was placed in a Catholic-run hospital for the insane in Baltimore, where he lived, supported by the diocese, for many years.[24]

The Third Provincial Council of Baltimore in 1837, faced with

[21]Bishop Tyler to Rev. J. Hand, August 15, 1844, Archives, All Hallows Missionary College. Hereafter cited AHMC.

[22]*Ibid.*, November 26, 1844, AHMC.

[23]Bishop Tyler to Dr. Woodlock, All Hallows, Dublin, December 26, 1847; Rev. Peter Taaffe to Dr. Woodlock, All Hallows, Dublin, October 24, 1847, AHMC.

[24]Bishop Tyler's "Diary," May 21; June 3, 1848, Hartford Archdiocesan Chancery Archives. Hereafter cited HChA; Bishop Tyler to Rev. B. Woodlock, All Hallows, Dublin, July 15, 1848, AHMC.

problems created by priests who were unsuited for missionary work or of unstable character, had issued a decree that young men wishing to work in the missions should take an oath that they would "perpetually" serve the diocese before being ordained sub-deacons.[25] For several years Bishop Tyler omitted receiving the oath from the candidates for his diocese. He felt that "if anyone became dissatisfied and wished to leave the diocese it would be better for them to be free to do so than be restrained by an oath." On learning from one of the older bishops that the clause requiring the oath was inserted at Rome, Bishop Tyler, on March 14, 1849, wrote to the president of All Hallows requesting him to ask his young men studying there to take the oath in the future.[26]

While he had some success in bringing men into his diocese, Bishop Tyler had little, if any, success in securing candidates for the priesthood from among his own people. In a sermon he delivered in the autumn of 1848 he noted that there was not "a single man in the whole diocese who was educating his son for the church." The bishop informed his people that he was providing funds for the four young men who were then studying for the diocese at his own expense.[27] In spite of his need for priests, late in 1848, the bishop found that he could not accept any more students for the diocese than the seven he was already supporting. He simply did not have the money to pay their expenses.[28]

During the five years of his administration, Bishop Tyler succeeded in increasing the number of his clergy to fourteen. Together with their bishop these men ministered to twelve churches and a Catholic population which, during the same five years, had grown to about twenty thousand people.[29]

As the numbers of his clergy increased, Bishop Tyler was able to respond to the requests of his people for priests. The bishop labored for the people of SS. Peter and Paul, and Fr. Wiley, whose poor health had prompted him to take a six month tour of Europe, continued to minister effectively among the people of St. Patrick's. After the bishop came to Providence, Fr. Fitton began to make regular visits to Woonsocket, Pawtucket, Newport and Crompton in

[25]Peter Guilday, *A History of the Councils of Baltimore* (New York: The Macmillan Company, 1932), p. 115.

[26]Bishop Tyler to Very Rev. D. Moriarty, President, All Hallows, Dublin, March 14, 1849, AHMC.

[27]The text of the sermon is found among Bishop Tyler's papers in the Hartford Chancery Archives.

[28]Bishop Tyler to Patrick M'Gowan, October 2, 1848, HChA; Bishop Tyler to Very Rev. D. Moriarty, President, All Hallows, Dublin, March 14, 1849, AHMC.

[29]*Metropolitan Catholic Almanac,* 1849, p. 209.

Warwick. The size of the mission was determined by the hope of providing him with enough territory to yield him financial support. When Fr. John Brady, Jr. came into the diocese in October 1844, Bishop Tyler sent him to say Mass in Woonsocket and probably also Pawtucket, while Fr. Fitton began to serve the cities of New London and Norwich, Connecticut.[30] In April 1845, Fr. Fitton wrote friends in Boston that the prospects of Catholicism in his mission area were highly encouraging. With his characteristic energy he finished a church in New London and was building two others in Norwich and Warwick. On the first Sunday of the month he officiated in New London, the second in Norwich, the third in Warwick, the fourth in Newport, and the fifth ("when it happened") at Stonington.[31]

In May 1845, responsibility for the New London parish passed to the older Fr. Brady in Hartford and in August 1845, he also took charge of Norwich.[32] Freed from these responsibilities Fr. Fitton again assumed charge of the congregations in Woonsocket and Pawtucket while Fr. Putnam in Providence took charge of visiting Warwick. This arrangement continued until November 1, 1846, when the bishop assigned Fr. Fitton to Newport as his permanent residence. The fact that he could settle in Newport at this time suggests that the Catholic population there was again large enough to support a priest. On assuming his duties Fr. Fitton took a census of his new parish. He found that there were 111 heads of families and a total congregation of 375.[33] In 1847 he estimated his flock at over 500 and in 1848 at 560.[34] In the 1840s a few mills were built in the Newport area, but at this time the church seems to have depended more on the visitors attracted to the city as a "watering place" than on the support of year round residents.

Among the first problems that faced Fr. Fitton in Newport was the condition of the frame church completed by Fr. Corry in 1837. The builder was evidently a stranger to church construction. Though the materials used in its construction were of the highest quality, saw and chisel had been used so poorly that the building had become unsafe. On February 3, 1847, Fr. Fitton spent $4,000 for land on Spring Street as a site for a new church. The purchase price for the land was supplied by Mrs. Goodloe Harper and her daughter, Emily, whom Bishop Fenwick had visited often. Their annual donation together with the assistance of the other members

---

[30]*Catholic Almanac*, 1845, p. 93.
[31]*Boston Pilot*, March 1, 1845.
[32]Byrne, *Catholic Church in the New England States,* II, 406, 416.
[33]St. Mary's, Newport, "Baptismal Register," November 1, 1846.
[34]*Ibid.,* 1847, 1848.

of the parish encouraged Fr. Fitton to build a church that would be "a credit to the religion they loved so dearly." The plans for the new church were among the first drawn by Patrick C. Keely. Born in Kilkenny, Keely had begun as a carpenter in Brooklyn. Aside from receiving instructions from his father, a builder, he was self-taught.[35] While the Harpers supplied a large part of the funds, the people of Newport gave what they had including their own labor. On August 7, 1848, volunteers began digging the foundation trenches. The work took a week. On August 15th, the first stone was laid and the foundation walls begun the next day.[36]

Fr. Fitton received aid of another kind, thanks to the presence of Fort Adams. Among the officers there was a young engineer, Lieutenant William S. Rosecrans, who was later to serve as a Union general in the Civil War. A cheerful young man, noted for his piety and deep faith, he offered his help to Fr. Fitton in supervising the construction of the brown stone, gothic style church. The corner-stone was laid on June 14, 1849, and the building was dedicated on July 25, 1852, under the Holy Name of Mary, Our Lady of the Isle.[37]

November 1846, marked not only Fr. Fitton's appointment as pastor of Newport, but also the assignment of pastoral responsibilities in Woonsocket to Fr. Charles O'Reilly. Fr. O'Reilly was born in County Cavan, Ireland and educated in Irish schools, before going as a missionary to the West Indies. He had come into the diocese in June 1846. Previous to his going to Woonsocket, priests, particularly Fr. Fitton, had only visited the town. After purchasing land in October 1842, the Catholic congregation had by 1844 built a small sixty by forty foot frame building at the cost of about $2,000 in hopes that the bishop would soon be able to send them a pastor. Fr. John Brady, Jr. had come up from Providence on October 12, 1844, to perform the first baptism and recorded marriage in the new church.[38]

Fr. O'Reilly, on coming to the city, made his home in the basement of the church. A hard worker, he served all those he could reach regardless of diocesan boundries. He was only in the parish a short time, however, when he decided that the church was altogether too small to serve the needs of the fast growing congregation. In 1848 he built an addition twice as large as the original

[35]Francis W. Kerwick, "Patrick Charles Keely, Architect: A Record of his Life and Work," (South Bend, Indiana: privately printed, 1953), pp. 5-7.
[36]Fitton, *Sketches,* pp. 215-17.
[37]Byrne, *Catholic Church in the New England States,* I, 431. A description of the newly finished church is given in the *Boston Pilot,* June 23, 1849.
[38]Smyth, *Catholic Church in Woonsocket,* pp. 65-67; *Catholic Almanac,* 1845, p. 93.

structure. Like many other men who had the personal resources to endure the hard life of a missionary, Fr. O'Reilly was a man loved and respected by many. A simple, humble man yet he had an explosive personality and was quick to take and give offense. While Bishop Tyler lived, everything went well, for the bishop seems to have been a man who could understand and tolerate others.[39]

When in 1847 Fr. Joseph McNamee accepted Bishop Tyler's invitation to join his diocese, the bishop appointed him pastor of St. Mary's, Pawtucket. Born in County Tyrone, Fr. McNamee had come to the United States while a young boy. He was ordained in 1840 for the Diocese of Cincinnati and worked there until his health began to fail. He came East hoping that sea air and bathing would help his rheumatism. While the previous pastor, Fr. Ivers, lived in Pawtucket, he boarded in a tavern, much to the disgust of the local temperance advocates.[40] Where Fr. McNamee stayed on coming to Pawtucket is unknown. He is remembered as being a priest of great zeal, piety and a man endowed with a personality that made him a great favorite among his people.

The original church in Pawtucket had become too small by 1846 so that year Bishop Tyler purchased two parcels of land, and Fr. McNamee purchased additional land in 1847 in hopes of building a new church. The purchase of land suggests that the church debt had finally been paid. Bishop Tyler, in November 1847, came to Pawtucket to finally dedicate the old church.[41] It would remain for someone else to build a new one, for in 1853 the disease that had brought Fr. McNamee to the East Coast overcame him. His fellow priests rendered him what assistance they could, and his funeral reflected the esteem in which he was held by those he worked with and served.[42]

While the first Catholics who settled in the Pawtuxet Valley walked to church, the increasing numbers of established families created the possibility of their having a church of their own. In 1844 Mary Doran, the wife of an English calico printer at the Crompton Print Works, bought an acre of land on the hill east of the village as the site of the church. On October 15, 1844, Fr. Fitton laid the

[39]Smyth, *Catholic Church in Woonsocket,* pp. 66-67; Byrne, *Catholic Church in the New England States,* I, 415.

[40]*Rose and Lily,* April 20, 1844.

[41]Boston *Catholic Observer,* cited in John G. Shea, *A History of the Catholic Church Within the Limits of the United States 1843-1866,* Vol. IV (New York: John G. Shea, 1892), p. 166.

[42]*Metropolitan Catholic Almanac,* 1854, p. 268; McKenna, *The Centenary Story of Old St. Mary's,* p. 35. A Mass Intention Book—Diary kept by Fr. McNamee can be found in the Hartford Chancery Archives.

cornerstone for a projected fifty by thirty foot frame building.
Today on a tombstone at the rear of the church one can still read
the following: "Mary Doran, Wife of Paul Doran, Died October 1,
1849, Aged 33 Years. She was the first person who took a crowbar
in hand at the building of the church and the clearing of the lot."
The building was completed on January 4, 1845, and on January
19th, Fr. Fitton celebrated the first Mass there. A few months later
on July 20, 1845, Bishop Tyler came to dedicate the church and
administer the sacrament of Confirmation.[43] After Fr. Fitton moved
to Newport, Crompton became a mission of the cathedral parish,
and Fathers Putnam and Gibson paid monthly visits to the valley.[44]

Painful Growth of the Church in Rhode Island

Bishop Tyler had little to offer the priests who came to the new
diocese. So widespread was the knowledge of the poverty of the new
diocese that the Bishop of Philadelphia, Francis P. Kenrick, wrote
to the rector of the Irish College at Rome on June 5, 1846, that the
"unfortunate haste with which Little Rock and Hartford were made
Sees in a former Council, should cause us to pause when a New See
is to be erected."[45] The Leopoldine Mission Society of Vienna was
the first to offer aid to the new diocese.[46] On February 24, 1845,
Bishop Tyler wrote both the Leopoldine Society and the Society for
Propagation of the Faith in Paris requesting their financial assistance. The bishop explained to both societies that his people, mostly
Irish or of Irish descent, were "generally poor and dependent upon
their daily labour for subsistence." The diocese needed, in addition
to more priests, schools for children, and religious Sisters and
Brothers to staff them. The particular project for which the bishop
asked the aid of the societies was a much needed addition to his
cathedral church of SS. Peter and Paul. The church that Fr. Corry
finished in 1838 was now far too small to accommodate all who
wished to attend Mass, even now when there were two Masses
offered on Sunday. As he and Bishop Fenwick had done at the
cathedral in Boston, Bishop Tyler wished to add another wing to the

---

[43]*Boston Pilot,* July 12, 1845.
[44]Byrne, *Catholic Church in the New England States,* I, 422.
[45]Bishop Kenrick to Rev. Dr. Cullen, June 5, 1846, *Records of the Catholic Historical Society of Philadelphia,* VIII, 239.
[46]Bishop Tyler to Vincent Edward (Milde), Archbishop of Vienna, August 26, 1844, Leopoldine Mission Society Archives. Hereafter cited LMSV. On August 3, 1844, Bishop Tyler received a letter informing him that the Leopoldine Society was sending him four thousand florins.

church to form a T, thus about doubling its capacity and making it "at least something like a cathedral."[47]

A year later Bishop Tyler, in another letter to the Society for the Propagation of the Faith, returned to the concerns expressed the previous year. He spoke again of the poverty of his people and of his diocese. But he also spoke with pride of the fact that it was "only about 17 years since Catholics began to settle in (the diocese). . . . They all came here poor, seeking to make a livelihood by their labour. Their wages are generally low, and of course they must live poor, yet by their contributions they have supported the priests who have served them, and built all the churches we have without any help from abroad."[48]

The bishop's plea for help in rebuilding his cathedral created an impression in the society's central council in Paris that Bishop Tyler's needs were not pressing. In a letter written on January 20, 1847, the bishop attempted to correct this impression. He reported that "his people had contributed liberally towards enlarging the church in proportion to their means, yet the sum of their contributions amounts to only 2,300 dollars and the greatest contribution of any one is 20 dollars." As a result of lack of resources the diocese wanted for everything. "My only chalice," he wrote, "is brass and I have but one other at the cathedral and only four or five more in the whole diocese which belong to it. On last Christmas I said my first pontifical Mass, although with only one priest to assist and woefully deficient of suitable ornaments. These, however, are matters of less importance than others that afflict me."[49]

To the bishop's mind, the lack of Catholic schools was a far more pressing matter. In the city of Providence alone there were about one thousand children of Catholic parents between the ages of six and fourteen who were growing up "in a deplorable ignorance of religion." To provide religious teachers he needed to build a residence for which he did not have the money. He lacked money also to provide vestments, chalices and other necessities for the three priests from All Hallows that he was expecting that summer. He wished to send the men to several places "where the numbers of newly arriving poor Catholics made the presence of a priest necessary. . . . How happy would I be to be able to assist each of them with a few hundred dollars to get in small churches and also

---

[47]Bishop Tyler to the Society for the Propagation of the Faith, Paris, February 24, 1845, SPFA; Bishop Tyler to Archbishop Vincent Edward, February 24, 1845, LMSV.

[48]Bishop Tyler to the Society for the Propagation of the Faith, Paris, January 24, 1846, SPFA.

[49]*Ibid.,* January 20, 1847, SPFA.

abodes for themselves." The bishop ended his letter by listing his priorities; his cathedral, his poor children, and his mission stations.[50]

Through self-sacrifice and strict frugality with church contributions, Bishop Tyler was able to bring the construction work along far enough to rededicate the church on April 11, 1847. At first it seemed that he would have to modify his original plans for the church when he was unable to acquire all the land needed for the western wing. But the young bishop decided that it was better to go on and build in a defective manner rather than delay any longer, "so necessary is it for numbers of our poor people, hundreds of whom cannot get into the church as it now is, to hear Mass."[51] Shortly after penning these words, however, he acquired the desired land. The bishop was forced to forego the purchase of a house on the corner of Broad and Fenner streets that he had wished to buy as a residence and settle for a less expensive one. Bishop John Fitzpatrick came down from Boston to celebrate the pontifical Mass on the day of the rededication, and Fr. James Ryder, the president of Holy Cross College, preached that day to an immense crowd who jammed into the church.[52]

With his first goal achieved Bishop Tyler now sought to raise funds for another project that he felt was a pressing need—providing a Catholic education for the children of Providence. Providence in the 1840s had a very good public school system. But its teachers and the texts used were not without their bias. Rhode Island's Protestant heritage was promoted in the classroom.[53] Bishop Tyler's concern lay less with the bias of the schools than with the ignorance of Catholic children regarding their own faith. In a report he submitted to the Society for the Propagation of the Faith in Paris in January 1848, he noted that about half the citizens of his two state diocese were "infidels," that is, people, without denying God, simply had no religious affiliations.[54]

When he lived in Boston, Bishop Tyler witnessed the great work done by the Sisters of Charity from Emmitsburg, Maryland in educating the girls of that city. He wished to obtain a similar community for Providence and hoped that the superiors of the Sisters

[50]*Ibid.*

[51]*Ibid.*, January 20; February 22, 1847, SPFA.

[52]Fitton, *Sketches,* pp. 232-33; Clarke, *Lives of the Deceased Bishops,* II, 284-85; Byrne, *Catholic Church in the New England States,* I, 395.

[53]Americo Lapati, "A History of Catholic Education in Rhode Island" (unpublished doctoral thesis, Boston College, 1958), pp. 8-54; Charles Carroll, *Public Education in Rhode Island* (Providence: 1918), pp. 37-128.

[54]Bishop Tyler to the Society for the Propagation of the Faith, Paris, January 10, 1848, SPFA.

of Charity would include in the group one or both of his sisters who were members of the order. The superiors agreed to supply some sisters on condition that the bishop build a convent for them before they arrived. The bishop attempted to raise funds by beginning a special drive for that purpose and by appealing again to the Society for the Propagation of the Faith.[55] After consulting with his clergy and parishioners Bishop Tyler decided to sponsor a series of lectures during the winter months of 1847 as the best way of raising money for the purpose. Dr. Le Prohon gave the introductory lecture, but interest waned when difficulties arose regarding arrangements for the sisters' planned arrival in Providence.[56]

In light of the difficulties that arose with the Sisters of Charity, the bishop, during the course of a summer visit to Philadelphia in 1848, explored other possibilities. The Sisters of St. Joseph had established themselves in that city the previous year and the bishop thought that they would do well in his part of the country. He tried to speak with the Superior and with Bishop Kenrick, but neither was at home. On November 2, 1848, Bishop Tyler wrote of the intent of his visit to Bishop Kenrick. He asked his fellow bishop to assist him in procuring information regarding the Sisters of St. Joseph and instructions on how to obtain several nuns for his diocese.[57] At about the same time, Fr. Philip O'Reilly, an Irish priest who had come into the diocese in 1848 and now served in New Haven, took it on himself to write to friends in Dublin inquiring of the possibility of obtaining either a group of Sisters of Mercy or Sisters of Charity from that city. He was in the process of establishing a school of his own in New Haven, and wanted to secure the sisters for his parish. Fr. O'Reilly's initiative annoyed the bishop. Part of Bishop Tyler's difficulties with the Sisters of Charity was his insistence that the sisters be qualified to run "a decent school." He had no idea if the sisters Fr. O'Reilly was trying to obtain would be suitable for work in the American missions. Bishop Tyler wrote to Fr. O'Reilly informing him that, in view of the difficulty of finding or building a house for the sisters and of his lack of knowledge as to the sisters' suitability as teachers, he was not anxious at the moment to pursue the matter. However, on January 25, 1849, he did write to Rev. Bartholomew Woodlock of All Hallows College for copies of the rules of both orders.[58]

[55]*Ibid.;* Bishop Tyler to Sister de Sales, November 18, 1848, HChA.
[56][Catherine Morgan], *Mercy, A Little Sketch of the Sisters of Mercy in Providence, Rhode Island, from 1851 to 1893* (Providence: J. A. & R. A. Reid, 1893), p. 9. The author entered the Sisters of Mercy in 1854 and taught in the cathedral schools.
[57]Bishop Tyler to Bishop Francis P. Kenrick, November 2, 1848, HChA.
[58]Bishop Tyler to Rev. Philip O'Reilly, January 12, 1849; Bishop Tyler to Sr. de Sales, November 18, 1848, HChA.

In the bishop's mind the need for Catholic schools was so pressing that he decided in the autumn of 1848 to go ahead and open a school with a lay staff rather than wait any longer. In the basement of the enlarged cathedral church there were two large rooms. The room immediately under the old part of the church was designated the boys' school area. It was considerably smaller than the one occupied by the girls, but well lit compared with theirs which had only five small cellar windows to let in light and air. There was also a small chapel in the basement that was used for children's Masses.[59]

On October 12, 1848, the bishop reached an agreement with Hugh Carlin "to keep the school." He began work six days later. For teaching, playing the organ, and devoting his entire time to the bishop's service, he received an annual salary of $400. Carlin gladly took the appointment for the year and hoped that "he would long be retained in the situation now given him." On October 30th the bishop made an agreement with Mrs. Carlin to keep the girls' school, but apparently still hoping to receive the service of some sisters, agreed to pay her $3 a week. In addition to teaching, she was to devote one evening each week teaching catechism to adults.[60]

The money set aside for salaries for both teachers seems to have come, not from the parents, but out of the general church funds—a situation about which Bishop Tyler had some reservations. He told his congregation towards the end of the first year of the school's operation that the schools had been supported "at great expense during the last year, but I must acknowledge that I have my doubts of the propriety of supporting them out of the funds of the church, when these are needed for other things more intimately connected with religion." The bishop felt that *"parents themselves* ought to look to the *literary education* of their children, that is reading & writing & arithmetic & so forth." (italics Tyler's)[61]

In December 1848, Fr. Wiley opened a day school at St. Patrick's for boys in the schoolhouse in the rear of the church where the girls school had its lessons. The school started with about thirty-five boys, eight years old and up and was under the charge of John Coyle. The parents who were able paid $1.25 for each boy in addition to providing their books. No boy "if well conducted" was refused, until the total number of students reached eighty. Coyle received $300 a year for his service. His salary came from the money

[59]Morgan, *Mercy,* p. 126.
[60]Bishop Tyler, "Diary," October 12, 18, 30, 1848.
[61]Bishop Tyler, Undated Sermon, HChA.

paid by the parents who could afford it and from a semi-annual collection taken up in the church. The school could not accommodate all the children. Most remained limited to religious instructions in Sunday school as was the case with most of the other children throughout the diocese.[62]

Both pastors were aware that their efforts were insufficient to accomplish the task of bringing the knowledge of their faith to the children of Providence. Each in his own way sought the help of the people of the parish. On May 2, 1847, Bishop Tyler invited his congregation to join a "Confraternity of the Blessed Virgin Mary to Befriend Children." He gave as the object of the projected confraternity "the increase of piety in its members and the spiritual and corporal welfare of the children of the congregation." The immediate cause for concern, the bishop told his people, was to obtain a better attendance of the children at catechism. The first thing that needed to be done, he said, was to collect the children on Sundays and bring them to church. Some of the members of the confraternity would do this work, others would assist in the teaching and others would watch over the children during divine services. Secondly, the confraternity would "provide suitable clothing for very poor children, who now remain away from church on account of being destitute in this respect." The confraternity was also to assist the bishop in realizing his hope of bringing the Sisters of Charity to Providence to take charge of educating the female children of the congregation.[63]

Along different lines but in persuit of similar ends Fr. Wiley, on January 23, 1848, organized the Young Catholic's Friends Society "for the clothing of poor children & otherwise assisting in providing for them both spiritually and corporally." He notes in the parish records that a large number of male members of the congregation attended the organizational meeting and nearly one hundred enrolled as members. Later that year on October 25th the society sponsored the first in a series of lectures for "the moral and intellectual instruction of the hearers and to aid in raising a fund for the clothing and educating poor Catholic boys." About six hundred persons, among whom the priest noted were twenty or thirty Protestants, gathered in Mechanics Hall in the Washington Building to hear Orestes Brownson lecture on the importance of possessing a knowledge of the true religion of Christ and a simple, easy means of ascertaining which is the true religion. Six other lectures were

---

[62]"St. Patrick's Records," December 26, 1848.
[63]Bishop Tyler, Sermon, May 2, 1847, HChA.

given that year, all well attended, and proceeds, after all expenses
were paid, amounted to $110. Between thirty and forty boys were
helped the first year.[64]

Fr. Wiley's entries in his parish records reflect a rhythm of
parish life similar to the one known in contemporary parishes. St.
Patrick's was perhaps exceptional in the Hartford diocese in that the
parish had a resident pastor who was without responsibility for
outlying missions. Fr. Wiley, on January 6, 1845, had left for Europe
on a six-month tour "for the benefit of my health and relaxation
from missionary labor." His place was supplied by Rev. George
Haskins of the Boston diocese. Fr. Wiley celebrated all the liturgical
feasts and seasons with appropriate ceremonies and with good attendance on the part of his parishioners. Besides the Young Catholic's Friends Society, which attracted the men of the parish, there
was a Rosary Society that enrolled 350 women in 1849. The pastor
also had his problems with debt and at least one case of burglary
of church property.[65]

Bishop Tyler, in addition to his responsibilities to the Church
in Rhode Island, also was conscious of his responsibilities to the
Church as a whole. In May 1846, the bishop joined his fellow American bishops in deliberations on the concerns of the Church in America. In the years between the Fifth Provincial Council of Baltimore
in 1843 and the Sixth in 1846, religious freedom in America was
sorely taxed. Nativist organizations and preachers fanned the flames
of bigotry and prejudice as never before.

The granting of a request by Bishop Kenrick of Philadelphia to
the local school board to allow Catholic children to use their own
version of the Bible for daily reading in the public schools and to
excuse them from religious instructions in the schools proved to be
a long smoldering fuse that ignited in May 1844.[66] Although Philadelphia saw the worst violence during this period, almost all American cities with a large Catholic population felt the effects of nativist
agitators in some way.[67]

But by the time the fathers of the council assembled for their
first session on May 9, 1846, the attention of the country was already

---

[64]"St. Patrick's records," January 23; October 25, 1848; January 14, 1849.

[65]*Ibid.*, January 5, 6; September 5, 1845; October 12, 1847.

[66]Ray Allen Billington, *The Protestant Crusade 1800-1860: A Study of the Origins of American Nativism* (Chicago: Quadrangle Books), pp. 220-34; Dennis Clark, *The Irish in Philadelphia: Ten Generations of Urban Experience* (Philadelphia: Temple University Press, 1973), pp. 21-22 notes that there is convincing evidence that the violence in Philadelphia was essentially a clash between Irish Protestants and Irish Catholics, at least at its inception.

[67]Billington, *Protestant Crusade,* pp. 193-211.

being drawn away from the violence directed against the Catholics to the new political issues of the Oregon Boundary, the Mexican War, the Wilmot proviso and the entire question of slavery in the territories. Rather than reacting to the past, the bishops concerned themselves with internal matters of the Church. They gave expression to the rising devotion of the Church to Mary Immaculate by naming her patroness of the Church in the United States. Other discussions and decrees of the council dealt with problems of church organization and discipline.[68]

Rhode Island avoided the violence fed by anti-Catholic newspapers and orators. The *Providence Journal* followed the riots in Philadelphia closely and drew from them the lesson that the disturbances were a result of foreigners who "by perjury, fraud, forgery and violence became citizens and outvote natives."[69] The local Quaker-sponsored paper, the *Christian Soldier,* later *Rose and Lily,* did not approach the excesses of the *American Protestant Vindicator* of New York or the concern with exposing the errors of Catholicism shown in the pages of the *New England Magazine.* Occasionally, articles from these publications were reprinted in local papers, as were a few letters from local correspondents attacking popery and Romanism.[70]

The issue of the relative truth-value of Catholic and Protestant versions of the Bible that played a part in school controversies in New York and Philadelphia also received a public airing in Rhode Island. Fr. John Corry addressed a letter to the editor of the *Providence Journal* in response to an earlier letter in the *Journal* that accused Catholics in New York of burning bibles. Later, another series of letters and pamphlets appeared in local papers when Fr. Ivers in Pawtucket took issue with statements in an article by a Dr. Bromley of New York, who was joined in the controversy by Rev. Mr. Dowling, a Baptist preacher attached to the Pine Street church in Providence.[71]

For the most part, Rhode Islanders during these years maintained their traditional religious tolerance. However, the nativist tactic of joining anti-Catholic prejudices with hostility towards the immigrant served to open in the tolerant foundations on which the political structure of the state was built. The nativists throughout

[68]Guilday, *A History of the Councils of Baltimore,* pp. 143-53.

[69]*Providence Journal,* July 10, 16, 24, 1844.

[70]*The Christian Soldier,* September 8, 1842; May 19, 1843; *Rose and Lily,* March 30, 1844.

[71]*Providence Journal,* January 7, 1843; January 15, 1844; *Boston Pilot,* February 4, 25; August 12, 1843; Billington, *Protestant Crusade,* pp. 142-44.

the United States promoted the belief that an alliance existed between the immigrant and the Catholic church—an alliance dedicated to subverting traditional American freedoms. The conviction
arose that immigrants could not be trusted with the responsibilities
of the vote. Such arguments struck a responsive cord in Rhode
Island.[72]

The Rhode Island State Constitution adopted in November
1842, in the wake of civil strife caused by Dorr's forces provided that
a foreign-born citizen could be a voter only if he possessed the
traditional $134 in tangible property. Registered native-born citi-
zens could vote if they paid at least one dollar in taxes or served in
the militia. Only persons, whether native or foreign-born, who paid
taxes on a minimum of $134 worth of property, real or personal,
could vote in the election of the Providence City Council or on any
local proposition to impose taxation or to spend public funds.[73]

In April 1844, Henry J. Duff, along with seventy-five others,
wrote to the United States House of Representatives requesting an
investigation as to whether they, as naturalized citizens, had been
unjustly deprived of their rights by the Rhode Island Constitution.[74]
By July 9, 1845, the *Republican Herald* reported a meeting to further
the organization of the American Citizens Association. The organization of which Duff was the secretary had as its object the constitutional rights of naturalized citizens.[75] A series of petitions followed
from this agitation. At the January 1847 session of the Rhode Island
legislature, a committee of the House considered a petition submitted by Duff to amend the state constitution to permit naturalized
citizens of the United States to vote on the same terms, conditions
and qualifications as were required of native citizens. The group
based their contention on the fact that these rights were guaranteed
under the United States Constitution. The House committee a short
time later issued a twenty-four page report denying the petition on
grounds that completely avoided the issues raised in the petition.[76]
The continuing failure of the immigrants' leaders to secure changes
in voting requirements, in effect, left almost politically voiceless the
thousands of foreigners who would crowd into Rhode Island during
the next few years. Without a strong voice or political muscle, their

---

[72]Billington, *Protestant Crusade*, pp. 118–35.

[73]*Rhode Island Manual*, 1965-66, pp. 49-52.

[74]*Boston Pilot*, May 4, 1844.

[75]*Republican Herald*, July 9, 1845; Petitions Not Granted, May 1846, Rhode Island
State Archives. The petitioners protested that it was impossible for them to buy land
and that Negroes enjoyed more rights than they did.

[76]*Republican Herald*, March 3, 1847.

social and economic needs would long be ignored or only feebly met.[77]

Political control enabled the nativists to continue to influence the courts and the administration of justice. Here, too, the principles of toleration and religious freedom were severely challenged in a flood of emotion and prejudice. On December 31, 1843, the bloodied body of Amasa Sprague, owner of the A. and W. Sprague Company in the town of Cranston, was found by one of his handy men in a field near his home. Sprague, who employed several hundred Irish immigrants and native Yankees in his prosperous print works, was naturally a man of influence in the village around his mill. His brother, Senator William Sprague, was a leader in the "Law and Order" party which had put down Dorr's "rebellion." Like many mill owners of the day who built their mills near water sources and away from older settlements, Sprague owned not only the print works but company houses that he rented to his mill hands, a company store where the hands found it advisable to trade, and even a church where his Protestant workers worshipped. Sprague was concerned about his workers, particularly their drinking. Life in the mills was hard and dull. Many found recreation in the liquor bought in a small grocery store run by an Irishman named Nicholas Gordon.[78]

Gordon had immigrated from Ireland and settled in Cranston sometime in the middle 1830s. He had obtained a license from the Cranston Town Council to sell liquor along with the groceries, notions and candy he stocked in the small store attached to his house. His business prospered, and by July 1843, he had saved enough money to bring from Ireland the other members of his family—his aged mother, Ellen; his sister, Margaret; his three brothers, William, John and Robert and the seven-year-old daughter of the widower, William. The joy of the arrival of his family was marred by the power of Amasa Sprague. Convinced that the liquor sold in Gordon's store was affecting his production, Sprague blocked the renewal of Gordon's license in June 1843.[79]

When Sprague's body was found, suspicion immediately fell on the one man who had opposed him and reputedly threatened him

[77]Coleman, *Transformation of Rhode Island*, pp. 285-94. Note on page 294 the bibliography on suffrage after 1842.

[78]The details and background of the Gordon case are found in Edward C. Larned, William Knowles and Sidney S. Rider, "The Trial of John Gordon and William Gordon . . ." (Providence: 1884); Carroll, *Rhode Island*, II, 754-61; Benjamin Knight, *History of the Sprague Families of Rhode Island* (Santa Cruz: 1881); Conley and Smith, *Catholicism in Rhode Island*, pp. 52-55.

[79]*Providence Journal*, January 2, 1844.

—Nicholas Gordon. Investigation by the state's attorney general showed that Nicholas Gordon had been in Providence the day of the murder, first at Mass and later in the day, at a christening. However, neither John nor William Gordon could account satisfactorily for their whereabouts during the day. Anti-Irish and anti-Catholic sentiments, combined with the violent nature of the crime and the prominence of Sprague, created a climate where the Gordons's guilt was presumed before they were brought to trial.[80]

The Irish community rallied to the support of the Gordons as did many of the same figures who had supported Thomas Dorr. The chief defense counsel was General Thomas F. Carpenter who served without fee. Carpenter was a leading member of the Rhode Island Bar and a Dorrite sympathizer. Perhaps even then the Catholic leanings that would lead to his entrance into the Catholic church in 1850 were also apparent.[81] Samuel Y. Atwell, who would later in the year serve as a defense lawyer for Thomas Dorr against the charge of treason, also contributed his service to the Gordons's defense.

The state charged William and John with murder and Nicholas with being an accessory before the fact. Their attorneys managed to win separate trials on the charges, but throughout the trials of the brothers, the name of Nicholas Gordon was heard. The state's case against William and John was based on the contention that they acted for their brother in murdering Sprague. No witnesses were found who saw the murder and only circumstantial evidence was presented to show motive and opportunity. Witnesses were able to place John Gordon near the scene of the crime. On April 17, 1844, after one hour of deliberation, the jury found John Gordon guilty of murder. They could reach no decision on William's guilt, and he was later released. Nicholas Gordon also was released when juries twice could not agree on a verdict in his case.[82] Appeals to the court and the general assembly for a reprieve of John's death sentence were made in vain. On February 14, 1845, John Gordon was hanged in the yard of the old state prison in Providence. Fr. John Brady, who was with Gordon the morning he was executed is quoted in the *Herald* as saying; "Have courage, John,—you are going to join the noble band of martyrs of your countrymen, who have suffered before at the shrine of bigotry and prejudice."[83]

The sheriff turned the body over to the Gordon family for burial the next day in a grave in the North Burial Ground. The

---

[80]*Ibid.*, January 3, 22, 1844.
[81]*Boston Pilot*, November 16, 1850; July 22, 1854; Abraham Payne, *Reminiscences of the Rhode Island Bar* (Providence: Tibbits and Preston, 1885), pp. 1-6.
[82]*Providence Transcript*, April 27, 1844; *Republican Herald*, April 19, 1845.
[83]*Republican Herald*, February 15, 1845.

mourners in his funeral procession, who had come not only from Rhode Island but nearby Massachusetts and Connecticut, took thirty minutes to pass a given point.[84] Two months later Gordon's body was exhumed and carried to Pawtucket and buried in the Catholic cemetery there. Again, several thousand people joined in the walk to the cemetery. As the years passed, certainty over Gordon's guilt faded, and the irregularities of the trial were remembered. Gradually the realization dawned that perhaps an innocent man had been sacrificed in the name of intolerance.[85]

In January 1848, Bishop Tyler still hoped for good relations between Catholics and their neighbors. In a letter written that month he noted that "the Protestants, i.e. Americans despise the Catholics partly on account of their poverty and want of education and partly on account of old prejudices against the Catholic religion. Wherever we have decent churches, the Americans frequently go to Mass and listen to the discourses and although we have had few converts, yet there is a great improvement in the public feeling towards the Catholic religion.[86]

New Waves of Immigrants

Nativist fears of political and religious domination by and job competition from the growing immigrant population were only increased in the late 1840s by a flood of new immigrants driven from Europe by hunger and economic dislocation. In the late summer and fall of 1845, reports began to circulate in Europe of crop failures along the lower Rhine, in parts of England and Scotland and in Ireland. Many people suffered in the winter that followed, particularly in Ireland where food was not overly plentiful for the poorer classes even in good times.[87] When the potato crops on which many Irish families depended failed, the situation for many became desperate.

With the coming of spring and the return of the shipping sea-

---

[84]*Ibid.*, April 23, 1845.

[85]The conviction that an innocent man might have been hung provided renewed emphasis for a drive to abolish the death penalty. In January 1838, William R. Staples and Samuel Atwell petitioned the legislature to abolish capital punishment. This petition was reported as unfavorable by a legislative committee. After Gordon's death, juries were reluctant to sentence a man to hang. In 1852 the death penalty was abolished.

[86]Bishop Tyler to the Society for the Propagation of the Faith, Paris, January 10, 1848, SPFA.

[87]Marcus Lee Hansen, *The Atlantic Migration, 1607-1860* (New York: Harper and Row Torchbooks, 1961), pp. 242-44; Cecil Woodham-Smith, *The Great Hunger* (London: Four Square Books, 1965), pp. 1-65.

son, a small but important number of men and women made their
final decision to leave their homes and families in Ireland and on the
continent. Many of those who left early in 1846 were small farmers
who had been debating whether or not to leave for the last few
years. They had saved some money for their trip, and, after selling
many of their possessions, they raised the resources necessary to
reestablish themselves in their new homes.[88]

By the beginning of August 1846 it was evident that not only
had the Irish potato crop failed again but that it had failed completely. Throughout September the Irish thronged the embarkation
ports of Ireland and England. Their departure was not the result of
a thought out plan to seek better opportunities but flight to escape
what they regarded as the curse on the land that brought hunger
and disease to all who lived there. Those who left in the spring of
1846 often had enough money to purchase passage on shipping
traveling from Liverpool, England, to New York, the main port of
entry into the United States. Those with less money could usually
find the means to pay for passage on the numerous cargo vessels
that were beginning to dock in Ireland with cargoes of grain from
Canada and the United States that the British government was im-
porting to compensate for the crop failures. For the first time in
history, emigration from Ireland continued through the winter. Ice
closed the Canadian ports in the early fall, so most of these immigrants in the winter of 1846-1847 landed in New York.[89]

Whatever resources the people had on leaving Ireland, most
were gone when they reached America. Frightened by the influx of
people whom the natives feared would become public wards, petitions flooded Congress to enact stiffer regulations regarding the
number of passengers per ton which a ship might carry to the
United States. The several state legislatures demanded stricter enforcement of laws requiring shippers to pay a bond guaranteeing
that passengers would not become wards of the state. The effect of
these acts was to increase the price of the Atlantic passage to the
United States and divert the emigrant stream to Canadian ports.[90]

While the sight of poor Irish arriving in Boston and New York
filled some native Americans with fear and loathing and served to
increase tensions between Irish and American, reports of the hunger and disease in Ireland precipitated the first great nationwide

[88]Hansen, *The Atlantic Migration*, pp. 244-46; Woodham-Smith, *The Great Hunger*,
pp. 209.
[89]Hansen, *The Atlantic Migration*, pp. 249-50; Woodham-Smith, *The Great Hunger*,
pp. 210-11.
[90]Hansen, *The Atlantic Migration*, pp. 253-59; Woodham-Smith, *The Great Hunger*,
pp. 211-34; *Providence Journal*, July 8, 1851.

free-will extension of American generosity to a people struck down by a natural catastrophe. The Quakers of Dublin, on November 13, 1846, organized a Central Relief Committee, and when word of the famine that followed the crop failure in 1846 reached America with the first ships in January 1847, Americans also opened their hearts and pocketbooks to the sick and starving in Ireland. Although their goals were the same, Catholics and their neighbors made separate collections for Ireland. Relief efforts got underway in Providence a month later, and by March 10, 1847, the citizens of Providence had contributed over $6,300 for the relief of Ireland. The Catholics of the diocese raised $3,600, which Bishop Tyler forwarded to his fellow bishops in Ireland.[91]

Relief efforts did not stop the outward flow of immigrants. Many Irish farmers had a few coins put away for an emergency which now helped to pay for passage to England, Canada or America. Landlords, moved by conscience or self-interest, also paid the passage of their tenants, some on the cheapest and most unsanitary ships in Irish ports. Like the relief funds, most passage money came from friends and relatives in America. The young men and women sent out by the pooled resources of the family discharged their obligations as quickly as they could both for the sake of their family and for their own prestige. If it was done quickly it was a sign of their success in America. Frequently it meant taking the first job offered, low wages and cheap lodging. Their low standard of living often antagonized native American workers who did not understand their motives.[92]

It is an unfortunate fact of life that human suffering provides the occasion for some men to show great compassion, and for others to exploit the defenseless. Of all the frauds and swindles to victimize untutored Irish emigrants, none was more nefarious than those perpetrated by dishonest passenger agents. In a letter to a local paper, Fr. Charles O'Reilly of Woonsocket, described how his entire Irish congregation had been fleeced by such an agent. He told how they had placed their money in his hands to arrange the passage of their relatives "and lo! tis swindled." He spoke of a daughter who had paid for the passage of the Connelly family from Ireland. They had sold out their possessions and waited in vain for the passenger certificates which never arrived.[93]

If one wanted to leave Ireland badly enough, not a great deal

[91]*Republican Herald,* February 20; March 18, 1847; Potter, *To the Golden Door,* pp. 454-57; Woodham-Smith, *The Great Hunger,* pp. 236-42.

[92]Hansen, *The Atlantic Migration,* pp. 250-51, 281-82; Woodham-Smith, *The Great Hunger,* pp. 222-26.

[93]The incident is described in Potter, *To the Golden Door,* p. 471.

of money was needed. The cheapest way was to obtain passage on ships plying between Ireland and Canada. Such traffic was not burdened with the American laws regulating passenger size and provisions for the voyage. The death rate of the emigrants who took the Canadian route was very high in spite of the heroic efforts made by Canadian officials and doctors to care for the emigrants when they landed. For most Irishmen, Canada was but a stopping place on their way to the United States. As was true in other days, men would leave their families in Canada and walk across the border in search of work.[94]

Famine and hope for a better future were not the only spurs to emigration from Ireland in the 1840s and 1850s. In 1847, England's Parliament repealed the Corn Laws, thus exposing Irish farmers to overseas competition and forcing Irishmen to either abandon their land or turn it into pasturage. The Irish Poor Law of 1847 also had the effect of forcing the small farmer to abandon his land as did the Encumbered Estates Act of 1849. Besides the small landowners and tenant farmers who were men of some substance, the bulk of the immigrants were cottiers who lived on the fringe of the old style agricultural society. Along with them came the small shopkeeper, the wandering peddler and the semi-skilled artisan who depended on the trade of the farmers for their livelihood.[95]

The experiences that awaited the Irish immigrants were often as bitter as those they left behind. Immigrant aid societies could and did provide some assistance on the voyage over and on landing in America. Once the immigrant left the docks they either had to depend on relatives and friends for help or on their own talents and abilities to find work, lodging and assistance in making the adjustment to the new environment. Frequently the immigrants headed for towns and cities where Irish communities were already established. Here they crowded into whatever quarters they could find; most often it was a tenement. Those with skills or business experience found themselves forced to compete with natives with more capital and greater experience.

Many who came to Rhode Island found work in the expanding cotton and woolen industries. These mills provided work not just for the men, but employed large numbers of women and children whose labor was often necessary for the families to survive. The women also found work as maids, while the men found jobs unloading wagons and ships, pushing carts, cleaning yards, or on railway

[94]Woodham-Smith, *The Great Hunger,* pp. 212-34.
[95]Hansen, *The Atlantic Migration,* pp. 267-79.

and mill construction projects. Others took whatever they could get. As a result of the types of jobs and the nature of the industries many immigrants were irregularly employed and underpaid. Ill-housed, poorly paid, often socially and politically restricted, the Irish immigrant had few constructive outlets. Many Irish men and women sought relief and recreation in the only way open to them—through alcoholic indulgence.[96]

Excessive drinking was a problem that afflicted all segments of American society. Contemporary papers constantly note the frequent meetings of temperance societies and report the activities of those who favored state imposed restrictions, such as licensing, or outright prohibition. Catholics were suspicious of the many popular temperance movements because of their evangelical Protestant overtones, and they challenged the right of the state, moved by such groups, to legislate on the matter. The effect of the Catholic church's opposition was to identify the Irish in the eyes of reform elements with the liquor interests.[97]

Although shunning the civil temperance groups, Catholics attempted to deal with the problem by utilizing preaching and personal good example. The primary motive that led Fathers Fitton and Wiley to establish a city wide Catholic Temperance Confraternity in Providence was "the alarming increase" of the vice of intemperance. On July 4, 1844, the Temperance Confraternity marched fifteen hundred strong to a picnic grove on Smith Hill.[98]

The cause of temperance in Rhode Island received its greatest boost when Fr. Theobald Mathew twice visited the state in 1849. Fr. Mathew was an Irish Franciscan already famous for his ability to persuade his countrymen to abstain from liquor. He first came to the attention of the American people during his efforts to obtain food supplies for the victims of the famine in Ireland. In 1849, on the invitation of many prominent Americans, Fr. Mathew traveled to New York where he was warmly received by natives and Irish alike.[99] Temperance advocates in Providence prompted Mayor Thomas M. Burgess to extend the priest an invitation to visit the city.[100] Fr. Mathew accepted the invitation, and on Wednesday, September 19, 1849, he arrived in Providence. After meeting with

[96]"Census of 1850, Providence County," Mss. at Rhode Island Historical Society; Edwin M. Snow, "Statistics and Causes of Asiatic Cholera as it Prevailed in Providence, in the Summer of 1854 . . . ," Providence City Documents, No. 5, 1854-1855.
[97]Handlin, *Boston's Immigrants*, p. 134 and notes; Potter, *To the Golden Door*, pp. 517-21.
[98]"St. Patrick's, Records," November 19, 1843; July 4, 1844.
[99]*Republican Herald*, July 4, 1849.
[100]*Ibid.*, July 18, 1849.

the mayor and other prominent citizens among whom were several
Protestant clergymen, the priest addressed a large crowd in Howard
Hall who had gathered to welcome him. The following day he spoke
in the cathedral and at St. Patrick's, where over three thousand
persons pledged to abstain from liquor.[101]

Fr. Mathew made a second visit to the state in October. When
he arrived in Pawtucket from Boston, he was again accorded a warm
civic welcome by the prominent men of the town. On the following
day he spoke in the morning and afternoon to large crowds in St.
Mary's. Most of the mills stopped to allow their operatives to be
present, and great numbers came from the surrounding country.
The same scene was repeated the following week when Fr. Mathew
visited Woonsocket. On October 10, 1849, he organized a temperance society in Woonsocket that was to bear his name and for years
would claim the honor of being the oldest Catholic temperance
organization in the state.[102]

Temperance societies, however, could do little to get at the
conditions of life that were the main cause of intemperance.[103]
Bishop Tyler and his priests did what they could to help those who
could not help themselves. For special needs such as the care of
orphans there were mutual aid societies like the Young Catholic's
Friends Society, which was partly supported by collections taken at
Christmas and other feasts.[104] Those in need because of poverty,
sickness or desertion could make their needs known to their pastor
who shared what little in the way of material resources the generosity of others had put into his hands.[105]

The Death of Bishop Tyler

It would remain for another bishop to deal with the physical,
moral and spiritual problems the increasing numbers of Catholics
would create for the Church. Although in his letters he spoke cheerfully of the improvement of his health, Bishop Tyler knew in the first
months of 1849 that he would no longer be able to carry the full
weight of the responsibilities of his office.[106] When he left Provi-

---

[101]*Ibid.*, September 22, 1849.

[102]*Providence Visitor,* October 7, 1893.

[103]Brennan, *Social Conditions in Industrial Rhode Island,* pp. 80-87; Potter, *To the Golden Door,* pp. 517-25; Mathias Harpin, *Trumpets in Jericho* (West Warwick: Commercial Printing and Publishing Co., 1961), pp. 79-80.

[104]"St. Patrick's Records," December 25, 1848, 1849.

[105]Le Prohon, "Memorial," p. 5; Fr. Joseph McNamee, "Diary," HChA; *Providence Journal,* August 26, 1851.

[106]Bishop Tyler to Sister Mary de Sales, July 7, 1847, UNDA.

dence in May 1849, to participate in the deliberations of the Seventh
Provincial Council of Baltimore, Bishop Tyler was determined to
ask his fellow bishops to petition Rome to have a successor named
for him. He carried with him to the council a certificate signed by
Dr. Le Prohon to the effect that his health was failing.[107] The bishops at Baltimore, rather than accept his resignation, chose to petition Rome for a co-adjutor for the diocese. They recommended the
man that was apparently Bishop Tyler's own choice, Rev. Bernard
O'Reilly, then vicar-general of the new Diocese of Buffalo.[108]

Along with his request for resignation, Bishop Tyler carried
with him the reports he received from his priests regarding the
status of the devotion of clergy and laity of his diocese toward the
Immaculate Conception of Mary. Pius IX, in an encyclical letter to
the bishops of the world, had asked for this information. The bishop
in turn had asked his priests to read the encyclical letter of the Pope
and to report to him "the spirit of devotion" manifest in the various
congregations of the diocese towards the Immaculate Conception.[109] The conclusion of the reports of all the bishops of the
United States was included in the first decree of the council. Among
the other business treated by the council was a proposal to solicit
the Holy See for three new metropolitan Sees—New Orleans, New
York and Cincinnati. Hartford along with Boston, Albany and
Buffalo would be included in the archdiocese of New York. The
pope accepted the proposal and on July 19, 1850, created three new
archdioceses.[110]

On his return from the council Bishop Tyler slept in a cold
damp bed aboard the steamer that plied between New York and the
railhead at Stonington. When he arrived in Providence on Friday he
was his usual cheerful self but complained of fatugue after his journey. He said Mass the next day, but on Sunday when he went to
celebrate the Mass of Pentecost, he was too weak to go to the altar
after vesting. After assisting at Mass, he was helped to his bed.[111]
Dr. Le Prohon quickly recognized the illness as rheumatic fever.
Given his already weakened condition, death was only a matter of
time. The bishop slipped into delirium during much of the three
weeks he lingered. Seeing that the bishop was dying, Fr. Wiley
informed Bishop Fitzpatrick that his friend was near death. Al-

---

[107]Le Prohon to Bishop Francis P. McFarland, June 14, 1859, HChA.
[108]Shea, *Catholic Church in the United States,* II, 167. Hartford historians stress the
influence of Bishop Hughes in the selection.
[109]Bishop Tyler to Rev. William Wiley, April 16, 1849, "St. Patrick's Records";
Guilday, *History of the Councils of Baltimore,* p. 159.
[110]*Ibid.,* pp. 156-57, 161.
[111]Stephen Whelan to Rev. B. Woodlock, All Hallows, Dublin, August 20, 1849,
AHMC.

though he had not been fully conscious for several days, Bishop
Tyler opened his eyes after his friend came in to kneel at his bed-
side. Bishop Tyler realized what Bishop Fitzpatrick's visit meant and
piously received the sacrament of the sick. Since he had named his
friend in his will to take over the affairs and the property of the
diocese until a new bishop was appointed, Bishop Tyler took advantage of these few hours of consciousness to explain to Bishop Fitzpatrick how he had arranged the affairs of the diocese. "At the end
of which," wrote Fr. Fitton, who witnessed the scene, "he closed his
eyes and never spoke audibly more." The bishop died on June 18,
1849, at the age of forty-five.[112]

Bishop Tyler's death was a cause for mourning not only for
people he had served but for all the community who had come to
know him. The *Providence Journal* wrote that "Our Roman Catholic
fellow citizens have met with a great loss by the decease of their late
Bishop. He was a kindly, unassuming, devoted man and lived in the
most friendly and familiar relations with the people of his charge.
To the portion of Protestants who enjoyed his friendship here, his
name will have associations, in some respects, similar to those that
attach to the memory of Cheverus."[113]

On June 20th Bishop Fitzpatrick celebrated a Mass of Requiem
assisted by Fathers John McElroy, S.J. and John J. Williams. Fr.
Wiley, who would become administrator of the diocese over the
next few months, preached the sermon. After absolution the
bishop's body was borne on the shoulders of six priests and buried
in a tomb under the high altar of the church. Many of those who
knew him used the adjective saintly whenever they wrote of him in
later years.

[112]Le Prohon, "Memorial," pp. 8-9; Clarke, *Lives of the Deceased Bishops,* II, 287-90.
[113]*Providence Journal,* June 22, 1849.

Chapter III

The Episcopate of Bishop Bernard O'Reilly

The Bishop and His Priests

For a full year the Diocese of Hartford was without a bishop. During this year the affairs of the diocese were in the hands of Bishop Fitzpatrick of Boston to whom Bishop Tyler had willed the material possessions of the diocese. Locally, Fr. Wiley, who had been Bishop Tyler's vicar general, assumed administrative responsibility. Although the bishops of the Council of Baltimore had submitted Rev. Bernard O'Reilly's name to the Holy See for confirmation as co-adjutor bishop with the right of succession, the nomination was not acted upon until Pope Pius IV returned from political exile after French troops restored order in Rome in 1850. In the interval, since nothing was said publicly of Fr. O'Reilly's nomination, the priests and people of the diocese speculated as to a successor. Fr. James Fitton's name was often heard, as was that of Rev. George Haskins, a priest of the Boston diocese who had taken Fr. Wiley's place in St. Patrick's for a few months back in 1845.[1] Fr. Wiley's name was also circulated as a possible candidate.[2] Fr. Fitton was especially popular among the Catholics of Providence for his "zeal for temperance and other good works." His transfer to Providence in the spring of 1850 only fed the rumor of his possible nomination.[3] Rome appointed Fr. O'Reilly co-adjutor bishop with right of succession by a Papal brief of July 3, 1850, and after news of Bishop Tyler's death was received in Rome, Fr. O'Reilly was appointed bishop of Hartford by a brief dated October 5, 1850. He received the

[1]*Providence Journal*, June 22, 1849.
[2]McNamee, "Diary," December 25, 1849, HChA; *Freeman's Journal*, January 5, 1850.
[3]Byrne, *Catholic Church in the New England States*, II, 370.

bulls of appointment on October 14th through Bishop Fitzpatrick.[4]

Fr. O'Reilly was the first native of Ireland to be appointed as bishop in New England. He was born in County Longford, in 1803. Neither contemporary nor later sources speak of Fr. O'Reilly's parents except to say they were both pious and patriotic. Of his three brothers mentioned in surviving documents, one established a medical practice in Ireland and a second brother went to Mexico, where he made a successful living as a merchant. Fr. O'Reilly's younger brother, William, also became a priest and followed Bernard to the United States. Years later Rev. William O'Reilly in writing an obituary for his brother related that when Bernard, then twenty-two, informed his parents that he wished to be a priest; "at home, if it must be so," but that he would prefer "to minister at the altar that's free." Bernard's parents gave their consent and their blessing. On January 17, 1825, Bernard O'Reilly sailed for America. He began his studies for the priesthood in the seminary at Montreal and completed them at St. Mary's, Baltimore. The young man was ordained a priest on October 13, 1831, in New York City for the Diocese of New York.[5]

Fr. O'Reilly's first pastoral assignment was in New York City. Within a few months of his ordination an epidemic of Asiatic cholera struck the city. The young priest worked tirelessly night and day until he contracted the disease himself. After staying in bed long enough to partially recover, Fr. O'Reilly went back to ministering to his people only to be struck down again by the disease.[6]

In December 1842, Fr. O'Reilly was given the pastoral charge of St. Patrick's in Rochester, New York. His new mission area extended from Auburn in the east to Niagara Falls in the west. In serving his parish Fr. O'Reilly spent long days in travel and often had to contend with the discomfort of the seasons or endure deep-rooted prejudices towards the Catholic church. The zeal and devotion he showed earned him the respect of the people he served. Shortly after the Sixth Provincial Council of Baltimore recommended creation of the Diocese of Buffalo, the diocese's first bishop, John Timon, appointed Fr. O'Reilly to be his vicar general and superior of his seminary. Fr. O'Reilly left Rochester for his new residence in the bishop's house in Buffalo.[7]

---

[4]*Ibid.*, II, 137. The date of the appointment, given by Fr. James O'Donnell as July 23, 1850, is wrong.

[5]*Metropolitan Catholic Almanac,* 1857, pp. 294-97; Clarke, *Lives of the Deceased Bishops,* II, 391-93.

[6]*Metropolitan Catholic Almanac,* 1857, p. 295.

[7]*Ibid.*

During the next few years Fr. O'Reilly added to his reputation the qualities of an administrator and a willing defender of the Church against any who would allow prejudice to dominate their actions. When a young doctor, who had received a favor of some kind from Fr. O'Reilly, was ostracized by a part of Buffalo's population and verbal attacks were made against St. Joseph's hospital and the Sisters of Charity who staffed it, Fr. O'Reilly engaged the chief offender, Rev. John C. Lord in a debate carried on in a series of letters to local papers.[8]

Although he probably knew of his nomination as bishop of Hartford, the official notification of his appointment on October 14, 1850, caused Fr. O'Reilly to note in his "Journal" his "great anxiety as to accepting the appointment." Two days later, after offering Mass "to obtain light and aid in the matter from God," he concluded to accept and felt "relieved of much anxiety."[9] Bernard O'Reilly received episcopal ordination in St. Patrick's church, Rochester, on Sunday, November 10, 1850, from the hands of Bishop Timon assisted by Bishops John Fitzpatrick and John McCloskey of Albany. Bishop Fitzpatrick accompanied the new bishop to Providence where on Sunday, November 17th, a solemn procession of priests and acolytes accompanied Bishop O'Reilly to the cathedral church where he was installed as the second bishop of Hartford. In the afternoon a similar ceremony took place in St. Patrick's.[10]

Within two months of his ordination as bishop a resident of Providence noted that Bishop O'Reilly had already won over the people of Providence by his zeal, piety and watchfulness.[11] The bishop impressed his contemporaries as a man of fine physique and dignified deportment. But the strength of his appearance did not inhibit some of the younger sons of Providence from greeting him on the streets as "Paddy the Priest."[12] Bishop O'Reilly was quite a different man from his predecessor. Blessed with good health, he was a man of great activity. He was also impulsive and much swayed by his feelings. He enjoyed a reputation as an orator and did not spare himself in the pulpit. His two years as vicar general under Bishop Timon gave him an acquaintance with administration, and

---

[8]Byrne, *Catholic Church in the New England States,* II, 136-37.

[9]Bishop O'Reilly's "Journal," quoted in Byrne, *Catholic Church in the New England States,* II, 137.

[10]*Boston Pilot,* November 23, 1850; *Republican Herald,* November 20, 1850.

[11]*Boston Pilot,* February 15, 1851.

[12]Mary Teresa Austin Carroll, *Leaves From the Annals of the Sisters of Mercy,* Vol. II (New York: Catholic Publications, 1889), p. 386. Hereafter referred to as Carroll, *Annals.*

before long a new style was evident in the Hartford diocese.[13]

The same restless energy that had showed itself in Buffalo prompted the new bishop of Hartford to move quickly to meet the pastoral needs of his diocese. On December 2, 1850, Bishop O'-Reilly addressed his first pastoral letter to the clergy and laity of the diocese. He called upon his priests to minister and his people to receive the sacraments frequently and encouraged the Catholic community to watch over the education of their children, to care for orphans and to participate in the Jubilee proclaimed by Pope Pius IX.[14]

The new bishop well realized that it was his responsibility to supply priests to minister to the needs of the people. In 1849, Bishop Tyler had estimated the Catholic population of Connecticut and Rhode Island for that year's *Metropolitan Catholic Almanac* at about twenty thousand and noted that he had thirteen priests to serve their needs.[15] In a letter written on January 11, 1851 to the Society for the Propagation of the Faith in Paris, Bishop O'Reilly estimated that the recent influx of Irish immigrants had increased the Catholic population of his diocese to around forty-five thousand while the number of priests had remained the same. He had thirteen churches but at least thirty were needed and thirty priests to staff them.[16]

Several young men whom Bishop Tyler had supported in the seminary were ordained by Bishop O'Reilly within the first few years of his coming to the diocese. The first of these was Daniel Kelly. A native of Ireland, he had studied at Holy Cross College, Worcester, and Fordham College, New York. He had probably completed his studies before Bishop O'Reilly came to Providence. On December 1, 1850, the bishop ordained him a priest.[17]

With the need for priests so great in the first years of his administration, Bishop O'Reilly did not set any particular date for ordinations to the priesthood but ordained a man whenever he felt the person was ready. Often young men received the three major orders within a space of three weeks. As a result, candidates for the priesthood would at times meet the bishop at a particular church or follow in his company while he made his visits to the parishes of the

[13]*Boston Pilot,* March 1, 1851.
[14]Pastoral Letter, Providence, December 2, 1850, HChA.
[15]*Metropolitan Catholic Almanac,* 1849, p. 209.
[16]Bernard O'Reilly to the Society for the Propagation of the Faith, Paris, January 11, 1851, SPFA.
[17]Byrne, *Catholic Church in the New England States,* I, 422; Obituary, *Providence Journal,* February 20, 1877.

diocese.[18] Most, if not all these young men, whether they graduated from seminaries in the United States or not, were natives of Ireland.[19] Many of the first men ordained came to America either because they were attracted by the opportunities there, or because they sought to escape from the political or social troubles at home. Those ordained in later years came with their families for much the same reason.[20]

The pressing needs of his diocese prompted Bishop O'Reilly to receive into his diocese men who had served as priests in other parts of the United States. He refused, however, to accept priests who had served on the Irish missions because, as he wrote to the President of All Hallows, they in "matured age, with habits formed, seldom assimilate to our forms of society." These older Irish priests had concepts of the rights and privileges of pastors that were contrary to the way Bishop O'Reilly interpreted American practices. The bishop felt that these men "rarely rendered any service to religion" but served their own interests. To his mind, they lacked a spirit of "disinterestedness."[21]

On several occasions during the course of his administration, conflicts arose over ownership and management of church property between the bishop and several of his priests. The first such incident reached its climax on May 12, 1851, when Bishop O'Reilly removed Rev. Philip O'Reilly from the pastorate of St. Mary's in New Haven, Connecticut. Fr. O'Reilly, who had entered the service of the diocese under Bishop Tyler, seems not to have provided an *exeat* and any of the usual letters of recommendation. Bishop Tyler himself had experienced some difficulties with the impetuousness of Fr. O'Reilly. Bishop O'Reilly had none of his predecessor's patience with men who put their interests above that of the church as a whole.[22]

By the end of 1851 Bishop O'Reilly's relationship with Fr. Charles O'Reilly in Woonsocket had deteriorated also. Here again, the issue was management of church property. Fr. O'Reilly left the diocese, probably in February 1852, and took up pastoral duties in Blackstone amongst a congregation he had served while in Woonsocket. Fr. O'Reilly took his feud with Bishop O'Reilly to the courts

[18]Byrne, *Catholic Church in the New England States,* I, 371.

[19]Ordination Register, HChA.

[20]See obituaries in *Boston Pilot, Weekly Visitor, Providence Visitor.*

[21]Bernard O'Reilly to the President, All Hallows, Dublin, January 2; June 5, 1851; February 5, 1853, AHMC.

[22]Byrne, *Catholic Church in the New England States,* II, 334-35; Bernard O'Reilly to the President, All Hallows, Dublin, June 5; July 15, 1851, AHMC.

where the priest sued the bishop for salary, and the bishop responded with charges of mismanagement.[23]

The most difficult and notorious of all Bishop O'Reilly's confrontations with his priests occurred in July 1854, when the bishop removed Fr. John D. Brady from the pastorate of Trinity church in Hartford. Fr. Brady's parishioners took up the cause of their pastor after his death from cholera and, in an act of defiance, interred his body at the door of the church, a practice the Irish reserved for particularly beloved priests. Bishop O'Reilly objected because the site was unsuited as a burial place. The dispute was widely reported in the local press and seen as another instance of the tyranny of Catholic bishops.[24] The bishop's dismissal of priests such as Fr. Brady further lessened the number of clerics available to meet the needs of increasing numbers of Catholics. On April 21, 1854, he summed up his experience with his older priests when he wrote to Rev. Dr. Woodlock of All Hallows that he could rely "but on my own priests, this I am satisfied by sad painful experiences. Of all the others I received I was able to retain but three, the balance I had to dismiss after giving some scandal by their unpriestly conduct."[25] Because of such encounters, Bishop O'Reilly declined to accept any priest who did not have the proper credentials even if his decisions meant additional duties for those who remained.

For Bishop O'Reilly, as for Bishop Tyler, the main source of priests to serve the diocese continued to be the Irish seminaries, particularly All Hallows in Dublin. Bishop O'Reilly began his correspondence with the administrators of All Hallows on January 2, 1851. All Hallows sent Bishop O'Reilly four young priests during his first year as bishop and many others in the years to come.[26] Other young men were recruited with the aid of sympathetic Irish bishops either as students or as recently ordained priests. Others came to the Diocese of Hartford because a relative served among its clergy or lived in the diocese. By July 15, 1851, Bishop O'Reilly could write to the Propagation of the Faith in Paris that since he came to the diocese he had recruited fifteen additional priests to serve his diocese.[27]

Often in his letters to the Fathers at All Hallows, Bishop O'-

---

[23]Byrne, *Catholic Church in the New England States,* I, 415; *Providence Journal,* July 3, 1852.

[24]*Providence Journal,* November 20, 21, 22, 23, 24, 1854.

[25]Bernard O'Reilly to Rev. Dr. Woodlock, All Hallows, Dublin, April 21, 1854, AHMC.

[26]Bernard O'Reilly to the President, All Hallows, Dublin, January 2, 1851, AHMC.

[27]Bernard O'Reilly to the Society for the Propagation of the Faith, Paris, July 15, 1851, SPFA.

Reilly would speak of the qualities he looked for in his priests, qualities that probably were a projection of himself. He wished to have his seminarians "properly trained in the ceremonies of the church, as they are particularly necessary for our mission."[28] Pressed as he was for priests, Bishop O'Reilly urged the college to ordain his men as soon as possible. The college authorities, on the other hand, did not wish to recommend students for ordination until they were fully prepared and saw an advantage for the morale of the college in ordaining seminarians there. The bishop reluctantly acceded to the faculty's wishes while urging the departure of his newly ordained priests within three weeks of their ordination.[29]

When by 1853 the swelling tide of Irish immigrants into his diocese threatened to neutralize all the bishop's effort to recruit additional clergy, the bishop renewed his insistance on the prompt departure of his new priests for America. In writing of two young men who wished to spend some time in Ireland, the bishop pleaded with the authorities of All Hallows, "Do not permit them to wander about amidst their friends but direct them to me immediately. I really cannot understand how men devoted to God, should be looking forward to rest, whilst souls that they might possibly save are perishing."[30] When the two young men finally arrived the bishop wrote of his reasons for displeasure. "The wants of a diocese presses most heavily on a Bishop, and no one can feel this pressure but the Bishop. I have to labour at the Cathedral with one priest, where four were required whilst my young priests were taking what is called recreation." The bishop's solution was to ask that in the future the college authorities allow the young men to come to the United States before their ordination and to be ordained here.[31]

Another important avenue for recruiting priests was created when Bishop O'Reilly, drawing upon his experience as the superior of the seminary in Buffalo, opened his own seminary at his residence in Providence in September 1851, with eight theology and two philosophy students.[32] The bishop taught the students himself for the first week until Revs. Hugh Carmody and Patrick Lambe arrived fresh from All Hallows. Fr. Carmody became the seminary's superior and professor of moral theology and church history. At some time during the first year Fr. John Dowd joined the group as professor of philosophy. Fr. Carmody was superior of the seminary only

[28]Bernard O'Reilly to the President, All Hallows, Dublin, January 2, 1851, AHMC.
[29]Ibid., February 15; April 1, 1851, AHMC.
[30]Ibid., November 15, 1853, AHMC.
[31]Ibid., January 29, 1854, AHMC.
[32]Byrne, Catholic Church in the New England States, II, 138.

until February 1852, when Bishop O'Reilly assigned him to a mission. Fr. Lambe replaced him as superior.[33]

Finding funds to support his new seminary as well as to pay the expenses of the ten young men studying in other American seminaries proved as much a problem for Bishop O'Reilly as for Bishop Tyler. Sometime in 1851 the bishop appealed to his priests and people to support the new seminary. Again, on March 25, 1852, Bishop O'Reilly, through the medium of a pastoral letter, asked for support of a special collection on Easter Sunday for the seminary which he described as being in a "most prosperous condition."[34] In 1853, the seminary had eight students.[35] Housing even eight seminarians together with the clerical staff of the cathedral, all in the same dwelling with the bishop, must have posed a real difficulty. This factor, together with the pressing need for priests in other parts of the diocese, probably accounts for the notice that appeared in the *Metropolitan Catholic Almanac* for 1855: "The Bishop does not continue his theological seminary but has, at this moment, in various ecclesiastical institutions, 22 young men studying for the priestly state."[36] The seminary collection begun by Bishop O'Reilly continued to be an important source of funds for the education of seminarians in future years.

From the bishop's letters written when he first came to his new diocese, it is apparent that he expected to solve the problem of supplying sufficient clergy within the first year, if not by the summer of 1851. Although he was able to write to Paris that the twenty new priests who joined the diocese in 1851 constituted the "largest increase that one finds in any diocese in the country," the needs of his diocese pressed on him so that his hoped for visit to Europe to secure additional funds and religious brothers was postponed.[37] In October 1852 he was at last able to write to his clergy and people that "the moment . . . has arrived when, without injury to any interest, we may absent ourselves for a season; the Diocese is to a great extent supplied with efficient, disinterested, pious and zealous

[33]*Metropolitan Catholic Almanac,* 1852, p. 173; Bernard O'Reilly to the President, All Hallows, Dublin, February 9, 1852, AHMC; William Stephen Morris, *The Seminary Movement in the United States: Projects, Foundations and Early Development, 1833-1866* (Washington: Catholic University of America Press, 1932), pp. 26-28.

[34]Bernard O'Reilly, Pastoral Letter, Feast of the Annunciation, [March 25], 1852, HChA.

[35]*Metropolitan Catholic Almanac,* 1853, p. 132.

[36]*Ibid.,* 1855, p. 156.

[37]Bernard O'Reilly to the Society for the Propagation of the Faith, Paris, December 28, 1851, SPFA.

Priests; none are now famishing for the Bread of Life; the consolations of religion are brought within the reach of all."[38]

The bishop sailed for Europe on October 16, 1852.[39] After visiting Rome, Vienna, Munich and Paris where he spoke with anyone who had funds to aid the mission needs of his diocese, he took the opportunity to spend some time with his family in Ireland. While in Ireland Bishop O'Reilly visited with the seminary authorities with whom he had been corresponding. One afternoon he stopped at the college of Maynooth. A young student in his last year of theology, noticing that the bishop was a stranger on the grounds, offered to show him around. Before leaving the bishop invited the student to come to his diocese. The young man at the time intended to enter the Jesuits and serve the missions in China or Japan. After Bishop O'Reilly proceeded to narrate the hardships of his diocese, the long journeys required of a missionary, the rigors of the climate and the scattered nature of its population, the student, Thomas F. Hendricken, accepted the challenge offered by the bishop. On April 29, 1853, Bishop O'Reilly ordained him a priest.[40]

In spite of the vigor of his appeal to supply his diocese with priests, Bishop O'Reilly's efforts fell short of success until the flow of Irish immigrants into Connecticut and Rhode Island slowed after 1855. In addition to the loss of older priests occasioned by Bishop O'Reilly's insistence that his pastors administer their parishes in accordance with the guidelines laid down by the provincial councils and his tenets of good administration, sicknesses of one kind or another took their toll of the priests. In February 1853, while he was in Europe, Bishop O'Reilly received word from his diocese that three of his priests were "severely indisposed."[41] Later that year Fr. Hugh Carmody took sick and returned to Ireland to recover his health.[42]

Years later Fr. Austin Dowling would write of Bishop O'Reilly and his priests that he was "so exacting . . . so easily moved to act" that he no sooner took them in than he let them go. "Everybody knew of this characteristic hastiness of disposition which made him 'suspend' with absolute impartiality, the good and the bad, the worthy and the unworthy."[43] If Bishop O'Reilly demanded "disin-

---

[38]Bernard O'Reilly, Pastoral Letter, Feast of St. Francis Borgia, [October 10], 1852, HChA.

[39]*Boston Pilot*, October 14, 16, 1852.

[40]Clarke, *Lives of the Deceased Bishops*, III, 153-54; *Weekly Visitor*, October 23, 1875.

[41]Bishop O'Reilly to the President, All Hallows, Dublin, February 5, 1853, AHMC.

[42]*Ibid.*, November 15; December 14, 1853, AHMC.

[43]Byrne, *Catholic Church in the New England States*, I, 380.

terestedness and zeal" of his priests, he set an example of both
virtues. He began visiting the parishes of his diocese within the first
weeks of his administration. During the years he was pastor of the
diocese, the bishop spent countless days traveling and assisting in
the organizing of parishes, blessing churches, presiding at gradua-
tions, dedicating orphan asylums and looking after his priests. Coupled with the zeal that underlay his activity was a deep personal
courage in the service of the Church. The priest who ministered to
cholera victims until struck by the disease himself and who defended
the Sisters of Charity in Buffalo matured into the bishop who did
what he felt was right at whatever cost to himself. He was sensitive
to the criticism of his priests and people, but he remained firm in
his convictions.

In an effort to reach an understanding with his priests regarding the internal affairs of his diocese, Bishop O'Reilly convoked a
synod on October 22, 1854, in the cathedral in Providence. The
previous week he had gathered thirty-seven of his priests together
for a retreat—the first ever made by the diocesan clergy as a body.
The synod lasted two days. The chief item on its agenda concerned
a reading and discussion of the decrees and recommendations of
recent national and provincial councils as well as the diocesan statutes intended to implement the council's decisions. The topics discussed at the synod included the compensation that priests would
receive from their parishes and the bishop from the diocese. In
September 1855, Bishop O'Reilly sent a letter to all his priests
formally announcing that the decisions of the synod were in effect
and that in accordance with a desire expressed by the national
council at Baltimore, he had established a chancery office to handle
episcopal correspondence.[44]

The Search for Religious to Staff
Schools and Orphanages

In addition to increasing the number of priests, Bishop O'-
Reilly, from the first days of his administration of the diocese, hoped
to obtain the assistance of a community of religious women to staff
schools and orphanages in the diocese. In particular he sought out

---

[44]Byrne, *Catholic Church in the New England States*, I, 380-81; Bishop O'Reilly,
Pastoral Letter, Providence, September 17, 1855, HChA; Donna Merwick, *Boston
Priests, 1848-1910: A Study of Social and Intellectual Change* (Cambridge, MA: Harvard
University Press, 1973), pp. 89-99 provides some useful observations that can be
applied to the situation in the Diocese of Hartford.

the Sisters of Mercy "because their institute embraces the care of orphans and the sick, and the education of young girls."[45]

Bishop Michael O'Connor, the first bishop of Pittsburgh, had invited the sisters to establish the first house of their order in the United States in his see city. Led by Frances Warde, five sisters from the convent at Carlow, Ireland, left Liverpool on November 10, 1843. The community at Pittsburgh prospered, and in 1846, Mother Warde, as her sisters came shortly to call her, established a second house of the order in the frontier town of Chicago and another in Loretto, Pennsylvania in 1848.[46]

Early in 1851, Bishop O'Reilly exchanged letters with Bishop O'Connor asking his assistance in establishing a house of the order in Providence. Both bishops in asking and consenting had to search their consciences and balance the needs of the people against the personal risk to sisters living in a New England city with the surety of prejudice and at least the possibility of violence. Both bishops and the sisters agreed to take the risk. On March 10, 1851, because of a desire to establish the house on a feast of her patron saint Francis Xavier, Frances Warde, with four companions garbed in lay dress for the journey, boarded a stage for Providence.[47]

Bishop O'Reilly learned of their coming while visiting his priests in Connecticut. In his correspondence with the Mother Superior in Pittsburgh the bishop had been assured that the sisters would come as soon as arrangements could be made and a house in Providence provided. The bishop's efforts to provide the sisters with a suitable house were at first unsuccessful. When he received word that the sisters wished to come in March and would be content with any dwelling the bishop could secure, the bishop wrote to Providence directing that a small two-story house he owned on High Street be prepared for them. Arrangements were as yet incomplete when the sisters arrived in Providence on the evening of March 11th. The day after their arrival was the feast of the translation of the relics of Saint Francis Xavier. The sisters assisted at Mass on that day, which was celebrated on a temporary altar hastily erected in a house as simply and properly furnished as any in the city.[48]

---

[45]Bernard O'Reilly to the Society for the Propagation of the Faith, Paris, January 11, 1851, SPFA.

[46]Carroll, *Annals*, III, 43-49. Kathleen Healy, *Frances Warde: American Founder of the Sisters of Mercy* (New York: The Seabury Press, 1973), pp. 148-74.

[47]Carroll, *Annals*, III, 386-89; Healy, *Frances Warde*, pp. 226-29.

[48]Byrne, *Catholic Church in the New England States*, I, 373; Carroll, *Annals*, III, 388-89.

The bishop was delighted to have the sisters in his diocese, feeling that by their presence and assistance, "religion would be placed in a more respectable position."[49] The bishop's joy was shared by the Catholics of Providence. The sisters immediately took over the instruction of the cathedral Sunday school and soon after were instructing some three hundred girls in the cathedral "free school" and nearly forty girls in a "select school" opened in two rooms in the convent.[50] The sisters also offered daily catechism instruction for "a great number of adults." They also found time to visit the poor and the sick.[51]

As Bishop Tyler had anticipated, the presence of the sisters and the poverty of their house supplied the stimulus to collect funds for a convent large enough for the sisters' needs. In April, Bishop O'Reilly worked out an agreement with Mr. Jonathan Nichols, a Providence jeweler, to purchase his estate on the corner of Broadway and Carpenter streets. When word of the sale and the intended use of the house became known in the city, Mr. Nichols, according to an account published in the *Journal,* "was so beset by his neighbors—especially the fairer portion of them—that he had no peace of his life." As a result of the uproar, Mr. Nichols felt compelled to ask the bishop to release him from the contract. The bishop, "not wishing to disturb the peace of any neighbor," willingly gave up the bargain.[52]

The bishop continued to look for a suitable place for the sisters. On May 28, 1851, he purchased the Stead property at the corner of Broad and Claverick streets together with a frame house on an adjoining lot. Perhaps because of the publicity given the previous sale by the *Journal,* the purchase was made without incident. The estate was not vacated until October 1st, and after some remodeling, the sisters moved into their new, slightly larger home.[53]

Living and work space were serious considerations for the sisters because of the astonishingly rapid increase in the size of their Providence community. On July 20, 1851, Frances Warde noted in a letter that the community, in addition to the four professed choir

[49]Byrne, *Catholic Church in the New England States,* I, 373.

[50]The parish grammar school open to all was then referred to as the "free school." Select school referred to a high school level course offered by the sisters for young ladies whose parents could afford the tuition. The young ladies of the select school boarded with the sisters in the convent.

[51]Sr. Mary Francis Xavier [Warde] to the President, All Hallows, Dublin, Feast of St. Jerome [July 20, 1851], AHMC.

[52]*Providence Journal,* May 31, 1851.

[53]Byrne, *Catholic Church in the New England States,* I, 395; Carroll, *Annals,* III, 391-92.

sisters who came with her from Pittsburgh, consisted of three postulants and five postulant lay sisters. Some of the new members of the
community were friends of the bishop whom he had met while in
Buffalo. Some, Frances had known in Ireland, and others were
introduced to the community by mutual friends.[54] On August 15,
1851, the bishop officiated in the convent chapel at the reception
of four lay sisters into the community.[55] On August 21st the three
young ladies who had been postulants for the previous six months
received the white veil in the cathedral. Some two thousand people,
Catholics and non-Catholics, witnessed the ceremonies.[56]

For the Catholics of Providence the House of Mercy was a
source of pride. For the non-Catholic citizens of Providence the
sisters were a curiosity and a challenge. Within a few months of her
arrival Frances wrote back to Ireland that "the most respectable
Protestants are most kind and attracted to us."[57] For the most part
the leaders of Providence society, priding themselves on their
Rhode Island heritage of tolerance and religious freedom, graciously accepted the presence of the sisters in the city and supported
their efforts at bringing relief to the sick and poor. There were
others, however, among the citizens of Providence whose heritage
was one of prejudice, suspicion and even hatred of the Catholic,
especially of the "female Jesuits" as some called the sisters. During
their first year in Providence the sisters patiently endured the risk
and reality of harassment whenever they went about the city, as well
as the frequent breaking of the windows of their convent.[58]

As the size of their community grew the sisters took on more
responsibilities. The parishioners of St. Patrick's were unhappy that
the sisters taught in the cathedral school while their children remained neglected. When schools opened in the fall of 1851, the
sisters took charge of over five hundred children in both St. Patrick's
and the cathedral schools. By October 1851 the sisters were also
caring for nineteen orphaned youngsters—all female children of
Irish parents—in the small frame house adjoining the convent. The
girls came from many places throughout the diocese.[59]

The number of orphaned children in those years was great, as

[54]Sr. Mary Francis Xavier [Warde] to the President, All Hallows, Dublin, [July 20, 1851], AHMC; Carroll, *Annals*, III, 393.

[55]*Boston Pilot*, August 23, 1851.

[56]*Providence Journal*, August 22, 1851; *Boston Pilot*, August 30, 1851.

[57]Sr. Mary Francis Xavier [Warde] to the President, All Hallows, Dublin, [July 20, 1851], AHMC.

[58]Carroll, *Annals*, III, 391, 393-94; Morgan, *Mercy*, pp. 22-24.

[59]Sr. Mary Francis Xavier [Warde] to the President, All Hallows, Dublin, Feast of Saints Simon and Jude, [October 28, 1851], AHMC.

poverty, disease, the lack of medical aid available to the poor and
dangerous working conditions took their toll of the adult population in the state. In 1835, the citizens of Providence had established
the Children's Friends Society for the purpose of receiving "indigent children of both sexes not otherwise provided for, and who, for
want of parental care are in a suffering and dangerous condition."[60]
The society cared for the children and placed them out. Placing out
simply meant giving the children to those who were willing to take
them, sometimes for adoption, more often, for the sake of their
services. In the years before the Catholic community was in a position to look after its own, orphaned children of Catholic parents
were occasionally placed out to Protestant families to the great
agitation of many Catholics.[61]

The Catholic community in Providence had long been sensitive
to its responsibilities for the homeless children within its borders.
The Hibernian Orphans' Society, formed in 1839 by several of the
leading men in the Irish community in the north end of Providence,
was the earliest effort by the Irish to meet the needs of the orphans.
In 1841, the society had about two hundred members and raised
funds through payment of an initiation fee and monthly dues of a
few cents.[62] The society was apparently a victim of the dispute with
Fr. Corry. In February 1848, Fr. Wiley took the initiative of forming
from among many of the same men who had belonged to the Hibernian Society, an organization that he called the Young Catholic's
Friends Society. The object of the group according to its constitution was "to form a fund to clothe poor and destitute boys, to
procure books for those in need who attended the Sunday school
and premiums for rewarding and encouraging the meritorious and
to aid the pastor in teaching or searching out young people and
leading them to catechetical instructions." In addition to raising
funds through the collection of initiation fees and monthly dues,
there was to be an annual collection in St. Patrick's and special
events of interest to the whole community.[63]

On March 9, 1851, after having talked the matter over with Fr.
Wiley, Bishop O'Reilly issued an invitation to the Catholics of Provi-

[60]William Kirk, ed., *A Modern City, Providence, Rhode Island and Its Activities* (Chicago:
University of Chicago Press, 1909), pp. 303-305.
[61]Bishop O'Reilly to the Society for the Propagation of the Faith, Paris, February
17, 1853, SPFA.
[62]*Evening Chronicle,* September 14, 1843.
[63]Young Catholic's Friends Society, Records of Meetings, Meeting of January 14,
1849, PChA.

dence to combine in forming a society to aid in supporting and educating the orphans of the city. After the bishop had explained the purpose of the proposed Roman Catholic Orphan Asylum and School Society, many of the former members of the Young Catholic's Friends Society came forward to sign their names alongside the men of the cathedral parish and to pay a fifty cent initiation fee and twelve cents at each monthly meeting.[64] Perhaps to avoid any chance of a renewal of the antipathy among the Catholics of the city, the society's constitution provided that the bishop would be the president of the society and the two pastors in the city would be the vice presidents. An important source of funds for the society was initiated on December 20, 1851, when the Sisters of Mercy organized the first Orphan's Fair. This Orphan's Fair became a regular event and was patronized by Catholics and non-Catholics alike.

In 1853, the sisters opened orphan asylums in Hartford and New Haven, and the children who came from these cities were withdrawn from the cottage on Claverick Street. However, the procession of girls who, along with young lady boarders and two sisters, marched each Sunday morning from the school grounds up Broad and Fenner streets to the cathedral, continued to grow until the orphans alone numbered thirty-two or three. The bishop soon realized that the cottage was too small. He was hard pressed for funds but decided to make the effort to build a three-story brick building on the land between the cottage and the convent. When the bishop discussed his plans with Frances Warde, she asked him to add ten feet in the rear to the original plans to accommodate a boarding school. The bishop agreed to alter the plans after Warde volunteered to raise the money to defray the additional expense.[65]

In October 1853, Bishop O'Reilly, as he and other of his priests did several times, traveled to Boston to preach in that cathedral in behalf of the new orphan asylum. To his great disappointment the collection realized less than $300.[66] A collection for the orphans came to be taken up each year at Christmas in all the churches of the diocese. While helpful in maintaining the asylums, Bishop O'Reilly had to find additional funds to finance the buildings he constructed for the orphans. Work on the first building began in the

[64]Records of the Roman Catholic Orphan Asylum and School Society, Records of Meetings, Meeting of March 9, 1851. The records are found in the same book as those of the Young Catholic's Friends Society, PChA.

[65]Morgan, *Mercy,* pp. 89-90.

[66]*Providence Journal,* October 1, 1853; Byrne, *Catholic Church in the New England States,* I, 379.

spring of 1854 and was completed the following year. It was then
known as St. Mary's Orphan Asylum or simply the Orphan Asylum.[67]

In May 1852, within one year of the sisters' arrival, the community in Providence had among its members enough professed sisters
to enable Mother Warde to send out her first mission houses to
Hartford, and New Haven. There the sisters began again the direction of the education of Catholics, especially children, and the caring for orphans.[68]

New Parishes and Schools
in Rhode Island

As the number of priests and religious grew, Bishop O'Reilly
strove to meet the desires of Catholics on the fringes of his diocese
to have a priest residing among them. The first request was made
only three days after the bishop's arrival in Providence. On November 20, 1850, a delegation from the "Fox Cove" section of Providence called on their new bishop. The men had previously spoken
to Bishop Tyler about having a priest offer Mass on Sundays and
holydays in their neighborhood. The first Irishmen in the district
had settled around the terminus of the Boston and Providence
Railroad because of the cheapness of the land. The Catholic population, however, soon swelled with the arrival of another flood of
immigrants who found lodging in the tenements near the docks or
work in the mansions near Benefit Street. The Fox Pointers, who
attended Mass at St. Patrick's, received the support of Fr. Wiley for
their request, and a short time later Bishop Tyler gave his consent.
Arrangements were almost completed when the bishop was stricken
with his fatal illness. Matters remained unchanged until Bishop
O'Reilly arrived. The new bishop agreed to send them a priest and
urged the men who called on him to think of building a church.[69]
On January 24, 1851, the committee arranged to buy two lots of
land at Hope and Arnold streets for $1,500. The land was part of
the Arnold family graveyard that extended to Brooke Street.[70]

True to his promise, Bishop O'Reilly, on March 31, 1851, assigned Fr. Joseph Stokes to serve as the first pastor of the parish

[67]Morgan, *Mercy,* pp. 90-93; *Boston Pilot,* January 6; April 28, 1855. Sr. Catherine
asserts that the asylum was finished in 1855 but appears to be mistaken as to the date.
[68]Carroll, *Annals,* III, 407-408.
[69]*Providence Visitor,* February 20, 1893.
[70]Greene, *Providence Plantations,* p. 158.

whose church would be dedicated to St. Joseph. Fr. Stokes was a native of Ireland and had served in the dioceses of Charleston, Richmond, Nashville and Albany before coming to Providence.[71] The first Sunday Fr. Stokes celebrated Mass in a small building on the wharf of the Baltimore Steamship Line. Larger quarters were secured for the next Sunday at Lannigan's Hall on Benefit Street.[72] Bishop O'Reilly had initially advised construction of a small chapel at a cost of about $4,000. However, he allowed Fr. Stokes to persuade him to attempt a more ambitious project. The people of St. Mary's in Newport were then building the stone church designed by Patrick Keely. Fr. Stokes wished to build a similar church in Providence and had Keely draw the plans. The men of the parish after finishing their day's work, volunteered their labor to excavate the site. On August 3, 1851, Bishop O'Reilly blessed the cornerstone.[73]

Fr. Stokes' attempts to raise money to pay for the church began to lag behind his expectations. He seems to have overestimated the ability of his parishioners to pay for the work. Fr. Stokes left the parish late in 1851 to take charge of an established parish in New London, Connecticut.[74] In January 1852 Fr. James O'Reilly, who had served in Newport before transfering to St. Mary's in Boston in 1844, offered his services to Bishop O'Reilly. The bishop assigned him to take charge of St. Joseph's. Fr. O'Reilly encountered the same difficulties in raising money as did Fr. Stokes. In two years time he was able to collect only $1,200 towards paying the cost of construction, which, including the cost of the land and the organ, mounted to $40,000 before the project was finished. As the months passed, Bishop O'Reilly carefully watched the progress of the church. In August 1853, he lost patience with Fr. O'Reilly and personally took charge of supervising the construction. Services were held in the church for the first time on December 16, 1853, but the structure was not formally dedicated until July 15, 1855.[75]

Shortly after coming to the parish, Fr. O'Reilly opened a school for the children of the parish which he staffed with a lay teacher working under his supervision. After Fr. O'Reilly left the parish in March 1854, his successor, Fr. Hugh Carmody invited the Sisters of Mercy to take charge of instructing the girls while a gentleman continued to instruct the boys. At first the sisters held classes in the

---

[71]*Metropolitan Catholic Almanac*, 1854, p. 282.

[72]*Providence Visitor*, February 20, 1893.

[73]Byrne, *Catholic Church in the New England States*, I, 402.

[74]*Metropolitan Catholic Almanac*, 1852, p. 172.

[75]*Providence Journal*, December 12, 1853; *Boston Pilot*, July 14, 1855; Byrne, *Catholic Church in the New England States*, I, 402.

small vestry of the new church while the parishioners worked to complete a two-story wooden school house. Built on the north side of the church facing Hope Street, the building had one large room on each floor and cost $4,000. A depression had settled on the city of Providence in 1855. Burdened as the parish was by the debts on the church, Fr. Carmody reluctantly had to close the school. In 1856, the parish succeeded in re-opening it only to close it again on March 19, 1858. After that date the school was converted into a pastoral residence.[76]

Across the city the Catholic population around the mills in Olneyville was also asking for a priest. Fr. John Corry had accurately anticipated the need for a church in this area when he purchased land on the corner of Barton and Broadway in 1841. The land remained in Fr. Corry's name until Bishop O'Reilly purchased it from him in June 1852. During the same month Bishop O'Reilly blessed and laid the cornerstone for the new church. Parish boundaries extended for awhile out to Greenville and Georgiaville and included a large part of Cranston. Construction of the wooden frame church progressed under the supervision of Fr. James Hughes. Fr. Hughes, a nephew of Bishop O'Reilly, was ordained in Providence on July 4, 1852 and served as rector of the cathedral and vicar general. Bishop O'Reilly dedicated the church known as St. Mary's and offered the first Mass there on Sunday, May 29, 1853.[77]

The bishop asked Fr. John Quinn, a newly ordained twenty-four-year-old priest, to take charge of the parish. Born in Ireland and educated in the public schools of Lowell, Massachusetts, Fr. Quinn had studied theology in Rome. He would serve St. Mary's parish for his entire priestly life. Among the first actions Fr. Quinn took as pastor was the establishment of a mission in Cranston to serve about 140 Catholic families, many of whom worked in the A & W Sprague Mills.[78]

The two older parishes in Providence continued to prosper. Bishop O'Reilly visited St. Patrick's on the day of his installation and was very much pleased with the congregation. Fr. Wiley, however, found it difficult to work under Bishop O'Reilly. Much to the regret of his congregation, Fr. Wiley decided to leave the parish in August 1851.[79] In a letter to the *Journal* a parishioner called the commu-

[76]*Providence Journal,* March 2, 1854; *Weekly Visitor,* August 31, 1879; Morgan, *Mercy,* pp. 134.
[77]Parish deeds, June 17, 1852, PChA; *Weekly Visitor,* August 19, 26, 1882; Joseph A. Streker, "Centennial Commemoration, 1853-1953," pp. 17-19.
[78]Byrne, *Catholic Church in the New England States,* I, 409.
[79]*Providence Journal,* August 25, 1851.

nity's attention to Fr. Wiley's self-sacrificing service, "his courage in surmounting difficulties," and "his zeal in alleviating the wants of the poor."[80] Fr. Wiley's health had also been declining for several years and this undoubtedly influenced his decision. After several years as pastor of St. Nicholas's church in East Boston, Fr. Wiley succumbed to his illness on April 19, 1855.[81]

Under Bishop O'Reilly, the cathedral parish was served by a succession of newly ordained young priests working with and under their bishop. To assist in the teaching mission of the parish, Bishop O'Reilly in 1852 sought the aid of the Christian Brothers.[82] This year also marked the opening of the academy or select school by the Sisters of Mercy and the establishment of a boy's academy. The *Metropolitan Catholic Almanac* for 1852 states that "this institution, aided by three qualified teachers, is organized with a view of affording a cheap and thorough classical and commercial education, to the sons of those who anxiously desire the advancement of their children." The qualified teachers were the theology students who lived with the bishop.[83]

In 1848 Bishop Tyler had purchased property on Lime Street on which he intended to build a school. Probably in 1853, Bishop O'Reilly conveyed the property to the School Society of SS. Peter and Paul. Under the society's auspices a three-story brick building was constructed and completed in 1855. The first floor was occupied by the boys' free school, the second by the boys' academy and the third, a large hall, was reserved for school entertainments. The bishop's hope of obtaining the services of the Christian Brothers died with him in 1855. At the opening of the school year following his death, the diocesan administrator moved the youngest girls to the third floor hall. In 1858, the new bishop decided to close the boys' academy and merge it with the free school. The space it occupied was needed to accommodate the older girls and younger children. An "accomplished teacher, aided by an assistant under the supervision of a clergyman of the cathedral" continued the work of instruction in the boys' school after the closing of the seminary.[84]

The churches outside the city of Providence also experienced various degrees of growth. When Fr. Fitton went to Providence from Newport in March 1850, his place was taken by Fr. James

[80]*Ibid.,* August 26, 1851.
[81]*Boston Pilot,* April 20, 1855.
[82]Bishop O'Reilly to the President, All Hallows, Dublin, April 1; July 15, 18, 1851, AHMC.
[83]*Metropolitan Catholic Almanac,* 1852, pp. 173-74.
[84]Byrne, *Catholic Church in the New England States,* I, 396; Morgan, *Mercy,* p. 76.

Gibson, who left when Fr. Fitton returned to the parish eight
months later. Work on the new stone church which had begun in
1848 progressed slowly. The people of the Newport parish were
generous in their offerings but poor in resources. Fr. Fitton turned
to Mrs. Harper and her daughter and the people influenced by
them. In three or four years the Harpers and their friends contributed nearly $7,000 to the project. Fr. Fitton raised additional
funds on trips to Boston parishes to solicit for his church. By July
25, 1852, work on the church had progressed to the point where Fr.
Fitton assisted Bishop O'Reilly in the dedication of the new building. The bishop dedicated the church under the patronage of the
Holy Name of Mary, Our Lady of the Isle.[85]

Lay people had started a private Catholic school in Newport on
January 10, 1846. A schoolmaster instructed the boys and a school-
mistress the girls. On May 3, 1854, the Sisters of Mercy opened a
convent in the city. Frances Warde had hoped to establish the convent there in May 1852 but it appears that she decided that the
needs of Hartford and New Haven were more pressing. In coming
to Newport, the sisters revived an old acquaintance with Miss Emily
Harper. Miss Harper had been among those laity and clergy who
helped to welcome the sisters when Frances Warde and her companions stopped over in Philadelphia on their way to Pittsburgh in
1843.[86]

In projecting the establishment of the convent in 1851, Frances
Warde noted that "a fine benevolent lady of high rank and good
fortune Miss Emily Harper of Baltimore will assist in getting up the
establishment." Miss Harper's mother joined her daughter in the
hope of seeing a House of Mercy in Newport. When Mrs. Harper
approached Fr. Fitton with the proposal, the priest concurred in the
project. This generous lady purchased the plot of land where the
present St. Mary's convent sits. The small cottage, which Fr. Fitton
had used for Mass on weekdays while the new church was being
built, was moved to the site. Two wings were added to the building
so that the structure could serve as a parochial school as well as a
convent. Two sisters, who began teaching in the school in 1853,
were at first sufficient to instruct the fifty or sixty girls who attended
the school.[87]

Early in 1855 Fr. Wiley asked Bishop Fitzpatrick of Boston to

[85]Byrne, *Catholic Church in the New England States,* I, 432.
[86]Sr. Francis Xavier to the President, All Hallows, Dublin, October 28, 1851,
AHMC; Morgan, *Mercy,* p. 137; Byrne, *Catholic Church in the New England States,* I, 432.
[87]Sr. Francis Xavier to the President, All Hallows, Dublin, October 28, 1851,
AHMC; Morgan, *Mercy,* p. 138.

recall his friend Fr. Fitton to Boston to take charge of St. Nicholas and carry on the work of building the church he planned for the parish. Bishop Fitzpatrick conveyed the request to Bishop O'Reilly. The Hartford bishop granted the request asking only that Fr. Fitton remain at his post until another was found to take his place.[88] Fr. Fitton left Newport in August 1855. As his successor in Newport, Bishop O'Reilly arranged with the Bishop of Buffalo the "loan" of the services of the bishop's brother, Rev. William O'Reilly.[89]

Pawtucket experienced a measure of economic growth in the late 1840s and early 1850s attracting additional Irishmen to labor in its factories, mills and shops. The small church built with so much difficulty in 1828 now was unable to accommodate all the people who wished to assist at Mass.

In 1853, when Fr. McNamee of St. Mary's, Pawtucket, finally succumbed to the illness that brought him to Rhode Island, charge of the parish passed to Rev. Patrick G. Delaney, a young Irish-born priest ordained by Bishop O'Reilly in 1851.[90] Realizing that an addition to the church was needed immediately, Fr. Delaney proceeded to begin work on its construction. On November 8, 1857, the clergy of the neighboring parishes gathered in St. Mary's, which Fr. Delaney now called the church of the Immaculate Conception, to join with the parishioners in celebrating the rededication of the church.[91]

The proudest boast of the people of St. Mary's during those years was their school. In 1854, the people and their pastor built a two-and-a-half story schoolhouse near the church on the corner of Grace and George streets. The parish opened the school in January 1855, to protect the youth of the parish "from the baneful influences of proselytism and immorality."[92] Like the earliest schools in Providence and Newport, its first teachers were lay people. Such was the desire of the parents to have their children in a Catholic school that some children walked to the school from the outlying sections of the parish in Central Falls, Valley Falls and Lonsdale.[93]

It was in the 1850s that the growth of the textile industry in Rhode Island created a demand for more parishes in the mill villages that sprung up to house workers. In the first half of the nineteenth century, water power was the key to textile development and

[88]Lord, Sexton and Harrington, *History of the Archdiocese of Boston*, II, 510-11.
[89]Byrne, *Catholic Church in the New England States*, I, 432.
[90]McKenna, *The Centenary Story of Old St. Mary's*, pp. 35-36.
[91]*Boston Pilot*, November 28, 1857.
[92]*New York Tablet*, August 15, 1857.
[93]*Boston Pilot*, March 31, 1855; Morgan, *Mercy*, pp. 152-54.

water power was available particularly in the northern and western hill country of the state. Rhode Island water was soft and did not require treatment before cloth was washed or bleached, and dyes took easily. The state's climate was also ideal for textile manufacturing. The high relative humidity kept fibers supple enough to be spun without breaking, and the comparatively even seasonal distribution of rainfall provided a steady flow of water for power and other purposes.[94]

In Pawtucket, Fr. Delaney visited the mill towns on the Blackstone as far north as Ashton. He also offered Mass in the village of North Attleboro, although it was not only in another state but in another diocese as well.[95] In Woonsocket, Fr. Charles O'Reilly occasionally visited the mill workers in Pascoag, Albion and in Millville across the border in Massachusetts where Fr. McNamee had begun visiting the few Catholics there by 1850. Four years later, the bishop assigned an assistant to Woonsocket to cover the parish's "outstations." When there was a change of assistants in 1855 Bishop O'-Reilly included a notation that the new assistant, Fr. Bernard Tully "attends the French" as well as all the outstations.[96] According to a census taken in 1846, out of a population of 4,856 in Woonsocket, 332 were of French extraction. Most of these, if not all, were emigrants from French Canada.[97] The outstations served by Fr. Tully included the villages of Manville, Slatersville, Albion and Pascoag.[98]

Because of the immature nature of the American economy in the early nineteenth century, the population of mill villages could vary in response to the prosperity of the textile industry. The village of Pascoag in the town of Burrillville presents a good example. Irish Catholics had first begun to settle in the village in the early 1830s when the woolen mills there began operating. The construction of new mills in the 1840s created new jobs which the supply of native workers could not fill.[99]

As noted earlier, Fr. Charles O'Reilly came out from Woonsocket by 1850 to offer Mass in the town.[100] On March 15, 1851, Bishop O'Reilly appointed Fr. Christopher Moore, a young priest just two months ordained, as first resident pastor of the district. Fr. Moore's stay in the town seems short lived for in 1852 Pascoag

---

[94]Coleman, *Transformation of Rhode Island*, pp. 71-73.
[95]Statement of Fr. Patrick Delaney, quoted in Massena Goodrich, *Historical Sketch of the Town of Pawtucket* (Pawtucket: Nickerson, Sibley & Co., 1876), p. 185.
[96]*Metropolitan Catholic Almanac*, 1850, p. 103; 1854, p. 184.
[97]Bonier, *Debuts de la Colonie Franco-Americaine de Woonsocket, R. I.*, p. 288.
[98]*Metropolitan Catholic Almanac*, 1855, p. 155.
[99]Coleman, *Transformation of Rhode Island*, pp. 136-37.
[100]*Metropolitan Catholic Almanac*, 1850, p. 103.

became a mission visited by priests from the cathedral in Providence.[101] A year later, Fr. Patrick J. Lenihan, another recently ordained priest, took charge of the mission that eventually included the villages of Greenville and East Greenwich as well as Pascoag.[102]

While Fr. Lenihan was serving the district he began to lay plans for the construction of a church in Pascoag and even had Patrick Keely draw plans for it. In July 1853, Bishop O'Reilly went out to the village and preached on the subject of a church lot.[103] When Fr. Lenihan left Pascoag late in 1854, the pastoral responsibility there was assumed by Fr. Tully in Woonsocket. Fr. Tully abandoned the plan for a church in Pascoag because the building of the granite mill in the village of Harrisville in 1849 had attracted a sizable number of Irish Catholics there. Fr. Tully, against the objections of the families in Pascoag, decided to build a church for the district in Harrisville in view of that village's more central location. Until the church (which was first called St. Bernard's) was completed in 1857, the priests who visited the district said Mass in private homes, the old Pascoag Inn and the old Town House. Fr. Tully left the district in October 1856 and was succeeded by Rev. John Duffy under whose charge the church was completed.[104]

Further to the south in the town of Smithfield, the establishment of mills in the village of Greenville created an Irish Catholic community that was visited by the priests from the cathedral.[105] In August 1852, a resident of the village could write that the two hundred or three hundred Catholics there were preparing to build a church so that they might secure the permanent presence of a priest.[106] In 1854, Greenville became a mission served by Fr. Lenihan in Pascoag and in 1855, the village continued to be visited by Fr. Lenihan after his transfer to East Greenwich. Sometime in 1855, Bishop O'Reilly sent Rev. Philip Gilleck to serve as the village's first resident pastor. Fr. Gilleck had worked in the Diocese of New York and had entered the Hartford diocese on March 1, 1852.[107]

With approximately three hundred Catholics in his parish Fr. Gilleck found it difficult to raise the money from the mill workers

---

[101]*Metropolitan Catholic Almanac*, 1852, p. 172; Byrne, *Catholic Church in the New England States*, I, 418.

[102]*Metropolitan Catholic Almanac*, 1854, p. 184.

[103]Byrne, *Catholic Church in the New England States*, I, 418.

[104]*Metropolitan Catholic Almanac*, 1855, p. 155; Ryan, *Burrillville, R. I. and the Catholic Church*, pp. 74, 82, 83; *Boston Pilot*, November 6, 1858.

[105]*Metropolitan Catholic Almanac*, 1852, p. 172.

[106]*Boston Pilot*, September 4, 1852.

[107]*Metropolitan Catholic Almanac*, 1854, p. 184; Byrne, *Catholic Church in the New England States*, I, 436; II, 296-97.

in the village that was needed to build a church there. He went on
a collecting tour and in November 1855 returned with $1,200.[108]
The following year Fr. Delaney asked Bishop O'Reilly to assign
another priest to serve the needs of the people of Attleboro and a
short time later that town became a mission of Greenville. A year
after he finished the church in Greenville, which was dedicated
under the name of St. Philip, Fr. Gilleck succeeded in completing
a second church in the more prosperous town of Attleboro which
was dedicated on June 19, 1859.[109]

Still farther to the south and east, the pace of life in the Catholic
community in the Pawtuxet Valley also quickened in the 1850s. An
outbreak of cholera in Providence in 1849 had caused the closing
of the missions outside the city for nearly a year. The mission at
Crompton, then in the town of Warwick, was among those closed.[110]
On December 1, 1850, Bishop O'Reilly ordained for the first time.
The young man was Daniel Kelly, and it was he whom the bishop
sent to Crompton to serve the mission as its first resident pastor. Fr.
Kelly's stay there was short lived. In August 1851, Fr. James Gibson,
who had returned to the cathedral parish after a short stay in New-
port, moved to Crompton which he had often visited along with
Fathers Edward Putnam and Joseph McNamee in previous years.[111]

By 1853, the railroad from Providence to Hartford had pushed
into the valley and a number of Irishmen who labored on it stayed
to work in the mill villages along the Pawtuxet. Many millworkers
lived in tenements erected by the millowners because the mills were
built outside of existing villages. The church at Crompton was too
small and too remote to serve the needs of the increasing Catholic
population in the valley. On July 13, 1853, a deed was executed in
the name of Bishop O'Reilly that conveyed ownership of the "Rock
Chapel" in Phenix to the bishop for the sum of $450. The chapel,
built on a ledge for the use of the Episcopalians in the area, was sold
when their numbers attending the chapel did not justify keeping it.
The owner of the chapel sold only the chapel; he gave Fr. Gibson
the foundation and the lot of land.[112] In June 1855, Bishop O'Reilly
made SS. Peter and Paul, as the new church in Phenix at Riverpoint

[108]Byrne, *Catholic Church in the New England States,* I, 436.
[109]Lord, Sexton and Harrington, *History of the Archdiocese of Boston,* II, 306.
[110]*Republican Herald,* June 13; July 28, 1849.
[111]Oliver P. Fuller, *The History of Warwick* (Providence: Angell, Burlingame & Co.,
1875), pp. 371-75. Fuller's book contains a letter from Fr. Gibson in which he verifies
and completes the information on the parish printed in Fitton, *Sketches,* pp. 231-32.
[112]J. R. Cole, *History of Washington and Kent Counties* (New York: W. W. Preston &
Co., 1889), p. 1003; Fuller, *History of Warwick,* p. 374.

was called, a mission of the priest in East Greenwich so that he would have enough to sustain himself.[113]

Because of the increase in population of Crompton and its mission, Fr. Gibson, after taking charge of the parish, enlarged the amount of land surrounding the church. In 1856, he practically rebuilt the church, substantially increasing its size and its ability to accommodate his parishioners. One of the last entries in Bishop O'Reilly's diary concerns this parish. On November 17, 1855, the bishop notes that he "visited Crompton and River Point, and confirmed 350." He was "much pleased," he said, "with the congregation and pastor of Crompton."[114]

To the south of Warwick, the town of East Greenwich lacked water power sites but the unique qualities of its water made it attractive to cloth printers. By the 1850s, important strides had been made in using the steam engine as a power source in the textile industry. Steam power allowed manufacturers to construct mills in the villages of East Greenwich.[115] By 1851 the Catholics there were numerous enough to cause Fr. Gibson to visit them. In 1852 priests from the cathedral took over their care. By July the Catholics of the town were laying plans to build a church.[116] From the salaries of the millworkers and housemaids, funds were raised to purchase a lot in the northern part of the village. They had high hopes of beginning the task of laying a foundation in the fall of that year. As in many other cases, however, the people's dreams outdistanced the funds available for the enterprise. A letter published in the local *Kent County Atlas* in August 1852, by the Protestant employer of an Irish maid appealed to his fellow citizens who "valued the privilege of worshipping God in (their) own sanctuaries to accord the (Catholics) the same ability to worship according to their principles and feelings, in theirs."[117] The letter elicited a reply from a fellow townsman who signed himself, "Simplex." The author asked whether it was either " 'kind, just or politic' to aid in introducing and sustaining among us a system of religion which makes it a solemn duty on the part of all who embrace it to persecute even unto death all heretics."[118]

[113]Byrne, *Catholic Church in the New England States,* I, 424.

[114]*Ibid.,* I, 422; *Boston Pilot,* December 8, 1855.

[115]Coleman. *Transformation of Rhode Island,* p. 108.

[116]*Metropolitan Catholic Almanac,* 1852, p. 172; 1853, p. 131; *Kent County Atlas,* July 24, 1852.

[117]*Kent County Atlas,* August 21, 1852.

[118]*Ibid.,* August 28, 1852.

A few days after the letter appeared, Fr. Patrick Lenihan came
down on a visit from Pascoag and immediately sat down in his hotel
room to pen a reply to Simplex.[119] Whatever hopes the good will
of a few members of the Protestant community had raised among
the Catholics for help in building a church seem to have faded in
the exchange. A year later, on September 10, 1853, Fr. Lenihan
purchased a house and lot on Main Street and at once prepared the
building for Mass. He dedicated the chapel to the Holy Name of
Jesus. After he gave up the mission in Pascoag, Fr. Lenihan took up
residence in East Greenwich late in 1854. When prosperity returned
in 1857 and the town's Catholic population began to grow again, Fr.
Lenihan purchased a larger building on Marlborough Street to use
as a church.[120]

As the resident pastor of East Greenwich, Fr. Lenihan also
assumed responsibility for Peacedale and Wakefield as well as
nearly all of southern Rhode Island. Although in the 1840s leadership in the woolen industry began to pass from southwestern to
northern Rhode Island, the Hazard family mills at Peacedale continued to increase in production and employment. Peacedale and
the neighboring village of Wakefield began to attract Irish immigrants by the early fifties. Before 1852, the families in Peacedale and
Wakefield were attended by the priests from the parish at Stonington, Connecticut who also served the Catholic families on the
Rhode Island side of the Pawcatuck river in Westerly. The next year,
priests from the cathedral came down to offer Mass as they did in
East Greenwich.[121] Fr. Lenihan had visited Wakefield while he was
still in Pascoag and said Mass in the home of Mr. John O'Reilly and
occasionally at Willard's Hall, near Sugar Loaf Hill. A gentleman of
the town, Mr. Stephen Wright, in 1854, gave Catholics a lot of land
on High Street near the Town Hall on which Fr. Lenihan erected
a small church known as St. Mary's.[122]

The scattered settlements of Fr. Lenihan's parishioners did not
supply anything but the barest kind of living. After two years of
labor in the district, the mission at Phenix was added to Fr. Lenihan's responsibilities and increased his financial support. His missions were so distant that he had to neglect some of them, a fact that
displeased Bishop O'Reilly. The bishop valued the young priest for
his zeal and piety, though he thought him "a little singular."[123] As

[119]*Ibid.*, September 18, 1852.
[120]*Providence Visitor*, August 15, 1935.
[121]*Metropolitan Catholic Almanac*, 1852, p. 172; 1853, p. 131.
[122]*Ibid.*, 1854, p. 184; Byrne, *Catholic Church in the New England States*, I, 427.
[123]Byrne, *Catholic Church in the New England States*, I, 426.

a young man in Ireland, Fr. Lenihan abandoned his education to
fight as a Young Irelander for an Irish Republic. After some time
in exile in France he came to America. His article on the suffering
of passengers on an emigrant ship was rejected by all the papers to
which he submitted it until the *Irish American* published it. A poorly
paid assistant editor on a paper in Bridgeport, Connecticut before
entering the bishop's seminary in Providence, Fr. Lenihan was only
a priest five years when he died in 1857.[124] After his death, the
church in East Greenwich became a mission of SS. Peter and Paul
in Phenix.[125]

Across the bay in Bristol and Warren, the introduction of steam
power also played a role in the development of the towns. Because
steam power freed the millowners from the necessity of locating on
fast running streams, it allowed the entrepreneurs to locate mills
along the coast where the humidity was particularly high and where
supplies of Nova Scotian coal were readily available.[126] The Warren
Manufacturing Company was incorporated in 1847 and by 1850,
came to employ some 126 workers in its river front cotton mill at
the northern extremity of the town.[127]

In 1848, Fr. Hugh Mallon who was then stationed at the cathedral, visited the town. With the outbreak of cholera in Providence
in 1849, visits to the town lapsed until Fr. Hilary Tucker came in
1851 to serve the people there.[128] Born in Missouri in 1808, Fr.
Tucker had studied at a college of the Lazarists in Missouri before
completing his studies in Rome. After ordination he worked for ten
years in his native diocese before coming east to collect money for
a church he had built. He was persuaded to stay in the East and after
serving for a time in Lowell, came to Providence where he worked
with Fr. Wiley at St. Patrick's.[129]

When he first came to Warren, Fr. Tucker celebrated Mass in
Armory Hall. By August 1851, plans were underway to erect a
church in Warren to be called St. Mary's, and about $1,000 was
pledged for the project.[130] The church, a frame building in the early
English style of Gothic architecture, was dedicated by Bishop O'-
Reilly on January 11, 1852, a little over three months after the laying
of its cornerstone.[131]

[124]*New York Tablet,* June 18, 1867.
[125]Byrne, *Catholic Church in the New England States,* I, 426.
[126]Coleman, *Transformation of Rhode Island,* pp. 108-109, 128.
[127]Greene, *Providence Plantations,* pp. 410-11.
[128]Byrne, *Catholic Church in the New England States,* I, 435.
[129]*Boston Pilot,* March 30, 1877.
[130]*Northern Star,* August 16, 1851.
[131]*Boston Pilot,* January 17, 1852.

Although Fr. Tucker built his church in Warren, his responsibilities included the town of Bristol as well. The French Catholics whom Bishop Cheverus and Fr. Matignon visited in the early 1800s had long since drifted away. Railway construction and construction of two cotton mills in the town before 1850 attracted Irish immigrants. The Catholics of Bristol lent a willing hand to the building of the church in Warren, and after its completion continued to walk there to attend Mass.[132]

Fr. Tucker found his parish small and uncongenial. He wished to have a larger parish where he could do more. Bishop O'Reilly did not see his way to gratify his desire, so later in 1852, Fr. Tucker left to serve the Boston diocese. Fr. Patrick Lambe, who was ordained at All Hallows in June 1851, and who had served at the cathedral, came to Warren to take Fr. Tucker's place. Fr. Lambe served the people of Warren and Bristol until he was assigned to St. Patrick's in Providence on May 16, 1854.[133]

Fr. Lambe was succeeded by Fr. Michael McCallion, whose residence in the parish would last nearly forty years. It was Fr. McCallion who began to say Mass again in Bristol. On the first Sunday he visited the town, he was allowed to use the Town Hall, but anti-Catholic feelings forced him to seek other locations for Mass. Local sources record memories of Masses offered at the armory on State Street, and later in a little building on the Naval Reserve Wharf on Thomas Street. This small building lacked pews, so the people had to stand during most of the Mass, and when they knelt on the floor, it was often in sticky molasses. Still later, Mass was offered in a place called Alger's sail loft, which was cleared each Saturday night for Sunday Mass.[134] The search for a site for Mass was happily ended when on October 21, 1855, the Catholic families of Bristol witnessed the dedication of a plain, wooden building capable of seating about five hundred people, which was known as the mission church of St. Mary's.[135]

The arrival of increasing numbers of French Canadian and German Catholics into New England in the 1850s created particular pastoral problems for Bishop O'Reilly. By 1853, the number of French Canadians in the two state diocese had grown to a total

---

[132]Byrne, *Catholic Church in the New England States,* I, 434.

[133]*Ibid.,* I, 435.

[134]Frederick T. Goff, "St. Mary's Church, Bristol, Rhode Island: One Hundredth Anniversary, May 11, 1869—May 11, 1969." Mr. Goff following other writers ascribes these celebrations as occurring prior to the building of St. Mary's in Warren. However, they seem to more accurately describe the situation prior to the building of the church in Bristol.

[135]Byrne, *Catholic Church in the New England States,* I, 434-35; *Boston Pilot,* September 11, 1858.

which the bishop, in a letter to Bishop Ignatius Bourget of Montreal, estimated to be about four hundred. In his letter Bishop O'Reilly asked Bishop Bourget "to give him a good zealous priest to attend the Canadians." While Bishop O'Reilly had priests in his diocese who spoke French well, he felt that "one of their country will have more influence for good over them than any other." The bishop was concerned that the children of the Canadians would be lost to the Catholic faith because of what he concluded was a neglect of religion by their parents.[136]

Bishop Bourget appreciated Bishop O'Reilly's concern for the Canadians in his diocese, but, lacking sufficient priests to provide for his own people, he had to refuse O'Reilly's request for a priest. However, he offered to send down a man from time to time to lend assistance when Bishop O'Reilly thought such help would be useful.[137] Disappointed in his efforts to secure a Canadian priest, Bishop O'Reilly whenever possible assigned priests who spoke French to minister to French Canadian communities.

By the 1850s small numbers of German Catholics had settled in the diocese and Bishop O'Reilly again tried to provide pastoral care in their own language. At first he sought the assistance of a German-speaking Jesuit or Redemptorist priest from New York to visit the German communities, which were found particularly in Connecticut, to give the people a chance to receive the sacraments in a familiar context. As with the Canadians many Germans felt uncomfortable or even unwanted in "Irish" churches. As a result, some apostatized and others remained unchurched. When in 1855, Bishop O'Reilly did obtain the services of a German priest to minister to his countrymen, the people failed to raise funds enough to support his ministry and he left discouraged.[138]

Numbers and Need

The establishment of new parishes is but one sign of tremendous growth in the Catholic population of Rhode Island during the years Bishop O'Reilly served the diocese. Fr. Wiley's and Bishop O'Reilly's reports to the Catholic almanacs are at best approxima-

---

[136]Bishop Bernard O'Reilly to Bishop Ignatius Bourget, Montreal, July 28, 1853, Montreal Archdiocesan Archives. Hereafter cited MChA.

[137]Bishop Ignatius Bourget to Bishop Bernard O'Reilly, September 11, 1853, MChA.

[138]Byrne, *Catholic Church in the New England States*, II, pp. 354-55; Bishop Francis P. McFarland to the Society for the Propagation of the Faith, Paris, October 15, 1869, SPFA.

tions. Fr. Wiley reported the Catholic population of the Hartford diocese in 1850 as "about" twenty thousand and Bishop O'Reilly counted "about" fifty-five thousand in 1855.[139]

Although the municipal census of 1855 shows that the foreign-born population of Providence, which jumped from 10,275 in 1850 to 13,232 in 1855, found lodging in all the city's seven wards, the first, third, fifth and seventh showed the largest number of foreigners.[140] The first ward included the Randall's Square area and was the site of Philip Allen's print works and St. Patrick's parish. The third ward included what is today the Fox Point section of Providence, and the fifth and sixth wards included the area in the neighborhood of the cathedral. Many of the heads of the Irish families in the tenements of these wards listed their occupation in the 1850 census as laborers. The same census shows that in most cases both the mother and father of these families were unable to read and write although the children in some of the families were literate because of the opportunities for education that living in Providence afforded.[141]

When a cholera epidemic visited Providence in 1854, Edwin M. Snow, in a report to the Providence City Council, noted the highest percentage of fatal cases were in the tenement neighborhoods of India Street and Fox Point Hill. Nine-tenths of the deaths were among foreigners. The principal local causes of the pestilence, the report says, were the condition of the canal near Gaspee Street, the filth on Fox Point Hill due to the custom of keeping hogs, and the porous character of the soil in both these locations.[142]

The first reasonably accurate figures that exist for the Catholic population of Rhode Island date from a tour of the diocese undertaken by Bishop O'Reilly's successor in 1857. There are no figures for the cathedral parish, but the pastors of the other parishes in the city gave their parish populations as: St. Patrick's, 5,700; St. Joseph's, 2,500; and St. Mary's, 3,500. St. Mary's in Newport listed 1,500; St. Mary's, Pawtucket, 2,600; St. Charles's, Woonsocket, 2,000; and St. Mary's, Crompton, 1,360. Of the new parishes SS. Peter and Paul in Phenix gave its population as 1,000 and 100 at its mission at East Greenwich and 35 adults at Wickford. St. Patrick's,

[139]*Metropolitan Catholic Almanac*, 1850, p. 103; 1855, p. 232.

[140]Edwin M. Snow, Comp., *Census of the City of Providence taken in July 1855*, 2nd ed. (Providence: Knowles, Anthony & Co., 1856), pp. 16-17.

[141]"Census of 1850," Providence County, Manuscript at R. I. Historical Society.

[142]Edwin M. Snow, "Statistics and Causes of Asiatic Cholera as it Prevailed in Providence, in the Summer of 1854 . . ." *Providence City Documents*, No. 5, 1854-1855, pp. 10-12.

Harrisville noted 1,000 and had 23 families at its out-missions in
Albion and 15 families in Slatersville. St. Philip's, Greenville listed
a total population of 330 and in St. Mary's in Warren and Bristol,
there were 800 people.[143]

All churches in which these first Catholics of Rhode Island
worshipped were built through a combination of sacrifice and pride
of parishioners and the generosity of fellow Catholics in other parts
of the United States and Europe. Bishop O'Reilly's appeal for financial assistance for his diocese, which he described in a letter in 1853
as "the poorest with such a population certainly in America," was
answered by three mission societies, the Society for the Propagation
of the Faith in Paris and Lyon, the Ludwig Mission Association in
Munich, and the Leopoldine Mission Society in Vienna.[144] The
funds sent by these mission societies helped to build and furnish
many of the mission churches erected in the diocese at this time and
paid for the education of many priests who came to serve the diocese.

Bishop O'Reilly's frequent visits to his parishes made him
aware very quickly of the material needs of his people. In 1851 he
wrote to the Central Council of the Propagation of the Faith in Paris:
"My diocese is entirely composed of poor emigrants who have
recently come to the country."[145] Later in 1856 he again wrote
to the Central Council in Paris of the material conditions of his
people:

> The Catholics in these two states which comprise the diocese of
> Hartford have risen up to between 55,000 and 65,000 souls. The two
> states are sustained principally by factories of different kinds; a great part
> of our Catholics are employed in these establishments. As my diocese
> reaches almost to the city of New York where the great part of the immi-
> grants who come to the United States arrive, the poor come continually
> in such great numbers to look for employment in the factories of my area,
> so that the employers can always hire the poor at a wage which they wish
> to offer. For this reason our Catholic population is utterly poor; I can even
> say that there is not a Catholic family in the diocese which can live without
> working.[146]

[143]Bishop Francis P. McFarland, "Diary," 1857, HChA. A letter written in the
Boston Pilot, August 22, 1857 gave the Catholic population in Newport in 1853 as
about five hundred and noted that at the time of his writing Catholics numbered
nearly one thousand.

[144]Bernard O'Reilly to the Ludwig Mission Society, February 1, 1853, LMSA.
Letters to the other mission societies are found among Bishop O'Reilly's correspondence.

[145]Bernard O'Reilly to Central Council, Propagation of the Faith, Paris, December
28, 1851, SPFA.

[146]*Ibid.*, January 17, 1856, SPFA.

Many Irish immigrants lived so close to the subsistence level that only minor changes in the business cycle or sustained periods of severe weather were enough to create hardship and need.

Such consciousness of society's responsibility for the poor as existed at the time was concerned not with improving the lot of the poor but with keeping them alive. While in Ireland the pauper and the sick could look to the parish for support, in America civil authorities had come to assume these responsibilities. At first town meetings or city councils elected an Overseer of the Poor to care for the poor and ensure that they did not become a permanent burden on the community. Paupers were farmed out to local citizens on a contract basis. The citizens provided food and lodging in return for the pauper's work. In 1723, the town of Newport built the first poorhouse in the state and thereafter many other towns and cities provided the same kind of refuge for the poor. In 1850, under the provision of a resolution adopted by the legislature, Governor Henry B. Anthony appointed Thomas R. Hazard to study the provisions made by cities and towns of the state for the support of the poor and insane. Hazard's report, which he submitted to the general assembly at its January 1851 session did much to focus attention on the plight of the sick and the poor and led to some significant reforms.[147]

During the course of preparing his report, Mr. Hazard visited Dexter Asylum in Providence and compiled a list of inmates and the causes of their poverty. Of the 136 men, women and children in the asylum, sixty-one were born in Ireland, the rest were native American or immigrants from England, France or Portugal. There were 163 inmates in the asylum in July 1858; 103 of whom were natives of Ireland. They seemed to have been well cared for by the standard of the times, as were the insane poor in Butler Hospital and the indigent sick in the city hospital. Their expense fell upon the city.[148]

A month after Hazard issued his report to the general assembly a correspondent to the *Boston Pilot* provided a description of the lot of the poor in Providence who received outdoor relief rather than being provided for by residence in the poorhouse. He noted that there were large numbers of needy in the city owing, he felt, to the

[147]Edward Field, ed. *State of Rhode Island and Providence Plantations at the End of the Century: A History*, 3 vols. (Boston & Syracuse: The Mason Publishing Company, 1902) III, 389-408.

[148]Thomas R. Hazard, *Report on the Poor and Insane, made to the General Assembly at its January session, 1851.* (Providence: Joseph Knowles, State Printer, 1851); George W. Wightman, "Semi-Annual Report of the Overseer of the Poor with the Report of the Select Committee thereon," *Providence City Documents*, 1859, p. 7.

manufacturing character of the place. "The amount given to the poor, by the city, is a miserable affair. About $1,000 a month, leaving the creatures to famish from hunger and cold, unless relieved by private charity." The Overseer of the Poor was a man over eighty, a good man, but one faced with a difficult task.[149]

The efforts of public officials were supplemented by private sources. Several older Protestant churches in the city supported a "City Missionary" or Missionary-at-Large who helped when he could.[150] In November 1855, many leading citizens of Providence, among whom was Bishop O'Reilly, founded the Providence Aid Society. Its stated purpose was "to prevent and relieve pauperism, and promote the welfare of the poor." The aid society sought to accomplish its object "by personal intercourse with the poor, by affording aid when it is imperatively demanded, and especially by providing employment for the needy."[151]

The Overseer of the Poor for the most part felt that the Irish poor were in some way the responsibility of their bishop. Bishop O'Reilly became annoyed by the number of referrals of the poor and destitute sent to him by the overseer because he could do very little if anything for so great a number.[152] To assist the bishop, a small group of parishioners of the cathedral parish, on Sunday, November 27, 1854, organized a branch of the St. Vincent de Paul Society, a lay organization dedicated to the service of the poor. The men divided the city into districts, and a committee of two was elected for a period of three months to administer relief work in each of the districts. Those in need because of poverty, sickness or want would make their needs known to their pastor. He in turn would contact one of the men in whose district the person lived, and they would investigate the case. Money, food, clothing, fuel or shelter would be provided as circumstances dictated. Funds came from the poor boxes in the rear of the churches, from charity sermons, or from the proceeds of lectures or entertainments.[153]

The Sisters of Mercy also did much to alleviate the lot of the sick and destitute. The sisters were supported in their work by

---

[149]*Boston Pilot*, February 21, 1852.

[150]*Providence Directory*, 1853, p. 320; 1857, p. 397.

[151]*Providence Journal*, November 15, 1855. Others besides Bishop O'Reilly who were present at the organizational meeting of the Providence Aid Society were Bishop Clark of the Episcopal Church, Rev. Francis Wayland, President of Brown University, Rev. Dr. Hill, Hon. Thomas Davis, and Welcome B. Sayles, Esq.

[152]Byrne, *Catholic Church in the New England States*, I, 372.

[153]Daniel T. McColgan, *A Century of Charity: The First One Hundred Years of the Society of St. Vincent de Paul in the United States*, 2 vols. (Milwaukee: The Bruce Publishing Co., 1951) I, 265-66.

Catholics and non-Catholics alike. Often the donations to the sisters for their work were very small but large in view of the circumstances of the one giving. Most of this money was given privately and quietly.[154] In the severe cold of the winter of 1850-1851 the city's poor could turn to the Fuel Society, the Ministries-at-Large, the Sisters of Mercy, the Children's Friends Society, and the Shelter and Employment Society for help.[155]

There were times in the 1850s when all the normal sources of relief, both public and private, were insufficient to meet the needs of the people of Providence. When, in the fall of 1856, a disastrous financial panic rocked the entire country, Providence did not escape its effects. Men were thrown out of work, and without work for an extended time, they faced starvation. The city of Providence met the emergency by providing work and food for her poorer classes during the hard winter of 1856-1857. Those absolutely unable to work were given food and fuel without having to go to the poorhouse. The city employed those who were able-bodied in grading the high bluff on Smith's hill and filling in the Cove lands.[156]

The following winter 5,570 relief orders totaling $8,824.68 were drawn against the office of the Overseer of the Poor. In addition, the city expended $20,000 for filling the waste lands above the Cove basin. There were 1,900 families registered for aid. Of this number, 1,400 were Irish representing almost 6,300 persons. The Overseer of the Poor, in submitting his report to the Providence City Council in December 1858, concluded that foreign-born residents of Providence "furnished more than their just proportion of paupers." A particularly disturbing aspect of the problem was the fact that many of those receiving relief had deposits in the Savings Bank of Providence. The committee estimated that at least $50,000 was sent from Providence to Ireland every year. The overseer concluded his report with a recommendation for reform in the "outdoor relief system."[157]

There is in the report a hint that the city's troubles were probably aggravated by the influx of poor Irish and there is at least a hint of resentment. That resentment, together with confusion as to the cause of economic and social turmoil Americans encountered in the 1840s and 1850s served to create the conditions for a new outburst of violence against the "foreigners."[158]

---

[154]Morgan, *Mercy*, pp. 15, 35-37.
[155]*Providence Journal*, January 26, 1852.
[156]Greene, *Providence Plantations*, pp. 87-88.
[157]Wightman, "Semi-Annual Report," 1859, p. 7.
[158]Potter, *To the Golden Door*, p. 471-73.

Nativism in Rhode Island

In the aftermath of the Dorr rebellion, the Law and Order forces, as the anti-Dorr men were labeled, had dominated the state government throughout the 1840s through the medium of the Whig party. By the 1850s the Whig party nationally was in decline, and in the state elections of 1851, overconfidence and dissension so weakened the Whigs that the Democrats elected Philip Allen, Governor, Judge William Beach Lawrence, Lieutenant Governor, and a majority of the Senate, leaving only the House in Whig control. Governor Allen was re-elected in 1852 and 1853. In 1853, the state's voters also elected a complete Democratic state ticket and gave the Democrats a majority in both branches of the general assembly. In the election campaigns of the 1850s the Democrats had advocated a liberalizing of the constitution's provisions regarding voter qualifications. Although a call for a new constitutional convention passed the legislature in May 1853, the voters failed to give it the required sixty per cent majority. The same fate befell all attempts to amend the constitution.[159]

Although powerless to avert the Whig defeat, the *Providence Journal* was particularly vigorous in warning of the dangers to Rhode Island's traditions if the Democratic program of voting reform was successful.[160] One correspondent to the *Journal* held out the prospect that if voting restrictions were removed, "Rhode Island will no longer be Rhode Island when that is done. It will become a province of Ireland; St. Patrick will take the place of Roger Williams, and the shamrock will supersede the anchor and Hope."[161] The rhetoric of the *Journal* was directed particularly at the rural elements in Rhode Island's population who saw the voting restrictions as a bulwark protecting their interests against inundation by the growing numbers of foreigners gathering in Rhode Island's cities.[162] This fear that their values and place in society were endangered, when added to the traditional tension between the interests of the rural and urban commercial populations, caused enough Rhode Island Democrats to desert their party on all the constitutional questions that would have liberalized the voting requirements. In the elections of 1854 and 1855, significant numbers of Democrats cast their votes for candidates who campaigned for prohibition and continued legal

[159]Carroll, *Rhode Island,* II, 579, 581.
[160]*Providence Journal,* February 25; March 22, 25, 27, 31; April 1, 7, 1851. Conley and Smith, *Catholicism in Rhode Island,* pp. 76-83.
[161]*Providence Journal,* March 27, 1851.
[162]*Ibid.,* April 4; June 22; July 13, 1853.

restrictions on foreigners with the result that a coalition of former Whigs, prohibition advocates and nativists were elected to all state offices.[163]

One important issue that served to increase tension in the 1850s between natives and foreigners was the argument over support of the state public school system. Rhode Islanders were justly proud of their free public schools.[164] The Catholics of the state, however, did not share that pride. Bishop O'Reilly expressed the conviction of many of his people when he stated that the free education provided by the state was a Protestant education. He was so convinced of the danger to the faith of the children who attended the public schools that he set the establishment of Catholic schools as one of his first priorities. The bishop's concern was less that the children would convert to Protestantism than that, due to training in "uncatholic schools," they would lapse into indifferentism towards their faith.[165] The bishop's view was supported by the experience of the Irish with public education in British-dominated Ireland. One Providence letter writer to the *Boston Pilot* reminded his readers that the public schools of Ireland sought after Catholic children "not for the purpose of teaching, but corrupting them."[166]

There were some among the Catholic community in Providence who disagreed with the bishop's view and who advocated the continuance of the practice of Catholic children attending the public schools. Those who argued for the public schools, or "mixed education" as they called it, saw in the practice a chance to erase the stigma of being a foreigner. They argued that sending the children to the Sunday school would be sufficient to educate children in the faith.[167] The majority within the Catholic community, however, dismissed such arguments as coming from those who wished to accommodate themselves with their Protestant neighbors and indicated they felt that such people were Catholics in name only. "Franklin," one of the writers on the subject to the *Boston Pilot,* thanked God that the number of Catholics who admired mixed education were so few.[168] For some, at least, public education was not a matter

---

[163]Mario R. Di Nunzio and Jan T. Galkowski, "Political Loyalty in Rhode Island: A Computer Study of the 1850's." *Rhode Island History,* XXXVI (August 1977), pp. 93-95; Carroll, *Rhode Island,* I, 582-86.

[164]Charles Carroll, *Public Education in Rhode Island* (Providence, R. I.: E. L. Freeman Co., 1918), pp. 129-76.

[165]Bernard O'Reilly to the Society for the Propagation of the Faith, Paris, January 11, 1851, SPFA.

[166]*Boston Pilot,* July 10, 1852.

[167]*Ibid.,* February 21, 1852.

[168]*Ibid.,* March 6, 1852.

of principle, but an alternative to no education for their children.

After the opening of Catholic schools in Providence at St. Patrick's, SS. Peter and Paul's and St. Joseph's and the tuition school run by the sisters in their convent, most Catholic parents, who were able to do without the added income of their children's labor and who lived close enough to the schools, transferred their children from the public schools. The superintendent of public schools in Providence in 1854 estimated that less than one-tenth of the children of Catholic citizens continued to attend public schools, and those that did, he added, acted "in direct opposition to the will of the priests."[169] About half the Catholic children between five and fifteen attended either public or parochial schools in Providence by 1855.[170] The remainder, for the most part, worked in factories to supplement their families' income with their meager wages.[171]

While native Rhode Islanders might resent the refusal of some Catholics to send their children to the public schools, no cry was made against Catholic schools until the citizens of Rhode Island felt that the Catholics might destroy the public school system because of their opposition to its "Protestant" character. During the fall of 1852, the *Freeman's Journal* and other Catholic papers in New York began to urge Catholics everywhere to unite in demanding a share of public money for the support of their schools, or, if this could not be obtained, the passage of laws forbidding the reading of the Protestant bible in state-supported educational institutions. The Rhode Island secular press joined in the general outcry against such demands because they believed these concessions represented a possible threat to the financial stability of public education in Rhode Island. At least two Rhode Island Catholics, one who wrote in the *Newport Daily News* and a Providence Catholic school teacher, John Coyle, in a public address to the Irish nationalized citizens in July 1853, undertook to defend the justice of the Catholic position. The arguments of both men were similar and basically were an exposition of the need to establish Catholic schools.[172]

After Coyle's address was published in full by the *Providence Tribune,* the editor of the *Providence Journal* offered the citizens of Rhode Island a response to the Catholic objections to the public schools which he felt would be consistent with Rhode Island's reli-

[169]*Providence Journal,* February 16, 1854.
[170]Snow, *Census,* 1855, pp. 32-33.
[171]*Metropolitan Catholic Almanac,* 1855, p. 168.
[172]*Newport Daily News,* February 4, 9, 1853; *Providence Tribune,* July 8, 1853; *Pawtucket Gazette and Chronicle,* March 25, 1853.

gious heritage. "Let the Catholic children use the version which their parents prescribe, or let the reading of the Scriptures in the schools be confined to those portions which are undisputed . . . We would even consent to give up the bible in the schools rather than to drive out of them the Catholic children." In this instance the *Journal* editor acknowledged, in reporting the comments of one of his correspondents, that he "did not speak the sentiments of one in ten in this community." The sentiment of the community the *Journal* correspondent noted was, "very decided in favor of the bible in the schools."[173] An expression of that sentiment quickly appeared in a series of articles written for the *Providence Daily Tribune* by Rev. Mr. George R. Darrow. Rev. Darrow attacked John Coyle's argument sentence by sentence. The theme of his articles was that if Coyle had his way the public schools would be destroyed.[174]

The State Commissioner of Public Schools at the time, Elisha R. Potter, Jr., was a man who was more concerned with the quality of education than with settling religious controversies. In his report to the general assembly in 1853, Mr. Potter presented voluminous extracts from the arguments of both parties on the use of the bible in public schools. Commissioner Potter took the position in this report that "the reading of the Bible or conducting other devotional exercises at the opening or closing of schools is neither forbidden nor commanded by law, and rests with the teacher, who should respect his own conscience and the consciences of his pupils and their parents."[175] Potter's decision, as he pointed out in a letter published the following year in the *Journal*, allowed a teacher in a school where there were a large number of Catholic children leeway to avoid compelling the children to use a version of the bible they felt to be erroneous. Potter himself felt that, "Our school system is a part of the machinery of the State, supported by the funds of the State, and no one has a right to use it as a means to enforce upon others his own religious views."[176] Commissioner Potter's decision was slightly more acceptable to Rhode Islanders than was the *Journal*

---

[173]*Providence Journal,* July 30, 1853.

[174]*Providence Tribune,* July 11, 13, 14, 16, 1853. See also John Coyle reply to Rev. Mr. Darrow, July 21, 22, 1853; and Rev. Mr. Darrow reply July 25, 28, August 1, 9, 1853.

[175]"Report of the Commissioner of Public Schools," pp. 28-32, in E. R. Potter's *Reports and Documents upon Public Schools and Education* (Providence: Knowles, Anthony & Co., 1855).

[176]*Providence Journal,* August 25, 1854. Mr. Potter's decision arose out of his conviction expressed earlier in an address before the Rhode Island Historical Society on February 19, 1851, that people have a right to govern themselves and every person should be permitted to manage his own concern.

editor's proposal. A good number of Rhode Islanders continued to insist on the need and right to have the Protestant version of the bible read in the schools.[177]

The controversy over Catholic schools was but part of the rising uneasiness among native Rhode Islanders—an uneasiness that politicians, either out of conviction or opportunism, exploited during the annual campaigns for state offices. On February 24, 1853, with another election campaign about to begin, there appeared in the *Providence Journal* a lengthy letter to the editor that was printed under the lead; "What is the Church of Rome." The letter filled two entire pages of print. To accommodate it the *Journal* increased its usual four page edition to six. The author, who signed himself "Sentinel" and later acknowledged himself as a Portsmouth farmer, disclaimed any hostility towards particular persons in writing to the *Journal.* The occasion of his letter was an article that had appeared in the *Newport Daily News* under the caption, "Is the Catholic Opposed to Learning?" In the course of his response Sentinel took issue with the faith and practices of the Catholic Church.[178]

Two days after the appearance of Sentinel's letter, the *Journal* published two reactions. Fr. James Hughes labeled Sentinel's statements as "scurrilities" and criticized the *Journal* for issuing a supplement to publish it. The second letter writer who signed himself "Vindex," also criticized the *Journal* for publishing the letter, but devoted his space to a request addressed to Sentinel to prove certain of his allegations, the chief of which was that "there exists at this present time a most daring conspiracy against the civil and religious liberty of the world."[179] Sentinel took up Vindex's invitation to debate and submitted two more articles, the first to answer Vindex's questions, the second to discuss the original question of public education and the Catholics. Two other exchanges of letters followed. After Vindex's third reply, Sentinel embarked on a series of twenty articles, the last of which the *Journal* published on April 15, 1854.

Who Sentinel and Vindex were is unknown. Vindex might have been Bishop O'Reilly.[180] The editor of the *Journal* did note that Sentinel was not a clergyman or a citizen of Providence. Other articles he would write of similar style and tone indicate that he spoke for the nativist agricultural influences in the state who felt

---

[177]*Providence Tribune,* October 31, 1854.
[178]*Providence Journal,* February 24; June 14, 1853; *Newport Daily News,* January 19, 1853.
[179]*Providence Journal,* February 26, 1853.
[180]Byrne, *Catholic Church in the New England States,* I, 380.

their control over the politics of the state threatened by the large number of Catholics in the cities who could swing an election if allowed to vote.[181]

Publication of such lengthy articles as submitted by Vindex and Sentinel were an unusual practice for the *Journal.* A year earlier the *Kent County Atlas* declined to continue a series of letters from Fr. Patrick Lenihan over the validity of Catholic belief that flared as a result of an article on the Catholic church published by the paper's editor. Further, the editor of the *Newport Daily News,* in whose columns the seminal article appeared, expressed uneasiness with opening his pages to theological arguments but continued to print responses to the original article for a few days.[182] The practical economics of publishing a daily paper like the *Journal* mitigated against using space for theological and historical arguments that might be used for news or advertisements. The *Journal's* editor declined to publish any but the articles by Vindex and Sentinel.[183] But the fact that the paper published twenty articles by Sentinel in space usually reserved for popularly oriented fiction, book reviews, human interest pieces, or texts of recent legislation, indicates that the editor felt that the subject was one of popular interest and concern.

Among the pieces of reform legislation passed by the Democratic-controlled general assembly at its January 1854 session was an act re-organizing the Providence school committee. Prior to 1832 school committee members had been elected by the freemen of the town under the General School Act of 1828. In 1832, the general assembly passed a city charter that gave the Providence City Council the right to choose members of the school committee. The general assembly in 1854 reduced the number of school committeemen and made enough of its membership elective to divest the city council of control.[184] To some citizens of Rhode Island, the general assembly's decision to restore control over the school committee to the citizens of Providence was the first step in dividing public tax money between public and Catholic schools.[185]

Once roused, the fear of Catholic influence found further scope for expression when, during the same January session of the general assembly, a bill was introduced to remit taxation on the Infant

[181]*Providence Journal,* June 14, 1853.
[182]*Newport Daily News,* January 25, 26, 27, 28, 29, 31, 1853; *Kent County Atlas,* August 21, 28; September 18; October 2, 1852.
[183]*Providence Journal,* July 30, 1853. Several of Sentinel's articles were also printed in the *Providence Tribune.*
[184]*Rhode Island Acts and Resolves,* January Session, 1854. Carroll, *Rhode Island,* I, 579-81.
[185]*Providence Journal,* February 27, 1854.

Asylum Bishop O'Reilly was building with the support of the Catholic Orphan and School Society. The Act of Incorporation was modeled on that granted to the Children's Friend Society. The bill passed the House but ran into difficulties in the Senate. Before moving consideration of the House-passed measure, the Senate began debate on an act to empower local school committees to examine or visit any school or system incorporated by or receiving direct or indirect aid through tax exemption from the state. In the course of the debate it became clear that the act was directed at the Catholic Orphan Asylum. The bishop invited the members of the Senate to visit the asylum before the bill came to the floor, but the *Daily Tribune* held that one such planned visit was of no value in discovering the injustices it felt were being inflicted on the children at the school.[186]

The Senate passed the act to enlarge the powers of the local school committees and let it be known that until the House concurred with the Senate action it would not proceed with the matter of incorporating the Catholic asylum.[187] In the House's debate over the Senate's measure regarding school committees, one side argued that the Senate act was unnecessary and prejudicial. Defenders of the act made it clear that the bill originated in response to the suspicions that lay behind charges published in the *Tribune* "of crimes having been committed in that institution [and] of acts of intolerance on the part of Catholics."[188] The House voted to concur with the Senate measure and the Senate passed, with an amendment regarding the amount of tax exemption, the measure to incorporate the asylum.[189]

Debate over the incorporation of the asylum was not confined to the legislature. The *Providence Journal,* while deploring any kind of support for institutions that served to propagate the Romish faith, defended the right of Catholics to obtain the incorporation on the grounds of what they called the Roger Williams doctrine. By the Roger Williams doctrine, the *Journal* understood that "the Legislature should grant the same favor to all institutions, or no favor to any denomination."[190] The stance taken by the *Journal* was challenged by several Rhode Islanders whose letters the *Journal* printed.[191] The most vigorous opposition to the act of incorpora-

---

[186]*Providence Post,* February 18, 1854.

[187]*Providence Tribune,* February 16, 1854.

[188]Debate in the Rhode Island House of Representatives, reported in the *Providence Post,* February 18, 1854.

[189]*Acts and Resolves,* January Session, 1854.

[190]*Providence Journal,* February 2, 11, 1854.

[191]*Ibid.,* February 11, 16, 1854.

tion came from the *Providence Daily Tribune.* The *Tribune,* which began publication on June 13, 1853, was dedicated to reform causes, principally to the adoption of a "Maine" or prohibition law.[192] Within a few months of its initial appearance, its editors, Clement Webster and Benjamin Colby, were claiming the largest circulation of any daily paper in Providence. Although a vehicle for prohibition advocates, the paper championed most of the currently popular reforms among which was the public school movement and halting the growing influence of foreigners.

In line with their goals, the editors of the *Tribune* beginning in November 1853, ran articles "exposing" the activities of the Sisters of Mercy which, according to their arguments, posed a danger to the children of Providence. On the day before the Senate passed the Act of Incorporation of the Orphan Asylum, the *Tribune* ran a piece about a "Mysterious Disappearance, Probable Abduction" in which the *Tribune* repeated its suspicions that the Sisters of Mercy forced children into their convent. The *Tribune* article concluded by asking members of the general assembly for counsel on what they would do if their children were forcibly taken from them for the purpose of being confined within the walls of a nunnery.[193]

The actions of the *Tribune* caused alarm in the minds of some residents. One man who had lived in Boston at the time the Ursuline convent in Charlestown was burned wrote to the *Providence Post* of his fear at:

> seeing now in the public mind symptoms very similar to those that accompanied these events in Boston. A ferment is observable; the pulpit has thus far shown a most commendable discretion; but one of the most, if not the most, influential papers in the State, has been filled for months past, with communications of a nature so false and virulent, as to lead a disinterested observer to some doubts concerning the sanity of the writer.

The *Post* correspondent signed himself, A Protestant and native-born American.[194]

The prohibition cause for which the *Tribune* served as a trumpet drew together many who saw the Irish foreigners as among the chief contributors to the evils that hard drink brought on the community. The foreigners owned many of the rum shops and patronized most.[195] Rum shops and tavernowners spread money around at election time to see that anti-Maine law candidates were elected to

[192]*Providence Tribune,* June 13, 1853.
[193]*Ibid.,* November 8, 12, 1853; February 23, 1854.
[194]*Providence Post,* March 20, 1854.
[195]*Providence Tribune,* May 6, 1854.

public office. In May 1852, prohibition advocates whose strength lay in the rural towns, succeeded in securing from the general assembly the passage of an Act for the Suppression of Drinking Houses and Tippling Shops. The law was quickly ruled unconstitutional by the Rhode Island Supreme Court, but in 1853, the general assembly rewrote the act and submitted it to the people in the April election. The act passed by a narrow margin even though the Democratic party, which had consistently opposed liquor control, won the state elections by a landslide. The observance of the law and its enforcement in certain towns was lax. In spite of the numbers of people, usually Irishmen, who were arrested on charges of drunkenness and of selling liquor, drink was available to those who wanted it.[196]

In the state elections of 1854 the Maine law issue, the supposed threat to the public school system posed by Catholics whom the Democratic party might wish to court, together with the attempts of Democrats to reform suffrage requirements, helped to bring about a reversal of the Democratic victory of 1853. Enough voters, who had previously voted for the Democratic party, gave their votes to William Hoppin who ran at the head of both the Whig and Maine law slates. The election broke the power of the urban-rural coalition that had brought the Democrats to victory in 1851.[197]

Although there was considerable anti-foreigner, anti-Catholic feeling evident in the 1854 state elections, the pivotal issue was the Maine law issue.[198] With the agitation of the temperance groups quieted by the victories of their candidates, reformers began to turn their attention to other issues.

Before 1854, Rhode Island had witnessed little in the way of outbursts of physical violence against Catholics. Neither the *Providence Journal, Post* or *Tribune* initially paid much notice of the rabble-rousing rhetoric of Alessandro Gavazzi, an Italian Barnabite monk, who had been active in the fight for Italian liberation in 1848 and 1849 and who blamed the Roman Church for its failure. Gavazzi dedicated himself to the annihilation of the Church. He found a sympathetic audience in England for his anti-Roman charges and was invited by the American and Foreign Christian Union to come to America to lecture. Within months after his arrival on March 6, 1853, word reached the United States of the proposed visit of Archbishop Gaetano Bedini, Apostolic Nuncio to Brazil and a special emissary of Pius IX to President Pierce. The archbishop, who had

---

[196]Carroll, *Rhode Island,* II, 648-49.
[197]*Providence Post,* March 24; April 6, 7, 1854; *Woonsocket Patriot,* March 31, 1854.
[198]*Providence Post,* April 6, 1854; *Providence Tribune,* April 20; May 6, 11, 1854.

been papal governor of Bologna, proved a perfect target for
Gavazzi's invective against the Church.[199]

Archbishop Bedini came on a dual mission to the United States.
He was accredited as a papal nuncio and empowered to settle trusteeship conflicts in Buffalo and Philadelphia, and secondly, he
planned to tour the United States to observe the religious situation
of German Catholics. After quickly settling the trustee questions in
favor of the clergy, the archbishop began his tour. Spurred on by
Gavazzi, the Protestant press had prepared Protestants for the archbishop's coming by misrepresenting his innocent mission as a carefully planned journey that would end in the subjugation of American freedom.[200] When Archbishop Bedini arrived in Boston after a
visit to Washington and a second stay in New York, he was "in a
state of terrible trepidation under the fear of conspirators against
his life."[201]

Bishop Fitzpatrick hurried back from Worcester to meet the
archbishop. Thanks to his hospitality the archbishop completely
recovered from his fright within a few days. At the end of September
Bishop Fitzpatrick brought him down to Providence to meet Bishop
O'Reilly. Bishop O'Reilly showed him around the city, and together
with Bishop Fitzpatrick they journeyed to New York to meet Mrs.
Goodloe Harper. The *Pilot* correspondent who reported the archbishop's visit expressed his happiness that Archbishop Bedini was
"everywhere treated with the most marked respect."[202] In December 1853, Gavazzi's lecturing brought him back to Boston. Some
citizens of Providence expressed interest in inviting him to lecture
in Providence "but the project was abandoned at the earnest request of some of the 'solid men' of Providence, because they feared
a riot would ensue." The *Journal* objected. Its editor argued that the
fears of Providence citizens violated the principle of freedom of
speech.[203]

Gavazzi's importance lies principally in the fact that his activities convinced hundreds of others that nativism offered a fertile field
for their invective. Perhaps the most prominent New England fol-
lower of Gavazzi was John Orr. Orr was a street preacher who
dressed in a large white garment and carried a trumpet. Calling

[199]Potter, *To the Golden Door,* pp. 579-80.
[200]Billington, *The Protestant Crusade,* pp. 300-302.
[201]Msgr. Peter Guilday, "Gaetano Bedini: An Episode in the Life of Archbishop
John Hughes," U. S. Catholic Historical Society. *Records and Studies XXIII* (New York,
1933), pp. 101-102; Lord, Sexton and Harrington, *History of the Archdiocese of Boston,*
II, 661-63.
[202]*Boston Pilot,* October 8, 1853.
[203]*Providence Journal,* December 17, 1853.

himself the Angel Gabriel, he harangued crowds in New England and New York often inciting his listeners to violence.[204]

Rhode Island was spared any of the outbreaks of violence that followed in the wake of street preachers like Orr. The "solid men" of Providence out of principle respected the rights of ministers to speak their minds in their pulpits or of respectable citizens to lecture on the issues of the day. Out of principle, too, they accepted the right of Catholics among them to worship God undisturbed. However, the position of the traditional leaders in Rhode Island society was undermined in the 1850s by the disorganization of the Whig party and the appearance in the state of the Order of the Star Spangled Banner, a secret fraternal order dedicated to the suppression of any threats to American liberties posed by foreigners. The consciences and social position of the more responsible and respectable men of the state prevented them from joining the order and espousing its political aims. The result was the creation to a degree of a power vacuum that enabled the "middling class of Yankees," to use George Potter's phrase, to gain temporarily positions of influence and leadership. These "new men," who challenged the traditional Whig leadership, respected order too much to participate in acts of violence against the Catholics, but they had no scruples of conscience in condoning outbreaks after they happened. The temporary and partial eclipse of the older leadership gave wider scope to the lowest class of natives who had long ago convinced themselves that for the Irish, and particularly for the Catholics, the laws affording protection to person and property did not apply.[205]

In December 1853, Bishop O'Reilly, who had many times felt the personal animosities that the middling and lowest class of natives harbored against Catholics, wrote of the change in public feeling towards Catholicism created in part by the activities of Gavazzi and his native imitators to a supporter of his diocese in Europe. His anger is perhaps the cause of his poor grammar.

> Protestants never were so bitter as at this moment such as this is owing to our increase as also to the lies given forth in lectures by bad men and apostates from Europe. A riot is feared in New York just now; the Nuncio and Bishop O'Connor were lately insulted at Pittsburgh and here we hear as it were, growling around us, a feeling of the deepest hatred . . . One

[204]Billington, *The Protestant Crusade*, pp. 304-306; Potter, *To the Golden Door*, pp. 581-85; Lord, Sexton and Harrington, *History of the Archdiocese of Boston*, II, 669-72.
[205]Potter, *To the Golden Door*, pp. 283-85; *Newport Daily News*, March 30; April 2, 1855.

of the daily papers here publishes every lie, and will collect against us,
whilst there is ever some minister lecturing against us.[206]

In April 1854, the bishop returned to the same theme in writing
to the president of All Hallows, Dublin: "The nuncio was sadly
treated as you are aware; the good Providence of God has protected
us so far, yet there may be at any moment an avalanche outburst of
Protestant hatred against us. We have certainly to bear much in
every section of the country." The bishop then added his own
opinion that "this city and state is eminently puritanical and exceed-
ingly hostile to catholicity."[207]

Publicly Bishop O'Reilly and his priests did what they could to
allay the fears of their fellow Rhode Islanders about any possible
threat to their liberties from the Catholic community. In a lecture
to the St. Vincent de Paul Society in Providence, Fr. Thomas Quinn
spoke of the American Catholic's devotion to the principle of religious liberty and the many contributions of Catholics in building
American society.[208] Except for a letter in reply to an attack on the
Sisters of Mercy published by E. Z. C. Judson, alias "Ned Buntline,"
in the *Boston Bee,* Bishop O'Reilly refused to recognize the "lies" of
the *Tribune* by refuting them.[209]

In April 1854, some three hundred native Americans formed a
militia unit called the Guard of Liberty.[210] Under the state militia
law this organization could be supplied with arms from the state
arsenal and its officers commissioned by the governor. The mouth-
piece of the Democratic party—the *Providence Post*—raised a protest
calling the Guard of Liberty "a secret organization, professedly
intended for the more effectual suppression of the power and influence of those of foreign birth."[211] In other words, the editor, as did
many others, regarded the guard as a Know-Nothing organization.
The *Journal* answered the *Post* pointing out that the members of the
guard had the same right to organize as a militia company as anyone
else and affirmed its conviction of the effectiveness of the governor's

[206]Bishop O'Reilly to Rev. Ferdinand Muller, Ludwig Mission Association, December 19, 1853, LMSA.
[207]Bishop O'Reilly to the President, All Hallows, Dublin, April 21, 1854, AHMC.
[208]*Providence Journal,* July 18, 1854.
[209]*Providence Tribune,* May 10, 1854. Unlike the *Tribune* which found exposés of the
affairs of the Sisters of Mercy good copy, the *Journal* refused to publish letters
proposing to "expose the general character of nunneries," *Providence Tribune,* May
8, 1854. On February 8, 1855, Bishop O'Reilly also sent a letter to the *Providence Post*
correcting some false information about Bishop Rese of Detroit.
[210]*Providence Tribune,* May 1, 3, 1854.
[211]*Providence Post,* July 22, 1854. Cf. in the same paper the letter of "L.H.M."
explaining and defending the guard.

control over them as militia. The *Journal* ended its article with a caution that "such is the tide of public feeling at present, that there is danger of going too far, on the other side, and prudent men may be called upon to hold back."[212]

Given the secretiveness that surrounded the activities of the Order of the Star Spangled Banner and its political arm, the American or Know-Nothing party, it is not surprising that there is little information available concerning its advent in Rhode Island politics. While noting the activities of Know-Nothings in other states as news items throughout much of 1854, the *Journal, Post* and *Tribune,* as supporters of particular parties or special viewpoints, supply little information about the early local activities of that party. In perhaps June or July 1854, A. C. Greene began to publish a bi-weekly called *The Anti-Romanist and True Catholic* that served as a voice for the Know-Nothings. The paper proved short-lived, and only an except on nunneries exists to give any indication of its nature.[213] The Know-Nothing's American party officially surfaced on the Rhode Island political scene in December 1854, when it held a convention in Providence to nominate candidates for coming elections.

The Know-Nothings began making their influence felt during the January 1855, session of the legislature which had been elected under the old party labels the previous April. The following month, the legislature finished action on a joint resolution asking Rhode Island's senators and representatives to secure passage of laws imposing severe penalties on those introducing foreign paupers and criminals into the country "since the first impose unreasonable taxes and the second corrupt public morals and endanger public safety." The second part of the resolution urged the congressmen to press for revision of the naturalization laws so that twenty-one years residence rather than five would be necessary to apply for citizenship.[214] Among the charges lodged by the nativists against foreigners was the accusation that they often obtained naturalization by fraudulent means. In February the legislature amended Rhode Island laws to forbid the state courts to take up naturalization procedures, an action which went far beyond the demands for reform that originally inspired the legislation.[215]

More important in the minds of the nativists than reducing any future foreign influence was the neutralizing and removal, if possible, of oppressive foreign influences already operating within

[212]*Providence Journal,* July 25, 29, 1854; *Boston Pilot,* August 12, 1854.
[213]*Providence Tribune,* September 28, 1854.
[214]*Acts and Resolves,* January Session, 1855; *Providence Post,* February 16, 17, 1855.
[215]*Acts and Resolves,* January Session, 1855; *Providence Post,* February 26, 1855.

Rhode Island. There was no more suspect Catholic institution in
Providence than the convent of the Sisters of Mercy. Even the *Journal,* the voice of the Providence establishment, which as a rule
published only what it regarded as legitimate news, had its reservations about the convent. Its editor, however, refused to feed prejudice by publishing unsubstantiated articles derogatory of the Catholic church as its chief competitor, the *Tribune,* did so often.
Nevertheless, on November 25, 1854, there appeared in the *Journal*
a piece headlined, "Escape of a Novice." The article told of the
"escape" of Miss Josephine Buckley from the convent of the Sisters
of Charity at Emmitsburg. A few weeks later the *Journal* published
a short notice from the convent's Superior denying Miss Buckley's
claim that she was held against her will as well as Miss Buckley's
reply.[216]

With the news of Miss Buckley's adventures fresh in people's
minds, "Sam" as the Know-Nothing leaders and propagandists
signed themselves, began a propaganda campaign against the evils
of "nunneries." The *Tribune,* which ran the articles, either in the
name of fairness or to sell copy, opened its pages to a rebuttal by
a Philadelphian, Francis Fitzpatrick, which appears to have been
stock material.[217] When Mr. Fitzpatrick came to Rhode Island to
give a lecture in Woonsocket, a local Know-Nothing leader challenged him to a debate on the subject of nunneries and set a date.
Mr. Fitzpatrick refused to take the bait and failed to show.[218]

The Know-Nothings either believed or had convinced themselves of the charges, and in Rhode Island as in Massachusetts, they
attempted to expose the "immoral conditions" they felt existed
inside the convents. The means they chose was to propose state
inspection of the "nunneries." On March 1, 1855, Mr. Albert K.
Barnes, a representative from Scituate, introduced an act into the
legislature to give the school commissioner the right to enter any
school, "the properties of which were exempted from taxation."
The act was referred to the Committee on Education whose chairman reported the same day that the act would confer a power only
the Supreme Court could exercise by writ of Habeus Corpus. Action
on the bill was suspended indefinitely.[219] While Rhode Island legislators quickly and quietly handled the Know-Nothing challenge
to freedom of religion, Massachusetts, on the other hand, would
witness a comic-opera series of inspections of "nunneries" by a

[216]*Providence Journal,* November 25; December 13, 19, 28, 1854.
[217]Lord, Sexton and Harrington, *History of the Archdiocese of Boston,* II, 686.
[218]*Woonsocket Patriot,* February 16, 1855; *Providence Tribune,* March 2, 1855.
[219]*Providence Post,* March 2, 1855.

legislative committee which the *Journal* reported with glee.[220]

Undaunted by the legislature's rebuff, Know-Nothing agitation against the nunneries continued. On March 20, 1855, the *Tribune* published an article that it headlined, "An American Girl Confined in the Nunnery in this City." The *Tribune* charged that a young lady, Rebecca Newell, daughter and heiress of a respected citizen of Providence, the late Stanford Newell, had been induced by the sisters to enter the convent against the wishes of her family. With the family about to depart the city for the west, she was resisting their entreaties to leave the convent even for a visit to her family.[221] Recognizing the explosive potentialities of such charges, Edward P. Knowles, the mayor of Providence immediately called on Miss Newell at the convent and left convinced of the falsehood of the *Tribune's* implications that she was being detained in the convent. Hoping to quiet any anxiety about her freedom that the article might have raised among Providence citizens, Miss Newell, after the mayor's visit, asked Mr. Henry Anthony, the editor of the *Journal* to visit her. After conversing with her, Anthony left also satisfied of Miss Newell's freedom to leave the convent if she wished. He obtained a statement from Miss Newell denying the allegations of the *Tribune* which he ran in the *Journal* on the twenty-first.[222]

The mayor's anxiety was not misplaced as the *Tribune's* article created a minor sensation in the city. In the face of the evident inaccuracy of its charges, the *Tribune* retreated somewhat from the position that it had maintained regarding Miss Newell's being confined against her will. The *Tribune* explained that the intent of its article was to "show parents and guardians the danger to which those entrusted to their care are subject in visiting, merely to gratify an idle curiosity, such an institution as is growing up in our midst, under the name and pretense of a charitable and religious one."[223] The *Post* on the same day commented on the *Tribune's* article warning of the danger of mob violence that could develop as a result of the implications that Miss Newell was being detained by force. Perhaps the editor of the *Post* was thinking of the threats of violence that followed incidents of recent Know-Nothing Catholic encounters in other cities.[224]

The *Post's* concern was well placed. On March 22nd, placards

[220]*Providence Journal,* April 2, 3, 6, 11, 12, 18, 22, 1855.
[221]*Providence Tribune,* March 20, 1855.
[222]*Providence Journal,* March 21, 1855.
[223]*Providence Tribune,* March 21, 1855.
[224]*Providence Post,* March 21, 1855. See also *Providence Post,* March 19, 1855 for an account of disturbances in Brooklyn, N. Y.

and handbills appeared on Providence walls and in its streets calling on all true Americans to assemble the next evening in the vicinity of the convent at the corner of Claverick and Broad streets.[225] The *Tribune* had ended its original article with the hope that "Sam" would "look into Miss Newell's case, while he may visit the State on the fourth of April," the date of the upcoming state elections.[226] The opponents of the Know-Nothings charged them with calling the meeting to dramatize the fears that they had been expressing in their campaign. The Know-Nothings countered with the charge that their opponents had issued the call for the meeting in order to embarrass them. In any case the first placard was followed by one which attributed the call to "gather for a mob" to the enemies of the Know-Nothings. This second placard called on the order's members to take no further notice of the call.[227] Throughout the day of the twenty-third, rumors circulated that an assault on the convent would be made that evening.[228]

Spreading rumors brought varied responses from Providence's citizens. Some of the leading citizens contacted Bishop O'Reilly to offer the protection of their homes to the sisters. The bishop thanked them for their good will and concern but replied that he felt it better for the sisters to remain in their convent.[229] Bishop O'Reilly nevertheless realized that in the light of occurrences elsewhere in New England, certain precautions had to be taken because even a few irresponsible rowdies could ignite the situation. At the bishop's request city and state officials were called upon to ensure the sister's safety. On the evening of the twenty-third the mayor and the city marshall with a large force of police were on hand at the convent while several militia companies reported to their armories in the event of serious trouble.[230]

As further assurance of the sisters' protection, the bishop asked that some of the Catholics of the city be on hand. Either in response to the bishop's request or on their own initiative, several hundred Catholic workmen hurried home early from work, ate a hasty supper, grabbed a gun, club or anything they could get hold of and made their way to the convent grounds. The bishop along with Frances Warde saw to it that the convent grounds were barricaded,

[225]*Providence Journal,* March 22, 1855; *Providence Post,* March 22, 1855.

[226]*Providence Tribune,* March 20, 1855.

[227]*Providence Journal,* March 23, 1855; *Providence Tribune,* April 7, 1855.

[228]*Providence Tribune,* March 23, 1855.

[229]Morgan, *Mercy,* p. 26. Of the two secondary accounts written by the Sisters of Mercy relating the incident, Sister Mary Catherine's appears more reliable although less detailed than Mother Austin's published in the *Annals,* III, 395-406.

[230]*Providence Tribune,* March 23, 1855.

and the Irishmen took up positions inside the convent to defend its occupants.[231] The bishop made his own preparations sending his will, along with other important papers, to his nephew, Fr. Hughes in Hartford.[232]

By eight o'clock, the announced time for the gathering, a crowd of about two thousand people (some it was said came from Boston, Salem and Taunton) had assembled near the convent. Someone demanded Miss Newell's release, and when the demand was repeated a third time, Bishop O'Reilly replied; "The sisters are in their home, they shall not leave it even for an hour; I shall protect them while I have life, and, if needs be, register their safety with my blood."[233] A mixed chorus of cheers and jeers followed the bishop's response. The crowd stayed for about two hours in front of the convent until finally the mayor, "in a short but effective and judicious speech, appealed to the regard Rhode Islanders had for law and order and in a mild and persuasive manner, requested the crowd to disperse."[234] The crowd, which apparently was made up mostly of spectators and the curious, shortly thereafter dispersed and went home.

The city was exceptionally quiet the next evening. The incidents of March 23rd marked the closest point to a violent break with Rhode Island's traditional tolerance for religious beliefs. A few days after the state elections, the *Journal* declared that "a single angry word followed by a blow, might have led to an outbreak which would have been suppressed only by blood." The fact that violence did not erupt, the *Journal* felt, lay to the "good sense and prudence of the Mayor" and to the action of Bishop O'Reilly, "who was equally active and equally judicious among his own people." Also the *Journal* felt "a great deal must be attributed to happy accident."[235]

Agitation against the nunneries and against the Catholic church did not end with the dispersal of the crowd from the convent or with the election victory of temperance and nativist candidates over Democrats in the April election. The *Tribune's* exposé of nunneries continued to run for five more installments.[236] Apostate priests, such as Rev. P. J. Leo, continued to be invited to speak in Provi-

[231]Morgan, *Mercy*, pp. 26, 30-31.
[232]Byrne, *Catholic Church in the New England States*, I, 376.
[233]*Metropolitan Catholic Almanac*, 1857, p. 296.
[234]*Providence Tribune*, March 23, 1855.
[235]*Providence Journal*, April 7, 1855. Within a few months of the incident, Miss Newell decided that God was not calling her to lead the life of a religious. She left the convent and the city, but remained in contact with the sisters in Providence for many years.
[236]*Providence Tribune*, April 12, 13; May 1, 2, 3, 1855.

dence by the same American and Foreign Christian Union that had
invited Gavazzi to the United States.[237] In the tense atmosphere
created by the agitation, prejudice even more easily perverted the
administration of justice than it had in the 1840s. Irish men and
women were natural suspects in cases of violent crimes, and reports
of violence involving Irish men were well reported in the local
papers.[238]

In 1855, candidates jointly supported by the Whigs and the
Know-Nothings' American party swept the state elections. Although
the Know-Nothings as a result gained considerable influence in the
state government, they proved as powerless to impose further limitations on the political rights of foreign-born citizens as the Democrats, after their victory in 1853, had proved in enlarging them. The
impact of the Know-Nothing movement in the state was considerably lessened with the formation of a state Republican party in time
for the presidential election in 1856. The Republicans offered yet
another alternative to those Rhode Islanders frustrated with the
older parties. Candidates supported by both the American order
and the Republicans dominated every state election until 1860 and
nativist influence remained a powerful force in the state legislature
for years thereafter.[239]

The Death of Bishop O'Reilly

With the passing of the immediate crisis of the Know-Nothing
challenge, Bishop O'Reilly turned to the task which had occupied
his mind since the early days of his episcopate—the completion of
his plans to provide a religious education for the children of Providence by obtaining the services of Christian Brothers to teach in the
new school that was to be finished in the fall of 1855. On December
5th the bishop sailed for Europe to attempt to achieve in person
what he had not been able to achieve by letter. His trip met with
some success and, after visiting his parents, he embarked on the
steamer *Pacific* on January 23, 1856, for the return voyage home.[240]

Another man might not have risked a voyage to Europe in

[237]*Providence Journal*, April 10, 1855; *Providence Tribune*, April 30, 1855.
[238]John M. Ray, "Anti-Catholicism and Know Nothingism in Rhode Island,"
American Ecclesiastical Review, CXLVIII (January 1963), 27-36.
[239]Carroll, *Rhode Island*, I, 582-86.
[240]Propaganda Fide to Brother Philippe, F.S.C., Rome, December 10, 1851; Propaganda Fide to Archbishop Cullen, Dublin, Rome, December 24, 1854, Propaganda
Fide Archives, Rome. Hereafter cited PFA. *Boston Pilot*, October 27, 1855.

winter. But the bishop, who had criticized his young priests for spending a few weeks "vacation" with their parents after ordination when there was work to be done, was a man who practiced what he preached. Three weeks passed and the *Pacific* failed to arrive on schedule. Other vessels that were on the sea at the same time reported "boisterous weather" and on crossing the Grand Banks several encountered ice flows. Thanks to their iron hulls they made port but many wondered what would happen to wooden hulled ships like the *Pacific* if they encountered the same conditions.[241]

News that Bishop O'Reilly was on board the *Pacific* drifted into Providence. After a few weeks, when shipping officials were sure that the *Pacific* had not returned to Europe, they regretfully concluded that the ship had foundered.[242] Hope for the bishop's safety persisted because of confusion as to whether or not he was in fact on the *Pacific*. It was the bishop's custom when traveling to sign the manifest simply as Mr. O'Reilly. At last, word arrived from his brother in Ireland that Bishop O'Reilly was in fact a passenger on the ship. Sorrowfully, the Church of Hartford prayed for the eternal rest of its second bishop. On June 17, 1856, the clergy and people of the diocese joined Archbishop Hughes and the other bishops of the Province of New York in celebrating a solemn requiem Mass for the repose of Bishop O'Reilly's soul.[243]

[241]*Providence Tribune,* March 7, 1856.
[242]*Providence Journal,* March 21, April 12, 18, 22, 1856.
[243]*Boston Pilot,* June 28, 1856; Byrne, *Catholic Church in the New England States,* II, 147-49.

Chapter IV

The Episcopate of Bishop Francis P. McFarland

The Diocese Awaits a New Bishop

Since Bishop O'Reilly's death could not be confirmed, Roman authorities believed it prudent to allow a reasonable amount of time to pass before naming a successor. While the diocese waited, Rev. William O'Reilly, the bishop's brother and one of his two vicar generals, was appointed administrator of the diocese.

There was much to be done. The number of Catholics in the diocese continued to increase due to immigration. Although limited in authority, Fr. O'Reilly did take advantage of certain opportunities to ensure better pastoral care. Many of the first churches built in the diocese were now becoming badly overcrowded; this was particularly true of the cathedral parish. In 1857 Fr. O'Reilly purchased the meetinghouse of the South Baptist Congregation from the parties who held the mortgage. The meetinghouse was in the town of Cranston, about a quarter mile beyond what was then the city line of Providence. The area around the church was sparsely settled, but it was in an area where land was available cheaply and where many Catholic families were settling. On June 21, 1857, Fr. O'Reilly dedicated the church under the title of St. Bernard's—a title chosen in honor of Fr. O'Reilly's brother by the wife of one of the men who helped organize the parish. For two years the priests from the cathedral rode out to say Mass there.[1]

In 1849, a young inventor, George H. Corliss, had gathered together a group of Irish workmen on the Moshassuck River, just beyond the Providence-North Providence line to build a factory to manufacture steam engines of his design. This area, too, was sparsely settled and at the time was part of St. Patrick's parish. By

---

[1] *New York Tablet,* July 4, 1857; Munro, *Memorial Encyclopedia,* p. 411.

1857 so many families had moved into the neighborhood of the
Corliss Works that St. Patrick's was too small to accommodate all
who came on Sunday. The pastor of St. Patrick's began construction
of a second church, but before it was complete, Fr. O'Reilly set up
a separate parish in the district and appointed Rev. Edward J.
Cooney as its first pastor. Fr. Cooney had come to know the area
well as an assistant in the cathedral in Providence.[2]

During the long wait for news of Bishop O'Reilly, his friends
hoped against hope that some word would come regarding his
rescue and return. Anxiety as to the bishop's fate lay particularly
heavy on the heart of his brother, William.[3] The lack of news also
gave free play to rumors. One made the rounds that the bishop had
never really sailed on the *Pacific* at all, but that he was in fact a
prisoner in the castle of St. Angelo at Rome, a companion, perhaps,
of Bishop Reze, the former bishop of Detroit, whose alleged "im-
prisonment" had been reported in Providence papers years before.[4]

Among the clergy of the diocese, speculation centered on who
was to be their new bishop. The creation of the Archdiocese of New
York in 1850 had removed the Diocese of Hartford from the jurisdiction of the Archbishop of Baltimore and placed it under the care
of the Archbishop of New York, who was then John Hughes. On
May 15, 1856, the bishops of the Province met in New York to
consider the matter of the vacancy of the See of Hartford. Although
Rome chose not to act immediately on their advice, the Roman
authorities did accept the choice of Archbishop Hughes and his
fellow bishops.[5]

The man chosen to be the third bishop of Hartford, Francis
Patrick McFarland, was born in Waynesboro, Franklin County,
Pennsylvania on April 4, 1819.[6] His parents, natives of County
Armagh, Ireland, had come to the United States in the spring of
1806 and settled on a farm in Waynesboro. As a boy his father, John,
had studied for the priesthood, but the Irish Rebellion of 1798
forced him to abandon the idea.

Young Francis acquired a good common school education,

[2]Richard A. Walsh, *The Centennial History of St. Edward Church, Providence, Rhode Island, 1874-1974* (Privately printed, 1974), p. 22.
[3]Rev. William O'Reilly's obituary in the *Providence Journal*, December 21, 1868.
[4]Byrne, *Catholic Church in the New England States*, I, 381.
[5]There are many letters on the subject in the Congregation of the Propaganda Archives in Rome. See Fenbar Kenneally, *United States Documents in the Propaganda Fide Archives: A Calendar* (First Series, Vol. IV), under Bishop Francis P. McFarland, p. 398.
[6]Clarke, *Lives of the Deceased Bishops*, III, 117-27 gives Waynesboro as McFarland's birthplace. The *Providence Journal*, March 15, 1858 gives his birthplace as Chambersburg, Pennsylvania.

later working as a teacher in the Academy at Chambersburg, Pennsylvania. About 1839, with the support and encouragement of his
parents, friends and a priest he had known, McFarland entered
Mount St. Mary's College, Emmittsburg, Maryland to pursue his
studies for the priesthood. For a brief period after he finished his
course of study, McFarland served as a professor at the college. This
was perhaps due to the fact that he was canonically still too young
for ordination or perhaps simply because he was an excellent
teacher. Following his ordination by Bishop John Hughes in old St.
Patrick's Cathedral in New York on May 18, 1845, Fr. McFarland
was assigned to St. John's College, Fordham, New York, where he
served as a professor while also doing parochial duty in New York
City. After a year at Fordham, Fr. McFarland petitioned his bishop
for a full time parochial ministry and was assigned to St. Mary's
church in Watertown, New York. Watertown and its missions extended over the whole of Jefferson County in western New York and
was said by an eyewitness of McFarland's labors to require "labor
enough for three priests."[7]

During the time Fr. McFarland was at Watertown, Rome
created the Diocese of Albany and appointed John McCloskey as its
first bishop. In March 1851, Bishop McCloskey transferred McFarland to St. John's parish, Utica, where during his ministry, McFarland made a strong and lasting impression on his parishioners. The
letter files at the Hartford Chancery contain many long, friendly
letters sent by the people of St. John's to their former pastor. Fr.
McFarland's labors in Utica also impressed his ecclesiastical superiors for on June 9, 1857, he was appointed Vicar Apostolic of
Florida, then part of the Diocese of Savannah. Reluctant to leave
Utica, he declined the honor. A year later he again received an
appointment from Rome, this time to the vacant See of Hartford.
It was with mutual sadness that Fr. McFarland left St. John's. On
March 14, 1858, in the cathedral in Providence, Archbishop Hughes
and seven other bishops of the province ordained Francis P. McFarland, the third bishop of Hartford.[8]

Bishop McFarland was an impressive speaker, delivering long
and powerful sermons, lasting an hour. Although he is remembered
more for the doctrinal content of his sermons, he chose to record
in his "Diary" that he often preached to the children of the cathedral
school at the early morning Mass. He was in demand as a speaker

---

[7]Clarke, *Lives of the Deceased Bishops*, III, 119.
[8]Byrne, *Catholic Church in the New England States*, II, 151-53; *Providence Journal*,
March 15, 1858; *Boston Pilot*, March 20, 1858.

in parishes throughout his diocese and in the halls of civic and fraternal groups throughout the state.[9] He had a kind, fatherly manner that greatly endeared him to his people. His day, from early morning rising to retirement late in the evening, was filled with prayer, correspondence, visits and meetings. Often his "Diary" for a given day begins with a notation on how he felt. His stomach was a constant source of anxiety, and he frequently suffered from lung troubles, often having to give up work and retire to a sanitarium.[10]

The Pastoral Task

Within weeks after his ordination, Bishop McFarland began a series of pastoral visitations of his new diocese. As he traveled, he kept a small ledger in which he carefully recorded the assets and liabilities, both material and spiritual, of the parishes he visited. The ledger is ample evidence of the growth of the Catholic population of the diocese since the days of Bishop Tyler's arrival.

By the 1850s Rhode Island's transformation to an economy based on industry was almost complete. Providence had become the state's leading industrial center and had its best balanced manufacturing economy.[11] Irish and English immigrants and a sprinkling of French Canadians and Germans made up a large part of the labor force in the factories and mills built in formerly uninhabited places to take advantage of water power. In Providence, where manufacturing establishments were in operation before the European immigrants arrived, native workers dominated the factory labor force and immigrants remained laborers and unskilled workers.[12] There was a great deal of mobility among Irish laborers and unskilled workers, who each year went to new neighborhoods within the city and state as well as to cities in other states.[13] Those who reached or established themselves in non-manual positions did so by supplying their fellow countrymen with goods. Dry goods merchants and liquor dealers headed the list of leading men in the Irish community. If a

[9]Charles Howard Malcom to Bishop McFarland, April 8, 1861; Henry W. Diman to Bishop McFarland, February 8, 1861, HChA.

[10]Byrne, *Catholic Church in the New England States,* I, 382.

[11]Coleman, *Transformation of Rhode Island,* pp. 157-60.

[12]Robert A. Wheeler, "Fifth Ward Irish: Immigrant Mobility in Providence 1850-1870," *Rhode Island History,* XXXII (May 1973), 59.

[13]Stephan Thernstrom and Peter R. Knights, "Men in Motion: Some Data and Speculations about Urban Population Mobility in Nineteenth century America," in *Anonymous Americans,* Tamara K. Hareven, ed. (Englewood Cliffs, N.J.: Prentice-Hall, Inc., 1971), pp. 17-47.

laborer set his family to work, or was a skillful and resourceful man himself, he could build up a cash reserve and accumulate property as many did.[14] It was the more successful or skillful immigrants who made up the stable part of Rhode Island's cities and towns and thus the core of any parish.

During the early 1850s the booming economy of the United States enabled priests and people to make considerable progress in paying off existing debts on their churches, and many optimistically assumed new debts to enlarge their churches, or, in the more thickly settled parishes, to build schools.[15] The collapse of the economic boom in the Panic of 1857 severely affected the Catholic population of Connecticut and Rhode Island who were dependent on the factories for their livelihood. In 1858, in the midst of his year-long tour of his diocese, Bishop McFarland wrote that although schools and larger churches were needed, the depression had created a situation where "more thought is demanded for temporalities than for the spiritualities of many congregations."[16] The bishop's optimism that in "a few years" the diocese would be able to reduce its burden of debt was crushed when Confederate guns, which opened up on Fort Sumter, April 12, 1861, brought civil war to the nation and eventual economic dislocation to additional communities whose livelihood depended on Southern cotton supplies for their raw material.

Rhode Island Catholics and the Civil War

If Catholics in Rhode Island had any opinion on the war, it was one of opposition. The Dred Scott decision was generally supported by the Irish. When John Brown raided Harper's Ferry, his fanaticism shocked the Catholic Irish as it did conservative opinion in the North in general. Officially, the Catholic hierarchy neither condoned nor condemned slavery. The Church would have applied its ancient and massive patience to the solution of slavery in the United States.[17] As Bishop McFarland told a meeting of the St. Vincent de Paul Society in February 1862, " [Christ] did not preach emancipation at once and unconditionally. Such a measure would have

---

[14]Wheeler, "Fifth Ward Irish," p. 59 and the author's collection of Irish immigrant biographies for concrete examples.

[15]Byrne, *Catholic Church in the New England States*, I, 382.

[16]Bishop McFarland to Rev. Hugh Carmody, October 19, 1858, PFA.

[17]Potter, *To the Golden Door*, pp. 380-85, 620-22; Lord, Sexton and Harrington, *History of the Archdiocese of Boston*, II, 704-11; Thomas T. McAvoy, *A History of the Catholic Church in the United States* (Notre Dame: University of Notre Dame Press, 1969), pp. 183-87.

created a revulsion at once, and increased with tenfold the violence
the opposition to the Christian system. . . . Slavery whether we
consider it an evil or a sin, is to be cured by removing the cause and
eradicating the evil passions, which have made slaves and slavehold-
ers."[18] More than by slavery, Catholics were repulsed by the aboli-
tionists who appeared to Church leaders as wild, dangerous en-
thusiasts, risking the life of the Union for what many Catholics
considered their maddened morality. The thoughtful men of the
Church, when they listened to the proponents of abolition, heard
the echoes of the voices of the Know-Nothings railing against foreigners, for some of them had been associated with that cause as
well.[19]

Stephen Douglas, campaigning on the issue of popular sove-
reignty, received vigorous support from Irish wards in the elections
in 1859. Irish Catholic opinion in the North was strongly in favor
of preserving the Union but not at any price. The *Boston Pilot* spoke
for a large crosssection of Irish opinion when it proclaimed, "The
Union—It must be preserved. The *Pilot* knows No North, No
South."[20] On December 14, 1860, Bishop McFarland, fearing the
consequences of the increasing tensions between North and South,
asked the people of his diocese in an open letter "to unite in fervent
prayer for the preservation of the Union and peace of the country."[21] When the Confederate guns ended the efforts at political
compromise, the majority of Catholics in Rhode Island were able to
put aside their suspicions, resentments and doubts and line up with
native Rhode Islanders to volunteer for military service in response
to President Lincoln's call for militia.

The governor of Rhode Island at the time President Lincoln
called for troops for three month's service was William Sprague. A
young and energetic governor, he had been elected on the Democratic ticket with the support of conservative Republicans opposed
to their party's candidate. The same day that Lincoln asked for
troops, Governor Sprague summoned the general assembly into
special session to provide the necessary authorization and appro-
priations. While the assembly labored, Sprague, with dreams of a
military career as a spur, utilized the credit of his family's textile
operations, the A and W Sprague Company, to speed the organization and equipment of the First Regiment, Rhode Island Detached

[18]*Providence Post,* February 3, 1862; *Providence Journal,* February 3, 1862.
[19]Madeleine Hooke Rice, *American Catholic Opinion in the Slavery Controversy* (New
York: Columbia University Press, 1944), pp. 102-103.
[20]*Boston Pilot,* January 12, 1861.
[21]*Providence Post,* December 20, 1860.

Militia. Ambrose E. Burnside, who had resigned from the United
States Army to manufacture a breech-loading rifle of his own inven-
tion in Rhode Island, accepted Governor Sprague's offer of command of the regiment. The first contingent of troops left Providence
for the defense of Washington on April 20th aboard the steamer,
Empire State. [22]

Among those accepted for service with the First Regiment were
a number of Irish and a few French Canadian Catholics. Desire to
serve their adopted Country was not limited to the laity. Fr. Thomas
Quinn, at that time assigned to the cathedral, also volunteered for
service, moved, he said, "by the duty he owed to the people of his
communion in the Rhode Island regiment," but also, it seems, by
a restlessness that would prove a trial for his bishop. Fr. Quinn left
Providence by train on April 22nd and joined the Rhode Island
troops at New York as associate chaplain.[23]

By the time the Rhode Islanders moved south into Virginia
toward Manassas Junction, the First Rhode Island had been joined
by the Second Rhode Island, a regiment enlisted for three years or
the war's duration. Governor Sprague accompanied the regiments
as an aide to Colonel Burnside. At Bull Run, the Second Rhode
Island fought superbly, but the First, initially held in reserve, failed
to come to the support of the Second. In spite of the efforts of
Governor Sprague and the unit's officers to rally the regiment, the
First ultimately joined the general rout back toward Washington.
Shortly after the battle, Fr. Quinn wrote to the bishop giving the
casualty figures among Catholic soldiers and giving a short account
of his experiences in the action. Ignoring War Department pleas to
re-enlist, the First Rhode Island returned home to Providence on
July 28th and was mustered out of service on August 2nd.[24]

There were more volunteers for the first two Rhode Island
regiments than there were places in them. On May 27, 1861, the
Journal reported that the Irish in Providence had formed a military
organization they called the Sarsfield Guards. Among the resolutions the company adopted at their first meetings was one of invitation to their fellow countrymen of Rhode Island to cooperate in

[22]Donald A. D'Amato, "William Sprague, Rhode Island's Enigmatic Governor
and Senator" (Unpublished master's thesis, University of Rhode Island, 1956), pp.
19-25.
    [23]*Providence Journal,* April 22, 23, 1861; Edwin M. Stone, *History of the First Regiment,
R. I. Detached Militia and Also of the Second Regiment, R. I. Volunteers* (Providence:
Providence Press Co., 1866).
    [24]Thomas Quinn to Bishop McFarland, undated, HChA; D'Amato, "William
Sprague," pp. 25-26; Alice Hunt Sokoloff, *Kate Chase For the Defense* (New York: Dodd,
Mead & Company, 1971), pp. 66-68.

forming an Irish Regiment. However, a month later, the Sarsfield Guards and the Irish American Guards who met with them had second thoughts about a separate regiment of Irish. A resolution adopted by both units and concurred in by the Pawtucket Guards read, "We, adopted citizens, view with distrust the efforts of certain persons to raise an Irish Regiment in Rhode Island, and that while we would hail with pleasure such a Regiment, we have no confidence in its (would be) leaders, and consider their intrusion detrimental to the progress of our companies."[25]

The cause of the Irish Regiment had been taken over by a faction among the Irish led by Peter A. Sinnot. Sinnot, whom the *Journal* described as the man "chiefly instrumental in effecting the raising of this body," was a Providence liquor dealer and a leader of a revived movement to extend the suffrage. Elected colonel of the regiment, Sinnot was able to raise at least four companies from among the operatives of the mills and factories closed by the depression and the war. Without the full support of the Irish communities of Rhode Island, Sinnot's efforts to raise a full regiment ultimately failed.[26]

In August 1861, Colonel Ashur R. Eddy began to recruit a third regiment of three-year volunteers. Several officers and a good number of enlisted men were recruited from the disbanded First. Men originally recruited by Sinnot and his supporters, together with men from the other Irish companies, also joined those who enlisted in the Third. On August 14, 1861, Governor Sprague, after having talked with Fr. Quinn, wrote Bishop McFarland asking that Fr. Quinn accompany the regiment as chaplain. That evening, the bishop wrote both the governor and Fr. Quinn giving his consent.[27] The regiment, which Colonel Eddy drilled on the Spring Green Farm in Warwick, left Providence on September 7, 1861. Three months later the War Department ordered the regiment reorganized as a heavy artillery unit. For reasons that are not entirely clear, Fr. Quinn left his post sometime in October or November, and the position of chaplain was offered to a Protestant minister, Rev. Frederick Denison, the unit's historian.[28]

Colonel Eddy resigned before the regiment left Rhode Island,

---

[25]*Providence Journal,* May 27; June 28, 1861.

[26]*Ibid.,* June 28; July 1, 25, 1861; *Providence Post,* July 23; August 19, 1861.

[27]Gov. Sprague to Bishop McFarland, August 14, 1861; Bishop McFarland to Gov. Sprague, August 14, 1861; Bishop McFarland to Thomas Quinn, August 14, 1861, HChA.

[28]Bishop McFarland to Thomas Quinn, October 30, November 28, 1861; January 8, 1862, HChA; Frederick Denison, *Shot and Shell: The Third Rhode Island Heavy Artillery Regiment in the Rebellion, 1861-1865* (Providence: J. A. & R. A. Reid, 1879), p. 25.

and his place was taken by Colonel Nathaniel W. Brown. When
Colonel Brown died of yellow fever in 1862, command of the regiment eventually passed to a regular army officer of French descent,
Colonel Alfred N. Duffie, whom Denison describes as a "liberal"
Catholic. At least on one occasion when the regiment was paraded
for Sunday services which were conducted by Denison as the regiment's chaplain, one of the enlisted men asked Colonel Duffie to be
excused on the grounds that the services were Protestant services,
and he was a Catholic. Colonel Duffie denied the request, stating
that the services were Christian in nature and were not objection-
able to Catholics.[29] Such experiences were not unique to Rhode
Island regiments or unique to the Civil War period.[30]

In the early days of the war, Bishop McFarland came to believe
that the war had "dissipated the prejudices of our distrustful neighbors."[31] Although the national crisis, by uniting the North in a
common cause, did lessen the climate of prejudice against foreigners, it did not remove it. Discrimination, whether intentional or not,
appeared in a variety of ways.

As the war dragged on, Congress turned to conscription to
meet the continual manpower needs of the Union army. The Conscription Act of March 1863, initially made all men, between the
ages of twenty and forty-five, liable for military service. The act did
not allow for exemptions on any basis except that a man, by paying
$300, could avoid a particular draft call or, by providing a substitute
willing to enlist for three years, could be entirely exempt from
service. The American Church, as a whole, was concerned that
clergy would be called up for service in spite of the fact that Canon
Law prohibited clergy from bearing arms. Although no Rhode Island priests were in fact drafted, the possibility was a concern to
Bishop McFarland who, during the war, was in correspondence with
his fellow bishops about a revision of the draft law.[32]

The first draft under the Conscription Act, passed in March
1863, provoked four days of serious riots among the Irish population of New York City and smaller disturbances in Boston and other
cities. When, in July, a Newport police officer attempted to distrib-

---

[29]Frederick Denison, "A Chaplain's Experience in the Union Army," *Personal
Narratives of Events in the War of the Rebellion,* Fourth Series, No. 20 (Providence: The
Society, 1893), 18-19.

[30]Lord, Sexton and Harrington, *History of the Archdiocese of Boston,* II, 715; Duggan,
Catholic Church in Connecticut, pp. 90-93; Byrne, *Catholic Church in the New England States,*
II, 141-47.

[31]Bishop McFarland to Propagation of the Faith, Paris, December 20, 1862, SPFA.

[32]*Freeman's Journal,* August 1, 1863; Bishop John Timon to Bishop McFarland,
December 12, 1863, UNDA.

ute draft notices from the provost marshall to men in the predomi-
nently Irish Fifth Ward, the wives of the drafted men refused to
receive the notices. When the officer persisted, he so provoked the
women that they pelted him with mud and stones. All was quiet
when a detachment of police arrived on the scene, and the militia
men the mayor kept in readiness that night spent a peaceful evening.[33] Conscription would prove particularly hard on millworkers
and laborers whose families were solely dependent on their wages.
With the men gone, their families would have to support themselves.

The Newporters were not alone in objecting to the draft or
refusing to show for induction on the day specified. The failure of
Irishmen to appear provoked disparaging remarks from some citizens. Fr. Michael McCabe of Woonsocket was never one to let
injustice pass unchallenged, and he had a sympathetic forum in the
Woonsocket Patriot. After the first draft had been held, word spread
that Fr. McCabe had advised his parishioners whose names were
drawn to leave the town immediately, and that he was organizing his
parishioners to resist the law. Fr. McCabe vehemently denied the
charges.[34] The list of delinquent men published in the *Patriot* in
September 1863, contained the names of natives as well as Irishmen.[35]

Renewed Attempts to Remove
Constitutional Limitations

The nation's need for men to fill the ranks of its regiments
proved the occasion for another attempt at eliminating the discrimination against the foreign-born written into the Rhode Island constitution.[36] In June 1860, John Myers and Peter A. Sinnot began
publishing a weekly, *The Adopted Citizen,* in Providence "to elevate
our adopted citizens to their proper position in the State." Sinnot
hoped to achieve this end "by consolidating the scattered strength"
of the foreign citizen. The venture failed for lack of financial support
within a few months.[37]

Sinnot erred in suspecting that Rhode Island's growing for-

[33]*Newport Daily News,* July 17, 1863.
[34]*Woonsocket Patriot,* July 24, 1863.
[35]*Ibid.,* September 25, 1863.
[36]Conley and Smith, *Catholicism in Rhode Island,* pp. 97-103; Charles E. Gorman,
An Historical Statement of the Elective Franchise in Rhode Island (Providence, 1879).
[37]*Providence Post,* June 25; September 21, 1860.

eign-born population would support his paper in its campaign to secure equal rights for the foreign-born. However, the Rhode Island General Assembly, faced with the need to fulfill the Federal call for new troops and seeing the initial readiness of the Irish and others to serve, moved in the special session of the legislature Governor Sprague called on August 8, 1861, to show the good will of the state. The purpose of the session was to raise new regiments and revise the militia law of the state. To spur enlistments from among the foreign-born, the assembly proposed an amendment to the constitution to allow "aliens who enlist or volunteer in any of the regiments of the state, and shall be honorably discharged therefrom and who are now or may become naturalized citizens of the United States, shall be admitted to vote at all elections in this state on the same terms as native-born citizens of the state."[38]

The assembly's proposal set in motion in the winter of 1861-1862 a vigorous campaign by Sinnot and his associates to rally support among the adopted citizens of the state for the assembly's proposal. At the end of February 1862, delegates representing the foreign-born citizens of towns throughout the state met in convention in the State House in Providence to perfect their association and to give evidence of their strength. The names of the delegates suggest that the convention attracted a fairly representative cross-section of foreign-born residents of Rhode Island, Irish as well as Germans, with only the relatively small portion of the French Canadian population unrepresented. The convention elected Michael J. Brennan of Providence as president of the state association, Isaac Lawrence of Newport, vice-president, and six secretaries to represent the various interests, among whom was Sinnot.[39] Since the Democratic party, in its convention a week earlier, had adopted a resolution to "secure to the adopted citizens in this state their just political rights," the chances of success were bright.[40]

In a special session called by the governor in June 1862, the proposed amendment, in a slightly modified form, passed both houses of the legislature.[41] However, while the more tolerant of the state held a majority of the votes, the right of debate gave the minority a chance to voice their feelings, as happened on September 4, 1862, when they introduced a motion to strike the word native from a piece of legislation. The outburst in the Senate against Irish in general and Catholics in particular, sparked prompt objections

[38]Carroll, *Rhode Island,* II, 604.
[39]*Boston Pilot,* February 1, 22; March 1, 1862.
[40]*Ibid.,* March 1, 1862.
[41]*Acts and Resolves,* Special Session, June 1862.

from clerical and lay spokesmen and from the Democratic press of Providence.[42]

Since any proposed amendment to the Rhode Island Constitution had to be passed in two separate legislative sessions, the amendment was submitted to the general assembly in its May 1863, session and again passed. When submitted to the voters in October 1863, the proposal was rejected 1,346 to 2,394. The defeat of the proposed amendment did not mean the immediate end of the Adopted Citizens Organization. It limped on for another year. When its members met in convention in March 1864, Mr. Sinnot noted a "general apathy of such as had heretofore taken a deep interest in the cause of the Adopted Citizens." Lacking a quorum, the convention delegates resolved to meet to consider the best policy to pursue at the "present important juncture." In the end they resolved not to support at the polls any candidates who did not "pledge themselves to the support of our cause."[43] After April 1864, there is no further mention in the local press of the association.

Demands for revision of the suffrage provisions of the Rhode Island Constitution surfaced again after 1867. General Burnside, governor from 1866 to 1868, and Thomas A. Doyle, multi-term mayor of Providence and a Protestant of Irish descent, led a movement for a constitutional convention aimed at suffrage revision. In 1867 and 1868 the state senate refused to concur with the house on the question of calling a convention. Proposals in other sessions did not get beyond the house. Appeals for redress to the United States Congress were also rejected.[44] In October 1871, suffrage advocates switched tactics and succeeded in having an amendment extending the right of suffrage to naturalized foreign-born citizens on the same terms as natives put before the state's voters. It was again rejected. Whenever the question of suffrage extension was raised in these, as in previous years, debate ranged over the fitness of the foreign-born to vote and raised anew the question of the loyalty of Catholics.[45] Commenting in 1871 on the lack of success of the suffrage movement, the Providence correspondent to the *Boston Pilot* berated his fellow citizens for their apathy and indifference in political affairs.[46] The editorial writer of the *Journal* was probably closer to the reality

[42]*Boston Pilot*, September 13, 27, 1862; *Woonsocket Patriot*, September 19, 1862.
[43]*Providence Journal*, April 2, 1862.
[44]*Boston Pilot*, May 28; June 11, 1870.
[45]See for example *Boston Pilot*, March 28; September 5, 1868; March 18, 1871; *Providence Journal*, December 3, 1868; October 6, 9, 1871.
[46]*Boston Pilot*, May 6, 1871.

of the situation in explaining the continuing frustration of the efforts of foreign-born to obtain equal rights with the natives when he observed; "It is a waste of time to argue upon the qualified suffrage for naturalized aliens in this state. There is no other controverted provision of the constitution of which the people are so divided." Opposition to the enlargement of the suffrage "is a prejudice too deep to be easily eradicated."[47]

The agitation for suffrage further heightened a felt need among foreign-born citizens of Providence for a newspaper that could be their voice. In February 1870, the *Rhode Island Lantern,* a weekly, devoted to suffrage and "intended for the foreign-born" began publication.[48] In June 1870, another weekly, the *Weekly Review,* took up the cause of Catholic journalism. The paper, published on Saturday by Michael A. Walsh and James E. Hanrahan, was to be "a first class family newspaper," providing a weekly resume of the week's foreign and domestic news and comment on the issues of the day.[49] Financial difficulty led the publishers of the *Lantern* to merge their paper with the *Weekly Review,* giving birth to a new paper, the *Weekly Democrat.* The combined paper continued on until December, when it folded, and Michael Walsh resumed publication of the *Weekly Review.* Later, Walsh, too, ceased publication.

While the war both quenched and stirred anti-Catholic and anti-foreign emotions, the economic dislocations caused by the war served to further aggravate the hardships of the people of the diocese whose livelihoods were dependent on or related to cotton manufacturing and other industries. In writing to the Society for the Propagation of the Faith in Paris in January 1862, Bishop McFarland lamented that many of his people were reduced to begging while others were so hard pressed financially that they could no longer contribute anything in the way of alms for others.[50] The further loss of employment caused by the war brought about a drastic decline in the revenues of several parishes in the diocese and, to some degree, affected them all. Rather than sell some of the churches whose parishioners could no longer pay the interest on their mortgages, Bishop McFarland attempted to stretch his own revenues in order to help them and appealed to the less seriously affected parishes and the Society for the Propagation of the Faith for aid. Because of the drain on his resources, the bishop, in 1862, felt

---

[47]*Providence Journal,* December 3, 1868.
[48]*Boston Pilot,* February 12, 1870.
[49]*Weekly Review,* June 18, 1870.
[50]Bishop McFarland to the Society for the Propagation of the Faith, Paris, January 18, 1862, SPFA.

obliged to close four mission churches, among which was St. Ann's in Cranston.[51]

Probably the most seriously affected of the Rhode Island parishes was St. Joseph's in Providence. The people of the parish had been struggling with a heavy debt incurred in building their church. The Panic of 1857 forced the new pastor, Fr. Peter Brown, to close the parish school in March 1858, since the high interest payments on the church's debt left no monies for other expenses. Only the bishop's intervention on the parish's behalf, the generosity of their fellow Catholics in Providence and the timely return of prosperity to the working classes in Providence saved the church.[52] By 1863, some measure of prosperity had returned to the Catholics of the diocese.

Renewed Growth in Rhode Island

The increasing population of his two-state diocese created continual demands on Bishop McFarland to provide the people with priests and parishes. Among the first Rhode Island parishes to receive the bishop's attention was the newly established parish near the Corliss and Nightingale factory in what would eventually be called the North End of Providence. On July 29, 1857, Bishop McFarland blessed the cornerstone of the new church Fr. Cooney was prepared to build. The people of the parish were comparatively poor. Many of them had found work initially in the Corliss shops and later the section attracted railroad workers and employees of other industries that grew up in the district. In spite of the relative poverty of the parish, Fr. Cooney and his people erected a brick church from designs supplied by Patrick Keely at a total cost of around $18,000. Bishop McFarland dedicated the church on July 4, 1859 under the title of the Immaculate Conception.[53]

Even with his debt, Fr. Cooney felt the need to provide a Catholic school for his people. In 1862, the Sisters of Mercy began to conduct daily visits to the North End to instruct the girls of the parish, while a layman was employed to instruct the boys.[54] The schoolhouse was a non-descript structure attached to the church. In July 1867, the Superior of the Sisters of Mercy withdrew her sisters

---

[51]*Ibid.*, May 8, 1862.

[52]Byrne, *Catholic Church in the New England States,* I, 409; Bishop McFarland to the Society for the Propagation of the Faith, Paris, May 8, 1862, SPFA.

[53]*Providence Journal,* July 5, 1859.

[54]*Sadlier's Catholic Almanac,* 1864, p. 114, notes that the 150 boys and 200 girls attended the free day school and that the Sunday school enrolled 500 children.

from the parish because of the need for their services in other parishes already provided with convents.[55] Undaunted, Fr. Cooney succeeded that year in building a convent on Walling Street. Rather than invite the Sisters of Mercy to return, Fr. Cooney turned to the Sisters of Charity who were able to send sisters from their Mother-house in New York to staff his school.[56]

Although the Civil War seriously affected the cotton industry in Rhode Island, it proved a boon to the woolen interests. In 1864, the Wanskuck Company put up a new mill a short distance upstream from the Geneva Mill, then in the town of North Providence. This served as a catalyst for the village of Wanskuck which grew up around the mill. In 1865, Fr. Cooney began to collect funds for a church in this district of his parish. The Wanskuck Company offered the use of land which Fr. Cooney refused since he found none of the company land suitable, and he could not obtain a clear title to it. Two years later he bought a site on Branch Avenue near Douglas and in August began construction of a sixty by thirty-two foot wooden church. On Christmas day, 1867, Mass was celebrated for the first time in the yet unfinished church, initially dedicated to St. Joseph. After the church was finished, Geneva, Wanskuck, Tool-ville, Eagle Park and Woodville were set up as a mission of the Immaculate Conception, and a priest rode out from Providence on Sunday to say Mass in the new church.[57] To accomplish so much required an extraordinary man. Fr. Edward J. Cooney was such a man.[58]

When the financial crisis began to lessen after 1863, the diocese at last was able to deal effectively with its rapidly increasing population. Pastoral care required both creation of new parishes and the expansion of the older ones. In 1867, when the bishop sat down to review the situation of his diocese for the information of the diocese's benefactors in Paris, he felt it beneficial to explain the need for new churches so soon after the original ones were built. He reminded the society that the first churches constructed in his diocese reflected the poverty and small numbers of the first wave of Catholic immigrants. These churches were of wood and several of them were so badly built that they were already "irreparably in ruins."[59] Although the number "in ruins" included one or two

---

[55]Morgan, Mercy, p. 170.
[56]Byrne, Catholic Church in the New England States, I, 400.
[57]Walsh, The Centennial History, pp. 22-25.
[58]See Bishop Hendricken's Eulogy of Fr. Cooney, The Weekly Visitor, December 8, 1878.
[59]Bishop McFarland to the Society for the Propagation of the Faith, Paris, July 6, 1867, SPFA.

churches purchased by Catholics from other congregations, at least three of the churches built in southern New England were in such condition that the need for their eventual replacement was soon obvious.[60] Even those churches that were relatively well constructed simply could not accommodate the number of people who had arrived in the 1850s to live within the boundaries of older parishes.

In 1859, Bishop McFarland sent Fr. Bernard Coit, a convert ordained to the priesthood the previous June, to take charge of the mission church of St. Bernard, just south of the old Providence city line. As the parish's first pastor, Fr. Coit's ministry was hampered by his poor health, and he died in 1863. His successor, Fr. Daniel Mullen, recently returned from service as chaplain to Union troops, served the parish less than a year before being transferred in October 1864 to Valley Falls. A former missionary among the Indians in Nova Scotia, Fr. Michael Wallace came up from Phenix to take charge of the parish. Fr. Wallace found himself faced with the familiar problems of a growing congregation and an old church in need of repair, but wartime poverty, rising prices and a large debt forced him to delay any action to replace the church. By the spring of 1867, the parish debt had been paid and a pastoral residence built. The old church was then moved to the grounds of the new infant asylum in anticipation of using it as a schoolhouse as soon as the new church was finished.[61] The work went swiftly, and on November 28, 1868, Bishop McFarland rode out to Prairie Avenue to dedicate the new brick structure as the church of St. Michael the Archangel.[62]

Except for those who lived near St. Michael's, the Catholics of Cranston were parishioners of St. Mary's, Providence. In 1858 Fr. John Quinn had bought land for a church in the vicinity of the Sprague Print Works, where many of his parishioners worked, and proceeded to erect a mission church. By July 18, 1858, when Bishop McFarland dedicated the small frame building, the population of the mission was estimated at five hundred people.[63] The population in the area grew rapidly after 1858. Early in 1860 Bishop McFarland, realizing the need to establish the mission as a separate parish, appointed Fr. Patrick F. Glennon, a young priest on the Cathedral staff as the first pastor of St. Ann's. Fr. Glennon served the parish

[60]Among these churches are St. Patrick's, Providence; St. Mary's, Taunton, where the roof fell in 1850; and churches in Fall River and Newport that decayed prematurely.

[61]*Boston Pilot,* July 20, 1867.

[62]*Providence Journal,* November 28, 1868; Oscar R. Ferland, "One Hundred Years, St. Michael's Parish, Providence, Rhode Island, 1859-1959."

[63]*Providence Post,* July 17, 1858.

only until the fall of 1860 when a more experienced priest, Fr.
Richard O'Gorman, came up from Connecticut to take charge of the
parish. Fr. O'Gorman's tenure as pastor was cut short when the
shortage of cotton supplies forced the Sprague Mills to lay off their
workers. Without work, the people of St. Ann's could no longer
support a resident pastor. In July 1861, Bishop McFarland closed
the parish and sent Fr. O'Gorman to a new parish in Valley Falls.[64]
In 1863, when the Print Works were again in operation, Bishop
McFarland sent an elderly priest, Fr. Michael Lynch, to reopen the
parish. Fr. Lynch's health proved unequal to the task. To accommodate Fr. Lynch and yet still provide Mass for the people, the bishop
sent one of his cathedral assistants, Fr. Philip Grace, to assist the
pastor. The bishop himself went out to Cranston to introduce Fr.
Grace and make the necessary arrangements. When Fr. Lynch died
on January 17, 1864, Fr. Grace took charge of the parish until Fr.
Joseph O'Brien succeeded him in the summer of 1867.[65]

Although the establishment of St. Ann's as a separate parish
reduced the size of its mother parish, St. Mary's, the increasing
population of the Olneyville section crowded the wooden church
built by Fr. James Hughes. In 1863, Fr. Quinn felt he could no
longer wait to start construction on a new church. The old church
was moved back with the hope of converting it to a schoolhouse
when the new structure was finished.[66] The parishioners began to
dig the foundations in the evenings after their day's work in the mills
of Olneyville. Bishop McFarland laid the cornerstone on Sunday,
November 5, 1865 and dedicated the new church, constructed of
Westerly granite, on July 11, 1869.[67] Because Fr. Quinn wished to
have the finest building possible, he refused to accept the bishop's
advice to cut back on his original plans in the face of rising costs.
The result was a heavy debt on the parish.[68]

The prosperity of St. Mary's and its daughter parish in Cranston depended on job opportunities and revenue generated by the
Sprague enterprises. In the late 1860s, as more and more people
filled the neighborhood of the mills in Olneyville, it seemed as
though the adjoining section of Elmwood would soon become a
thickly settled district. As the houses went up, there was talk of
creating a new parish in Elmwood so that the residents of the sec-

[64]Bishop McFarland to the Society for the Propagation of the Faith, Paris, May 8, 1862, SPFA.
[65]Bishop McFarland, "Diary," December 1, 11, 1863; January 18, 1864.
[66]*Providence Journal*, April 29, 1864.
[67]*Providence Journal*, July 12, 1869; Streker, "Centennial Commemoration," p. 21.
[68]Bishop McFarland, "Diary," May 3, 1865.

tion would not have so far to go to attend Mass at St. Mary's. In 1868 Fr. Michael Clune, a newly ordained priest, was sent to St. Mary's as a second assistant to the ailing and frequently absent Fr. Quinn. Fr. Clune sympathized with the wishes of the people of Elmwood to have a parish of their own and began taking a collection to purchase a site for a church. With the money collected he bought land on Linwood Avenue. However, since Bishop McFarland was away at Rome attending the First Vatican Council, the affairs of the diocese were in the hands of Fr. James Hughes, whom Bishop McFarland had appointed vicar general after the death of Fr. William O'Reilly in 1868.[69]

Fr. Hughes thought a site on Potters Avenue was preferable to Fr. Clune's choice, and in April 1870, the chancellor of the diocese, Fr. Michael Tierney, purchased the second site.[70] With the land in hand the residents of the area undertook the task of a monthly collection to raise money for building a church. As usual, the parishioners contributed more than money. Those who owned horses and wagons volunteered their use along with their own labor to dig the foundation. By September, the site was ready for the masons and carpenters hired to do the actual building.[71]

Fr. Clune was not there to share the labor. At the end of April 1870, he was transferred to St. Michael's to assist the ailing Fr. Wallace. Construction on the new frame church progressed slowly. When Fr. Wallace was able to resume his duties at St. Michael's in January 1871, Fr. Clune moved to St. Patrick's to assist there until the new church in Elmwood was far enough along to conduct services.[72] When in June 1871, Bishop McFarland named him pastor of the Church of the Assumption, Fr. Clune rented a house on the corner of Potters Avenue to use as his residence. It was evidently a small place. When Bishop McFarland came out to dedicate the church on August 20, 1871, Fr. Clune erected a tent on the lawn adjacent to the church to entertain his guests.[73]

Among Bishop McFarland's cherished hopes was that of building a new cathedral in Providence. Bishop Tyler's "enlarged" cathedral was at best a poor affair, not too well built to begin with and too small even when it was finished. On December 20, 1863, the bishop announced a collection to raise the money he would need to

---

[69]"Twenty-Fifth Anniversary of the Organization of the Parish Named in Honor of Our Lady," *Providence Visitor*, August 15, 1896.

[70]*Providence Journal*, April 9, 1870.

[71]"Assumption, Providence," *Providence Visitor*, May 16, 1935.

[72]*Weekly Review*, February 4, 1871.

[73]*Providence Journal*, June 22, 1871; *Boston Pilot*, February 11, 1871; *Providence Visitor*, August 15, 1896.

purchase additional land for a new cathedral.[74] Although the bishop was able to purchase several lots at inflated prices on all sides of the cathedral property, the people of the diocese did not take kindly to the idea of a larger cathedral church, and nothing much was done.[75]

The failure to enlarge the cathedral led to the formation of yet another parish in Providence. A large part of the cathedral congregation lived on Federal Hill in 1870. Bishop McFarland had for a few years given some thought to building a church on the hill. He was unable to act on the idea before the Vatican Council opened so that the task of organizing the new parish was passed to Fr. Hughes. In April 1870, Fr. Hughes published a meeting notice of Catholics of the hill to be held in the cathedral. During the meeting, Fr. Hughes outlined the need for the new parish, which was to be called St. John's, and introduced the parish's first pastor, Fr. John McCabe. Fr. Tierney, the chancellor, then rose to discuss the plans for the new building. Until the new church was built, the parishioners of St. John's would attend Mass at the cathedral at an hour set aside for them.[76] Work on the new structure was sufficiently well along for Bishop McFarland to lay the cornerstone in June 1871.[77]

Outside the city of Providence the same pattern of rapid payment of debts, some wartime disruption and new construction and post-war prosperity prevailed as pastors struggled to provide for the needs of the people entrusted to their care. After Bishop McFarland's installation as bishop, Fr. William O'Reilly was able to devote more of his time to his parish of St. Mary's in Newport. By January 1, 1859, Fr. O'Reilly had succeeded in completing the furnishing of the church and the construction of the church tower although a debt of $20,000 still remained.[78]

The parish school was a source of pride for both pastor and the teachers. Examinations at the end of the school year were times for exhibitions before parents and guests of the knowledge and accomplishments of the students and were well reported in the local papers.[79] The parish population had increased to 1,500 by 1857, and the school enrolled 175 boys and 150 girls while another 175 boys and 160 girls attended the Sunday school. A letter writer to the *Boston Pilot,* who claimed to be "creditably informed," noted that

[74]Bishop McFarland, "Diary," December 20, 1863.

[75]*Providence Journal,* April 29, 1864; Byrne, *Catholic Church in the New England States,* I, 384.

[76]*Providence Journal,* April 22, 1870.

[77]*Providence Journal,* June 26, 1871; *Boston Pilot,* July 8, 1871; "St. John's, Providence," *Providence Visitor,* October 3, 1935.

[78]Byrne, *Catholic Church in the New England States,* I, 432; *Boston Pilot,* August 22, 1857.

[79]*Boston Pilot,* August 1, 8, 1857; August 8, 1863; Morgan, *Mercy,* pp. 139-41.

only five Catholic children attended the city public schools.[80] By
1863, the number of boys enrolled had increased to 234. William
Delaney, the teacher of the upper grades of boys, could claim a large
measure of credit for the success of the school. The number of girls
attending the school probably showed a like increase.[81] The increased number had to be accommodated in the limited space of the
sisters' convent, where classes were held. Among the new students
to enroll in the girl's department at this time were the daughters of
several naval officers and professors attached to the Naval Academy
which the government moved to Newport at the outbreak of the
Civil War.

During the first years of the Civil War, Fr. O'Reilly, with his
already large debt, was unable to do anything about overcrowding
in the schools. But as elsewhere, with the change in economic conditions in 1863, Fr. O'Reilly began to make plans to build a schoolhouse on the lot in back of the church. It was not until 1865 before
construction of the new building actually got underway. When it
did, granite was used in its construction and not the brick originally
proposed. Bishop McFarland laid the cornerstone in July 1865, and
the building was ready for use in the spring of 1867.[82] It was an
imposing building and an ambitious one for the parish, even with
the help received from wealthy summer residents. The parish took
fifteen years to pay off the debt on the school.[83] Construction of the
schoolhouse allowed the Sisters of Mercy to renovate the rooms in
the convent formerly used by students of the parish school. In
October 1867, they opened in the convent a private academy or
select school for the young ladies of Newport.[84]

During the Civil War the military established a hospital at
Portsmouth Grove that became the responsibility of the priests in
Newport. During this time they also took over from the pastor of
Fall River the charge of the Portsmouth mission that served the coal
miners. When the mines in Portsmouth were worked, as they were
intermittently during the nineteenth century, there were hundreds
of Catholics in the district. When they were shut down, only a few
Catholic farmers or farm-hands formed the congregation.[85]

To the north, Warren and Bristol continued under the care of

[80]Boston Pilot, August 8, 1857.
[81]Ibid., April 16, 1859; August 8, 1863; "The Late William R. Delaney," Providence
Journal, February 27, 1879.
[82]Providence Journal, July 25, 1865; Morgan, Mercy, pp. 139-40.
[83]Byrne, Catholic Church in the New England States, I, 432.
[84]Morgan, Mercy, pp. 144-51.
[85]For an historical sketch of the coal industry in Rhode Island see Providence
Journal, April 20, 1878.

Fr. Michael McCallion. Of the two towns, Bristol, thanks to the influx of Catholics drawn by the new mills and factories there, grew faster. By 1867 the number of Catholics was such that the original church could not accommodate them. Fr. McCallion set about enlarging the structure, providing adequate space for the Sunday school. The rededication of St. Mary's in September 1879, was one of the first services Bishop McFarland performed after his return from the First Vatican Council.[86]

Along the Blackstone River in the northern part of the state, the mill villages on its banks were becoming the home of increasing numbers of Catholic families in the 1850s. The Catholics of Valley Falls and vicinity initially traveled to Pawtucket each Sunday, while those farther away were visited by the priest from St. Mary's who celebrated Mass in a house in Ashton. By 1859, the number of parishioners in the area had grown to between 1,400 and 1,500 people. Fr. Delaney, the pastor at Pawtucket, realized that he could not, in justice to his own health, give adequate attention to their growing spiritual wants. When he expressed his wish to divide his parish, the people of Valley Falls requested him not to do so, preferring to remain connected to the Pawtucket parish. However, as Pawtucket alone demanded so much of his time, Fr. Delaney went ahead in 1859 and purchased land for a church in the village of Valley Falls near the road to Lonsdale and Woonsocket.[87]

On September 9, 1860, Bishop McFarland laid the cornerstone for the wood frame church designed by James Murphy. The bishop returned less than a year later on July 21, 1861, to dedicate the finished structure in honor of St. Patrick.[88] Before he passed on the responsibility for the people of the district to the parish's first pastor, Fr. Richard O'Gorman, Fr. Delaney, in a manner typical of him, published in the *Boston Pilot* a notice to the people of Valley Falls and Lonsdale, rendering an account of the money he had collected and spent on the new church.[89] Besides Valley Falls, the new parish included the villages of Lime Rock, Manville and Ashton, and later the pastor at Valley Falls took over responsibility for the people of Albion from the pastor of Harrisville.

Fr. Richard O'Gorman suffered from a problem fairly common among the people of the diocese but relatively rare in excessive form among the priests of his day—for a time he drank too

[86] *Boston Pilot*, September 5, 1870; *Providence Journal*, September 6, 1870.
[87] *Providence Visitor*, October 24, 1935; *Boston Pilot*, August 3, 1861.
[88] *Providence Journal*, September 15, 1860; *Boston Pilot*, August 3, 1861.
[89] *Boston Pilot*, July 20, 1861.

much. When Fr. O'Gorman could no longer be relied on to perform his ministry, Bishop McFarland removed him and, on October 5, 1864, replaced him with Fr. Daniel Mullen who had recently
asked the bishop for a better assignment.[90] Later, Fr. Cooney at
the Immaculate Conception in North Providence, asked to have
Fr. O'Gorman live with him. The bishop himself took Fr. O'Gorman into the cathedral rectory for a time. Fr. Mullen served at
Valley Falls until February 15, 1868, when he was transferred to
Norwich, Connecticut, and Fr. Hugh J. O'Reilly, who had already
ministered for many years in parishes in Connecticut, came to take
his place. Under Fr. O'Reilly's administration, St. Joseph's mission
was established at Ashton and Mass was celebrated on alternate
Sundays at Albion and Manville. By March 1871, the congregation
at Ashton had grown large enough to undertake the building of a
church also dedicated to St. Joseph which was situated a few minutes walk from the village.[91]

With his responsibilities lessened, Pawtucket's Fr. Delaney
could turn his energies towards developing his parish school. In
1859 he had added a two-story ell to the school building in order
to relieve the overcrowding of the girl's school. During the summer vacation of 1861, Fr. Delaney made arrangements with the
mother superior of the Sisters of Mercy in Providence to have two
sisters travel to Pawtucket on the stage each day to take over instruction of the girls. As it was less than ideal to have the sisters
come from Providence each day, in the spring of 1862 the men
and boys of St. Mary's dug out a foundation hole and built a cellar
for a convent. On Easter Sunday that year, the people of the parish contributed $800 towards the cost of construction. To ensure
that the building was properly constructed, Fr. Delaney called a
parish meeting that selected men experienced in building to inspect the work of the contractors. The ladies of the parish contributed to the effort, as they often did, by running a parish fair.
When the convent was complete in July 1862, three sisters came
out from Providence to live there. Within a year or so the gentleman teaching the boys resigned and two more sisters arrived to
assume his responsibilities. Shortly after they settled in the convent the sisters opened a Select Academy there for girls whose
tuitions helped supplement what the parish could contribute to
the sister's support.[92]

---

[90]Bishop McFarland, "Diary," November 29, 1863; September 2, 3; October 5,
1864.

[91]*Providence Journal*, March 21, 1871.

[92]*Boston Pilot*, May 3, 1862; Carroll, *Annals*, p. 420; Morgan, *Mercy*, pp. 154-60.

In Woonsocket Rev. Michael McCabe, since coming to the parish in February 1855, had reduced the debt on St. Charles parish and added a vestry to the church. In 1859 he moved and enlarged the rectory and built a parochial school on Earle Street which he called St. Michael's. For the first ten years of the school's existence, the faculty was comprised of lay teachers among whom Miles Sweeney was a prominent figure.[93] As in many other towns in the diocese many of Fr. McCabe's parishioners worked in mills eleven or twelve hours a day, six days a week. Since Sunday, their day off, was taken up with attendance at Mass, Vespers and Sunday school for their children, there was little in the way of opportunity for a parish outing without the co-operation of the millowners. In August 1859, several factory owners in Woonsocket stopped their works for a day so that their operatives could join their wives and children on a sail down Narragansett Bay to the picnic groves at Portsmouth. Apparently this was not an uncommon practice.[94]

The Civil War proved a severe blow to the cotton manufacturers in Woonsocket. The *Woonsocket Patriot,* on September 12, 1862, reported that of the thirteen cotton mills in Woonsocket, only three or four were in operation. As late as the fall of 1865, the *Patriot* reported that twelve cotton mills were still idle. While cotton manufacturing was severely curtailed by the hostilities, the wartime demand for woolens proved strong. Some measure of the prosperity of mill hands in Woonsocket by 1863 can be gleaned from the fact that in that year Fr. McCabe began to collect funds to build a new church. The original church was now far too small and inconveniently located. By 1866, when Bishop McFarland asked him to take charge of St. Patrick's in Providence, he had collected just over $10,000.[95]

Fr. Francis J. Lenihan, a young Irishman ordained by Bishop McFarland in 1859, took Fr. McCabe's place and almost immediately began to concern himself with construction of the church. The energetic pastor raised funds through fairs and personal solicitation of parishioners. In July 1866, Fr. Lenihan purchased a lot on Earle and Snow streets as a site for the new church.[96] Located as it was in a secluded and quiet part of the village, the purchase did not meet with popular approval. After considerable debate the parish made

93 *Woonsocket Patriot,* August 26, 1859; Morgan, *Mercy,* pp. 170-71.
94 Brennan, *Social Conditions in Industrial Rhode Island,* pp. 48-49; *Boston Pilot,* September 3, 1859; *Woonsocket Patriot,* August 12, 1859.
95 *Woonsocket Patriot,* January 29, 1864; Smyth, *History of the Catholic Church in Woonsocket,* p. 69.
96 *Woonsocket Patriot,* July 6; August 3; October 5, 1866; June 21; August 9, 1867.

the decision to build on the original site, and in October 1866, the old church was moved a short distance north to land owned by Nathaniel Elliot, who had agreed to purchase the building after the new church was completed. That winter Fr. Lenihan went south hoping to regain his health which was slowly failing. He returned in the spring but because he still needed rest he felt obliged to give up his pastoral labors. On June 21, 1867, Bishop McFarland came to Woonsocket to lay the cornerstone for what was to be a light colored granite structure. Work on the basement was completed by the end of the summer. Fr. Lenihan never saw the completion of the church; he died on August 3, 1867, at the age of thirty-three.[97]

Fr. Lenihan's successor at St. Charles was a well-known scholar, a former professor of Rhetoric at Fordham and a Civil War chaplain to New York's Sixty-Ninth regiment. On taking charge of St. Charles, Fr. Bernard O'Reilly proceeded with the building of the new church. He wrote frequently to Bishop McFarland reporting his progress and asking advice on his ministry. On May 22, 1868, the old wooden church was destroyed by fire and Fr. O'Reilly had to find other quarters for Mass. Services were held at the old Armory Hall for two Sundays, then in Harris Hall and finally late in 1868, in the new church when construction was sufficiently well advanced.[98] Fr. O'Reilly left Woonsocket in 1869 to devote himself full-time to scholarly work. His departure was the occasion for the return of Fr. McCabe, under whose administration the new church was completed in October 1870.[99]

By 1860 the growth of industry had served to shift the balance of population from those towns important when Rhode Island's economy depended on agriculture to those expanding with the growth of industry. The population of the town of Burrillville grew between 1810 and 1860 by 126 per cent.[100] The growth of Catholic parishes in those once-rural areas of the state reflected this shift of population as many of the new factory hands were Catholic immigrants. In Harrisville, Fr. William Duffy had supervised completion of the small church his predecessor had started. The church was dedicated under the title of St. Patrick on October 17, 1858. The parish, served the Catholics of Mapleville, Pascoag and Glendale as well as Harrisville, and two mission stations brought the sacraments

[97]*Woonsocket Patriot,* August 9, 1867; *New York Tablet,* June 18, 1867.
[98]*Woonsocket Patriot,* October 16, 1868.
[99]*Ibid.,* September 6, 1867; May 29, 1868; October 21, 1870; Smyth, *History of the Catholic Church in Woonsocket,* pp. 84-89, provides a good deal of biographical information on the extraordinary ministry of Fr. Bernard O'Reilly.
[100]Coleman, *Transformation of Rhode Island,* p. 225.

to some five hundred Catholics at Slatersville and twenty-three families at Albion.[101] In 1858 the Catholics in the four villages, which comprised the bulk of the parish, succeeded in raising enough money to purchase the lot next to the church and presented Fr. Duffy with the deed and $1,100 in cash to build a rectory so that he would no longer have to board out.[102] In 1858 or 1859 Fr. Duffy added Manville to the places he visited for Mass and would continue to travel there until 1864. The largest mission served by Fr. Duffy was at Putnam, Connecticut, where he offered Mass to a mixed congregation of Irishmen and French Canadians from 1858. It was a twenty-eight mile trip to Putnam over difficult country roads but the dedicated priest made the trip each Sunday until he left Harrisville in 1866.[103]

Fr. James O'Reilly came to Harrisville from service as an assistant in the cathedral in February 1867, and became the parish's next pastor. He served the parish for less than two years during which time his labors were hampered by his poor health. He died in August 1868, at the age of thirty-three. His successor, Fr. William Bric, another young priest, energetically took charge, improved the parish's facilities and cleared it of debt.

After 1865, French Canadians began to make up the larger part of the operatives in Slatersville. Fr. O'Reilly, by 1868, had begun visiting the village every other Sunday saying Mass in a large hall in the "Navu," a group of tenements on North Main Street.[104] Three years later millowner William Slater made a gift of a large tract of land bordering the lower reservoir to Sarah Devlin, who had served the Slater family for many years. On September 14, 1871, Miss Devlin donated the land to Fr. Bric. Two months later construction of a church was begun and the cornerstone was laid in December of that same year.[105]

During the same time, to the south in Greenville, Fr. Philip Gilleck invited the bishop on September 19, 1858, to dedicate the chapel he had succeeded in building in honor of his patron saint, Saint Philip. Although the Greenville mills gave steady employment to many in the parish, Fr. Gilleck's mission in Attleboro, Massachusetts, grew faster than the Greenville parish. Greenville's entire

[101]Bishop McFarland, "Diary," 1858.

[102]*Boston Pilot,* September 3, 1859.

[103]The history of the church in Harrisville in these early years has been well told in Ryan, *Burrillville, R. I. and the Catholic Church,* pp. 84-97.

[104]George Harvey, *North Smithfield Centennial, 1666–1971* (Privately printed, 1971), p. 68; Walter A. Nebiker, *History of North Smithfield* (North Smithfield Bicentennial Commission, 1976).

[105]Byrne, *Catholic Church in the New England States,* I, 421.

population probably never grew very much beyond the 350 people Bishop McFarland found on his visit there in 1858.[106] By 1860, Fr. Gilleck began to devote his full attention to the Attleboro mission and Rev. Michael O'Reilly came out from Falls Village in Connecticut to take charge of Greenville. In 1868, Fr. O'Reilly gave way to Fr. Michael Roddon who added Georgiaville to the responsibility of the pastor of St. Philip's parish until he returned to his former assignment, Bristol, Connecticut in early 1871. His place was taken by Rev. Bernard Plunkett.[107]

Along the Pawtuxet in the town of Warwick the parishes were also expanding as the mills and factories put on additional hands. When Fr. Patrick Lenihan of East Greenwich died in 1857, the focus of his mission was reversed, and East Greenwich, along with Wickford and Wakefield, became a mission station of SS. Peter and Paul in Phenix. Fr. Michael Wallace came up from Connecticut on July 22, 1857, to become Phenix's first resident pastor. Shortly after coming to the village, he bought a house at 12 Ames Street and enlarged it to meet his needs. The old Rock Chapel, purchased in 1853, was already too small so in July 1859, Fr. Wallace purchased the Baptist meeting house on Highland Street. The old chapel was sold and converted into a tenement by its new owner. Bishop McFarland dedicated the newly acquired building on October 9, 1859.[108]

By 1863, Fr. Wallace had decided to give up the mission at East Greenwich, which he was attending every other Sunday, in part because of his inability to reduce the parish debt.[109] However, in October 1864, Bishop McFarland sent Fr. Wallace to Providence and appointed a young priest, Fr. John Couch, to take over at Phenix and its missions. Fr. Couch would serve SS. Peter and Paul for the next twenty years. Shortly after coming to Phenix he began visiting the Catholic families in the mill village of Pontiac and in 1865 he added Shady Lea to the list of mission stations.[110]

The rapid growth of the Catholic population in East Greenwich by September 1866, resulted in the purchase of land for a church on Main Street. In November of the following year the bishop set off East Greenwich as a separate parish with missions at Apponaug, Wickford and Wakefield and sent Fr. William Hart to serve as its

[106]*Providence Visitor,* November 24, 1911.
[107]*Sadlier's Catholic Directory, 1866-1871.*
[108]*Providence Post,* July 27, 1859; *Boston Pilot,* October 22, 1859; Cole, *History of Washington and Kent Counties,* 1004.
[109]Bishop McFarland, "Diary," December 14, 1863.
[110]*Sadlier's Catholic Almanac,* 1865, p. 114; 1866, p. 169.

William B. Tyler, first Bishop of Hartford.

Bernard O'Reilly, second Bishop of Hartford.

Francis P. McFarland, third Bishop of Hartford.

Thomas F. Hendricken, first Bishop of Providence.

The first cathedral of Sts. Peter and Paul.

Interior view of the early cathedral at the time of the consecration of Thomas F. Hendricken as the first Bishop of Providence.

Artist's rendering of the new cathedral (Courtesy, Rhode Island Historical Society, Rhi, x3, 4430).

The new cathedral of Sts. Peter and Paul, consecrated June 1886
(Courtesy, Rhode Island Historical Society, Rhi, x3, 4432).

The spacious interior of the new cathedral (Courtesy, Rhode Island Historical Society, Rhi, x3, 2281).

pastor. The parish was then known by the title Fr. Lenihan had given it—Holy Name of Jesus. The traveling demanded of the pastor quickly sapped Fr. Hart's health, and in February 1868, he left for a long vacation leaving his pastorate to Fr. Thomas Kane who came up from Bridgeport, Connecticut.[111]

For several years the parishioners continued to use the building on Marlborough Street but it was so small that all readily saw the need for a larger place to accommodate their increasing numbers. By May 1869, Fr. Kane collected over $1,000 towards construction of a church. Later that year a fair held at the Masonic Hall raised an additional $1,700. On August 1, 1869, Fr. Kane broke ground and one year later the diocese's Vicar General, Fr. James Hughes, dedicated the neat, white frame building.[112] Earlier, when the cornerstone of the building was laid on December 5, 1869, the new church was dedicated to Our Lady of Mercy. A vote of the parish corporation on that day changed the legal name of the parish also.[113]

When Bishop McFarland visited Westerly in 1858, he noted there were 150 adult Catholics in the town that straddled the Connecticut-Rhode Island border. At that time, Westerly was served by Rev. Michael O'Reilly who lived in Stonington, Connecticut. Prior to 1860 the Catholics of Westerly attended Mass in a private home. In 1861 their numbers had grown to the point where Fr. O'Reilly began building a church on the Connecticut side of the Pawcatuck which the bishop dedicated on May 26, 1861 under the title of St. Michael's.[114] After completing the church, Fr. O'Reilly moved his residence to Westerly and Stonington became an outmission. From about 1858, Wakefield, which had been attended first from East Greenwich, then for a time by a priest from Providence, also became one of the outmissions of Westerly. The church in that village, built by Fr. Lenihan, quickly became too small so in 1861 Fr. O'Reilly purchased a Baptist meeting house. Later that year when Bishop McFarland visited Westerly, he stopped in Wakefield on May 28th to dedicate the newly acquired building as the mission church of St. Francis.[115]

Unfortunately, Fr. O'Reilly was another priest who drank too

---

[111]*Rhode Island Pendulum,* February 5, 1869. To appreciate the difficulties of this mission see *Providence Visitor,* September 12, 1892.

[112]*Rhode Island Pendulum,* May 28, 1869; August 5, 1870; *Weekly Review,* August 6, 1870.

[113]*Providence Journal,* December 7, 1869; "Our Lady of Mercy Parish Celebrates One Hundred and Five Years . . . 1867-1972," pp. 5-7.

[114]*Boston Pilot,* June 15, 1861.

[115]Bishop McFarland, "Diary," May 28, 1861.

much. When the bishop visited Wakefield in October 1863, a committee of men of the parish came to him to complain of Fr. O'-
Reilly.[116] A few days later Governor Sprague criticized the priest for
using abusive language.[117] Shortly thereafter, Fr. O'Reilly was replaced by Fr. Patrick Sherry, who quickly and ably went to work to
rebuild the spirit and finances of the ailing parish. In 1870 Wakefield again became the responsibility of the pastor of East Greenwich who also assumed responsibility for the families living in the
vicinity of the Carolina mills.[118]

Bishop McFarland took special delight in caring for the orphans of his diocese. The bishop expressed his concern for the
progress of the girls in their studies and in the care they received
by his frequent visits to the orphan asylum in Providence. That he
could not provide the same care for the boys of his diocese worried
the bishop, as did the fact that the building Bishop O'Reilly had
constructed only a few years before, was rapidly becoming overcrowded. After deciding that the sisters could successfully care for
boys as well as girls, Bishop McFarland bought land on Prairie
Avenue near the old church of St. Bernard's for a new asylum
building large enough to house both.[119] On May 19, 1861, he laid
the cornerstone of the new building. During its construction the
bishop often went personally to inspect its progress. By April 1862,
the three-and-a-half story brick building that was to house the
Rhode Island Catholic Orphan Asylum, better known as St. Aloysius
Home, was ready for occupancy.[120]

The construction costs were considerable, but the bishop gave
the asylum one of the highest priorities even as the conditions
created by the Civil War diminished his revenues. The war added
to the bishop's burdens in another way; the number of children
recommended to the asylum increased as battle and disease took its
toll of their fathers, and the towns, especially the rural towns, only
reluctantly, if at all, took up the burden of support of Catholic
servicemen's families.[121] While each pastor was financially responsible for the care of the children from his parish in the asylum and
each year took up a collection for it, the sums collected did not
touch the debt incurred in its building or its improvement. The
Orphan's Fair, begun by the Sisters of Mercy, continued to be the

[116]*Ibid.,* October 28, 1863.
[117]*Ibid.,* November 8, 1863.
[118]*Sadlier's Catholic Directory,* 1870, p. 198.
[119]Rev. James O'Connor to Bishop McFarland, August 10, 1860, HChA.
[120]*Providence Post,* May 17, 1861; *Providence Journal,* April 23, 1862.
[121]*Woonsocket Patriot,* November 26, 1863; February 19, 1864.

chief source of funds. With the return of good times after 1863, total
receipts of $10,000 to $12,000 were not unusual. The orphan asylum was a popular charity not only among Catholics but non-Catholics as well, many of whom generously patronized the fair or contributed in other ways.[122]

In 1864 the construction of St. James Orphan Boys' Asylum in
Hartford relieved some of the pressure on St. Aloysius. But there
was in the bishop's mind always the desire to do more for the
children. In writing to Bishop McFarland after the bishop's arrival
in Rome in 1862, Fr. Carmody, then the bishop's secretary and
chancellor, gave more space to details of the day-to-day life of the
asylum than to any other topic.[123] There was always more to be
done at the asylum. After the work on the new St. Michael's church
was sufficiently well along to allow the use of the building for Mass,
the sisters began converting the old St. Bernard's for the varied uses
of the children of the asylum.

Although the orphans received a good deal of the bishop's time
and attention, his interest encompassed children generally. The
Sisters of Mercy recall in their *Annals* the fact that Bishop McFarland
paid frequent visits to the parish schools. It was the bishop's pride
and delight to watch the progress of the students and to see his
schools rise steadily to a higher standard in aim and scope.[124] The
newspapers record that he was a familiar figure among the clergy
and other guests who witnessed the public examinations of the
students at the end of each school year.

Just after his consecration, Bishop McFarland visited the cathedral parish's Lime Street school, which Bishop O'Reilly had built as
a boy's academy. The bishop's brother, Fr. William O'Reilly, had
moved the girl's department of the cathedral school from the basement of the cathedral to the large hall on the third floor of the
building. Since the prospect of securing the aid of teaching brothers
was slight, Bishop McFarland decided to close the boy's academy
and utilize its space to relieve the cramped conditions of the girl's
department.[125] In 1864, yet more room was needed. After some
deliberation land was purchased on South Street in the Fifth Ward
near the river and a two-story frame building was erected. One
consideration in selecting the site was the fact that a large number

[122]*New York Tablet,* January 21, 1865; Morgan, *Mercy,* pp. 92-97.
[123]Fr. Hugh Carmody to Bishop McFarland, May 8, 27, 1867, HChA. See also
Bishop McFarland to the Society for the Propagation of the Faith, Paris, December
20, 1862 and the many references to visits at the asylum in the bishop's "Diary."
[124]Carroll, *Annals,* III, 418-22.
[125]Morgan, *Mercy,* pp. 76-77.

of children of school age lived in the South Street area who were too young to walk the distance to the Lime Street school.[126] In 1870, Fr. Christopher Hughes, at St. Patrick's, moved his old schoolhouse and began construction of a new building that would be completed in September 1871.[127]

In closing the boy's academy Bishop McFarland did not abandon the idea of one in the future. In 1865, Fr. Hughes at St. Patrick's, Hartford, erected a "spacious and solid schoolhouse" along with a house for Christian Brothers who arrived there in September 1866.[128] The next year Bishop McFarland wrote to the head of the Christian Brothers in New York asking for brothers for the cathedral parish. His request received a favorable reply, in part, because of the assistance he had given the brothers in Utica. However, his request could not be met immediately because the order lacked the trained personnel.[129]

In anticipation of the coming of the brothers, Bishop McFarland in September 1868, purchased land on Fountain Street as the site for a three-story brick building that would be an "academy for the more advanced scholars from the different Catholic schools of the city and also a parish school for the larger boys" of the cathedral parish. The bishop originally hoped that the brothers would be in Providence the following August and would take charge of the younger boys at the Lime Street school as well as staff the academy.[130] However, construction of the building did not begin until March 1870. When the building was nearly completed in September, the brothers were still unable to supply teaching personnel. Nevertheless, the Fountain Street school did open that fall as soon as it was completed with a faculty of lay teachers headed by the brilliant Rev. Henry F. Kinnerney, a newly ordained priest of the cathedral staff.[131] Three brothers headed by Brother Ptolemy arrived in Providence in September 1871, to join a layman, Mr. Goodwin, and Fr. Kinnerney who continued at the school as teacher of Latin and Greek until July 1872.[132]

Although schools were a costly burden on the Catholic commu-

---

[126]*Ibid.*, p. 78.

[127]*Providence Journal,* September 8, 1871; *Boston Pilot,* September 23, 1871.

[128]Bishop McFarland to the Society for the Propagation of the Faith, Paris, July 6, 1867, SPFA.

[129]Brother Patrick, F.S.C. to Bishop McFarland, New York, September 11, 1867, UNDA.

[130]*Providence Journal,* September 9, 1868.

[131]*Morning Herald,* March 7, 1870; *Providence Journal,* September 5, 1870.

[132]*Boston Pilot,* September 23, 1871; "La Salle Academy, A History: 1871-1971," *Providence Visitor,* September 24, 1971. The author of this article was seemingly not aware of the existence of the school a year before the Christian Brothers arrived.

nity, it was a burden the people generously shouldered. By 1872 the Catholic population of the Hartford diocese supported twenty-two free schools for boys and twenty-three for girls in addition to one academy or select school for older boys and nine for young ladies. The total number of students in Catholic schools was recorded in round figures as five thousand boys and fifty-five hundred girls.[133] When, in 1862, Bishop McFarland had written out a complete report on the situation of his diocese for the Congregation for the Propagation of the Faith in Rome, he estimated that two-thirds of the Catholic children of his diocese attended public schools.[134] Even with the number of new schools built in the 1860s, the ratio of Catholic children in public schools remained the same. All the select academies, both male and female, were staffed by religious. Of the twenty-three primary schools, ten, all in Connecticut parishes, were staffed by lay teachers, and one, St. Mary's, Newport, had a lay teacher for the boy's department.[135]

Because so many parishes did not have schools and those that did could not accommodate all the children of the parish, Sunday schools were, from the earliest days of parish life, an important part of the educational effort of the church.[136] In his 1862 report, Bishop McFarland noted that Sunday schools existed in every mission and that Christian doctrine was diligently taught, and he estimated that about twelve thousand attended these schools.[137]

Many of these Sunday schools were organized, staffed and directed by laymen and women working under the supervision of the parish priest. Their quality varied but among the best organized were the Sunday schools of the cathedral parish in Providence which in 1870 registered sixteen hundred children. The St. Peter and St. Paul Christian Doctrine Society, which directed the boy's department, held semi-annual meetings to elect officers for the society and for the boy's Sunday school. The officers of the Sunday school included a superintendent and two assistants plus a chairman of the Truant Committee.[138] The men of the parish supplied the teachers.

[133]*Sadlier's Catholic Directory,* 1872, pp. 204-205 for a list of the schools and the number of students attending them.

[134]Bishop McFarland to the Congregation of the Propaganda, Rome, May 16, 1862, PFA.

[135]*Providence Visitor* for the obituaries of several laymen who taught many years in the Catholic schools of Rhode Island. For example see *Weekly Visitor,* August 24, 1879; *Providence Visitor,* October 7, 1893.

[136]Guilday, *A History of the Councils of Baltimore,* pp. 94, 179.

[137]Bishop McFarland to the Congregation of the Propaganda, Rome, May 16, 1862, PFA.

[138]*Providence Journal,* March 21; April 4, 1870; January 30, 1871.

The Sisters of Mercy assisted by young ladies of the parish organized and instructed the girls.

In other parishes of the diocese where there were sisters in the day schools, the nuns either assisted the lay people in running the Sunday schools or were given complete charge.[139] In the absence of religious, which was the case for most of the parishes, the responsibility for the instruction of the children continued with the pastor and the laymen and women of his parish.

A glance at the statistics published by Bishop McFarland the first year he was bishop with those published at the time his diocese was divided provides perspective on the growth of the diocese and on the strain placed on the administrative structure in meeting the ever-increasing demands of a growing Catholic population. In the 1859 *Metropolitan Catholic Almanac,* which reflected the status of the diocese in 1858, Bishop McFarland reported that there were 52 churches in his diocese and 39 mission stations served by 42 priests. There were 11 schools for boys, 12 for girls, 3 female academies and 3 orphan asylums. The total Catholic population in 1858 was listed as 90,000. In 1872, when the bishop sent in a summary of the diocese's statistics to *Sadlier's Catholic Almanac,* he noted that there were 95 churches in the diocese, with 10 under construction, 64 chapels and stations served by 105 priests. There were now 22 free parochial schools for boys, 23 for girls, 1 male academy and 9 female academies and 4 orphan asylums. The Catholic population was listed at 200,000.

Perhaps the most valuable Catholic resource during this period of remarkable growth was the zeal and the faith of the people, sisters and priests. Many priests, including the first three bishops who lived in Providence, died at relatively early ages due to weakness caused by their labors and lack of attention to their health. The sisters for their part often had their living quarters in attics that were unbearably cold in winter or sweltered during the summer's heat. Their lunch often consisted of a sandwich wrapped in brown paper. For the sisters who taught during the early years of St. Patrick's school in Providence, their day began with a walk to school which at that time required a trip around the tidal basin and up Smith Hill. When he did not have a funeral, Mr. McNamee, a Providence undertaker, would send his carriage, but more often than not the sisters walked the entire distance. Their schools were at first old poorly ventilated church basements or shabby wooden buildings converted for school purposes.[140]

[139]Morgan, *Mercy,* pp. 132, 137, 160.
[140]Carroll, *Annals,* III, 427-28.

The growth of Catholic institutions in the two-state diocese during and before Bishop McFarland's time, while a tribute to the devotion and sacrifice of the church in Connecticut and Rhode Island, was in large measure assisted by the generosity of fellow Catholics in France, Bavaria and Austria. Between 1845 when Bishop Tyler first received monies from European mission societies until Bishop McFarland received the last such assistance in 1866, the Society for the Propagation of the Faith in Paris and Lyon alone contributed a total of $51,000.[141] The monies raised by the mission societies went to support priests who conducted roving ministries, to educate major seminarians and to support orphans.

The Incorporation of the Diocese in Connecticut and Rhode Island

It was not long after he took over administration of the new diocese that Bishop McFarland realized that his predecessor's policy that title to church property be held in fee simple by the bishop had become inadequate and even dangerous. Bishop O'Reilly's un- timely death had created a particularly difficult situation. A writer in the *Hartford Times* in 1856 suggested that under Connecticut law, Bishop O'Reilly's property (which meant all Catholic church prop- erty in the state) could be confiscated because the bishop died "without heirs capable of inheriting such real estate."[142] There were ambiguities in Rhode Island law too, particularly in the tax laws, which could be used, if state officials so chose, to cause serious difficulties for the bishop.

While the civil officials in both states never used the laws to take advantage of the bishop, a member of his own flock proved not at all reluctant to attempt to extort money from the diocese.[143] In March 1859, Mary Hannity brought suit against Fr. William O'Reilly as administrator of the estate of his brother to recover $3,000 on a promissory note she alleged Bishop O'Reilly had signed and which since had been stolen from her. The initial court verdict was in favor of Mrs. Hannity since the lawyers hired by the bishop to argue Fr. O'Reilly's case chose to make their defense on an appeal to the Circuit Court. The appeal was heard in October 1858, but the

[141]Theodore Roemer, *Ten Decades of Alms* (St. Louis and London: B. Herder Book Co., 1942), p. 106; *The Ludwig Missionsverein and the Catholic Church in the United States, 1838–1918* (Washington: Catholic University of America Press, 1933); Benjamin J. Blied, *Austrian Aid to American Catholics, 1830–1860* (Milwaukee: the Author, 1944).
[142]*Hartford Times* quoted in the *Providence Journal,* April 23, 1856.
[143]*Providence Journal,* February 27, 1857.

jury was unable to reach a unanimous verdict.[144] In May 1860 the
case was heard a third time and again the jury decided in favor of
the plaintiff.[145] Bishop McFarland, however, refused to concede. He
felt that the jurors had ignored the the preponderence of the evidence presented against the plaintiff, and there was suspicion that
one of the witnesses had lied under oath. He was unwilling to see
the diocese "robbed" and reluctant to see the character of its clergy
"spoiled" even though the expense of continuing the case was particularly difficult for the diocese.[146]

In January 1861, Bishop McFarland presented his petition for
a new trial before a three-judge panel of the Supreme Court. Before
doing so, his lawyers compiled a considerable dossier on all facets
of the case to support their contention that the jury was prejudiced
against the bishop and that perjury had been committed by one of
the witnesses.[147] It was probably small consolation to the bishop
that a reply he received from Philadelphia reported that the same
sort of suit had been tried there by other parties.[148] The judges
granted the motion for a new trial but the case does not seem to
have been retried.[149] The witness, Thomas Asten, accused of perjury, was tried and convicted.[150]

The most effective solution to the problem of securing title to
church property appeared in March 1863, when Archbishop
Hughes of New York obtained a general act of incorporation from
the New York legislature.[151] Recognizing the importance of the New
York precedent, Bishop McFarland, on January 11, 1864, called on
Senator Benjamin Eames and Representative Benjamin Lapham,
both of Providence, to discuss the matter of incorporation of the
churches of the Hartford diocese based on the New York model.
The same day he engaged James Ripley, his Providence attorney, to
draft the necessary petition and other documents.[152] The process
moved slowly and it was not until June 1865, that the bishop had
a draft of the act to study and approve.[153] The act passed the Rhode

[144]*Ibid.,* October 14, 15, 17, 1859.
[145]*Ibid.,* May 21, 1860.
[146]*Ibid.,* January 3, 1861; Bishop McFarland to the President, All Hallows, Dublin,
July 17, 1860, AHMC.
[147]See Hannity Case File, HChA.
[148]Anon., June 2, 1860, HChA.
[149]*Providence Journal,* January 3, 1861; *Providence Post,* February 4, 1861.
[150]Petition of Bishop McFarland to Governor William Sprague in behalf of
Thomas Asten, inmate of State Prison, March 14, 1861, HChA.
[151]Patrick J. Dignan, *A History of the Legal Incorporation of Catholic Church Property in
the United States, 1784-1932* (New York: P. J. Kenedy and Sons, 1935), pp. 207-10.
[152]Bishop McFarland, "Diary," January 10, 11, 1864.
[153]*Ibid.,* June 3, 4, 1865.

Island legislature in January 1866, and the Connecticut legislature six months later. Under its provisions the bishop and vicar general of the diocese together with the pastor and two laymen of any Roman Catholic church or congregation, upon complying with the requirements of the law, would constitute a body corporate with power to sue and be sued, and to purchase, hold and convey real and personal property.[154] Three years later, in August 1868, the bishop filed incorporation papers for all the parishes of Rhode Island and conveyed the property he held in his name to each of the new corporations for the sum of one dollar.[155]

Recruitment of Clergy and Funding their Education

Among the other administrative problems the bishop had to face was the seemingly endless one of finding enough qualified young priests to serve his diocese. The number of priests in the diocese in Bishop McFarland's time increased by sixty-three to a total of 105 by 1872. Most of the new men continued to be of Irish background, but an increasing number of them, although born in Ireland, received the better part of their education in American schools and colleges. While the bishop experienced little difficulty in finding young men who wished to study for the priesthood, he discovered that given the number studying, the number of men ordained for the diocese was fewer than he hoped, and the expense of their education was greater than the resources available.[156]

The funds for the education of seminarians continued to be raised in a yearly collection on Easter Sunday. However, having to constantly ask the people for money was an embarrassment for Bishop McFarland and there were also complaints on the part of some as to the expense of education of seminarians. Shortly after coming to the diocese Bishop McFarland adopted the rule requiring the men studying for the diocese to refund what the diocese paid for their education. The bishop believed they could easily do this

---

154*Acts and Resolves,* January Session, 1866; *Public Acts Passed by the General Assembly of the State of Connecticut* (New Haven, 1866), pp. 57–58; Byrne, *Catholic Church in the New England States,* II, 153-54.

155Incorporation Papers, Office of the Secretary of State, August 27, 1869.

156Bishop McFarland to the President, All Hallows, Dublin, August 2, 1865, AHMC. A partial listing of priests ordained under Bishop McFarland, their place of birth, education, ordination dates and a list of assignments can be found in the Ordination Register in the Hartford Archives.

within two years of their ordination, for they were usually generously supported by their parishioners.[157]

When the economic disruptions and inflation caused by the
Civil War cut deeply into diocesan revenues, Bishop McFarland
chose to use the money collected for the seminary fund for the more
pressing needs of the poor and orphans of his diocese. By 1863,
inflated American money had suffered so severely in foreign money
exchanges that the bishop found it impossible to send what funds
he did have to pay the debts of his seminarians in foreign seminaries. The bishop appealed for help in his annual reports to the
Society for the Propagation of the Faith. As it had done so often in
the past, the Society came to his aid.[158] The financial crisis eased
after 1863 and after 1867, so did the squeeze on personnel. During
that year the number of clergy increased by ten men, fifteen were
ordained in 1868, nine in 1869 and ten in 1871.[159]

Ministry to Canadian and German Catholics

The 1860s brought into the diocese a rapidly increasing number of immigrants from French Canada and smaller numbers from
the Catholic areas of Germany and Italy. In 1862, Bishop McFarland
estimated they made up a tenth of the approximately one hundred
thousand Catholics of his diocese.[160] These new immigrants, especially the Canadians, created an increasingly difficult pastoral problem for Bishop McFarland because the diocese lacked priests capable of ministering to them in their own language. Shortly after
becoming bishop, McFarland asked Fr. Dubruel, the rector of St.
Mary's Seminary in Baltimore, for assistance in securing the services
of a French priest.[161] Dubruel's failure prompted Bishop McFarland
to turn in time to Bishop Bourget of Montreal in search of a Canadian priest. In March 1861, McFarland wrote to the Canadian prelate asking the bishop to allow one of his priests, Rev. James Quinn,
who had been in McFarland's diocese for a short time, to remain if
the bishop saw fit to recommend him.[162] Bishop Bourget replied
favorably to McFarland's request, providing Fr. Quinn with his *exeat*
and a good recommendation. Beyond releasing Fr. Quinn, Bishop

[157]*Ibid.*, April 13, 1857, AHMC.
[158]Bishop McFarland to the Society for the Propagation of the Faith, Paris,
May 8; December 20, 1862; May 8, 1863, SPFA.
[159]*Sadlier's Catholic Almanac*, 1868-1872.
[160]Bishop McFarland to the Congregation of the Propaganda, Rome, May 16,
1862, PFA.
[161]Fr. Dubruel to Bishop McFarland, January 9, 1860, UNDA.
[162]Bishop McFarland to Bishop Ignatius Bourget, March 15, 1861, HChA.

Bourget could only offer McFarland a vague promise of additional Canadian priests at some future date when the Lord had increased the number of priests in Montreal.[163] Bishop McFarland also wrote to the Bishop of Quebec asking for assistance. He received a reply in September 1862, from a French priest serving as a missionary in Canada offering his services, but there is no record that he in fact came to the diocese.[164]

Bishop McFarland found a more fruitful source of clergy fluent in French and German in 1861, when he became a patron of the American College in the university city of Louvain, Belgium. The college had been established in 1857 with the assistance of Bishops Spalding of Louisville and Lefevre of Detroit to train young Belgian, Dutch and German students for the American missions. In April 1862, during a trip to Rome to attend to diocesan business, Bishop McFarland stopped in Louvain to see the college. From Louvain the bishop went on to England, where the college's Vice Rector, Fr. Florimond DeBruycker was engaged in preaching missions. Bishop McFarland persuaded him of the need for help in the diocese of Hartford. Later that same year Fr. DeBruycker began a roving ministry among the French and German communities in Connecticut and Rhode Island.[165] During his tenure as bishop, Bishop McFarland obtained the services of six young priests from Louvain in addition to those of one of their professors and Fr. DeBruyker. The bishop sent two of his own seminarians to study there.[166]

The idea of securing students from Louvain particularly appealed to Bishop McFarland because several would be fluent in both French and German. The bishop's hopes for the Louvain priests, however, proved illusory within a few years. Their pronounciation of German was so poor that they did not succeed as well as the bishop wished. In July 1868, the bishop obtained the services of a German priest, Fr. Henry Windelschmidt from Louvain, to minister to the Germans in New Haven and other parts of the diocese whose total numbers he estimated to be about thirty-five hundred. The priest was not able to support himself from the money he collected and the bishop had to make up the deficiency from his own funds. Another German priest, Fr. Joseph Schaele, came to the diocese in November 1871 and took up his duties in Providence.[167]

---

[163]Bishop Bourget, Montreal to Bishop McFarland, March 20, 1861, HChA.

[164]Fr. Duiroun to Bishop McFarland, September 23, 1862; Bishop McFarland to Fr. Duiroun, November 3, 1862, Quebec Archdiocesan Chancery Archives.

[165]Bishop McFarland to the Society for the Propagation of the Faith, Paris, December 20, 1862, SPFA; Duggan, *The Catholic Church in Connecticut*, p. 539.

[166]Ordination Register, American College, Louvain.

[167]Bishop McFarland to the Society for the Propagation of the Faith, Paris, October 15, 1869, SPFA; Byrne, *Catholic Church in the New England States*, II, 354-55.

Fr. DeBruycker's initial success in bringing many Canadians back to the sacraments encouraged the bishop and convinced him of the need to have priests who could minister to the Canadians in their own language and sympathize with their customs.[168] However, the possibility of obtaining the services of Canadian clergy to assist in the ministry to the Canadians in the diocese seemed bleak because of the reluctance of the hard pressed Canadian bishops to release any men when their own dioceses were understaffed. Since he could afford to pay the tuition of only a limited number of students in European seminaries, Bishop McFarland reluctantly had to continue to rely on the expediency of sending his own students to the French-speaking Sulpicians at Montreal and to request his students in Baltimore and at the Provincial Seminary in Troy, New York to learn French as well.[169]

French Canadians had left Canada and drifted into southern New England in the first decades of the nineteenth century. Some came because of their uneasiness under British rule in Canada that culminated in an ill-fated revolt in 1837–1838 and seethed in some hearts long after. Others came in search of adventure or work; many of these planned to stay only until they had earned a stake. To those who put off returning or who chose to stay, the United States was a strange place with a strange language and customs. Some were content to be different, but others, isolated or with only a few other Canadian families in the neighborhood, chose to assimilate with the Americans, anglicizing their French names, abandoning their language and culture and sometimes, their faith. Even for those Canadians who continued to go to church, it was the Irish church they attended and they were uncomfortable there.[170]

By the 1850s the rural areas of Quebec Province had become increasingly overpopulated. The soil on many farms had become exhausted and the farms were simply too small to support the large families that were traditional among the Canadians. It was also in the 1850s that American businessmen, searching for new supplies of labor, discovered that the rural French Canadian—the *habitant*— made an excellent laborer for new construction projects and a reliable and properly grateful operative in the factory. Like the Irish

[168]Bishop McFarland to the Society for the Propagation of the Faith, Paris, December 20, 1862, SPFA; Byrne, *Catholic Church in the New England States,* I, 417.
[169]Fr. Dubreul to Bishop McFarland, December 28, 1860, UNDA; Bishop McFarland to the Society for the Propagation of the Faith, Paris, December 20, 1862, SPFA.
[170]E. Hamon, *Les Canadiens Francais de la Nouvelle-Angle-terre* (Quebec, 1891); Mason Wade, "The French Parish and Survivance in Nineteenth-Century New England," *Catholic Historical Review,* XXXVII (July 1950), pp. 163-69.

before them, the French Canadians sought out places where they
heard by word of mouth that there were jobs. Often this meant
villages and towns where there were already small communities of
French Canadians, communities that could help the newcomers get
settled and find jobs.[171]

As their numbers increased, the Canadians became anxious to
have their own parishes where they could worship in the way they
had known in Canada. As with the Irish, the faith of the Canadians
was bound to their culture. They missed the Gregorian Chant and
full measure of religious rites that the Irish parishes, sensitive to
Yankee prejudices against "popish pageantry," had often played
down. What solemn religious celebrations there were, reflected
Irish folk traditions or, as on St. Patrick's day, celebrated saints
especially important to the Irish. There was also the problem of pew
rents and offerings for baptisms, burials or marriages which the
pastors of the well-endowed parishes of Quebec Province did not
demand of their people but which the pastors of the Hartford diocese depended on for their existence and to help them in the building and support of churches and schools.[172]

In Rhode Island, Woonsocket had one of the oldest French
Canadian communities. A census taken in 1846 had counted 332
persons as the total Canadian population in the villages of Woonsocket. By 1860, however, there were at least one hundred Canadian
families there.[173] The number of Canadians increased significantly
after 1861 as Canadians came to take up jobs opened with the
construction of new woolen mills.[174] After replacing Fr. McCabe in
January 1866, as pastor of St. Charles, Fr. Francis Lenihan grew
increasingly concerned about his inability to administer the sacraments in an effective way to his Canadian parishioners. Other
American bishops had found that the best way to provide effective
ministry to the Canadians was to comply with their requests to have
a church and priest of their own. Accordingly, in February 1866,
Bishop McFarland began the process of establishing a Canadian
parish by securing an act of incorporation of the "Roman Catholic
Church of St. Joseph of the village of Woonsocket" from the Rhode
Island General Assembly. Among the incorporators were the bishop

171Iris S. Podea, "Quebec to 'Little Canada', The Coming of the French Canadians
to New England," *New England Quarterly,* XXIII (1950), pp. 365-80. Harpin, *Trumpets
in Jericho,* pp. 60-77.
172Wade, "The French Parish and Survivance," pp. 168-77; Fr. Bernard O'Reilly
to Bishop McFarland, January 29, 1868, HChA.
173Bonier, *Debuts de la Colonie Franco-Americaine de Woonsocket, R. I.,* pp. 79, 288.
174*Woonsocket Patriot,* June 10, 1864; November 23, 1866.

and his Vicar General, Fr. O'Reilly, two French Canadian residents of Woonsocket and Fr. Eugene Vygen, a Belgian priest and former student of Louvain.[175]

For some reason, possibly because the Canadians preferred to have a priest of their own nationality as pastor, Fr. Vygen never arrived in Woonsocket. During the following months, Bishop McFarland continued to search for a Canadian priest to serve the parish. While the bishop pursued his search, several leaders of the Canadian community, thinking that the responsibility was theirs to set up a parish, also requested an act of incorporation from the general assembly. When word of their action reached the bishop, he saw it as an act of disobedience and promised to have nothing to do with them if they received their act of incorporation.[176] On April 1st, the men involved in securing the second act wrote to the bishop assuring him that they meant no disrespect but had acted "from a misunderstanding of the matter" and sent him the act along with their apology.[177]

By June 1866, Bishop McFarland was even more convinced that he could not rely on the Canadian bishops to loan him priests to serve Canadian parishes. His only alternative was to send a priest such as Fr. Lawrence Walsh to Woonsocket to assist Fr. Lenihan in ministering to the French. Fr. Walsh had studied in Montreal and was able to begin holding religious services for the Canadians in French.[178] In 1867, to the regret of the French community, Fr. Walsh was transferred to a parish in Hartford, and a Belgian, Fr. Arnold Princen, took his place.[179] Fr. Princen stayed only a short time, giving way in 1868 to an elderly Canadian, Fr. Ferdinand Belanger.

Although plans for a church of their own failed to materialize, the French Canadians in Woonsocket initially contributed along with the Irish towards the construction of the new St. Charles.[180] However, Fr. Lenihan's successor, Fr. Bernard O'Reilly, did not relate well to his French Canadian parishioners, and there was a certain amount of tension between him and Fr. Belanger.[181]

When the Sisters of Mercy opened their select academy in their

---

[175]*Acts and Resolves*, January Session, 1866.

[176]Fr. Francis Lenihan to Bishop McFarland, March 26, 1866, HChA.

[177]Joseph Daigle, *et al.*, to Bishop McFarland, April 1, 1866, HChA.

[178]Bonier, *Debuts de la Colonie Franco-Americaine de Woonsocket, R. I.*, p. 307, note; *Providence Journal*, May 25, 1868.

[179]*Woonsocket Patriot*, November 22, 1867; Smyth, *History of the Catholic Church in Woonsocket*, p. 119.

[180]Fr. Bernard O'Reilly to Bishop McFarland, October 20, 29, 1868, HChA.

[181]*Ibid.*, October 26, 29; November 13, 1868, HChA.

convent after coming to Woonsocket in 1868, the majority of the
academy students came from the French Canadian families in the
town because French studies were at least part of each day's instruction.[182]

Elsewhere in Rhode Island small French Canadian communities at Slatersville and in the villages of the Pawtuxet Valley experienced an influx of new arrivals drawn there by word of good
wages in the mills. At the same time, significant numbers of French
Canadians were establishing themselves in Providence and in the
mill areas along the Blackstone in Pawtucket, Central Falls, Manville
and Ashton. On the east side of the Bay, Warren also attracted a
number of families.

The Missionary Church

The Catholic church in the United States was a missionary
church in the nineteenth century. Both Bishops Fenwick and O'-
Reilly had looked forward to many conversions among the natives
of America once they came to know and understand the Catholic
faith. With the great influx of Catholic immigrants, the emphasis
of most bishops and priests shifted to preserving the faith among
their own people. One of the Church's constant worries was that
the children, especially the poor and those without parents, would
fall away from the Church because of their placement in the
homes of Protestant employers or in the care of the state orphan
asylums. Like his predecessors, Bishop McFarland considered the
public schools a distinct threat to the faith of the Catholic children
who were forced to attend them because of the poverty of their
parents and failure the of many parishes to support their own
schools.

From the available evidence, the number of those who publicly
left the church ("perversions" in the terminology of the day) were
few, although both the Catholic and Protestant writers made much
of occasional converts. Bishop McFarland, in 1859, wrote of his
gratitude that many of the children who were presumably lost to the
faith because of their placement in Protestant homes or institutions
were later reconciled to the Church.[183] As for adults, mixed marriages could and did lead to both conversions to the Catholic faith

---

[182]Morgan, *Mercy,* p. 175.
[183]Bishop McFarland to the Society for the Propagation of the Faith, Paris, January
21, 1859, SPFA.

and "perversions," that is, a public renouncing of the Catholic faith by joining a Protestant church.

In 1859 Bishop McFarland included statistics on conversions in the notes he took on his tour of all parishes in his diocese. Rhode Island pastors reported only twenty converts and four "perverts."[184] Two pastors, Fathers Delaney at Pawtucket and Quinn at St. Mary's, Olneyville, had each received six converts. In January 1859, Bishop McFarland recorded 320 "adult baptisms or actual conversions" for his diocese and a year later he recorded 200.[185] In January 1862, the bishop in a letter to the Society for the Propagation of the Faith reasoned that the number of conversions was not large because almost all the care of the church was directed towards the Catholic people, who, because of their lack of religious instruction were "given to intemperance and to other faults and are exposed to great temptation."[186]

What conversions there were seem mainly to have been the result of yearly missions given by visiting priests, often members of religious orders, in the larger parishes of the diocese. The missions served chiefly to reawaken the faith of those who had fallen away from the church and also served as the occasion of interesting non-Catholics in the Church. Sermons of at least an hour in length were common in most churches during missions and good speakers could always find large and attentive audiences.

Popular Devotions, Organizations and Causes

Until the late 1860s the devotional life of the Catholic population centered mainly on attendance at Mass on Sunday, either at the early Mass at seven or at the main Mass at ten. Large numbers would return again in the afternoon for Vespers. For important feasts, choirs and elaborate classical choral programs added to the solemnity. Observances of jubilees and missions saw large numbers around the confessional boxes and at the communion rails. Various religious societies became increasingly important in parish life in the more settled communities. Mention of the purgatorial society, organized to pray for the souls of the faithful departed, and scapular and rosary societies first appeared in the Catholic Directory listings

---

[184]Bishop McFarland, "Diary," 1859.
[185]Bishop McFarland to the Society for the Propagation of the Faith, Paris, January 21, 1859; January 1, 1860, SPFA.
[186]Ibid., January 18, 1862, SPFA.

for the Hartford diocese in 1852 and were said to be flourishing.[187] Societies of children of Mary, St. Aloysius and the guardian angel came to provide a devotional framework for the children of the parish. Altar societies looked to the care of sanctuaries as well as to the spiritual concerns of its members.[188]

The Catholic organizations of men tended to stress fraternal, benevolent and literary goals. The St. Vincent de Paul Society founded under Bishop O'Reilly in November 1853, had by March 1857, taken on a decidedly literary bent. Its members decided during that month to set aside time each week for literary exercises and study of informative topics. In July 1857, a few members of the society formed the Brownson Literary Institute, later to be known as the Brownson Lyceum. It was the leading Catholic literary society in Rhode Island and many prominent and successful Catholics of Providence were found among its members.[189]

Interest in benevolent societies did not completely fade. In April 1860, Fr. Coit drew some of the men of St. Michael's parish together to establish a branch of the St. Vincent de Paul Society. However, the economic depression that was already being felt and that was to get worse with the coming of the Civil War, contrived to overwhelm any attempt to meet the needs of the Catholic people of Providence from their own resources.[190]

In 1863, with the return of prosperity to some parts of Rhode Island, a group of men from St. Patrick's parish in Providence formed the St. Patrick's Benevolent Society to foster the faith of its members, provide aid in time of sickness, and help for the care of widows and orphans. Among its noted activities was the organization of the first public celebration of St. Patrick's Day held in the state in March 1863.[191] A similar benevolent society was formed in Burrillville in 1869.[192]

By 1869 the Irish community in Providence had matured socially and economically to the point where in September it was

---

[187]*Metropolitan Catholic Almanac,* 1862, p. 174.

[188]For a list of societies and confraternities and the number of members enrolled in each see *Sadlier's Catholic Almanac,* 1867, pp. 105-106.

[189]*Providence Visitor,* May 8, 1897; Daniel T. McColgan, *A Century of Charity, The First One Hundred Years of the Society of St. Vincent de Paul in the United States,* 2 vols. (Milwaukee: The Bruce Publishing Co., 1951), I, 267.

[190]McColgan, *A Century of Charity,* I, 267-68.

[191]*Boston Pilot,* March 30, 1867.

[192]Martha Julie Keenan, "The Irish Catholic Beneficial Societies Founded Between 1818-1869" (Unpublished master's thesis, Catholic University, 1953), pp. 63–69.

proposed to the convention of delegates from the religious and
fraternal societies of the city that they form an immigrant aid society. A committee was appointed and at a second meeting on October 7th the proposal for the creation of the Society for the Protection of Irish Immigrants was accepted and a list was distributed for
prospective members to sign.[193]

Social Concerns of the Bishop and His Clergy

Intemperance still ranked high among the chief concerns of
Bishop McFarland and his priests. Only a small number of temperance organizations remained in the 1860s to remind the Catholic
population of the enthusiasm for the cause generated by the visit of
Fr. Mathew to the state in 1849. In Woonsocket, the Father Mathew
Total Abstinence Society continued in existence, and there were
societies in St. Mary's, Pawtucket and St. Patrick's in Providence.
The cause of temperance lay dormant until the spring of 1870 when
the Passionist Fathers preached a series of missions in the state that
served to spark renewed dedication. Within a short time the state
counted nine Catholic temperance societies which in October 1870,
met in Providence to form a state organization.[194]

By the middle 1860s the militancy of the Irish communities in
the United States found expression in such organizations as the
Fenian Brotherhood and the Ancient Order of Hibernians. The
Fenian Brotherhood, organized in New York in 1857, was dedicated
to freeing Ireland from British rule by force of arms. Bishop McFarland held at least one meeting with Fenian delegations, but they
never received his support or that of a particularly large number of
the Irish in Rhode Island, although they did enjoy some popularity.[195] December 1870, saw the organization of a division of the
Ancient Order of Hibernians as a benevolent society.[196] Because of
the violence associated with the order and its activities, its reputation among some of the clergy was such that they discouraged their
people from joining.

While the newer immigrants, especially the French Canadians,
might occasionally join one of the parish temperance societies, they

[193]*Providence Journal,* September 24; October 8, 1869.
[194]*Boston Pilot,* March 12, 1870; *Providence Journal,* September 12; October 31,
1870.
[195]Bishop McFarland, "Diary," July 31, 1865; *Providence Journal,* April 5, 1866;
August 17, 1867; January 28; February 18; May 7, 1868.
[196]*Acts and Resolves,* May Session, 1869.

chose as a rule to form their own organizations. For example, in
1869, the growing French Canadian community in Woonsocket established and incorporated the Society of St. John the Baptist which
combined the features of a religious, national and aid society. Under
the society's auspices the Canadians paraded in Woonsocket on St.
Jean Baptiste Day in 1870.[197]

Taken up as they were with the responsibility of instructing and
providing suitable places for worship for their fast-growing and
frequently moving parishioners, the Catholic clergy did not, as a
rule, become involved in the civic affairs of their state and localities.
From time to time, local pastors such as Fr. Henry Kinnerney, did
speak out on civic issues; but for the most part, creative contact with
other social and religious groups was limited to the activities of
Bishop McFarland and the leading laymen of the state.

Bishop McFarland would be applauded by his successor as a
"valuable citizen," who during the Civil War "was not wanting in
patriotism and in a proper method of showing it."[198] The bishop
had the church bells rung at the news of the capture of General Lee,
and his associates, without hesitation, woke him with the news of the
assassination of Lincoln and the attempted assassination of Secretary Seward. The next day, in his Sunday sermon, Bishop McFarland
spoke of "Father Abraham's death."[199]

In September 1860, Bishop McFarland was among the speakers
on the platform of a meeting called to ratify the doings of a convention on Indian affairs that had recently met in Providence.[200] When
in 1863 the Rhode Island Hospital Society was formed by leading
physicians and citizens of Providence to promote the construction
of Rhode Island Hospital, Bishop McFarland joined in the effort,
contributed $500 towards the erection of the hospital's first build-
ing and urged support for the project among the Catholics of the
city.[201] The bishop hoped that by supporting the project, Catholics
would be guaranteed admission there, and priests and sisters might
visit patients to console and pray with them.[202]

McFarland's "Diary" records his conversations with governors
and mayors, and at least once on election day, aspiring office hold-
ers made it a point to call on the bishop.[203] In 1864 he attended the

[197]*Woonsocket Patriot,* June 17, 1870.
[198]Byrne, *Catholic Church in the New England States,* II, 157.
[199]Bishop McFarland, "Diary," April 9, 15, 16, 1865.
[200]*Providence Post,* September 19, 1860.
[201]Bishop McFarland, "Diary," November 3, 4, 1863.
[202]Bishop McFarland to the Society for the Propagation of the Faith, Paris, December 29, 1863, SPFA.
[203]Bishop McFarland, "Diary," April 6, 1864.

commencement at Brown University, a commencement which he
described as "a medley of bigotry and stupidity." The experience
only served to harden his conviction about the importance of Catholic schools, for on the next Sunday he spoke of "the importance of
supporting schools and guarding children as shown by the spirit of
bigotry and intolerance around us."[204]

During his years in Rhode Island, Bishop McFarland earned the
respect of its chief citizens. He co-operated with them in civic projects and they with him in the generous support the non-Catholic
population continued to provide for the care of orphans. Not all
Catholic children of the state, however, could be cared for by the
bishop. But his concern for their welfare followed them wherever
circumstances led them. Among the institutions in which Providence citizens took pride was the Providence Reform School. Established in January 1850, it was intended to receive children under
eighteen convicted of certain offenses by the courts of the state, or
who were admitted there at the request of parent or guardian and
with the consent of its board of trustees.[205]

In February 1868, Bishop McFarland wrote to James McMaster
of New York, editor of the *Freeman's Journal,* expressing his concern
for the moral and spiritual condition of the young inmates of the
reform school and asking McMaster's advice of how to proceed to
remedy the situation there. The bishop wrote of allegations of
moral mistreatment of the boys, of whom he said a majority were
Catholics, and of the refusal of the authorities of the school to allow
the boys to have Catholic books or to attend Catholic services.[206]

What course McMaster advised is not known. But in September
1868, Bishop McFarland addressed a meeting of his parishioners in
the Sunday school room of the cathedral. He noted that Connecticut allowed the children in its reform schools to attend Catholic
services and recounted in detail his efforts to ameliorate conditions
at the Providence school up to that point. Those attending the
meeting drew up a series of resolutions protesting the denial of
boys' access to Catholic services and appointed a committee to draw
up a constitution and bylaws for an organization to work towards
securing protection of Catholic children in the school.[207] The group
also resolved to petition the state legislature to allow Catholic children in the reform school access to Catholic religious services. To

[204]*Ibid.,* September 7, 11, 1864.
[205]Greene, *The Providence Plantations,* pp. 169-70.
[206]Bishop McFarland to (James A.) McMaster, New York, February 13, 1868,
UNDA.
[207]*Morning Herald,* September 21, 1868.

deal with the moral conditions at the school and the physical treatment of the children confined there the bishop, through his legal counsel, presented a petition to the Providence Board of Alderman from a group of prominent Catholic residents protesting conditions at the school.[208] Both efforts, however, proved unsuccessful.

The Division of the Diocese

In the fall of 1869 Bishop McFarland reluctantly set aside the particular concerns of his diocese and prepared for the opening of the First Vatican Council that was to convene in Rome on December 8, 1869. The priests of his diocese gave him $5,000 to help pay his expenses.[209] During the opening weeks of the council's deliberation Bishop McFarland joined his fellow American bishops in an effort to prepare a list of proposals for the council's consideration that would have the united support of all English-speaking bishops present.[210] One significant issue that divided the religious conclave concerned the argument over the definition of papal infallibility. Bishop McFarland was among the minority group within the English-speaking contingent who felt that such a definition would be inopportune. The bishop, however, would not vote his opinion. Ill health prompted him to leave the council before a formal vote on the question was taken.[211]

While in Rome the bishops of the Archdiocese of New York took up again a matter they had considered months before they had left for Rome. On June 16, 1869, at the annual meeting in Archbishop McCloskey's house in New York, Bishop Williams of Boston, concerned that his diocese was becoming too large to provide the necessary spiritual care, had proposed dividing his diocese setting off the western half as a separate diocese. The bishop's colleagues readily accepted his proposal. Bishop McFarland, whose diocese had seen a similar surge in population after the return of prosperity to the mill towns of New England, asked his fellow bishops a similar favor. Never having enjoyed good health, Bishop McFarland's task of administering his diocese was aggravated by the burden of travel necessitated by his increasing responsibilities and the location of his residence at one end of the diocese. Feeling himself increasingly

---

[208]Charles E. Gorman to Bishop McFarland, September 1, 1870, HChA.

[209]*Boston Pilot*, September 11, 1869.

[210]James J. Hennesey, *The First Council of the Vatican: The American Experience* (New York: Herder and Herder, 1963), p. 55.

[211]*Ibid.*, pp. 100-101, 230.

unable to carry his responsibilities in the manner his conscience
dictated, Bishop McFarland shared with his fellow bishops his desire
to lighten the burden either by resigning, or by obtaining a coadju-
tor, or by seeking a division of the diocese. At the meeting on June
16th, the third plan was urged upon him by his confreres, but as he
preferred one of the other alternatives, no decision was reached.[212]

During the bishops' gatherings at Rome, Bishop McFarland
again raised the question of his resignation but again no decision
was reached. The impasse between Bishop McFarland's wishes and
those of his fellow bishops was not resolved until the first meeting
of bishops of the province after their return from Rome. At this
meeting on April 19, 1871, Bishop McFarland agreed to retain his
see on condition that its area be reduced. The most natural division
was along the boundary between Connecticut and Rhode Island.
While it would create a compact and adequate diocese in Connecticut, the Rhode Island portion with Providence as its see city, was,
according to the standards of the time, too small. Apparently the
difficulty was removed on this occasion when Bishop Williams spon-
taneously offered to enlarge the projected diocese by transfering to
it most of Southeastern Massachusetts. Satisfied with the arrangements, the bishops agreed to recommend the creation of the Diocese of Providence to Rome.[213]

By the first of August 1871, the local papers had reported the
impending split of the Hartford diocese and the names of the men
selected by Bishop McFarland as candidates for the new bishopric.
The three priests recommended by Bishop McFarland to his fellow
bishops of the Province of New York for their consideration were
Fr. James Hughes, the diocese's vicar general; Fr. Matthew Hart of
St. Patrick's, New Haven, who had accompanied Bishop McFarland
to the Vatican Council; and Fr. Thomas F. Hendricken, pastor at
Waterbury, Connecticut.[214] On August 25, 1871, Archbishop
McCloskey, as spokesman for the bishops of the Province, wrote
Bishop McFarland about withdrawing Fr. Hart's name and sub-
stituting another. He also proposed recommending Fr. Hendricken
as *dignissimus.*[215] When Bishop McFarland agreed, Archbishop
McCloskey sent the recommendations to Rome together with their
petition to erect the new diocese. The Holy See accepted both the
petition and recommendations. In a document dated February 16,

[212]Lord, Sexton and Harrington, *History of the Archdiocese of Boston,* III, 43-44.
[213]*Ibid.,* III, 45.
[214]*Providence Journal,* August 1, 1871.
[215]John (McCloskey) Archbishop of New York to Bishop McFarland, August 25,
1871, HChA.

1872, Pope Pius IX formally established the new diocese and later selected Fr. Hendricken as its first bishop.[216]

Less than two years had passed since the Catholics of Providence and its environs had joyfully welcomed Bishop McFarland with a parade and speeches on his return from his twelve month absence at the Vatican Council.[217] On Sunday, February 25, 1872, the last Sunday he was to officiate at the cathedral in Providence, Bishop McFarland, troubled by a recurring illness, found the strength to preach to his people a final time. He briefly reviewed the events that had led to the division of his diocese and told the people of his concern that they have a younger and more zealous bishop to labor among them.[218]

It was with mutual sadness that the bishop and congregation took leave of each other. The bishop's kindness and affability were deeply appreciated and admired. His people turned to him as a father and his feeble health and frail habit drew them even closer to him. The poorest member of his flock could approach him without hesitation and would receive the kindest treatment. A scholar, he was also a man of extraordinary piety.[219] When he died on October 2, 1874, the *Boston Pilot* wrote of the funeral ceremonies; "The deceased Bishop was deserving of all these manifestations; for he was one of uncommon ability and self-sacrificing zeal, the untiring projector of churches and charities, and a father at once to the clergy of his diocese, whom he stimulated by faithful attention and the little ones whom he gathered under his religious care. It is known that much of his episcopal duty was done at some personal sacrifice and he did not spare himself even during ill health."[220]

[216]Shearer, *Pontificia Americana*, pp. 355-56.
[217]*Weekly Review*, August 20, 27, 1871.
[218]*Boston Pilot*, March 9, 1872.
[219]Bishop Hendricken's Eulogy of Bishop McFarland in Byrne, *Catholic Church in the New England States*, II, 156-57.
[220]*Boston Pilot*, October 22, 1874.

Chapter V

The Episcopate of Bishop Thomas
F. Hendricken

Thomas F. Hendricken—First Bishop of the Providence Diocese

Thomas Francis Hendricken was ordained first bishop of the new Diocese of Providence on Sunday, April 28, 1872 by Archbishop John McCloskey of New York who was assisted by Bishops David W. Bacon of Portland and John Williams of Boston. The new bishop was born on May 5, 1827, in the city of Kilkenny, Ireland. His parents, John and Anne (Maher) Hendricken, lived on Chapel Street in St. John's parish.[1] Among the earliest known ancestors on his father's side was a German officer who served with the army of the Duke of Ormond and took part in the battle of the Boyne. Thomas was the second of the Hendricken's three sons. John Hendricken died when Thomas was a mere boy, leaving his wife to care for James and William, his eldest and youngest sons and the family's three daughters. Most of Thomas's early years were spent with his family on a farm in the township of Triangle, about a mile northeast of Kilkenny.[2]

The young boy was a favorite of his uncle, Mr. James Fogarty, who was employed in a mercantile firm in Kilkenny. Together with Thomas's mother, Mr. Fogarty and his wife took an interest in the boy's education and shared the hope that he might one day be a priest. Hendricken began his studies in the schools of Kilkenny and in 1844 entered Kilkenny's St. Kiernan's College for a course in rhetoric and mathematics. When, in 1847, he took the examinations for admission to the Royal College of Maynooth, Hendricken so impressed the faculty that he was immediately placed on the Dunboyne Establishment—an honor reserved for the best students. In

[1]*Providence Visitor,* June 19, 1886.
[2]*Boston Pilot,* May 11, 1872.

the six years he pursued his studies of philosophy and theology, young Hendricken earned a high reputation for scholarship as well as for piety and devotion.[3]

As he approached the end of his course of studies at Maynooth, Hendricken decided to join the Jesuits and serve in the missions of China or Japan. But his chance encounter with Bishop Bernard O'Reilly of Hartford on the seminary grounds led to a change of plans. Hendricken had not previously considered going to the American missions. But before Bishop O'Reilly left Ireland he had won over the young seminarian and had the joy of ordaining the young man for the Diocese of Hartford on Easter Monday, April 25, 1853, at All Hallows College, Dublin.[4]

As Bishop O'Reilly thought little of long vacations after ordination, Fr. Hendricken, on May 27, 1853, boarded the sailing ship *Columbia* of the Black Ball line for the voyage to America. Among his fellow cabin passengers was another young priest, Fr. Walsh, and Rev. Samuel Davies, a young Protestant clergyman returning home from Germany. A warm friendship soon grew among the three. Berthed in separate quarters on board the vessel were some seven hundred German and Irish emigrants among whom the clergymen mingled. Although many of the emigrants were Catholics, the recent upsurge in Know-Nothing sentiment coupled with the *Columbia* captain's hatred of Catholicism prevented the two priests from holding services for their fellow passengers.[5]

Seventeen days out, Rev. Davies learned of an Irish woman who was on the point of death and was asking for the sacraments. The Protestant clergyman went below to the quarters of the Irish. When the woman asked for a priest Davies promised help. Fr. Hendricken was the first of the two he met. Hastily putting on his cassock and stole, Hendricken took the "Viaticum" and was on his way to the "Irish Quarter" when the captain, his anger roused by the sight of Hendricken's vestments, stopped him. Only the intervention of Davies and Fr. Walsh kept the angry captain from harming Hendricken. On the advice of his friends Fr. Hendricken did not openly defy the captain. Hendricken's failure to appear later at dinner seemed to confirm the captain's assertion that the priest was a coward. Together with his officers he joked of the beliefs and prac-

---

[3]*Ibid.*

[4]Francis X. Reuss, *Biographical Cyclopaedia of the Catholic Hierarchy of the United States, 1784-1898* (Milwaukee: M. H. Wiltzius & Company, 1898), pp. 52-53; *Weekly Visitor,* October 23, 1875.

[5]These details and those that follow were given by Rev. Davies in an interview shortly after Bishop Hendricken's death. *Providence Sunday Telegram,* June 20, 1886.

tices of Catholics. The meal was almost over when a sailor pushed open the cabin door with the news that the priest was down with the woman. Fr. Hendricken was just coming up the hatchway from below when a blow from the enraged captain knocked him back below decks. Davies and Walsh, held back by the crew, watched as more blows fell on their friend. Rev. Davies was able to wrench himself free and rushed to the German emigrant quarters. Knowing German he explained what was happening and asked the Catholics among them for help. Fifty veterans of the German armies grabbed whatever weapons they could lay hold of and followed Davies. Coming up the hatchway they heard the captain order his victim's body thrown overboard. Before the seamen could comply the Germans were on them, knocking them down and wresting Hendricken free.

Seeing the interference as mutiny, the captain was nonetheless warned by Davies that if he wished to finish the business, the Catholics, who outnumbered the crew and were aroused by the attempt to murder a priest for ministering to the sick, were ready for a fight. With the Irish emigrants now clamoring to get on deck there could be but one end to the affair. The captain, seeing his danger, ordered Hendricken to be put in irons but his German rescuers would not allow it. They took the battered priest to their quarters and tended his wounds. When Fr. Hendricken regained consciousness the next morning they took him back to his cabin. Fearing an attempt to poison him, they fed him from their own rations, and throughout the rest of the voyage to New York, the Irish and German emigrants mounted guard outside his cabin door.

On his arrival in Providence, Hendricken, like most of the newly ordained priests of the Hartford diocese, joined the four priests who, together with Bishop O'Reilly, made up the cathedral staff. The young priest served a few months in Providence before spending varying periods of time at St. Joseph's in Providence, St. Charles, Woonsocket and St. Mary's, Newport. On January 17, 1854, Bishop O'Reilly appointed Hendricken pastor of St. Joseph's church in Winsted, Connecticut, a parish established in 1852, where he served for more than a year.[6]

In July 1855, the bishop sent Fr. Hendricken to a new assignment in Waterbury, Connecticut. The church in Waterbury, though only built in 1846, had been damaged by fire in December 1854. Fr. Hendricken before long set out to raise the money to replace it. The cornerstone was laid on July 5, 1857 and the church was dedicated by Bishop McFarland under the title of the Immaculate Conception

---

[6]Byrne, *Catholic Church in the New England States,* II, 288-89.

of the Mother of God on December 19, 1858. Fr. Hendricken proved a talented administrator and builder. During his pastorate in Waterbury the parish witnessed the construction of a rectory, the opening of a parish school in the old church, the coming of the Sisters of Notre Dame from Montreal and the building of a convent where they conducted an academy for young ladies, and the purchase and laying out of a cemetery.[7]

His executive ability was only one of the talents Fr. Hendricken possessed in his ministry. He is remembered as a man of marked faith and piety, a man whose enthusiasm knew no bounds, whose constant aim was to build a parish second to none in the diocese. Like many other parishes in the diocese, Immaculate Conception daily grew in numbers. The poor and weak were Hendricken's special charges. Those of his parishioners who sought refuge from the burdens of life in drink, found in him a kind, considerate and sympathetic friend, and at the same time, a zealous promoter of temperance. The children of the parish also received his particular care and in their company he was one of them.[8]

Early during his residence in Waterbury, Fr. Hendricken identified himself with the cause of education, and was a member of the public school board for many years. Although the poverty of his people prevented the parish from employing a teacher, such was Fr. Hendricken's zeal for education that shortly after his arrival in Waterbury he opened a school and added the labors of teaching to his missionary duties.[9] Years later he would have the satisfaction of seeing at least one of his young students ordained to the priesthood.[10] In 1868, in recognition of his work as pastor, Fr. Hendricken received from Pius IX the degree of Doctor of Divinity, then the common way of recognizing ability and accomplishment.[11]

Other recognition awaited him. When the bishops of the Province of New York deliberated on whom to nominate as bishop of the new Providence diocese, a consensus emerged that Hendricken "was the most fitting candidate in every respect, health alone excepted."[12] Fr. Hendricken, who suffered from an asthmatic condition, was well aware of the limitations that his health imposed on him. In 1866, when Bishop McFarland was considering transferring Fr. Hen-

[7]*Ibid.*, II, 385-87.
[8]Joseph Anderson, D.D., ed. *History of Waterbury*, 3 vols. (New Haven, 1896), III, 740-41.
[9]*Providence Journal*, June 12, 1886.
[10]*Ibid.*, June 14, 1886.
[11]*Ibid.*, June 12, 1886.
[12]Archbishop John McCloskey to Bishop McFarland, August 25, 1871, UNDA.

dricken to the financially troubled St. Joseph's parish in Providence, the priest noted that, "When on former occasions, I hinted to yourself in person, my desire of leaving this parish, it was not by any love of novelty I was actuated. I considered my poor health and the great work that might be accomplished in a place of such importance as this is; no wonder then that I grew uneasy at the sight of so many responsibilities and so little strength to meet them."[13] In 1871 the bishops of the Province would conclude that even with his delicate health, Hendricken would be the best candidate as "the labors of the new diocese would not be very onerous."[14]

Hendricken's health would prove a cross to him in his fourteen years as bishop since it would force him to curtail his activities at certain times. On the night before his consecration an asthma attack so alarmed his friends that they feared he would choke to death. As a result of his asthmatic condition, his voice was often thin and wheezy and his sermons were punctuated with coughs, an unfortunate malady when one considers the fact that he was a speaker and writer of considerable talent.[15] When his asthma troubled him, he would be compelled to spend the greater portion of the night sitting up. At these times he would seek alleviation from physical pain by reading and thinking out the many details of his pastoral work.[16]

Before his ordination and installation as bishop, Fr. Hendricken worked out and signed an agreement with Bishop McFarland that stipulated that the priests and sisters in the diocese, with certain stated exceptions, would continue to serve the parishes where they were presently assigned. They also agreed on a division of responsibility for the infirm priests and sisters and on the division of diocesan funds.[17] A similar agreement was worked out with Bishop Williams of Boston.[18]

The Pastoral Task and the Panic of 1873

In his first published report on the condition of his new diocese Bishop Hendricken estimated that the total Catholic population was 125,000. He listed 43 churches with 5 under construction, 53 priests, 1 male and 5 female academies, 9 parish schools with 4,225

[13]Rev. Thomas Hendricken to Bishop McFarland, January 15, 1866, UNDA.
[14]Archbishop John McCloskey to Bishop McFarland, August 25, 1871, HChA.
[15]Byrne, *Catholic Church in the New England States,* I, 386.
[16]*Providence Visitor,* June 19, 1886.
[17]Agreement, March 11, 1872, HChA.
[18]"Memoranda," March 20, 1871, BChA.

students, and 1 orphan asylum with 200 orphans.[19] The geographical area of the diocese included the state of Rhode Island and the southwestern Massachusetts counties of Bristol (including the rapidly growing industrial cities of Fall River, Taunton and New Bedford), Barnstable (the "Cape" region), Dukes (the island of Martha's Vineyard), and Nantucket, plus the towns of Wareham, Marion and Mattapoisett in Plymouth County along Buzzard's Bay. Of the total diocesan figures, the Massachusetts portion of the diocese had, in 1872, an approximate Catholic population of 30,000 with 15 churches and 15 clergymen.[20]

As southern New England in the 1870s and 1880s became even more heavily an industrial area, the economic health of the nation became an increasingly important factor in the lives of factory workers and general laborers, among whom most of the Catholics of the new diocese were found. In January 1873, Fr. Joseph Reid, Bishop McFarland's secretary and a priest who had served for a time in Providence before the division of the diocese, prepared a statement for an author of a book intended for prospective Irish immigrants in which he described conditions which were typical of most of the manufacturing districts of New England.

Mechanics command good wages, and generally find employment, if they choose to work.

Average wages for mechanics per day, $3.50; for laborers per day, $1; for girls in service per week, $3.50. Help in factories for the most part work by the 'piece,' and secure for themselves fair wages when business is good. Although employment is easily found by the industrious, and fair wages are given for labor, still food, rents, clothing and other ordinary necessities and comforts of life cost less in Western States. Here, it is true, all these things can be found and secured, but at a greater outlay; and for the laboring classes only where domestic economy is made a pet household virtue.

Close confinement in factories, especially in cotton and woolen mills, impairs the health of many, and those who are forced to seek employment in such places when young generally lose soon the health bloom and vigor of youth, and live short lives.

To Catholics of Connecticut, the situation in Rhode Island is similar, there is everywhere an ample opportunity of leading good Christian lives, if they wish to do so. Nearly every town and village in the State has a Catholic priest living within its limits, or is frequently visited by him. Christian instruction is therefore secured and for this reason, our people are content to build homes for themselves and children in any portion of the diocese in which they may be found.[21]

[19]*Sadlier's Catholic Directory,* 1873, p. 288.
[20]"Memoranda," March 20, 1872, BChA.
[21](Bishop) F. P. McFarland per Joseph B. Reid, Secretary, to (Rev.) Stephen Byrne, Hartford, January 22, 1873 found in Stephen Byrne, *Irish Emigration to the United States* (New York: The Catholic Publication Society, 1873), pp. 72-74.

By the 1870s the older Irish Catholic population of Rhode Island and neighboring Massachusetts, which now contained an increasing number of native-born citizens, came to include also an increasing number of middle and upper middle class residents as the sons of the earliest immigrants and the abler of the immigrants established themselves as business and professional men.

The prosperous economic conditions described in Fr. Reid's letter ended in the fall of 1873, when the overextended economy of the United States slid into a sustained period of depression that gripped the nation and New England for nearly six years. Among the firms severely affected by the collapse of the post Civil War economic boom and the contraction of credit was that of the textile empire built by the Spragues. Before the A & W Sprague Manufacturing Company suspended operations in October 1873, the Spragues operated twenty-five per cent of the 1,142,000 spindles in Rhode Island. In addition, the Spragues boasted the largest and finest finishing mill in New England employing over ten thousand operatives.[22] The Sprague mills would reopen and continue operation under trusteeship, but confidence was destroyed and recovery slow.

Unfortunately, they were not the only Rhode Island establishment to be affected by the panic. Thousands of workers lost their jobs as concern after concern failed. The blow to Rhode Island's cotton industry was so severe that the state scarcely recovered from the effects of the depression until the end of the century.[23] Fortunately for Rhode Island other established industries such as machinery and metals came to employ increasing numbers of workers. By 1879, jewelry manufacturers in the state had made Rhode Island the chief center of their industry. Several industries new to the state, such as the manufacture of rubber goods at Providence, Woonsocket, and Bristol and chemical products at Rumford created job opportunities for willing workers.[24]

The relationship between job opportunities and growth in population is reflected in federal census reports and the Rhode Island state census reports which the general assembly in 1865 ordered taken every tenth year at mid-decade. In 1870, Rhode Island's total population stood at 217,353. Thanks to the relatively prosperous years at the beginning of the decade, the state's population had risen to 258,238 by 1875, an increase of 18.8 per cent. During the depres-

[22]A New York newspaper quoted in Cole, *History of Washington and Kent Counties,* pp. 1013-15.
[23]Greene, *The Providence Plantations,* pp. 96-97; Carroll, *Rhode Island,* II, 863-64.
[24]Kurt Mayer, *Economic Development and Population Growth in Rhode Island* (Providence: Brown University, 1953), pp.43-44.

sion years between 1875 and 1880 the population rose only seven
per cent to 276,531. Between 1880 and 1885, with the weakening of
the effects of the depression, the state's population rose ten per cent
to a total of 304,234. While rural areas in Rhode Island remained
relatively stable, the cities and industrial villages showed the greatest
increase in population between 1870 and 1875. This trend slackened
somewhat between 1880 and 1885 when only Providence and Pawtucket showed appreciable increases in population. A survey of the
federal census statistics for the Massachusetts cities and counties that
formed other parts of the diocese reveal a parallel situation.[25]

Studying the depression-caused fluctuations in the growth of
Rhode Island's total population does not reveal the essence of the
pastoral problems confronting Bishop Hendricken. By 1875, foreign-born comprised 27.7 per cent of the state's total population.
When the parentage of those listed in the census as born in Rhode
Island is also considered, the 1875 census figures reveal that 37.5
per cent of the population of Rhode Island were either foreign-
born or had at least one foreign-born parent. By 1880, Rhode
Island had the largest proportion of foreign-born of any state of
the Union—a distinction which it was to retain for thirty years.[26]

Not only did the percentage of foreign-born, and thus Catholic
citizens of Massachusetts and Rhode Island increase during these
years, but the composition of the foreign-born population would
also undergo considerable changes. Natives of Ireland during the
1870s and 1880s still comprised the largest contingent, but Irish
immigration had reached its peak before 1860 and the proportion
of Irish natives among the total foreign-born population would
decline from 68 per cent in 1860 to 48 per cent in 1880. The influx
of French Canadians, which had begun after the Civil War, would
continue and, although the rate of immigration would drop during
the depression period, the total increase of natives of Canada in the
twenty-year period between 1860 and 1880 would be larger than
that of the natives of any other country.[27] The increasing ethnic
diversity of Rhode Island's population is reflected in Rhode Island's
1885 census. In that year, the census takers noted that of 304,234
Rhode Islanders, 38,395 were born in Ireland; 15,785 in Canada;
2,614 in Germany; 814 in Portugal and its Western Islands and 760
in Italy.[28] Certainly, all of these were not Catholics; yet significant

[25]*Ibid.*, p. 45.
[26]*Ibid.*, p. 48.
[27]*Ibid.*
[28]Amos Perry, comp., *Rhode Island State Census,* 1885 (Providence: E. L. Freeman
& Sons, 1887), p. 231.

percentages of these, plus Irishmen born in England, Scotland and Canada who later immigrated to America, were.

During these years the pattern of high mobility among the lower economic groups which characterized American society in the late nineteenth century would continue as men and women, particularly French Canadians, would move about in search of work, better conditions, or out of sheer restlessness. Bishop Hendricken listed an increase of 16,000 Catholics in the total estimate of 136,000 in his 1879 report to *Sadlier's Catholic Directory*. At the time of his death, the Catholic population of the diocese totaled approximately 160,-000.[29]

Under Bishop Hendricken the number of priests serving the diocese would rise from the 53 who assisted him in ministering to 43 churches in 1873 to 104 who served 55 churches by 1887.[30] While in 1862 Bishop McFarland would report that only 6 of his 51 priests were native-born, better than half the young men Bishop Hendricken ordained during his years as bishop were born in the United States and many others came to America as young boys.[31] Among both the native and foreign-born clergy, many received their classical training at Holy Cross College in Worcester, at any one of many Canadian colleges and at a scattering of other American colleges and seminaries. Bishop Hendricken thought it a great advantage to send his Irish students to the major seminary at Montreal so that they could minister to both the English and French Catholics and many of his seminarians studied there.[32] Others studied their philosophy and theology at St. Mary's in Baltimore; St. John's in Brighton, Massachusetts after that school opened in April 1881, or at one of several other major seminaries in the United States and Canada.

After becoming bishop, Hendricken was confronted with the challenge of supplying clergy not only for the already existing Irish parishes of the diocese and for the new ones the diocese needed, but also of supplying priests capable of ministering to the Canadians, Portuguese and German immigrants whose number had swelled the diocese's total population. The bishop's task was complicated by a number of resignations, both spontaneous and re-

[29]Stephan Thernstrom, *Poverty and Progress: Social Mobility in a Nineteenth Century City* (Cambridge, MA: Harvard University Press, 1964).

[30]*Sadlier's Catholic Directory,* 1873, p. 288; 1887, p. 299.

[31]Bishop McFarland to the Congregation of the Propaganda, May 16, 1862, PFA. Statistics on the clergy who served under Bishop Hendricken are incomplete. These conclusions are based on biographical information accumulated by the author.

[32]Byrne, *Catholic Church in the New England States,* I, 386.

quested, among the clergy he had inherited from the Diocese of
Boston. To meet the immediate need for ministry, the bishop advanced the ordination of several men to orders by a few months. By
March 1874 the critical need for clergy prompted Bishop Hendricken to ask the rector of Maynooth Seminary to recruit five Irish
seminarians for a period of three years' service in the diocese. Earlier that year the bishop had written to major seminary superiors in
Canada looking for priests to serve the Canadians, and he would
also write to acquaintances and contacts in Portugal and Belgium in
hopes of securing clergy for the Portuguese and Germans of his
diocese.[33]

The depression that settled on the nation in the 1870s had its
effect on the recruitment of clergy. As immigration slowed down,
the need for expanding parish staffs and establishing new missions
also diminished. Yet in Bishop Hendricken's sixteen years of service, the number of young men studying for priesthood remained
constant. Beginning in June 1877, and continuing intermittently
thereafter, the bishops of Providence began to loan priests to other
dioceses for short periods of service.[34] With so many of his own
priests available, many of whom had studied in Canadian seminaries, the bishop, with varying degrees of success, elected to assign
them to Canadian parishes until such time as sufficient priests of
Canadian background and good character were available to serve
their own people.

In his dealings with priests, Bishop Hendricken showed a fraternal concern and compassion. He was, however, strict with himself
as far as his duties were concerned and expected his priests to follow
his example. He frequently called his young priests to account for
their actions and chastised his pastors for any neglect of their responsibilities. While in his first years as bishop he accepted priests
into his diocese from religious orders and other American and
Canadian dioceses, he preferred, as did his predecessors, to recruit
and train his own clergy. The bishop was well served by his first
Vicar General, Fr. Lawrence McMahon, whom he appointed on
June 30, 1872, and who, seven years later, was consecrated as the
fifth bishop of Hartford.[35]

[33]Bishop Thomas F. Hendricken, "Diary," January 19, 20; March 4; April 17; May
11; June 19, 1874, PChA. Hereafter referred to as Bishop Hendricken, "Diary."
[34]*Ibid.*, June 20; August 2, 1877.
[35]*Ibid.*, June 26, 1872.

First Expansion of the Diocese Under Bishop Hendricken

Bishop Hendricken, on assuming his office, had not only to provide priests but also places of worship for the people of his diocese whose increasing numbers had dictated the establishment of the diocese. The bishop's activities as a parish builder were divided in two spurts separated by the tight money times of the depression. Most of the parishes created in the early 1870s were set up in the industrial towns and villages whose Catholic population had grown as new mills were built and older ones expanded to supply the booming demand of the post Civil War Industrial Revolution.

On September 4, 1870, Bishop McFarland dedicated the rebuilt and enlarged church of St. Mary's in Bristol, made necessary by the growing Catholic population of that factory center. Three months later Fr. Charles Rogers, the nephew of the pastor of Warren and Bristol, joined his uncle as assistant in the parish. This was Fr. Rogers's first assignment after his ordination. On March 7, 1874, Bishop Hendricken appointed Fr. Rogers as the first resident pastor of St. Mary's, Bristol.[36]

To the north, the town of East Providence had become part of Rhode Island in 1862 when Massachusetts ceded the area in return for jurisdiction over the Fall River sections of Tiverton. The town's Catholic population increased substantially in 1873 as the result of the decision of the city of Providence to improve its sewerage system on the east side which was the cause of a significantly higher percentage of disease in that section of the city. The city excavated historic Fox hill, graded the point and filled in land along the shore of the Seekonk. A number of Fox Pointers were forced out of their homes and moved across the India Point bridge to the Watchemoket section of East Providence.[37] There was already a substantial Catholic population in Watchemoket who attended Mass at the cathedral or at St. Joseph's, while those near Rumford were part of St. Joseph's parish in Pawtucket. Because of the distance involved in getting to Mass, the pastor of St. Joseph's in Fox Point, Fr. Daniel Kelly, in March 1874, made arrangements to rent a hall in Watchemoket where he would come over to say Mass. The number of

---

[36]*Ibid.*, March 7, 1874.
[37]Greene, *The Providence Plantations,* p. 96; Joseph Conforti, *Our Heritage: A History of East Providence* (White Plains, New York: Monarch Publishing, Inc., 1976), pp. 74-88.

Catholics in the village was large enough then to contemplate building a church, and in 1874 he purchased a potential building site on
the corner of Anthony and Taunton Avenue.

Fr. Kelly at the time was in poor health and his parish was in
the process of building a new school. These factors, together with
the impact of the depression, probably combined to prevent him
from proceeding further with plans for a mission church at Watchemoket. In July 1874, the Sisters of Mercy purchased a large residence at "Bayview" which they opened as a boarding school the
following September as more room was needed in Providence to
accommodate their day students.[38] Initially, the priests from the
cathedral came out to offer Mass for the sisters and girls, but for a
time in 1875 Fr. Kelly or his assistant attended to their needs. In
1876, however, Fr. Kelly's health again began to fail so that priests
from the cathedral resumed responsibility for offering Mass at Bayview.

When Fr. James Brennan returned to duty at the cathedral in
the spring of 1876 after an extended illness, Bishop Hendricken felt
the time was right to carry out the postponed plans to establish a
mission at Watchemoket. In June the bishop asked Fr. Brennan to
offer Mass for the Catholics in East Providence following Mass at
Bayview. The priest first said Mass in Monroe's Hall, but within a
few weeks it was evident that Monroe's was not nearly large enough
for all who wished to attend and Lyceum (later known as Watchemoket) Hall became the regular place for Mass. On the third Sunday
after Fr. Brennan began going to Watchemoket, Bishop Hendricken
visited the village to enroll a large number of members into the
sodalities of Mary and the Sacred Heart.[39]

Fr. Brennan was as strong minded as he was energetic. An
Irish-born priest who had been ordained by the bishop in May 1872,
Fr. Brennan's hour-long sermons often attracted the notice of the
local papers.[40] Just over a year after he began offering Mass in East
Providence, Fr. Brennan and the people began talking of building
a church on the land purchased in 1874.[41] Plans for a church did not
progress beyond the fund-raising stage while the cathedral priest
attended the place. By 1880 the town demanded a full-time pastor.
Bishop Hendricken, on February 5th of that year, appointed Fr.
Farrell O'Reilly, the rector of the cathedral, to take charge of the

[38]Carroll, *Annals*, III, 424-25.
[39]*Weekly Vistor*, June 17; July 8; August 5, 1876; Bishop Hendricken, "Diary," June
25, 1876.
[40]*Providence Journal*, July 25, 1877; *Weekly Visitor*, May 24, 1879.
[41]*Providence Journal*, October 23, 1877.

parish as its first pastor and established its boundaries to include all of East Providence.[42] The parish broke ground for the church on July 6, 1880. Designed by Patrick Keely, the new wooden structure could accomodate as many as five hundred parishioners. Bishop Hendricken dedicated the church to the Sacred Heart on November 7, 1880.[43]

The land adjoining Pawtucket, on the east bank of the Blackstone River, was also part of the land acquired from Massachusetts in 1862. Here also the increasing number of houses in that pleasant section indicated a need for a church. By May 1872, Fr. Delaney of St. Mary's had bought land on Wolcott Street, and with $8,000 contributed by the people of St. Mary's, began construction of a new church in October of that year.[44] The following May, Bishop McFarland, in the absence of Bishop Hendricken who was in Europe, came out to Pawtucket to lay the cornerstone and dedicate the new church to St. Joseph.[45] Fr. Henry F. Kinnerney, the parish's first pastor, received news of his new assignment on January 24, 1874, his birthday. The learned Fr. Kinnerney had spent the last year traveling from hamlet to hamlet on Cape Cod before his former teacher, Bishop Hendricken, called him to Pawtucket. While waiting for the church basement to be roofed over, Fr. Kinnerney celebrated Mass for his parishioners in the old town hall on School Street until April 1874.[46] The parish had a debt of $52,000 when the pastor arrived, and with the collapse of credit after 1873 and the poverty of the people, progress on the church was slow. It was not until November 10, 1878, shortly after Bishop Hendricken had returned from a second trip to Europe, that the new church was dedicated.[47]

By 1873 the number of Catholics around the mills near the Pleasant View section of Pawtucket and in the village of Central Falls had also grown to the point where they could support a church and pastor of their own. On August 5, 1873, Bishop Hendricken appointed one of Fr. Delaney's assistants, Fr. James L. Smith, as pastor of that section. Fr. Smith first said Mass in Union Hall and later in Battery Hall on Exchange Street. His coming was welcome news as the people of Pleasant View and Central Falls would no longer have to travel the considerable distance to St. Mary's.[48] By the end of

[42]Bishop Hendricken, "Diary," February 5, 1880.
[43]Bishop Hendricken, "Diary," July 6; November 7, 1880; *Weekly Visitor*, October 30; November 13, 1880.
[44]*Providence Journal*, May 4, 1872; *Central Falls Weekly Visitor*, October 25, 1872.
[45]*Providence Journal*, May 26, 1873.
[46]*Providence Visitor*, February 2, 1895.
[47]*Weekly Visitor*, November 3, 1878; *Providence Journal*, November 11, 1878.
[48]*Central Falls Weekly Visitor*, August 9, 23; October 25, 1872.

August the parish had a site for a church and with the thawing of the ground the next spring, work was begun on a foundation. Funds for the church came from the usual collections and a fair.[49] By June 1873, the church, which would be dedicated to the Sacred Heart, had progressed to the point where Fr. McMahon, the diocese's vicar general, could lay its cornerstone.[50] Unfortunately, the labors of building the church and ministering to his parish proved too great for Fr. Smith's health and he resigned on February 6, 1875.[51] Another young priest, Fr. Michael Fitzgerald, formerly assistant and later rector of the cathedral in Providence, saw the church through to its completion and dedication by Bishop Hendricken on June 10, 1876.

Further up the Blackstone, the villages of Ashton, Berkeley, Albion and Manville were mission stations of St. Patrick's, Valley Falls. On November 1, 1872, Bishop Hendricken assigned Fr. James A. FitzSimon as pastor of the four places.[52] Fr. FitzSimon made Ashton and its new church the focal point of his mission. However, the completion of a new mill in Manville in the spring of 1873 attracted nearly three thousand new operatives to the site, most of them French Canadians. Fr. FitzSimon had studied in the New York Provincial seminary at Troy in the days when Bishop McFarland wanted his students there to learn French. His knowledge of French helped influence Bishop Hendricken's decision to alter Fr. FitzSimon's assignment and give him the responsibility of building a new church in Manville. Although also hampered by the effects of the Panic of 1873, Fr. FitzSimon and his parishioners, after little more than a year, were ready to dedicate a new church building to his patron, St. James. Bishop Hendricken consecrated the church on April 26, 1874 in the midst of a snowstorm that was, according to the bishop, "about as fierce and wild as came this winter."[53] The following summer, Fr. Antoine Bernard came down from Woonsocket to take charge of the new parish and Fr. FitzSimon returned to devote his full attention to Ashton and its remaining missions.

Further to the north and west, Bishop Hendricken, on June 9, 1872, solemnly dedicated the new church of St. John's, built by the people of Slatersville.[54] The next year, on April 18, 1873, he sent

[49]*Providence Journal,* June 23, 1873; *Central Falls Weekly Visitor,* June 27, 1873.
[50]*Central Falls Weekly Visitor,* February 12, 1875.
[51]Bishop Hendricken, "Diary," February 6, 1875.
[52]Byrne, *Catholic Church in the New England States,* I, 1872.
[53]*Providence Journal,* April 27, 1874; *Woonsocket Patriot,* April 24; May 1, 1874; Bishop Hendricken, "Diary," April 28, 1874; "St. James Church, Manville: Joy, Thanksgiving, Hope" (Hackensack, N.J.: Custombook, 1974), pp. 3-4.
[54]Bishop Hendricken, "Diary," June 9, 1872; Harvey, *North Smithfield Centennial,* p. 68.

Fr. James Berkens to Slatersville as the village's first resident pastor.[55]

To the south in Greenville and Georgiaville the center of Fr. Plunkett's mission shifted in 1873 after a fire destroyed the Stillwater Woolen Company and forced many of the Catholics who attended Mass at St. Philip's in Greenville to move elsewhere in search of employment. To compensate for the loss of parishioners, Bishop Hendricken removed the small chapel of St. Joseph in Wanskuck from the jurisdiction of Fr. Cooney at the Immaculate Conception and gave the charge to Fr. Bernard Plunkett. By September of 1873, Fr. Plunkett, who was in poor health, had moved his residence to Wanskuck which was his native place. The young priest died there on June 27, 1874 and was buried in front of the chapel.[56]

After Fr. Plunkett's death, the bishop returned charge of the Wanskuck chapel to the pastor of the Immaculate Conception, and sent Fr. Andrew Brady to serve as pastor of St. Philip's. Fr. Brady served only a few months. On November 18, 1874, he was appointed pastor of the parish in Sandwich on Cape Cod. His replacement was Fr. William Wiseman, a priest who recently came into the diocese and had served as an assistant at the cathedral and in New Bedford. Fr. Wiseman concentrated his efforts among the mixed congregation of Irish and Canadian people in Georgiaville, and within a few months of his appointment he had secured financing and purchased land for a new church in that village. On May 16, 1875, Bishop Hendricken blessed the cornerstone and on October 24th of that same year, dedicated the church under the patronage of St. Michael.[57] The following month, Fr. Wiseman apparently left the diocese and the bishop asked the French-speaking Fr. Berkens to succeed him. The new pastor continued to visit the chapel at Greenville and on occasion said Mass in a hall at Stillwater.[58] Fr. Berkens, however, was soon at odds with the Canadians of his congregation.[59] Failing eyesight finally prompted him to take a leave of absence in 1882 and return to his home in Belgium.

Although the bishop had again given Fr. Cooney charge of St. Joseph's at Wanskuck, the pastor of the Immaculate Conception realized that with the proposed expansion of the Wanskuck mill, the

[55]Bishop Hendricken, "Diary," April 18, 1873.

[56]*Providence Journal,* June 30, 1874; Bishop Hendricken, "Diary," September 16, 1873; Walsh, *Centennial History,* p. 27.

[57]Bishop Hendricken, "Diary," May 16; October 24, 1875; *Woonsocket Patriot,* May 21, 1875; *Weekly Visitor,* October 30, 1875; Paul Campbell, *et al.,* "St. Michael's Church, Georgiaville, Rhode Island: A Century of Faith and Sacrifice, 1875-1975" (Privately Printed, 1975).

[58]*Weekly Visitor,* December 8, 1877; *Providence Visitor,* November 24, 1911.

[59]"Georgiaville," Rev. James P. Gibson, "Scrapbook," p. 139, PChA.

village would soon attract a large enough population to support its own priest. With the help of two fellow pastors, Fr. Cooney persuaded Bishop Hendricken to appoint his young assistant, Fr. James A. Finnigan, as first pastor of the new parish. As the general assembly had, in 1874, given a huge section of the town of North Providence to Providence and Pawtucket, the chapel at Wanskuck was now part of Providence and that city already had a church named in honor of St. Joseph. Fr. Cooney rectified the situation by placing the chapel under the patronage of his own patron saint. When, on November 30, 1874, Bishop Hendricken raised the mission to the status of a separate parish, Fr. Finnigan became the founding pastor of St. Edward's. Setting himself three goals at the onset of his pastorate—the construction of a rectory, a school and church—Fr. Finnigan had by 1885, with the generous support of his millworker congregation, accomplished the first two of his goals. On August 21, 1885, he broke ground for a new and spacious brick church. However, it would be several years before the parish had the funds to complete this last task.[60]

In Our Lady of Mercy in East Greenwich, Fr. William Halligan, transferred from service as an assistant in St. Joseph's, Providence, succeeded Fr. Thomas Kane who was sent to Valley Falls in June 1872.[61] In the parish's Wickford mission the mills in Wickford, Belleville and Shady Lea had attracted a significant number of French Canadians in addition to the Irish who had arrived earlier. The priests from East Greenwich had initially said Mass in town in the homes of residents but when their numbers increased they moved services to the Saunderstown schoolhouse and on two Sundays a month, used the North Kingstown Town Hall, then on West Main Street. In 1874 Fr. Halligan decided that the people were numerous enough to build a church and on the first day of June arranged to purchase a half-acre of land on the Post Road.[62] By the end of November he succeeded in completing the construction of a small frame church that Bishop Hendricken dedicated under the title of St. Bernard on July 4, 1875.[63]

Fr. Halligan's northern-most mission in Apponaug also saw its Catholic population increase, attracted to the Warwick village by the

[60]Walsh, *Centennial History,* pp. 23-27, 79.

[61]Bishop Hendricken, "Diary," July 1, 8, 1872.

[62]"St. Bernard Church, Wickford, Rhode Island: A Century of Change and Growth" (Hackensack, N.J.: Custombook, 1975), pp. 5-7; *Providence Visitor,* September 10, 1936.

[63]*Rhode Island Pendulum,* November 20, 1874; Bishop Hendricken, "Diary," July 4, 1875.

lure of employment in the Oriental Print Works. By 1872 the priest from East Greenwich was coming to the village twice a month to offer Mass in the old Warwick Town Hall. Aware that he would soon need to build a church in Apponaug, Fr. Halligan in 1873 began looking for a site near the village only to find that no one was willing to sell land to a priest. One of the plant managers of the Apponaug mill, John D'Arcy, himself a non-Catholic, purchased a lot near the pond on Pontiac Road north of the present Apponaug Four Corners. Mr. D'Arcy then turned the land over to Fr. Halligan. Two years later, on November 25, 1875, Fr. Halligan dedicated a small frame church he had built on the site in honor of St. Catherine.[64]

During the summer months the congregation at Apponaug was swelled by Catholics who came from Providence with their employers to take up summer residence in the coolness of Warwick Neck or who might be working or vacationing themselves at Rocky Point or Oakland Beach. In April 1875, a Warwick Neck resident offered Bishop Hendricken a lot of land on which to build a church so that the Catholics who vacationed there during the summer would not have to travel the five miles to Apponaug.[65] The bishop could not accept his offer, perhaps because of limited funds. The early promise of the Apponaug mission in turn faded when the print works closed down in March 1883, and the workers had to go elsewhere to find work.[66]

The Catholics near the Carolina mills were properly the concern of the pastor of St. Michael's in Westerly. There were in 1877 some ninety Catholics in the village who complained to the bishop through a representative on December 19, 1877, that they had not had an opportunity to receive the sacraments in a long time. The bishop promised to go down to see them. Although Carolina would remain part of the Westerly mission, in May 1878, the *Visitor* mentions that Fr. Halligan had visited Carolina village to offer Mass in the home of Andrew Davey.[67]

In the Massachusetts portion of the new diocese with its large industrial and commercial centers of Fall River, Taunton, and New Bedford, the need for new parishes and additional clergy was perhaps most pressing. Only four new parishes had been erected in the area since 1856 even though the resumption of immigration after

[64]*Rhode Island Pendulum,* November 17, 1875; *Providence Visitor,* December 19, 1935.

[65]Bishop Hendricken, "Diary," April 30, 1875.

[66]Cole, *History of Washington and Kent Counties,* p. 951.

[67]Bishop Hendricken, "Diary," December 19, 1877; *Weekly Visitor,* May 5, 1878; "St. Mary, Carolina: A Heritage of Holiness" (Hackensack, N.J.: Custombook, 1972).

the depression of the 1850s and early 1860s had greatly increased the populations of the existing parishes.

The history of Catholicism in southeastern Massachusetts goes back at least to 1811 when Bishop Cheverus visited the port town of New Bedford. As in Providence, the Irish Catholic workmen the bishop met in New Bedford would stay only as long as there were jobs, of which there were few after 1815. No more is heard of Catholics in New Bedford until 1820 when an Irish Augustinian, Fr. Philip Lariscy, visited the town. The Irish laboring men raised enough money to purchase a forty-rod lot on the easterly part of Edward Wing's land off what would become Allen Street, a few rods above the Dartmouth road, and built a small frame church building.[68]

After Fr. Lariscy left the Boston diocese, other priests visited New Bedford on occasion. Fr. Woodley from St. Mary's in Newport visited once every two months for awhile to offer Mass in Fr. Lariscy's little church which was completed and enlarged back in 1829.[69] The missionaries stayed in the home of Cornelius McAleeney who proudly remembered opening his home to the priests.[70]

During this time New Bedford was chiefly a whaling town and consequently few Irishmen and other Catholics settled there for long. In 1832 Bishop Fenwick made New Bedford, Wareham and Sandwich, with its glass factory, part of the same mission. Seven years later Fr. Francis Kiernan, the newly appointed priest in charge of the district, reported to Bishop Fenwick that nearly all the Catholics had left New Bedford in quest of work and he had nothing to live on.[71] The bishop altered Fr. Kiernan's mission and appointed him to take charge of Waltham, Canton and Randolph and to "occasionally visit the people of New Bedford."[72] By the end of 1837 New Bedford was again one of the missions of the pastor of Newport and remained so until the Diocese of Hartford was created in 1844.

In June 1844, Bishop Fenwick sent Fr. Patrick Byrne to New Bedford as the town's first resident pastor. He ministered to the Canadians in the town until January 1845, when Fr. James Maguire succeeded him. Fr. Maguire would in time complain to the bishop that he could not live there. The inhabitants were a lawless crowd,

[68]Wheelock Craig, et al., History of the Churches of New Bedford (New Bedford: E. Anthony and Sons, 1869), p. 102; Lord, Sexton and Harrington, History of the Archdiocese of Boston, I, 731-32.
[69]Lord, Sexton and Harrington, History of the Archdiocese of Boston, II, 88.
[70]Weekly Visitor, February 12, 1881.
[71]Bishop Fenwick, "Memoranda," September 5, 1837.
[72]Ibid., October 23, 1837.

he said, and reported that he but narrowly escaped a beating from one of them because he reproved the fellow with the best of reason.[73] The bishop complied with his request for a transfer and in March 1846, sent Fr. Thomas McNulty, a young priest, just ordained, to the New Bedford mission with the responsibility to look after Sandwich as well. The arrangement lasted for a year. In 1847 either financial difficulties or personal animosities prompted Fr. McNulty to move to St. Mary's, Fall River.[74]

In the 1840s the railroad reached New Bedford and brought a good number of Catholics to the town, necessitating an enlargement of the "pitiful little structure" built there twenty years before. Although now living in Fall River, Fr. McNulty continued to attend New Bedford as its pastor. Sometime early in 1849 he secured the bishop's permission to buy the Universalist meetinghouse on the corner of Fifth and School streets for use as a church. After completing the purchase in March 1849, Fr. Lariscy's church, now old and decayed, was then sold and moved and the land used for a cemetery. The new church became known as St. Mary's.[75]

Fr. McNulty was reassigned to South Boston in 1853 and Fr. Henry E. S. Henniss, a former reporter and editor, took up residence in New Bedford. After healing some wounds that had divided the parish, Fr. Henniss, in 1854, enlarged the church to double its original capacity. But even the enlarged church was inadequate and he, in time, bought land on Hallman Street as a site for a new church. Fr. Henniss suffered from consumption and in June 1857, he went to Cuba. His place was filled by Fr. Joseph Tallon. Fr. Tallon began preparations for the church but the Civil War interrupted his collecting efforts. When he died in September 1864, he left some $13,000 to his successor, Fr. Lawrence McMahon, who took up his duties in New Bedford on January 1, 1865. On November 1, 1866, Bishop Williams laid the cornerstone of another Keely-designed church. On Christmas day, 1870 St. Lawrence's opened its doors for services.[76]

By the late 1860s New Bedford had become a polygot city. Fr. McMahon's parishioners came not only from Ireland but also from French Canada and Portugal. Of the two later arriving groups, the

[73]Byrne, *Catholic Church in the New England States,* I, 452.
[74]*Ibid.*
[75]Lord, Sexton and Harrington, *History of the Archdiocese of Boston,* II, 500; Byrne, *Catholic Church in the New England States,* I, 452.
[76]Lord, Sexton and Harrington, *History of the Archdiocese of Boston,* II, 501; Byrne, *Catholic Church in the New England States,* I, 452-53; Craig, *History of the Churches in New Bedford,* pp. 103-104.

Portuguese were the more numerous. Portuguese merchants had
first settled in southeastern New England in 1658 when a group of
fifteen Sephardic Jewish families had settled in Newport, Rhode
Island as refugees from the Spanish Inquisition.[77] As noted earlier,
at least one of the members of this mercantile community which was
composed of both Spaniards and Portuguese, was a Catholic subject
of Portugal and there were possibly others. The bulk of the community was scattered during the Revolutionary War.

While Newport declined after the Revolution, the Massachusetts port of New Bedford had by the 1830s become the most prominent whaling port in the Country. Hard pressed to find in New
Bedford or Nantucket enough men willing to sign on for the long
and arduous voyages, whaling captains often put out with skeleton
crews and made for the Azores, an archipelago of nine inhabited
islands and small rock formations in the Atlantic, eight hundred
miles off the European coast. At Horta, on the island of Fayal, the
whalers could take on food and water as well as fill out their crews
with islanders who were lured to whaling either by the prospect of
adventure or as a chance to escape the poverty of the islands. Other
captains put into Brava, another island under the Portuguese crown,
in the Cape Verdean group to the south of the Azores and some 320
miles off Africa. The island's dark skinned inhabitants came to form
a minority group within the Portuguese colonies in New England.[78]

Many Portuguese crewmen sailed to New Bedford with their
ships and came to form part of the fluctuating population of single
men. Some of the Portuguese sailors settled down, working as coop-
ers or carpenters, stevedores or laborers on the docks, or at a
number of other trades or jobs and in time, sent for their families.
By 1868 there were some eight hundred Portuguese living in New
Bedford.[79]

Pastoral ministry to the Portuguese residents of New Bedford
became a particular concern of Fr. Lawrence McMahon after he
came to New Bedford as pastor in 1865. Soon after his arrival, Fr.
McMahon estimated that between one-third and one-half of his
parish was Portuguese, most of them seamen in the whaling fleet
and other enterprises. To discharge his duty towards them, he set

[77]Morris Gutstein, *The Story of the Jews in Newport* (New York: Bloch Publishing Co.,
1936).

[78]"The Portuguese Colony: Peeps at the Azores and Cape Verdi People at Fox
Point," *Providence Sunday Journal,* October 28, 1888; William Gushue, "Whaling in
New Bedford, Massachusetts and Its Decline During the Civil War" (Unpublished
seminar paper, Providence College, 1977), pp. 88-108.

[79]Zephaniah W. Pease, ed., *History of New Bedford* (New Bedford, 1906), I, 295.

out without a teacher, to learn Portuguese and learned it well enough to hear confessions and listen to their problems. For two years he wrote letter after letter to the bishops of Portugal and priestly acquaintances of some of his Portuguese parishioners in hopes of securing the assistance of a Portuguese priest.[80] In 1866 his efforts appeared about to succeed when Fr. Antonio Felisberto Diaz arrived in the city only to fall sick and die there on September 13, 1866.[81] A second Portuguese priest, a "Father Noya," is said to have come to New Bedford in 1868, but apparently stayed only a short time.[82] Finally, in January 1869, Fr. Joao Ignacio Azevedo da Encarnacao, a native of the Azores, was sent to New Bedford by the bishop of Angra at the request of Bishop Williams.[83]

Fr. Azevedo first said Mass for the Portuguese people of New Bedford on the feast of the Epiphany in January 1869, in old St. Mary's.[84] As Fr. McMahon had hoped, the zealous young priest soon brought back to the sacraments many of his compatriots who had become lax because of the strangeness of religious customs and lack of knowledge of English.[85] With Fr. Azevedo's coming, the Portuguese began worshipping as a separate congregation, but it was not until September 1871, that Bishop Williams thought their numbers large enough to create a new parish to be known initially as St. Mary's, with Fr. Azevedo as pastor. Over the years Fr. McMahon had set aside the small contributions of his Portuguese parishioners. These funds, together with the monies collected by a special committee, were used to buy land on the corner of Wing and Fifth Street (now Pleasant) as a site for a church.[86]

During these early years, the priests of New Bedford also ministered to the Catholics on the islands of Nantucket and Martha's Vineyard. The first Mass on Nantucket was said in October 1833, by Fr. Patrick Canavan, who from 1832 to 1834, had charge of the missions at Sandwich, New Bedford, and Wareham after the transfer of the district's first pastor, Fr. Connolly. Fr. McNulty made his first visit to Nantucket in 1846 and continued to go there four times a year saying Mass in the house of one of his converts, Mrs. Lucy Sullivan, and also in a building that the Sons of Temperance erected

[80]Byrne, *Catholic Church in the New England States,* II, 169.
[81]*Boston Pilot,* September 26, 1866.
[82]Francis J. Bradley, *A Brief History of the Diocese of Fall River* (Fall River, MA., 1931), pp. 30-31.
[83]Lord, Sexton and Harrington, *History of the Archdiocese of Boston,* III, 217.
[84]Byrne, *Catholic Church in the New England States,* I, 454.
[85]"St. John the Baptist Church: The First Portuguese Church in the United States, 1871-1971" (Privately printed, 1971).
[86]Byrne, *Catholic Church in the New England States,* I, 454; II, 169.

in 1846. When Fr. Hennis became pastor of New Bedford, he visited the island in the fall of 1853, and in 1854 said Mass in the Sullivan home. He continued the custom of saying Mass there four times a year and finally, on April 8, 1856, purchased Harmony Hall from David Thrain for $18,000.[87]

Fathers McNulty and Henniss also visited Martha's Vineyard, Fr. McNulty going there in 1848. In his *Notes* on this station, Fr. Henniss wrote that he went to the island on September 5, 1854, and said Mass at Holmes's Hole in Mr. Dorian's Great House. At Edgartown, according to these *Notes,* he also said the first Mass in the house of Joseph Sylva in 1854. After this he continued to minister twice a year to the forty Catholics living on the island.[88] After the creation of the Diocese of Providence, Nantucket became, or continued to be the responsibility of the pastor at Harwich, and Martha's Vineyard remained one of the missions of New Bedford. The priests at New Bedford also occasionally ministered to the Catholics in the neighboring mainland villages of Dartmouth, Fairhaven, Tisbury and Westport.[89]

Fall River also is a name that appears at an early date in the history of Catholicism in southeastern Massachusetts. Initially the first bishops of Boston seem to have designated it an area rather than a place since it included the coal pits at Portsmouth, Rhode Island. Many of the first Catholic residents of the settlement at Fall River were probably the children or relatives of the people who originally went to Portsmouth.[90] Until about 1864, when a military hospital was set up at Portsmouth Grove, Portsmouth was one of the missions of St. Mary's, Fall River.

By the 1820s Fall River's excellent hydraulic power and navigable waters began to attract industries that in turn provided jobs for Irish immigrants. In the fall of 1822, Patrick Kennedy, his wife, Helen, and their five children came to the town and became the first Catholic family to settle there. Kennedy secured a job as a watchman in the Anawan Mill in 1825 and met his death in an accident a few years later. To support herself and her children, Mrs. Kennedy started a boarding house. In 1828, when Fr. Robert Woodley came to Fall River, he offered Mass in the Kennedy's kitchen, the largest room in the house, for the twenty or so Catholics of the place.[91]

[87]Fr. Henry E. S. Henniss, "Notes on the Nantucket Mission, 1857," cited in Lord, Sexton and Harrington, *History of the Archdiocese of Boston,* II, 162, 501.

[88]*Ibid.,* II, 501-502.

[89]*Sadlier's Catholic Directory,* 1873, pp. 286-87.

[90]Harold E. Clarkin, "Pioneer Catholicism: The Life and Times of Fr. Edward Murphy, 1840-1877." A paper read before the Fall River Historical Society, May 16, 1949, p. 5.

[91]*Ibid.,* pp. 5-6.

In 1830 Fall River was one of five Massachusetts and Rhode Island towns given to the charge of Fr. John Corry. By 1835 the town's Catholic population had begun to grow and it was time to think of building a church. Purchasing a site in 1835, which was then near the boundary line dividing Rhode Island and Massachusetts but near the center of town, Fr. Corry, by August of 1837, succeeded in erecting the church of St. John the Baptist for the estimated four hundred Catholics of the briskly growing town.[92]

Since the construction of the church in Providence was not going smoothly, Bishop Fenwick sent Fr. Corry there on August 24, 1837, just a few weeks after Fr. Corry had finished overseeing the building of St. John's. From the baptismal records of the church it is clear that Fr. Corry continued to care for the spiritual needs of the people of Fall River while he labored in Providence. Occasionally Fr. Wiley from Taunton or Fr. O'Reilly from Newport visited the place when Fr. Corry could not. By November 1838, however, the rapid growth of the textile industry in the town necessitated the assignment of a full time pastor. On November 25th, Bishop Fenwick sent Fr. Richard B. Hardey, an old Maryland friend who had been serving in the Boston cathedral, to Fall River. He became the first priest to minister exclusively to the congregation of that town and its environs. Fr. Hardey stayed only until April 1840, when he returned to the cathedral. A young Irishman, Fr. Edward Murphy, just two years ordained, came to take his place and began a pastorate that was to span nearly forty years.[93]

In 1841 there were about two thousand Catholics in Fall River and Fr. Corry's church was much too small to minister to their needs. Enlisting the aid of the men of the parish who would labor on the church after finishing their day's work in the mills, Fr. Murphy enlarged the church and equipped it with a basement, sacristy and rooms for the priest. On August 30, 1840, Bishop Fenwick visited the town and dedicated the renovated church.[94] Since the church was built near the state line, its expansion put the altar and the first few pews across the line into Rhode Island. In 1862 the two states adjusted their boundaries so that the Fall River section of Tiverton became part of Massachusetts, and the town of East Providence and the Massachusetts section of Pawtucket passed to Rhode Island jurisdiction.

Within a few short years, the growth of Fall River as an industrial city, caused the church again to become overcrowded. Even

---

[92]Lord, Sexton and Harrington, *History of the Archdiocese of Boston,* II, 163-64.

[93]*Ibid.,* II, 283-84; Bradley, *A Brief History of the Diocese of Fall River, Mass.,* pp. 16-17.

[94]Bishop Fenwick, "Memoranda," August 30, 1840.

additional Masses did little to accommodate all the people who
wished to attend services. In addition, the men who initially built the
church had done a poor job or had used poor materials and by the
late 1840s, the building was rapidly deteriorating. Fr. Murphy set
out to build a new church of stone according to the best plans
Patrick Keely could draw. Again, the men of the parish contributed
their labor, and the cornerstone of the church was blessed by Bishop
Fitzpatrick of Boston on August 8, 1852. The east, west and south
walls of the new church rose slowly around the little church of St.
John's. When it came time to put the roof on, the old church was
cut in two, lengthwise, and moved to the southeast corner of Spring
and Second streets where services continued to be held until the
new church was finished. The new building was dedicated to St.
Mary of the Assumption on December 16, 1855, but was not completed until 1856.[95]

In the 1860s Fall River as well as the other cotton textile centers
in New England witnessed a remarkable expansion of production.
To secure hands for the expanding mills and for new ventures, the
millowners sent representatives to canvass for help throughout the
rural areas of the Province of Quebec. When in August 1868, Fr.
Edward Murphy, pastor of St. Mary's, Fall River, became ill a French
priest, Fr. Antoine J. Derbuel, came to the city to fill his place. Fr.
Derbuel stayed until October and while he was there, counted about
one hundred Canadian families in the city.[96]

The following April, another French priest Fr. Olivier Verdier,
whom the Bishop of Quebec had loaned to Bishop Williams, came
to assist Fr. Murphy when he again became ill. Fr. Verdier stayed
until July 1869. Convinced of the need for a second parish in Fall
River, Bishop Williams that same July sent another French missionary, again on loan from the Bishop of Quebec to found a parish for
the Canadians. Fr. Adrien de Montaubricq had already performed
a similar service for the bishop of Chicago in 1864. Arriving in Fall
River, Fr. Montaubricq found some 500 to 600 Canadian families
living principally in the vicinity of the lower end of Williams and
Division streets. The priest took up residence in Connolly's block
on Second Street and began saying Mass for the Canadians in St.
Mary's church.[97]

[95]Clarkin, "Pioneer Catholicism," pp. 11-15; Lord, Sexton and Harrington, *History of the Archdiocese of Boston*, II, 502.
[96]"St. Anne's Centennial, 1869-1969" (Privately printed, 1969). The author, Fr.
Pierre Lachance, O.P. has done considerable research on the Canadian immigration
to Fall River and has made his research available for the writing of this section; *Le
Rosaire*, June 1969, p. 13.
[97]*Le Rosaire*, June 1969, pp. 13-17.

In January 1870, the Canadians broke ground for a church at the corner of Hunter and Williams. Work on the construction of the foundation went forward rapidly so that Fr. Montaubricq was able to announce the laying of the cornerstone for his small church for March 13th. A storm delayed the ceremony one week. Some 75 to 100 people gathered for the ceremony on a platform necessitated by the eight-foot-high basement wall. The platform's supports had been laid on frozen ground which, by the time of the ceremony, had thawed causing the platform to give way, sending those on it crashing down. Fortunately, no one was seriously injured and after calm returned, the stone was laid. Fr. Montaubricq had originally intended to dedicate the church to St. Clothilde but in gratitude and recognition of St. Anne, to whom he attributed the near miraculous protection from serious injury, he decided to dedicate the church to her. Bishop Williams blessed the finished church on November 13th.[98]

Knowing that southeastern Massachusetts would soon become part of the new Diocese of Providence, Archbishop Williams, while realizing that the area's population necessitated the creation of new parishes, left this challenge to the new bishop of Providence.[99] Shortly after his ordination as bishop on April 28th, Bishop Hendricken traveled to Taunton and Fall River. He wrote in his "Diary" for June 5th that there were "beautiful churches in these cities but not enough of them." Fr. Murphy, who felt most keenly the pastoral responsibility for the now widely scattered population of Fall River, had for several years been asking Bishop Williams to establish new parishes in that city. Mills built at the extreme ends of the city created neighborhoods at considerable distance from St. Mary's which was and continues to be in the heart of Fall River. A few days after Bishop Hendricken visited the city a notice appeared in the *Fall River Evening News* that a new Catholic church was soon to be erected in the city on the lot belonging to St. Mary's church at the corner of Linden and Pine streets. "It is to be built of brick and will be somewhat larger than St. Mary's church."[100]

Bishop Hendricken returned to Fall River on Sunday, October 27, 1872, to lay the cornerstone for the new church of the Sacred Heart.[101] But, before long, dissatisfaction appeared among the people because of the site chosen and the plans for the church. Believing that the situation would best be handled by the appointment of

---

[98]*Fall River Evening News,* January 17; March 7, 19, 21, 22, 26, 1870; *Le Rosaire,* June 1969, pp. 17-19.

[99]"Catholicity in Rhode Island," *Providence Visitor,* December 22, 1895.

[100]*Fall River Evening News,* June 17, 1872.

[101]*Ibid.,* October 28, 1872.

a pastor, Bishop Hendricken, at the end of December, transferred Fr. Francis J. Quinn from North Easton to take charge of the parish and the construction of its church.[102] The following March, Bishop Hendricken together with James Murphy, a Providence architect, met with Fr. Quinn and some builders "about the security of the foundation" which had been laid and which was only one-foot below the ground. They decided to take it down and begin again.[103] On August 31, 1873, Bishop Hendricken again laid a cornerstone for the church of the Sacred Heart.[104] When late in 1874, ill health forced Fr. Quinn to resign, Fr. Mathias McCabe was transferred from Sandwich to take charge of the parish, its half-finished church and its $80,000 debt. The church was not dedicated until September 1883.[105]

Shortly after the affairs of Fr. Quinn's parish settled into some semblance of order, Bishop Hendricken on April 14, 1873, transferred Fr. William Bric from his parish in Harrisville to be the first pastor of the section of Fall River known as Mechanicsville or Bowenville as the area's name more commonly appears.[106] The area contained large Irish and French Canadian settlements. Fr. Bric, an Irishman, had studied classics in Cambrai, France and theology in Baltimore. He bought land on North Main Street and built a temporary church and a rectory while he went about the business of collecting funds for a more suitable church. On August 15, 1880, a week before Bishop Hendricken laid the cornerstone of a new church in honor of St. Joseph, Fr. Bric died. His successor, Fr. Andrew Brady, labored for five years ministering to the needs of the parish and overseeing the construction of the brick church, which was dedicated on May 30, 1885. Like Fr. Bric, he was to die before he saw the fruits of his labors.[107] From the time St. Joseph's was formed, until 1879, its pastor had responsibility for the Catholics in Somerset which lay just across the Taunton River from Fall River. At that time Somerset was an industrial center. On September 18, 1873, Fr. Bric laid the cornerstone of a small church and on November 2, 1873, Bishop Hendricken dedicated the building in honor of St. Patrick.[108]

On April 17, 1873, three days after the bishop asked Fr. Bric

[102]*Providence Visitor,* December 22, 1895.
[103]Bishop Hendricken, "Diary," March 24, 1873; *Fall River Evening News,* March 25, 1873.
[104]*Boston Pilot,* September 6, 1873.
[105]*Weekly Visitor,* October 13, 1883.
[106]Bishop Hendricken, "Diary," April 17, 1873.
[107]Byrne, *Catholic Church in the New England States,* I, 440.
[108]*Ibid.* I, 443; *Providence Evening Press,* November 1, 1873.

to build a new parish in the northern part of Fall River, he officially assigned Fr. John Kelly, an assistant of Fr. Grace in Newport, the responsibility of building a parish in the Globe section of the city.[109] Seemingly even before he received his appointment, Fr. Kelly had arranged to lease for a year, a vacant building on South Main Street, known as the "broom factory," for use as a meeting place for Mass.[110] In 1874 the parish built a wooden church dedicated to St. Patrick which would suffice until they raised the money for a building worthy of the name. Like his brother priests in Rhode Island, Fr. Kelly's efforts at raising funds were hampered by the panic and depression. But Fr. Kelly was a most economical man whose one desire was to provide funds for the new church whose cornerstone was laid on September 18, 1881.[111] Fr. Kelly died on January 15, 1885, with the church yet unfinished but with sufficient funds in the treasury to see the work well along. Fr. Thomas Grace succeeded him and saw the church finished and dedicated in 1889.[112]

Farther north from Fall River along the Taunton River, the building of the Taunton Manufacturing Company's immense plant after 1823 attracted numbers of Irish Catholics to the place. When in 1828 Fr. Woodley made a tour of the leading towns of southeastern Massachusetts, he visited Taunton on Sunday, February 19th, where he probably said Mass for the first time for the eighty or so Catholics he found there. After this, he continued to visit the town about once every two months, officiating in a rented schoolhouse. Many of the Irish there apparently were skilled laborers employed in the Print Works for they seem to have been more well to do and more enterprising than most groups their size. By June 1830, they were petitioning Bishop Fenwick for permission to build a church. At that time Taunton was part of the charge of Fr. John Corry who made the building of a church there his first concern. Fr. Corry came to live in the town and on June 24, 1831, purchased land for the church. On October 28, 1832, Bishop Fenwick dedicated the neat wooden gothic church of St. Mary's and paid tribute to the one hundred and fifty or so Catholics whose efforts went into its construction.[113]

In August 1837, Fr. Corry went to Providence and Fr. William

[109]Bishop Hendricken, "Diary," April 17, 1873.
[110]*Fall River Evening News,* April 16, 1873.
[111]Bishop Hendricken, "Diary," September 18, 1881.
[112]Byrne, *Catholic Church in the New England States,* I, 439-40.
[113]Lord, Sexton and Harrington, *History of the Archdiocese of Boston,* II, 87-88, 163; Byrne, *Catholic Church in the New England States,* I, 443; [Maydell Murphy], "All in the Family: An informal sketch of St. Mary's Parish, 1828-1958" (Taunton, MA., 1959).

Wiley came to live in Taunton as its resident pastor. The increasing
number of Catholics prompted Fr. Wiley in 1838 to enlarge the
church. However, the growth of the community was checked shortly
after as a depression settled on the town.[114] When in January of
1842, Fr. Wiley was made pastor of St. Patrick's in Providence, there
was a brief outburst of opposition to the appointment of his successor, Fr. Dennis Ryan.[115] The feeling died down and the people
accepted the "new" priest although as it turned out, he did not stay
long. Towards the end of 1842, he was succeeded by Fr. John
O'Beirne.

By 1846 Fr. Corry's church was in a terribly dilapidated condition. When Bishop Fitzpatrick discovered this, he ordered Fr. Richard A. Wilson, who had replaced Fr. O'Beirne as pastor in the
summer of 1846, to make only necessary repairs on the building and
to begin preparations to build a new church. Land opposite the old
site was purchased in February 1848, and a year later construction
began. Shabby workmanship, however, soon resulted in tragedy.
On December 1, 1849, just after the carpenter had put on the roof,
a high wind completely wrecked the structure. The people put the
blame on the architect in charge who happened to be Bishop Fitzpatrick's brother-in-law. The anger of the people created an impossible
situation for Fr. Wilson who was forced to give up his charge on
February 5, 1850. For two years the parish was without the services
of a priest.[116]

Early in 1852 Fr. Daniel Hearne, who had come out to collect
for the Catholic University of Ireland and decided to stay in the
diocese, was assigned to the embittered Taunton parish. His mission, besides Taunton proper, included East Taunton, Mid-
dleborough, Norton, Westville, North and South Dighton. Fr.
Hearne tried to persuade the parish to accept the new church which
had been rebuilt but they refused. In June 1854, yet another church
was begun with Keely as architect. It was to be an exact counterpart
of St. Mary's church, Taunton, England, but due to controversy,
financial problems, and legal complications, it would take eighteen
years to construct. On June 1, 1856, the old church burnt to the
ground and a temporary structure had to be built. Ill health caused
Fr. Hearne to leave the parish in 1864, and Fr. Thomas H. Shahan

[114]Lord, Sexton and Harrington, *History of the Archdiocese of Boston,* II, 166.
[115]Bishop Fenwick, "Memoranda," January 17, 21, 1842.
[116]Lord, Sexton and Harrington, *History of the Archdiocese of Boston,* II, 503; Byrne,
Catholic Church in the New England States, I, 444-45. Fr. Sexton corrects Byrne's work
which states that Bishop Fitzpatrick at this time had placed the church under interdict.

of Salem came to replace him on January 1, 1865. Fr. Shahan stopped all construction work while he applied himself to the reduction of the parish's $80,000 debt. In 1871 Fr. Edward Sheridan succeeded him and oversaw the completion of the church and its dedication by Bishop Hendricken on November 3, 1872.[117]

Industrial growth in Taunton and in neighboring towns also meant an increased population necessitating division of the parish. On April 17, 1873, the same day as he noted in his "Diary" the establishment of two new parishes in Fall River, Bishop Hendricken officially assigned Fr. Hugh J. Smyth, Fr. Sheridan's assistant at St. Mary's, Taunton, to be the pastor of the Weir section of Taunton and to take temporary charge of East Taunton.[118] East Taunton or Squawbetty had been a mission of St. Mary's since at least 1855 when the church of the Holy Family was built. Fr. Smyth's responsibility also included the Catholics in the Dightons and Myricks, villages to the south and southwest of Taunton. Norton, to the northwest of Taunton, where Mass was said on a monthly basis by the priests from St. Mary's at least since 1852, would continue to be their responsibility for another year.

Initially, Fr. Smyth said Mass in the Staples Block on West Water Street, but after purchasing the old district school on First Street, he had the building renovated and enlarged to serve as a church. The diocese's vicar general, Fr. Lawrence McMahon, dedicated the building to the Sacred Heart on November 15, 1874.[119]

Closer to the Rhode Island border, Fr. Philip Gilleck had been giving his full attention to Attleboro and the missions at Wrentham, Walpole and Mansfield since he left Greenville and settled in North Attleboro about 1866.[120] Ill health forced Fr. Gilleck to retire on June 31, 1874, and his replacement, Fr. Edward J. Mongan, was appointed on February 16, 1874.[121]

In 1877 Fr. Mongan abandoned the old church near Peck's Mountain in Falls Village and bought the Tifft estate in North Attleboro where there was an octagonal stone barn that he remodeled for a church.[122] Sometime in 1874 Fr. Mongan took charge of St. Mary's in Norton and that same year ground was broken for a

---

[117]Lord, Sexton and Harrington, *History of the Archdiocese of Boston*, II, 503-504; Byrne, *Catholic Church in the New England States*, I, 445.

[118]Bishop Hendricken, "Diary," April 17, 1873.

[119]Byrne, *Catholic Church in the New England States*, I, 445; *Taunton Daily Gazette*, August 11, 1960.

[120]Lord, Sexton and Harrington, *History of the Archdiocese of Boston*, II, 506.

[121]Byrne, *Catholic Church in the New England States*, I, 448; Bishop Hendricken, "Diary," February 16, 1874.

[122]Bradley, *A Brief History of the Diocese of Fall River, Mass.*, p. 35.

church between Hebronville and Dodgeville on land donated by the
Hebronville Manufacturing Company in 1872.[123] Mass was first said
in the unfinished basement on Christmas day, 1874. The building
was completed and dedicated to St. Stephen the following summer.[124] By 1880 the number of Catholics in the two villages, among
whom were many Canadians, had increased enough to justify sending a priest each Sunday to offer Mass. The mission was given to St.
Joseph's in Pawtucket perhaps to give the priests in North Attleboro
the opportunity to open a new mission in the east village or Attleboro proper.[125] Mansfield, where St. Mary's church was built in
1871 and dedicated the following year, continued to be a mission
of Attleboro after the division of the diocese.

To the northeast of the Attleboros, the town of Easton first
welcomed a priest when Fr. Connolly, then pastor of Sandwich,
visited North Easton about 1832 on a tour of factory towns in the
area. Mass was not said regularly at least until 1840, when Fr. Wiley
from Taunton first offered Mass for about fifteen Catholics of the
place. After that, services were held with some regularity at the
Ames Company's boarding house.[126] In 1851, the Ames Company
gave the land by the side of the pond on which Fr. Terrence Fitzsim-
mons, the pastor of South Boston, who had charge of the town, built
a church under the name of the Immaculate Conception. In June
1853, North Easton and Bridgewater became part of a new mission
under Fr. Aaron F. Roche. In 1856, in a general revision of assignments, Fr. Thomas B. McNulty was sent to Easton but took up his
residence in North Bridgewater (now Brockton). In 1864, Fr.
McNulty bought land for a new and larger church in which he
celebrated the first Mass a year later. In 1871, Bishop Williams made
the place a parish and sent Fr. Francis Quinn to be its pastor.[127] On
August 18, 1871, when Bishop Hendricken visited Easton to give
first communion and confirm, he dedicated the new church to the
Blessed Virgin. At that time, nearly all the Catholics of the town
worked in Ames's shovel works while the younger people worked in
the shoe factories of Brockton.[128]

In the Cape Cod section of the new diocese, Sandwich was,
along with New Bedford and Fall River, among the oldest mission

---

[123]*Providence Journal,* October 27, 1874.

[124]Bishop Hendricken, "Diary," August 30, 1875.

[125]Byrne, *Catholic Church in the New England States,* I, 450.

[126]William L. Chaffin, *History of the Town of Easton, Massachusetts* (Cambridge: John
Wilson & Son, 1886), pp. 413-14; Byrne, *Catholic Church in the New England States,* I,
449.

[127]Lord, Sexton and Harrington, *History of the Archdiocese of Boston,* II, 162, 272,
494.

[128]Byrne, *Catholic Church in the New England States,* I, 447-48.

centers. Fr. William Tyler visited the place in September 1829, shortly after his ordination and in March 1830, he was there again on a sick call.[129] In 1825, Deming Jarves had begun to use the sands of Sandwich as raw material for the manufacture of glass. He recruited his operatives largely from the Irish glassblowers of East Cambridge and within a short time about a score of Catholic families had settled there.[130]

The seventy Catholics in Sandwich asked the bishop on his visit there in June 1830, to build a church and send a priest. After the people raised $600 with which to purchase a lot, the bishop had a small forty by thirty foot frame church built in Boston and sent down by water. Then, on September 19, 1830, after a rough passage by packet, the bishop dedicated the little church under the patronage of St. Peter.[131] On October 2nd the newly ordained Fr. Peter Connolly was sent to Sandwich to take charge of the church and with it, all of Cape Cod. Wareham, where the nail factories were drawing immigrants, and New Bedford were also part of the mission. Fr. Connolly also extended his concern to the factory towns of Easton, Foxboro and Walpole to the west.[132]

In November 1832, Bishop Fenwick decided to change the boundaries of the mission and its pastor. After visiting Sandwich and its neighboring towns with Fr. Connolly and his replacement, Fr. Patrick Canavan, the bishop redrew the mission boundaries to include only Wareham and New Bedford. The bishop remarked in his "Memoranda" that "the Catholics in all these places were mostly single people who come and go and have no attachment to any residence."[133] When hard times came to the glass industry after 1834, Fr. Francis Kiernan, who succeeded Fr. Canavan in July 1834, reported to the bishop the following January that there were only thirty-four Catholics at Sandwich and the same number at Wareham.[134] Fr. John Brady took charge of the district in 1835 but in 1837 Fr. Kiernan was back again. In 1839 and for a few years afterwards, the Cape Cod area became part of the mission of Newport and was looked after by a succession of priests from other missions.[135] About 1847 the glass industry rebounded and Fr. William Moran was sent to take residence as pastor of Sandwich and the

---

[129]Bishop Fenwick, "Memoranda," September 4, 1830.
[130]Raymond B. Bourgoin, *The Catholic Church in Sandwich, 1830-1930* (Boston: E. L. Grimes Pub. Co., 1930), p. 6.
[131]Bishop Fenwick, "Memoranda," September 18, 19, 1830.
[132]Lord, Sexton and Harrington, *History of the Archdiocese of Boston,* II, 84, 89-90, 162; Byrne, *Catholic Church in the New England States,* I, 456-57.
[133]Bishop Fenwick, "Memoranda," November 6, 1832.
[134]*Ibid.,* January 14, 1835.
[135]Lord, Sexton and Harrington, *History of the Archdiocese of Boston,* II, 284.

Cape villages. He attended eleven stations scattered along the
Cape. In 1854 he began to build a new church at Sandwich but for
some years it remained unfinished and unused. In 1864 Fr. Peter
Bertoldi was placed in charge of Sandwich. He finished the church
and it opened for services on May 14, 1865. Bishop McFarland
visited Sandwich on June 18, 1865 to formally dedicate the church.
The Catholics of Wareham had for many years attended Mass in
halls hired for the occasion, but on August 14th Fr. Bertoldi acquired a Baptist church which came to be called St. Patrick's. In
October, he bought land on the Cape at Harwich where, with the
considerable assistance of Mr. Patrick Dunn, he built the church of
the Holy Trinity in 1866. By 1868, the growing Catholic population
on the outer Cape caused Archbishop Williams to divide the parish.
By September, Fr. Thomas Sheehan had taken up his residence
there to take charge of the territory extending from Yarmouth to
Provincetown. The next year Fr. Sheehan was replaced by Fr. Cornelius O'Connor.[136]

Mass had first been said at Provincetown in August 1852, for
a congregation of Irish fishermen. On that occasion, Fr. Joseph
Finotti had come down from Boston to give a mission to the Irishmen. In January 1854, he returned and took the opportunity to buy
a house on a large lot of land that he and other priests who visited
the mission used as a residence and as a place for Mass. After 1864
the mission became the responsibility of the pastor at Sandwich.[137]

After the creation of the Diocese of Providence, Bishop Hendricken, on July 8, 1872, sent Fr. Henry Kinnerney "to take charge
of Sandwich for a few days" until he could decide on a priest to
replace Fr. Bertoldi who had resigned. Shortly after coming to
Sandwich Fr. Kinnerney wrote the bishop that there were six hundred Catholics in Sandwich and four hundred in Wareham.[138] Fr.
Kinnerney's "few days" stretched out to more than a year. In November 1872, the bishop sent Fr. Edward Mongan as assistant to Fr.
Kinnerney. Together, the priests were given responsibility not only
for Sandwich but also for the Catholics at Falmouth, Nantucket
Island, Orleans, Tisbury, Wellfleet, Wareham, Wood's Hole and
Yarmouth.[139] In January 1874, Fr. Kinnerney was called to assume
the pastorate of St. Joseph's in Pawtucket and Fr. Mathias McCabe

[136]Bourgoin, *The Catholic Church in Sandwich,* pp. 25-26; Lord, Sexton and Harrington, *History of the Archdiocese of Boston,* II, 499.
[137]"St. Peter the Apostle Church, Provincetown, The First Hundred Years, 1874-
1974" (Privately printed, 1974).
[138]Bishop Hendricken, "Diary," July 15, 1872.
[139]*Sadlier's Catholic Directory,* 1874, pp. 294-95.

came down to Sandwich to succeed him. Fr. McCabe soon informed the bishop of his disappointment with his assignment. Bishop Hendricken let him stay there a few months but in November 1874, he gave him a larger city parish and sent Fr. Andrew Brady to take charge of Sandwich.[140] In March 1874, the people in St. Patrick's, Wareham, petitioned the bishop for a pastor of their own, but he evidently felt the time was not right to establish a separate parish and refused their request.[141]

In Cape Cod's other parish at Holy Trinity in Harwich, Fr. Cornelius O'Connor's ministry was not as successful. Wishing to learn more about the situation in the parish, Bishop Hendricken, on September 20, 1873, sent his Vicar General, Fr. McMahon, to see Fr. O'Connor and to investigate the situation. The report he received evidently prompted his decision on October 15, 1873, to send Fr. John McGeough, the assistant at St. Mary's, Fall River, to replace Fr. O'Connor. Apparently Fr. O'Connor soon left the diocese and Holy Trinity again became one of the missions of Sandwich.[142]

Ministry to the French Canadians

While Bishop Hendricken during the first years of his episcopacy was concerned with continuing the task of parish building begun by Bishop McFarland, he soon had to face a problem that Bishop McFarland had wrestled with but only partially solved—providing ministry to the increasing number of French Canadian Catholics in Rhode Island. Bishop McFarland had only minimal success in recruiting French Canadian clergy for his diocese because the Canadian bishops lacked enough priests to serve their own needs. Beginning in the 1870s, increasing numbers of French Canadian priests began to volunteer for service in American dioceses, but their numbers were still too small to meet the need.

The first French Canadian priest who offered his assistance to Bishop Hendricken was Rev. Charles Dauray. Ordained less than two years, he came to the Pawtucket area in the fall of 1872 at his brother's invitation to rest and recover his health. A day or two after his arrival in Pawtucket, Fr. Dauray called on Fr. Patrick Delaney at St. Mary's to request permission to offer Mass in his church. Fr.

[140]Bishop Hendricken, "Diary," January 21, 23; November 18, 1874.
[141]*Ibid.*, March 4, 1874.
[142]*Ibid.*, September 20; October 15, 1873.

Delaney gladly gave permission and extended as well an invitation to have breakfast after Mass before he walked the considerable distance back to his brother's home in the village of Central Falls. According to Fr. Dauray's biographer, this invitation to breakfast carried the seeds of significant events.[143]

One morning as Fathers Delaney and Dauray sat at the table, Fr. Delaney reportedly spoke of his concern for the spiritual welfare of the Canadians in his parish. Fr. Henry Spruyt, a Belgian who had served as assistant in St. Mary's, had gone to the cathedral and his place was taken by Fr. John Keegan, a young priest ordained the previous July in the major seminary in Montreal. With some fluency in French and acquaintance with Canadian customs, Fr. Keegan could provide a minimum of care for the Canadians although apparently there was not a Mass offered in Pawtucket where the sermon was preached in French.

It was common for a pastor to invite a visiting cleric to offer one of the Sunday Masses in a busy parish. Fr. Delaney thought rather to ask Fr. Dauray to offer a special Mass for the French Canadians in the area. When his guest consented, word quickly spread that Mass would be celebrated in St. Mary's by a Canadian priest. On the designated Sunday, St. Mary's was filled. Impressed by the turnout, Fr. Delaney asked his guest to hold a retreat for the Canadians and again Fr. Dauray obliged. The retreat served both to call back to worship many of those French Canadians who had been absenting themselves from services and to show by the numbers of those who attended the exercises that the Canadians were numerous enough for a parish of their own. Shortly after the retreat was over, several leaders among the Canadians approached Fr. Delaney about establishing a parish and securing Fr. Dauray as their pastor.

Fr. Delaney informed Bishop Hendricken of Fr. Dauray's work and a few days later a delegation of French Canadians from the Pawtucket area called on the bishop with their request and the assurance that they were ready to support both church and priest. Bishop Hendricken received them cordially and listened with interest, but cautioned them on the financial difficulties involved. Not wishing to make a decision on the spot, the bishop promised to give their request serious consideration.

While these events were taking place, Fr. Dauray, his health improved, was preparing to return to Canada. Before he went, he

---

[143]Ambrose Kennedy, *Quebec to New England: The Life of Monsignor Charles Dauray* (Boston: Bruce Humphries, Inc., 1948), pp. 44-54. The biography is undocumented but appears to be accurate.

called on Bishop Hendricken to thank him for his kindness. At the close of their meeting the bishop invited Fr. Dauray to remain in the diocese. He spoke of his desire to help the Canadians but also of his conviction that they were too poor to maintain a parish. He asked Fr. Dauray to stay until the people realized this themselves. While it was possibly true that the French Canadians had contributed little to the support of the parishes where they lived, Fr. Dauray realized that the problem lay not with their poverty or lack of generosity but with the difference between the American and Canadian customs of supporting their churches. In Canada, many of the parish churches were endowed and the people were accustomed to contributing little to their support. Furthermore, Canadian parishioners had a greater voice in their parish affairs than the Irish had. Fr. Dauray believed that once the Canadians understood the American system, they would willingly support a pastor. Aware too, that he was in part responsible for creating the situation the bishop was now trying to deal with, Fr. Dauray asked for twenty-four hours to consider the matter. After stopping later that day to talk the matter over with Fr. Delaney, Fr. Dauray made up his mind to stay and returned to Providence the next day to tell the bishop. Gratified at his decision, Bishop Hendricken assured him of his confidence in him and approved in advance whatever he might do. Fr. Dauray returned to Canada for two months to say his good-byes and wind up his affairs there before beginning his new work.

In September 1873, Fr. Dauray assumed, according to the *Catholic Directory*, "temporary charge" of the French in Pawtucket and Central Falls.[144] At first he offered Mass in Armory Hall on Exchange Street in Pawtucket while the Canadians searched for a suitable site for a church. By March 1874, the new pastor bought land on Fales Street in Central Falls and later contracted with Henry Page of Woonsocket to build a church. The cornerstone was laid on September 13th and the new church was solemnly dedicated under the title of Notre Dame du Sacre Coeur on October 2, 1875.[145]

On November 12th, a few weeks after the dedication, Bishop Hendricken sent Fr. Dauray to Woonsocket and a newly ordained priest, Fr. A. Leon Bouland, came to fill Fr. Dauray's place.[146] Fr. Bouland was born in Lyons, France, and had only served a few

---

[144]*Sadlier's Catholic Directory*, 1874, p. 294.

[145]*Central Falls Weekly Visitor*, July 3, 1874; *Weekly Visitor*, October 9; November 7, 1875; Bishop Hendricken, "Diary," September 13, 1874, October 2, 1875; "Notre Dame Church: The Seed Has Grown to Harvest" (Hackensack, N.J.: Custombooks, 1974), p. 5.

[146]Bishop Hendricken, "Diary," November 12, 1875.

232 Catholicism in Rhode Island

months as an assistant in Woonsocket when he received his assignment. The priest served the parish until June 1880, when an Irish-American priest, Fr. Charles Mahoney, took charge of the parish and Fr. Bouland went on to a rather colorful career in the Boston diocese.

Fr. Dauray's assignment as pastor of the French parish in Woonsocket was to prove a test of his abilities as administrator and mediator. The French Canadians in Woonsocket had initially worshipped in St. Charles parish where a French-speaking assistant had ministered to their needs since 1866. By 1875 the French Canadians in Woonsocket made up at least a quarter of the town's total population of 13,543. It was obvious that St. Charles, even enlarged as it was, could not accommodate their numbers since there was need for two French Masses. Sometime in early 1872 Fr. McCabe, the pastor of St. Charles, arranged that the monies collected at the French services would be set aside for the day when the Canadians could purchase land and build a church.[147]

There was among the French Canadians a faction, of which Dr. Gideon Archambault was a leader, which dearly wanted to recreate the type of parish and be served by the kind of priest that they had known in Canada.[148] In its desire for a separate parish this group had the support of the majority of the Canadians and continued to ask Bishop Hendricken to address their need for a separate parish. In March 1873, the bishop finally yielded to their request and appointed Fr. Antoine Bernard, the French Canadian assistant at St. Charles, the first pastor of the Canadians in Woonsocket. French Canadian leaders, anticipating the bishop's decision, had already arranged to hold services in the large hall owned by the Harris Woolen Company on North Main Street.[149]

The parishioners considered two sites for their new church. They first thought of building on Hamlet Avenue near Bernon village, but then they had an opportunity to buy what was for them a more attractive site on the corner of Earle and Social streets. However, Bishop Hendricken probably thought the price was beyond their means and instead approved the purchase of the land on Hamlet Avenue in August 1873.[150] Soon thereafter, the men of the parish began excavating for the basement but the work did not progress very far.[151]

[147]*Providence Journal,* March 31, 1873.
[148]Robert Rumilly, *Histoire des Franco-Americains* (Woonsocket: L'Union Saint-Jean-Baptiste D'Amerique, 1958), p. 63.
[149]*Providence Journal,* March 27, 31, 1873.
[150]*Ibid.,* April 25, 1873; *Woonsocket Patriot,* May 9, 1873.
[151]*Providence Evening Press,* June 3, 1874.

The Panic of 1873 dealt another severe blow to the textile workers who had just recently returned to work following a strike to protest reduction of their daily working hours. As a result of the work stoppages, many French Canadians returned home until times got better.[152] The bishop visited Woonsocket on April 21, 1874, to assess the situation first hand.[153] A month later Bishop Hendricken assigned Fr. James Berkins from Slatersville to be the parish's second pastor, while Fr. Bernard went on to St. James in Manville. In June, masons began work on the basement and by October, work had progressed to the point where the basement could be used for Mass.[154] Bishop Hendricken, amid considerable ceremony, came on October 25, 1874, to bless the cornerstone of the church of the Precious Blood.[155]

Fr. Berkins, born in the Duchy of Limburg, a province of Belgium, and supposedly of Irish descent, found a cold welcome among the group in Woonsocket that had originally pressed for a separate parish. Some refused to attend his Masses or contribute to his support. The dissatisfaction culminated on the night of September 1, 1875, when someone hung an effigy of the pastor in the church yard. The next Sunday, Bishop Hendricken came up to Woonsocket to discuss the situation with the parishioners.[156] The bishop listened to their complaints but refused to transfer Fr. Berkins under pressure. After the dissidents returned to their "good behavior," the bishop consented in November 1875, to move Fr. Berkins to the parish in Georgiaville and brought Fr. Dauray from Central Falls to be the next pastor of Precious Blood.[157] In speaking of Fr. Berkins's change of assignment in its November 6th issue, the *Visitor* expressed what was probably Bishop Hendricken's own view of the situation in Woonsocket:

> Fr. James Berkins, the respected pastor of the French parish, Woonsocket, will go to another field of labor next week. During the time he ministered to this congregation, he labored with great zeal and leaves as a monument to his work, as beautiful a church as there is in the diocese. The French congregation of Woonsocket may find a more eloquent priest, perhaps, but we doubt if another can have their true interests more at heart than the good priest who leaves them.[158]

[152]*Providence Journal*, May 9, 1873; *Woonsocket Patriot*, December 5, 1873.
[153]Bishop Hendricken, "Diary," April 21, 1874.
[154]*Providence Evening Press*, June 3, 1874; *Woonsocket Patriot*, October 9, 1874.
[155]*Woonsocket Patriot*, October 30, 1874.
[156]Bishop Hendricken, "Diary," September 2, 3, 4, 5, 1875; *Woonsocket Patriot*, September 10, 1875.
[157]Bishop Hendricken, "Diary," September 10, 1875; *Providence Journal*, December 1, 17, 1875.
[158]*Weekly Visitor*, November 6, 1875.

Under Fr. Dauray, construction of the church proceeded and was nearly finished when, on February 2, 1876, a winter gale roared through Woonsocket, ripping the roof off the structure.[159] The loss stunned the people but did not quench their desire to finish their church. The Canadians used the basement of St. Charles while they repaired the storm-caused damage. They were able to reoccupy the basement again by the beginning of March.[160] Undaunted but burdened with heavy debt, the people of Precious Blood completed the church and witnessed its dedication on July 17, 1881.[161]

Besides Woonsocket, French Canadians settled early in the Pawtuxet Valley in the western part of the town of Warwick. By the 1870s the Canadians in the village along the Pawtuxet also numbered in the thousands. In November 1871, Bishop McFarland granted Fr. Gibson's request for a French-speaking assistant and assigned the newly arrived Fr. James Berkins to Crompton. When one Sunday, a year later, Fr. Berkins failed to appear at a Mass he was scheduled to offer and preach at, a number of French Canadians gathered after Mass under the pines besides St. Mary's and decided to ask Bishop Hendricken for a priest and parish of their own. They formed a committee to push their plan and obtain signatures among the French Canadians in the valley.[162]

The committee wasted no time in calling on Fr. Gibson to inform him of their plans. Fr. Gibson was not surprised at their request, he rather had anticipated it. He promised his support and his intercession with the bishop.[163] All this apparently happened at the end of 1872, for in his "Diary" on January 9, 1873, the bishop wrote, "Fr. Spruyt to be pastor of French at Crompton." Fr. Henry Spruyt, like Fr. Berkins, had come from Belgium and was of Flemish descent. Archbishop Martin J. Spalding of Baltimore had written to Bishop McFarland in December 1870, expressing his reservations regarding Fr. Spruyt.[164] Evidently Fr. Spruyt had served well enough as an assistant and the services of French-speaking priests were badly needed. Tradition has it that Fr. Gibson called a meeting of the French in Odd Fellows Hall in Riverpoint to introduce Fr. Spruyt to his new parishioners.[165] The parish numbered about two thousand and by the first part of January had raised some $5,000.[166]

---

[159]*Providence Journal*, February 3, 1876; *Woonsocket Patriot*, February 4, 1876.
[160]*Weekly Visitor*, March 4, 1876; *Woonsocket Patriot*, March 10, 1876.
[161]*Weekly Visitor*, July 23, 1881; Bishop Hendricken, "Diary," July 17, 1881.
[162]*Providence Evening Telegram*, March 19, 1911.
[163]Harpin, *Trumpets in Jericho*, pp. 88-90; "St. John the Baptist Church: Faith and Sacrifice Build a Parish." (Hackensack, N.J.: Custombook, 1974), pp. 9-13.
[164]Archbishop M. J. Spalding to Bishop McFarland, December 1, 1870, UNDA.
[165]Harpin, *Trumpets in Jericho*, p. 90.
[166]*Boston Pilot*, January 11, 1873.

Construction of a church probably got under way on a site on Quidneck (now Washington) Street with the coming of good weather. During construction, services were held in the Odd Fellows Hall. Progress on the church was slow. Many of the French Canadians in the Pawtuxet Valley worked in the Sprague mills which stopped when the company went bankrupt in the late fall of 1873. While the mills did resume operation within a short time and actually expanded, a strike in April 1875 against wage cuts only added to the problems of raising funds for the church. By July 1874, the upper part of the church was raised and partly boarded and in October, enough was complete to allow Mass to be celebrated in the basement.[167] On Sunday, October 18, 1874, Bishop Hendricken came down to Arctic and laid the cornerstone.[168]

During his pastorate Fr. Spruyt met with what a local paper described as "some trouble in church affairs," trouble that again centered with the continued desire of the Canadians of Arctic to have a priest of their own nationality. The weakness that Archbishop Spalding had warned of struck Fr. Spruyt in September 1878 when he temporarily suffered a mental breakdown.[169] Fr. George Mahoney served the parish while the ailing priest recovered. Fr. Spruyt returned to the parish in May 1879, only to be stricken a second time. On July 26, 1879, Fr. Spruyt resigned as pastor and Fr. Mahoney continued in temporary charge of the parish.[170] Following Fr. Spruyt's death that August, Bishop Hendricken appointed an Irishman, Fr. James Smith, to be the parish's second pastor. Following his resignation from his pastorate at Sacred Heart in Pawtucket, Fr. Smith had served as an assistant in Taunton and for over a year as an assistant to Fr. Dauray in Woonsocket. It was under Fr. Smith that the church was completed and formally dedicated in honor of St. John the Baptist on June 20, 1880.[171]

Sometime after 1870 new mill construction brought an influx of French Canadians into Natick, a small village on the Pawtuxet in Warwick. Despite the fact that the state census of 1875 was taken after a strike and a shutdown of the mills that forced many of the village's inhabitants to move away, there were still 330 of English, Scottish and Irish parentage and 749 of French Canadian parentage recorded as residents of the village. In 1873, at about the same time as construction began on the church in Arctic, Fr. Spruyt estab-

167 *Providence Journal*, July 24; October 18, 1874.
168 Bishop Hendricken, "Diary," October 18, 1874; *Providence Visitor*, October 17, 1935.
169 *Rhode Island Pendulum*, September 13, 1878.
170 Bishop Hendricken, "Diary," May 18; July 26, 1879.
171 *Ibid.*, June 20, 1880; *Pawtuxet Valley Gleanor*, June 26, 1880.

lished a small chapel in Natick near the railroad depot. In March 1875, a delegation of men from Natick and nearby Pontiac called on Bishop Hendricken to ask for a resident pastor. On June 26th the bishop acted on the request by combining the two congregations of the village—the French and the Irish—into one parish. Fr. John Couch of Phenix had begun building a church in Natick in 1870. As pastor, the bishop assigned a Canadian priest, Fr. Napoleon Rivier. He was also to serve temporarily as an assistant in the cathedral.[172] The Canadian chapel was boarded up and both the Irish and French attended Mass in the basement of Fr. Couch's unfinished church. Fr. Rivier offered Mass at different times for each community, preaching once in French and once in English.[173] Among the responsibilities of the new pastor were the Catholics at the State Farm at Howard. Bishop Hendricken apparently made the first visit there to offer Mass in October 1874. Fr. Rivier thereafter made weekly visits to the farm.[174]

In November 1882, the Canadian priest went to Wittenden, Massachusetts to take charge of a new parish there, and Fr. Patrick McGee, a recent graduate of the Grand Seminary at Montreal, came to Natick. Fr. McGee served until October 1884, when Fr. James Gleason was appointed pastor. During all this time the Natick church remained uncompleted. After Fr. William Meenan became pastor on July 18, 1887, he enlarged the original foundation and, aided in particular by the Knight family who owned the Natick mills, built and on April 20, 1890, dedicated the new church of St. Joseph.[175] It is evident from the baptismal records of the parish that after Fr. Rivier left, many of the French Canadians ceased attending Mass at St. Joseph's and went instead to St. John's in Arctic.

The first French Canadian family had settled in Providence in the early 1860s and made their home on Eddy Street, near the old steam mill. This section of the cathedral parish became the "French colony" until the 1870s. The building of the new woolen mills in the Olneyville district attracted many French Canadians to that locality where they soon formed a sizable part of the population.[176]

In May 1873, Bishop Hendricken brought Fr. Spruyt from Pawtucket to the cathedral where he served until the end of the year when the bishop sent him to Arctic as pastor. In September 1873,

[172]Bishop Hendricken, "Diary," March 2; June 26, 1875.
[173]Fuller, *The History of Warwick*, p. 375.
[174]Bishop Hendricken, "Diary," October 4, 1874.
[175]*Providence Visitor*, December 10, 1881; Byrne, *Catholic Church in the New England States*, I, 425.
[176]"Tour of the Nations," *Providence Sunday Telegram*, December 27, 1903.

Fr. Napoleon Hardy arrived in Providence "on trial," and took up duties in the cathedral parish.[177] Bishop Hendricken, on February 8, 1874, created a new parish for the French Canadians of Providence with Fr. Hardy as pastor. Initially, it was known as St. John the Baptist parish. The bishop at that time estimated the number of French Canadians to be about fifteen hundred but that figure proved grossly exaggerated.[178]

Fr. Hardy gathered the French Canadians for Mass in St. Ann's chapel in the Christian Brothers' Academy on Fountain Street. Sometime after April 23, 1876, the date of his last baptism in Providence, Fr. Hardy left the city for service in the Diocese of Portland.[179] In the Catholic directories for both 1877 and 1878 there is no mention of the parish. Quite possibly the depression had significantly reduced the size of the parish. In any case, there is no further mention of ministry to the French Canadians of Providence until April 1878, when Fr. L. G. Gagnier of Springfield preached a mission in the Fountain Street chapel during which five hundred people received communion.[180] Probably, the mission demonstrated the need for finding another priest to minister to the French. Accordingly, Fr. Dauray secured the services of Fr. Charles Gaboury who took charge of the congregation in August 1878.[181]

There were reportedly about one hundred families in the parish when Fr. Gaboury arrived.[182] But when in July 1879, Bishop Hendricken visited the French in St. Ann's chapel to confirm their children, he counted some two hundred families. The increase was not the result of immigration but of the zeal of Fr. Gaboury. The *Visitor* remarked on that occasion that "many are beginning to attend to religious duties who had previously neglected them."[183] The increasing numbers attending services soon caused the little chapel to be overcrowded but indicated also their ability to build a church. In January 1880, the parish held a fair as part of their effort to raise necessary funds.[184] By November 1880, Fr. Gaboury had purchased land on Harrison Street between Olneyville and West Elmwood near the present day Cranston Street Armory and on July 10, 1881, Bishop Hendricken dedicated the wooden church in honor of St. Charles. The *Visitor* described the men who formed the

---

[177]Bishop Hendricken, "Diary," September 24, 1873.
[178]Byrne, *Catholic Church in the New England States,* I, 406.
[179]*Weekly Visitor,* July 15, 1876.
[180]*Ibid.,* April 14, 1878.
[181]Kennedy, *Quebec to New England,* p. 90.
[182]*Weekly Visitor,* July 16, 1881.
[183]*Ibid.,* July 19, 1879.
[184]*Ibid.,* January 31, 1880.

core of the parish at that time as "mostly all mechanics in good circumstances and some families are property owners. They attend punctually the services on Sunday and are attached to the church. Although scattered throughout the city they all attend their own church."[185]

In Fall River, where the parishes of Sacred Heart, St. Joseph and St. Patrick's had already been erected for the Irish, the large colony of French Canadians in the vicinity of the Flint mill in the southeastern section of the city wished to have a church in the neighborhood rather than make the trip to St. Anne's. Following an informal gathering one July afternoon, a committee of French Canadians collected signatures on a petition which they presented to Bishop Hendricken. Although recognizing the need for another parish in Fall River, the bishop, hard pressed at that time to find clergy for the Irish parishes, did not know where to find a French Canadian priest to meet the need that the Catholics in Flint expressed in their petition.[186] He found a solution to his problem in Fr. Dauray. After explaining his concern of satisfying the wishes of the Canadians in Fall River, the bishop asked Fr. Dauray to make what would be the first of several trips to Montreal to find a priest willing to serve in the diocese. Fr. Dauray started the next day for Montreal, stopping for the night at Worcester to visit a classmate from the Grand Seminary at Montreal. In Worcester, Fr. Dauray met yet another classmate, Fr. Pierre J. B. Bedard, who had seen many of the people of his parishes in Canada emigrate to the United States and had come south himself looking to establish a mission to serve the Canadians.[187] Fr. Dauray was easily able to interest him in the Fall River parish that the bishop was anxious to establish. After reporting to Bishop Hendricken in Providence, the two priests went to Fall River to examine the situation there and to decide on a site for a church.[188] Land was purchased on October 9, 1874, and while a church was being built, Fr. Bedard offered Mass in the home of Mr. Henry McGee on Flint Street. Only a few people could actually get into the house; the rest stood outside in the hot sun. Since the parish was to be made up of both French Canadians and Irish, Fr. Bedard preached first in French and then in English. On the first Sunday of November a new wooden church was far enough

---

[185]*Ibid.*, July 16, 1881.
[186]P. U. Vaillant, "Notes Biographiques sur L'Abbe P. J. B. Bedard, Le Pretre Patriote, Fondateur de la Paroisse Notre Dame de Lourdes a Fall River" (Fall River, 1886), pp. 10-11.
[187]Vaillant, "Notes Biographiques," pp. 8-9.
[188]Kennedy, *Quebec to New England*, pp. 80-83.

along so that Mass could be said under the protection of a roof.[189]
The cornerstone of the church, which was to be dedicated to Our
Lady of Lourdes, was laid on December 1, 1874.[190]

By the 1870s New Bedford also had a growing French Canadian
community. Fr. Lawrence McMahon, pastor of St. Laurence, had
grown anxious over the laxness of French Canadians due to their
living in a strange environment. Knowing his limitations, he had at
various times, three French priests living with him in his rectory
which he loved to call his "petit seminarie."[191] One of them, Fr.
Thomas A. Chandonnet, was sent to New Bedford by Bishop Hendricken on March 28, 1873.[192] Two months later Fr. McMahon
began keeping a separate account book for "the Canadian
church."[193] In 1875 a French gentleman of New York City, living on
Lexington Avenue, gave Fr. McMahon a plot of land on the corner
of Robeson and Ashland streets as a site for a French Canadian
church. The work of building was begun at once and on January 1,
1876, Bishop Hendricken appointed Fr. George Pager, until then
one of Fr. McMahon's assistants, as pastor of the new church. The
cornerstone was laid in August 1876, and the church was dedicated
to the Sacred Heart in December. At that time the parish counted
not more than sixty French Canadian families but that number
would quickly increase.[194]

The French Canadians in the Diocese of Providence shared the
desire of French Canadians everywhere in the United States, not
only to have priests of their own background but also parish schools
where their language and traditions, both religious and cultural,
could be passed on to their children. Fr. Bedard in Fall River took
the lead in establishing schools within the French Canadian parishes
when he opened one in his parish in 1876. Staffed initially with lay
teachers, their place was soon taken by the Sisters of Jesus and Mary
from Sillery, Quebec. The sisters arrived on May 21, 1877, shortly
before Bishop Hendricken came down to Fall River on the thirtieth
to dedicate their convent.[195]

In St. Anne's, Fall River, the resignation of Fr. Adrien Montaubricq in June 1878, led to the appointment of Fr. Thomas Briscoe.

---

[189]Vaillant, "Notes Biographiques," p. 11.
[190]Byrne, *Catholic Church in the New England States,* I, 441.
[191]Bradley, *A Brief History of the Diocese of Fall River, Mass.* pp. 34-35.
[192]Bishop Hendricken, "Diary," March 28, 1873.
[193]C. J. Ertremont, "Centenaire de la paroisse du Sacre-Coeur de New Bedford, Mass." *Le Travailleur,* November 1974.
[194]Byrne, *Catholic Church in the New England States,* I, 445.
[195]*Fall River Evening News,* May 31, 1877; Byrne, *Catholic Church in the New England States,* I, 441.

Irish born, yet fluent in French, Fr. Briscoe opened a school in the
low, damp basement of the church in September 1879 and secured
the assistance of two French-speaking Sisters of Mercy who taught
all grades in the day school in both French and English and took
charge of the Sunday school.[196] Previous to the sisters' arrival, lay
people had taught catechism and in 1877–1878 two Sisters of Jesus
and Mary from the convent in Flint had taken on the task. In 1882
Fr. Briscoe started construction of a combination school and convent. While the work was in progress he went to Montreal and
obtained the services of the Sisters of the Holy Cross who arrived
in the parish shortly after Bishop Hendricken dedicated the convent
and school in August 1883.[197]

The Canadians in Rhode Island, lacking the numbers of their
countrymen in Fall River and hard hit by the depression of the
1870s, had to bide their time before they could start parish schools.
In the meantime those who could afford it sent their children to one
of the private schools opened by private citizens in Woonsocket
sometime before 1877 and in Arctic in 1887. These schools often
had the active support of the priests who allowed classes to be given
in the basement of the church in both Woonsocket and Arctic.[198] In
Woonsocket parents could also send their children to the academy
conducted by the Sisters of Mercy where classes were taught in both
French and English.[199]

By the 1880s Rhode Island had a truant law that required all
children under fourteen years of age to attend school at least twelve
weeks a year. In Woonsocket, at least, this law was well enforced.[200]
Since many, if not most, Canadian parents could not afford the
tuition, their children went to public schools or Irish Catholic
schools—a situation which created a dilemma for the Canadians. "It
is most especially in school," a Canadian wrote, "that the immigrant
son learns that his race is contemptible, that his parents are vulgar,
crude people; it is there that he forms the habit of reddening at their
name and of hating anything that reminds him of the land of his
forefathers."[201]

Only three years after the dedication of Precious Blood, Fr.
Dauray felt that in spite of the debt on the parish, the time had come

[196]Morgan, *Mercy*, p. 226.
[197]*Weekly Visitor*, August 25, 1883; *Fall River Evening News*, August 21, 1883; "Les Dominicains a Fall River," *Le Rosaire*, June 1969, p. 20.
[198]*Woonsocket Patriot*, August 11, 14, 1877; *Pawtuxet Valley Gleaner*, September 10, 1887; Harpin, *Trumpets in Jericho*, p. 132.
[199]Morgan, *Mercy*, p. 175-76.
[200]*Providence Journal*, October 14, 1888.
[201]Rumilly, *Histoire des Franco-Americains*, p. 52.

to open a school. After obtaining Bishop Hendricken's consent, he asked the Sisters of Jesus and Mary to come to Woonsocket. When the first group of sisters arrived on September 8, 1884, the parish had no place ready for them. They spent their first year in Woonsocket with the Sisters of Mercy at St. Charles. While construction of the three-story wooden combination school and convent on Hamlet Avenue went forward, classes were held in the basement of the church. The building was ready in November 1885.[202]

As in the other Canadian parishes, Precious Blood school was bilingual. There were some in Woonsocket as elsewhere opposed to the idea of separate Catholic schools. They saw a bilingual parochial school as an even more foreign institution out of harmony with American practices and ideals and inferior to American schools. Fr. Dauray was able to dispel doubts about the quality of his school by inviting a committee of citizens to form a board and to question the children in a public examination as was the common practice of the day. The youngsters did credit to themselves, their teachers and their pastor, proving in this instance that teaching in French did not hinder their progress in English or in other subjects.[203]

A similar pattern would develop in Arctic after Fr. Charles Gaboury, a Canadian, took charge when Fr. Smith was transferred in July 1887. In September, Fr. Gaboury opened the church basement as a place where lay teachers could offer classes. A short time after his arrival, Fr. Gaboury, in consultation with his parishioners, embarked on a project of building a large, three-story brick school similar to those he had known in Canada. The people of Arctic could not imagine how the French could need all that room and how they could staff and pay for it. When the school was ready in 1888, seven Sisters of Jesus and Mary arrived in Arctic to staff the school.[204]

In Central Falls, Fr. George Mahoney had taken charge of Notre Dame parish after Fr. Leon Bouland left in June 1880. In 1883 Fr. Mahoney invited the Sisters of Mercy to care for the day and Sunday schools of his parish. Two sisters came out that year to reside in the convent of St. Patrick's in Valley Falls and conduct bilingual classes as well as visit the sick. Years later, in 1891, after a Canadian priest had been appointed pastor, the Sisters of Mercy would leave the parish in favor of the Canadian order of the Sisters of St. Anne.[205]

---

[202]Kennedy, *Quebec to New England,* pp. 94-95.
[203]*Ibid.,* pp. 97-98.
[204]*Pawtuxet Valley Gleaner,* September 10, 1887; Harpin, *Trumpets in Jericho,* pp. 140-42.
[205]Morgan, *Mercy,* p. 238.

Ministry to the Portuguese

The growing number of Portuguese emigrants in the port towns of Massachusetts and Rhode Island also claimed Bishop Hendricken's immediate attention. Although Bishop Williams of Boston had established the first Portuguese parish in the United States in New Bedford in 1871, the pastor, Fr. João Azevelo, had not yet succeeded in erecting a church. Frustrated by his lack of progress in the New Bedford parish, Fr. Azevelo asked permission to leave the diocese. The bishop was reluctant to release him without having another priest to take his place.[206] However, by June 1873, Fr. Azevelo was transferred to the Diocese of Boston to take charge of the Portuguese parish there and Fr. Anton Mattos Freitas of Calheta, St. Jorge in the Azores, came to take charge of the parish in New Bedford. Under Fr. Freitas, ground was broken for a church in the spring of 1874. The cornerstone was laid on September 27, 1874, before ten thousand people and on June 27, 1875, Bishop Hendricken dedicated the church in honor of St. John the Baptist.[207]

There was a second Portuguese colony in Massachusetts on the Cape at Provincetown where Portuguese fishermen had been settling alongside the Irish. By 1869, the Portuguese had so swelled the number of Catholics in the place that the building in Snow's Block, where the priests had long gathered the people for Mass, was becoming too small. In April 1869, Fr. Cornelius O'Connor, the pastor of Harwich, who also had responsibility for Provincetown, bought land near present day Bradford Street as a site for a new church. A month later, however, work on the building site was apparently abandoned. In December of that year Fr. O'Connor leased a building known as Adams Hall as a place for Mass. By 1873, the number of Portuguese residents of the town had grown to the point where the bishop listed them as a separate national parish in *Sadlier's Catholic Directory* under the title of Our Lady of Refuge.[208]

Fr. O'Connor proved a poor administrator and he resigned in October 1873. Before appointing a new pastor, Bishop Hendricken altered the boundaries of the mission, giving the pastor at Sandwich responsibility for Harwich and appointing Fr. John McGeough to take charge of Provincetown with a mission at Truro. A year later,

    [206]Bishop Hendricken, "Diary," January 17, 1873.
    [207]*Ibid.*, September 27, 1874; June 27, 1875; Byrne, *Catholic Church in the New England States,* I, 454; *Rhode Island Country Journal,* July 2, 1875.
    [208]"St. Peter the Apostle Church, Provincetown: The First Hundred Years, 1874-1974," pp. 13–15.

Wellfleet, where there was a group of French Canadians, also became a mission station of Provincetown.[209] The pastor again altered the place for Mass in March 1874, when Fr. McGeough began using Masonic Hall for services. Also that month the parish reached a decision to begin as soon as possible construction of a church sufficient to meet their needs and allow sufficient space for an addition and decorations as funds allowed.[210]

Fr. McGeough served in Provincetown only a short time and was transferred on June 4, 1874. His place was taken by Fr. John Maguire, a priest just eighteen months ordained.[211] His mission was a particularly challenging one as the majority of his parishioners, being fishermen, were away from home and their families for weeks on end. In an incredibly short time the scholarly priest learned Portuguese and proved an extremely effective pastor to his people "who turned to him for advice and counsel in almost every matter of the slightest concern."[212] Under Fr. Maguire the parish was able to complete construction of their church, which Bishop Hendricken dedicated to St. Peter on October 11, 1874.[213]

Bishop Hendricken's approach to providing clergy to minister to the Portuguese Catholics of his diocese paralleled that of his efforts to recruit clergy for other nationalities. He preferred to have zealous and prudent priests from the homeland of the immigrants, and the bishop did succeed in recruiting one or two. But because of the limited success of his efforts, he was obliged to have his own priests trained in the language of the immigrants so that they could administer the sacraments. In the bishop's "Diary" for 1872 and 1873 there is frequent mention of James A. Ward whom the bishop sent to Lisbon and later to Santarem, Portugal to learn Portuguese. In December 1874, the bishop planned to send another young seminarian to Portugal but for some reason, he never carried this out.[214] Also, in 1874 the bishop persuaded Fr. Henry B. M. Hughes, O.P., a Welsh-born convert versed in languages, to come to Providence. Fr. Hughes arrived in October for a six-months stay and conducted services for the Portuguese of Fox Point in St. Joseph's in Providence.[215]

Fr. Ward was ordained on December 18, 1875 and assisted

[209]*Sadlier's Catholic Directory,* 1874, 1875; *Weekly Visitor,* April 1, 1876.
[210]"St. Peter the Apostle Church," pp. 16–18.
[211]Bishop Hendricken, "Diary," June 10, 1874.
[212]*Providence Visitor,* September 8, 1894.
[213]Byrne, *Catholic Church in the New England States,* I, 459; Bishop Hendricken, "Diary," October 11, 1874.
[214]Bishop Hendricken, "Diary," December 11, 30, 1874.
[215]*Ibid.,* January 15; October 6, 1874; *Providence Journal,* March 23, 1885.

initially in the cathedral parish in Providence. With the coming of
spring, he began a series of visits to the Portuguese colonies in the
diocese, visiting Provincetown, Fall River, New Bedford, Taunton,
as well as the Fox Point section of Providence.[216] In time he would
become an assistant in Taunton and Provincetown. In December
1878, he went out to Provincetown to replace Fr. Maguire as pastor.[217] Fr. Ward's health, however, proved to be poor. In January
1878, Fr. Francis Tuite replaced him in Provincetown for a short
time and in 1886 he gave up the pastorate there to Fr. Thomas P.
Elliot.[218] It would not be until 1893 that Provincetown would be
served by a Portuguese pastor.[219]

Ministry to the Germans, Italians
and Black Catholics

A few days before his death in 1886, Bishop Hendricken estimated that there were only one thousand Germans, Italians and
black Catholics in Providence.[220] The Germans of Providence and
in other parts of the Hartford diocese had attracted Bishop McFarland's attention since many of them had grown lax in their faith
because of the lack of clergy who spoke their language.[221] Shortly
before the division of the Diocese of Hartford, Bishop McFarland
had obtained the services of a young German priest, Fr. Joseph A.
Schaele. Under his direction, the Germans formed themselves into
the Society of St. Boniface, and he said Mass for them in the old
wooden church of St. Mary's on Barton Street.[222] In the summer of
1872, however, Fr. Schaele responded to Bishop McFarland's invitation to minister to the German Catholics in Connecticut.[223]

On September 25, 1873, another German-speaking priest, Fr.
James Marshall, a Pole by birth, arrived in Providence, but left a
week later after informing the bishop that he had not found enough
Germans in Providence to justify remaining.[224] In June 1874,
Bishop Hendricken wrote to the rector of the American College in

[216]*Weekly Visitor,* April 1, 22; May 1; June 17, 1876.
[217]*Ibid.,* April 1, 1876; December 22, 1878.
[218]*Ibid.,* January 19, 1879.
[219]Byrne, *Catholic Church in the New England States,* I, 459.
[220]Greene, *The Providence Plantations,* p. 159.
[221]Bishop McFarland to the Propagation of the Faith, Paris, December 20, 1862,
SPFA.
[222]Greene, *The Providence Plantations,* p. 159.
[223]Byrne, *Catholic Church in the New England States,* II, 444.
[224]Bishop Hendricken, "Diary," September 25; October 2, 1873.

Louvain asking him to recruit a German-speaking priest for his diocese. As in all his dealings with his clergy, the bishop would not accept any priest or seminarian who did not come well recommended. Two Belgian priests applied to come to Providence when they learned of the bishop's search. But one changed his mind and the other was apparently too old.[225] Finally, in April 1876, Bishop Hendricken accepted as a candidate for his diocese a Louvain student, William Stang.[226] After his ordination in June 1878, Fr. Stang served first as an assistant in the cathedral, and in March 1879 he began holding prayer services and instruction for the German Catholics in the cathedral on Sunday and Tuesday evenings. Later, the meetings were held in the chapel of the French Congregation on Fountain Street.[227] In 1883, some Catholics of German background complained to the Congregation of the Propaganda that they were being deprived of spiritual assistance because they lacked a priest of their own nationality.[228] Fr. Stang did what he could to meet the needs of the Germans in Providence and in other parts of the diocese. The *Providence Journal* in April 1885, mentions that he gave a mission to the German Catholic population of New Bedford and that the services were well attended.[229]

The Italians also began to receive particular attention during Bishop Hendricken's episcopacy. Until 1832 only isolated individuals had found their way to Rhode Island from Italian lands.[230] After 1832 a small colony of probably a dozen Italians established themselves in Providence. Among these was George Arduini, a Genoese seaman, who became the leading caterer in Providence before his death in 1878. The political and social upheaval that swept the Italian states in 1848 enlarged the Providence colony slightly, but it was not until 1857 that the Italians began to arrive in Rhode Island in any numbers.[231]

The earliest Italians were seamen like Arduini, wandering harp players, vendors of plaster statuaries, farmers, groups of street organ players, specialized artists and others.[232] By 1885 immigrants from

---

[225]*Ibid.*, June 19; September 22, 1874; February 25; March 2, 1875.

[226]*Ibid.*, March 1; April 27, 1876.

[227]*Weekly Visitor*, March 9; June 21, 1879.

[228]Cardinal Simeoni to Bishop Hendricken, April 17, 1883, PChA.

[229]*Providence Journal*, April 25, 1885.

[230]Ubaldo U. M. Pesaturo, *Italo-Americans of Rhode Island: An Historical and Biographical Survey of the Origin, Rise and Progress of Rhode Islanders of Italian Birth or Descent*, 2nd ed. (Providence, R. I.: The Visitor Printing Co., 1940).

[231]"The Italians: Their Colony in Providence," *Providence Journal*, October 7, 1888.

[232]Pesaturo, *Italo-Americans*, p. 10.

Tuscany, Genoa and the province of Naples swelled the numbers of
the Italians in Rhode Island to about 760 people, nearly all of whom
resided in Providence.[233] By 1887 the Italian population was estimated by a *Journal* writer to number about thirty-five hundred.[234]
While the earliest Italian immigrants from the Italian provinces of
Liguria and Tuscany mixed easily with the Yankees and Irish, in the
1870s the Italian colony was large enough and distinct enough to be
the object of occasional Irish animosity.[235] In 1888 a local reporter
observed that within the Italian community itself there was some
antagonism between Neapolitans from the south of Italy and the
Tuscans from the north, while the Genoese objected to both.[236]

How many of these early Italian immigrants to Rhode Island
considered themselves Catholics is unknown. In Providence they
settled mostly in the area around Spruce, Acorn, Cedar and Dean
streets and so were within the boundaries of St. John's parish after
it was established in 1870. The first notice of any ministry explicitly
to the Italians appeared in November 1874, when Fr. A. P. Petrarra,
then an assistant at St. John's, gave a retreat for the Italian-speaking
of the city. Little is known of Fr. Petrarra beyond his name and the
fact that he served both at St. John's and later in St. Michael's,
Providence, before leaving the diocese for Ohio in June 1876.[237]
Two years later, in June 1878, Fr. Leo Saracena, an Italian-born
Franciscan from the Hartford diocese, spent a few days with Fr.
Christopher Hughes, the pastor of St. Patrick's in Providence. The
Weekly Visitor published a short notice at the time that Fr. Leo would
be "happy to see any of the Italian Catholics who may wish to call
on him."[238] In October 1883, the newly transferred assistant at St.
John's, Fr. Henry Conboy, who had studied theology at Rome,
began to hold Sunday services each week for the Italians. Fr. Conboy, however, did not preach in Italian and no more than 150 to 200
people attended the services.[239]

---

[233]Perry, *Rhode Island State Census, 1885,* p. 231.

[234]*Providence Journal,* August 29, 1887.

[235]*Ibid.,* August 18, 1873; *Woonsocket Patriot,* May 12, 1876.

[236]"The Italians," *Providence Journal,* October 7, 1888.

[237]Cathedral Announcement Book, November 22, 1874; *Sadlier's Catholic Directory,*
1875, 1876; *Weekly Visitor,* July 1, 1876.

An Italian priest, Fr. Anthony Cassese, O.S.F. served for a short time in the first
half of 1867 as an assistant in St. Mary's, Pawtucket. His name first appears on the
baptismal records on February 17, 1867 and the last record on May 28, 1867. The
children he baptized were all Irish. See Giovanni Schavo, *Italian American History, The
Italian Contribution of the Catholic Church in America.* 2 vols. (New York: The Vigo Press,
1949), II, 379.

[238]*Weekly Visitor,* June 23, 1878.

[239]*Providence Journal,* October 13, 1883; August 29, 1887.

By the 1880s the Italians of Providence had found better employment than that of peanut vendor, organ grinder or sidewalk
fruit peddler to which many resorted when they first arrived. Many
now had jobs in manufacturing concerns while smaller numbers
worked as tailors, barbers or on construction projects.[240] As they
acquired property and opened small businesses to service their own
community, the Italians of Providence quickly established themselves as permanent citizens of the state and growing numbers soon
necessitated a more organized ministry on the part of the church.

Bishop Hendricken's pastoral concern and missionary zeal encompassed in a particular way the black residents of his diocese. In
commenting on the 1874 census of the city of Providence, the *Providence Journal* noted that the "colored population" of the city had
shown "a steady increase and had more than doubled since 1865
when 1,311 persons were counted." In 1874 the black population
numbered 3,557 persons.[241] At the end of May 1876, Fr. Hughes at
St. Patrick's, acting on a request of Bishop Hendricken, invited the
black Catholics of Providence to a religious service on Sunday evening, May 28th. About thirty persons assembled in one of the
schoolrooms at St. Patrick's that first evening. Because of the interest shown at the meeting, a sodality and choir was formed and plans
laid for regular services.[242]

In January 1877, the charge of the group was transferred to Fr.
William J. Madden, an assistant at the cathedral and later to another
cathedral assistant, Fr. James Brennan. At the cathedral the group
met in the sacristy on Sunday afternoons for a recitation of the
rosary and the singing of hymns.[243] When in June 1877, Fr. Brennan
took charge of the Catholic population in East Providence, yet another cathedral assistant, Fr. Peter Carlin, took charge of the black
Catholics who now regularly counted between forty and fifty at their
meetings. After assuming his new responsibility, Fr. Carlin, in December, organized a Sodality of the Immaculate Conception under
the patronage of St. Augustine. On April 28, 1878, the day that he
celebrated his sixth anniversary as bishop, Bishop Hendricken presided at the first reception ceremony of members into the sodality.[244]

Many of the members of the black community were born Catho-

---

[240]"The Italians," *Providence Journal,* October 7, 1888.
[241]*Providence Journal,* July 16, 1874. There is no indication that immigrants from
the Cape Verdean islands were included within this group.
[242]*Weekly Visitor,* May 27; June 3, 1876.
[243]*Ibid.,* February 3, 1877.
[244]*Ibid.,* May 5, 1878.

lic but several were converts.[245] Although one or another of his
priests had immediate charge of the group, Bishop Hendricken,
throughout his years as bishop, took a special interest in the black
Catholics and his sensitivity and affection were returned in kind.[246]

Second Expansion of the Diocese
Under Bishop Hendricken

While the economic depression of the 1870s hindered the
efforts of Bishop Hendricken and his priests in providing adequate
care and facilities for their parishioners, it also slowed the influx of
new immigrants. When conditions improved, the flow of immigrants gathered strength again. The last few years of Bishop Hendricken's episcopacy saw a rapid increase in the diocesan population, creating a renewed need for additional parishes and more
clergy.

By 1879 Wakefield and the surrounding villages had grown to
the point where a full-time priest was needed in the area. On De-
cember 1st, Bishop Hendricken split the East Greenwich parish of
which Wakefield was a mission and appointed Fr. William J.
McComb to be the first pastor of the new parish of St. Francis of
Assisi. The parish included the villages of Wakefield, Peacedale and
Narragansett Pier and the mission at "Carolina and Plainville."[247]
Since 1850, Narragansett Pier had begun to acquire popularity
throughout the east for its beaches and climate. By the 1880s the
Pier attracted one thousand Catholic visitors annually during the
summer season. To accommodate them, Fr. Francis Tuite, who in
1882 succeeded Fr. McComb as pastor, built a chapel at the Pier in
1884.[248]

Catholics of the Westerly area had long attended Mass in St.
Michael's on the Connecticut side of the Pawcatuck River. By 1885
their number had reached between 1,100 and 1,300. Bishop Hendricken, in May 1885, organized the Rhode Island portion of the
town into the parish of the Immaculate Conception and appointed
Rev. William Pyne its first pastor.[249] Since the people of Westerly
were attached to the old church and the distance was small, there
was initially little enthusiasm for the division. Fr. Pyne first cele-

[245]Ibid.
[246]Ibid., November 3, 1878; Providence Journal, December 10, 1878.
[247]Weekly Visitor, December 13, 1879; Bishop Hendricken, "Diary," December 1,
1879.
[248]Cole, History of Washington and Kent Counties, p. 599.
[249]Providence Morning Star, April 27, 1885.

brated Mass in Hibernian Hall, which after a month, proved too small and the congregation moved to a larger hall on Main Street. The priest's attempts to buy land for a church were initially frustrated by the reluctance of the town's inhabitants to sell to a priest. Land was bought through an agency in 1887 and the church of the Immaculate Conception was opened for services in 1889.[250]

The spurt in the Catholic population of the state in the 1880s is perhaps best illustrated in the creation of four new parishes in Providence between 1882 and 1886. In November 1882, the *Providence Journal* carried the news of the division of St. Mary's and St. John's parishes to form a new parish in the northwest section of Providence and of the division of St. Patrick's and Immaculate Conception parishes to form a new parish on the east side of Providence.[251] Bishop Hendricken appointed Fr. James Brennan to take charge of the three hundred families of the east side parish. Among the parishioners who would gather for the first time on November 12th in Angell Hall at the junction of North Main and Benefit Street would be many of the oldest Catholic settlers of Providence or their descendents. Fr. Brennan informed the people of his plans for the parish and for the erection of a church on the corner of Jenkins and Camp streets.[252] Initially, the parish was known as St. James in honor of the patron saint of its pastor. But after six or seven weeks of census taking and collecting for the new parish, Fr. Brennan found his strength giving way and asked to resign his labors in favor of someone stronger than himself.[253] Fr. James C. Walsh, an assistant at St. John's, took charge of the parish from Fr. Brennan. At St. John's, Fr. Walsh had helped to found the first Holy Name Society in the diocese in 1877 and now in March 1883, he dedicated his new parish in honor of the Holy Name.[254] The new pastor delayed construction of a church until the parish had established firm financial stability. It was not until August 1883, that construction of the new building on Camp Street was far enough along that the parish could use the basement for Mass. The building that the parish formally dedicated in April 1884 was intended both as a school and a temporary church. The basement was to be used as a Sunday school and for society purposes while the first floor was divided into four schoolrooms and the second floor held the chapel.[255]

Fr. James Murphy, an assistant at St. Mary's, Providence, be-

[250]Byrne, *Catholic Church in the New England States*, I, 428.
[251]*Providence Journal*, November 11, 1882.
[252]*Ibid.*, November 13, 1882.
[253]*Weekly Visitor*, February 10, 1883.
[254]*Ibid.*, March 10, 1883.
[255]*Providence Journal*, February 4, 1884; *Providence Visitor*, April 12, 1884.

came the first pastor of the parish created by dividing St. Mary's and St. John's. He held the initial service for his new parish on January 14, 1883, in Iron's Hall in Olneyville Square.[256] Services continued there each Sunday until February when the congregation moved to Unity Hall on Manton Avenue. The parish laid the cornerstone for a church on Manton Avenue the following September and the basement was used for Mass for the first time on Christmas, 1883. Bishop Hendricken dedicated the new church in honor of St. Teresa on April 15, 1885.[257]

The growing population of the Manton area of Providence prompted the bishop in November 1882 to detach that district from the care of the priests at St. Mary's and place it under Fr. Thomas P. Carroll who had taken Fr. Berkins's place in St. Michael's, Georgiaville.[258] By April 7, 1886, the number of parishioners of the mission had grown to such an extent that the bishop formed a separate parish in Manton and appointed Fr. Carroll as its first pastor. The new parish would be known as St. Thomas.[259]

The fourth parish Bishop Hendricken established in Providence in the 1880s took shape in the Fox Point section of Providence and was intended for the Portuguese Catholics of the city. The Portuguese began settling near the waterfront in Providence in the late 1830s. Until the 1860s there were only a small number in the city. By 1885, however, their numbers had reportedly increased to nearly twelve thousand people, most of whom had come from the Azores.[260] The bishop had long been concerned for the spiritual welfare of the Portuguese who had until then received the sacraments at St. Joseph's.[261] The occasional services provided by Fathers Hughes and Ward were thought inadequate. After he became pastor of St. John's in New Bedford in 1878, Fr. Antonio Freitas traveled to Providence to hold special services for the Portuguese on the third Sunday of each month. When Fr. Freitas resigned his parish in early 1885, his successor, Fr. Antonio Neves, continued the practice of offering Mass in Providence.

Within the first months of 1885 the Portuguese of Providence purchased the Wickenden Street skating rink and converted it for use as a church. The bishop dedicated the building on March 22,

[256]*Providence Journal,* January 13, 15, 1883.

[257]*Ibid.,* April 17, 1885; *Providence Visitor,* May 2, 1885.

[258]*Weekly Visitor,* November 25, 1882.

[259]*Providence Visitor,* June 10, 1889; Byrne, *Catholic Church in the New England States,* I, 405.

[260]*Providence Journal,* March 23, 1885; October 25, 1888.

[261]*Weekly Visitor,* May 13, 1876. Bishop Hendricken administered Confirmation at St. Joseph's to 430 adults, 90 of whom were Portuguese.

1885, in honor of Our Lady of the Rosary.[262] Since Fr. Neves was well occupied with his duties in New Bedford, the bishop gave temporary charge of the new parish to Fr. Thomas P. Elliot who had previously served the Portuguese Catholics in Provincetown.[263] In February 1886, Fr. Antonio Serpa came over to Providence to succeed Fr. Elliot. Fr. Serpa, a native of the Azorean island of Pico, had studied in the Azores and St. John's Seminary at Brighton, Massachusetts before his ordination on December 19, 1885. He spent two months with Fr. Neves in New Bedford before taking charge of the Providence parish.[264]

In the mill villages to the northwest of Providence, the Catholic populations likewise saw an increase, especially among French Canadians. In the 1870s new mill construction in Pascoag attracted enough workers so that its Catholic population was soon large enough to build and support a church. Fr. John Maguire, who had arrived from Cape Cod in 1878 to succeed Fr. Keegan as pastor of St. Patrick's in Harrisville, recognized the need for a church in Pascoag and bought land there in December 1879. In 1880 he saw the cornerstone laid for a church that Bishop Hendricken dedicated in honor of St. Joseph on September 20, 1880.[265] In February 1884, the bishop sent Fr. Daniel Driscoll, an assistant at the Immaculate Conception parish in Providence, to Pascoag to be administrator of a new parish.[266] Fr. Driscoll was apparently unable to raise sufficient funds to run the parish successfully. In January 1886, he resigned and the village again reverted to the charge of the pastor of Harrisville.[267]

In March 1884, Bishop Hendricken added an assistant, Fr. Thomas Kenny, to the staff of the parish at St. Michael's, Georgiaville which then served Greenville and the Manton district. With Fr. Kenny's arrival, the pastor of St. Michael's, Fr. Thomas Carroll, was able to offer Sunday Mass at the village of Rockland in North Scituate for the Catholic population there which until then, he could only visit on weekdays to offer Mass.[268]

At the other end of the state in Newport, Fr. Philip Grace, the pastor of St. Mary's, had in 1883, broached the subject of the division of his parish but because of the ill feeling caused by the pro-

---

[262]*Providence Journal*, March 23, 1885; *Providence Visitor*, April 4, 1885.

[263]*Providence Visitor*, November 28, 1885; January 9, 16, 1886.

[264]*Providence Journal*, October 28, 1888.

[265]*Weekly Visitor*, October 2, 1880; Ryan, *Burrillville, R. I. and the Catholic Church*, pp. 98-99.

[266]*Providence Journal*, February 4, 1884.

[267]Ryan, *Burrillville, R. I. and the Catholic Church*, pp. 101-103.

[268]*Providence Visitor*, March 22, 1884.

posed division, he allowed the matter to drop for the time being.[269]
Nevertheless, St. Mary's nearly six thousand parishioners severely
taxed even the new church and some division had to be made.
Bishop Hendricken and Fr. Grace apparently talked of the division
in July 1884, when the bishop visited the city.[270] However, it was not
until January 18, 1885, that Fr. Grace announced to his parishioners
that a new parish in the Point section had been marked off encom-
passing the entire First Ward and a large share of the Second—an
area which included the homes of some of the first Catholic residents of Newport. There was a feeling of sadness among many who
heard the announcement and feelings of anger in a few. Some had
been parishioners of St. Mary's since Fr. Woodley first said Mass in
the town. They had contributed to the first subscription to build the
church and to all the many collections that followed. Others criticized the division as being unequal. The new parish would have only
about thirteen hundred members, too few a number they predicted
to pay off quickly any debts incurred in building a new church.[271]
From the beginning, the parish would be called St. Joseph's, the
name Fr. Corry had given to the church the Catholics had built in
Newport in 1837 on Mount Vernon Street.

Fr. Grace had made arrangements to rent the old Unitarian
church on Mill Street and there the new parish's congregation assembled the next Sunday to greet their pastor, Fr. James Coyle. The
rented church was too small to think of holding Mass there for any
length of time. Fortunately for them, the congregation of Zion
Church on the corner of Touro and Clarke streets had reluctantly
decided to sell their church and build a smaller church elsewhere.
The parishioners of St. Joseph's were willing buyers of the church.
Since the Zion church lay outside the original boundaries, Fr. Grace
graciously redrew the boundaries and the people of St. Joseph's
occupied their new building for the first time on March 8th.[272] On
September 6, 1885, Bishop Hendricken dedicated the new church
amidst impressive ceremonies.[273]

Since the last years of the Civil War, priests from Newport
regularly visited the coal mines at Portsmouth when the mines were
being worked, and occasionally visited the area to say Mass for the

[269]"History of St. Joseph's Parish," newspaper clippings in Fr. James Coyle,
"Scrapbook," UNDA, p. 36; John H. Greene, "The Story of Early Catholicism in
Newport and History of St. Joseph's Parish" (Newport, 1935).
[270]*Providence Journal*, July 26, 1884.
[271]Coyle, "Scrapbook," p. 40; *Providence Journal*, January 19, 1885.
[272]Coyle, "Scrapbook," p. 36.
[273]*Providence Visitor*, September 19, 1885.

local farmers when the mines were closed. In December 1882, Fr. Grace of St. Mary's built a chapel in Portsmouth and for awhile, said Mass once a month. After St. Joseph's was established, Fr. Coyle assumed responsibility for the mission.[274]

Across Mount Hope Bay, the French Canadian community in Warren had by the mid-seventies come to number some fifty families. Since the first Canadians arrived in Warren in the 1850s, they had received the sacraments in St. Mary's. As most did not speak English, a delegation from the community, sometime in 1878, called on Bishop Hendricken to seek permission to form a parish of their own. Acting on their request, Bishop Hendricken asked the Canadian assistant at St. Joseph's, Fall River, Fr. Edouard Nobert, to take temporary charge of the Fall River parish's mission of St. Patrick's in Somerset and minister also to the Canadians in Warren. Fr. Nobert took up his residence in Somerset and traveled to Warren each Sunday for Mass which he initially said on the third floor of the Bander Block at 435 Main Street. Later he seems to have said Mass in Independence Hall at 34 Croade Street and at last in a hall belonging to St. Mary's church.[275]

In May 1881, Fr. Nobert bought land for a church at the corner of Main and Hope streets and transferred ownership to a parish corporation formed in August. Ground was broken for the new church on April 11, 1882, and the building was dedicated by Bishop Hendricken under the title of St. John the Baptist on November 12th. In August 1887, the bishop wrote Fr. Nobert appointing him as full-time pastor of St. John's and directing him to turn over the books of the Somerset parish to Fr. James Masterson who was to be its first pastor.[276] At the time Fr. Masterson took charge of the parish, there were twelve hundred Catholics who worshipped in St. Patrick's. But the closing of the various iron industries in Somerset in the years ahead would cause a great decline in the parish's population.[277]

The Massachusetts portion of the diocese experienced the same kind of rapid growth in textile manufacturing as did Rhode Island. In April 1882, Bishop Hendricken officially announced the establishment of two new parishes in Fall River.[278] The approxi-

[274]*Weekly Visitor,* December 30, 1882; Byrne, *Catholic Church in the New England States,* I, 433.

[275]Ulysse Forget, *La Paroisee Saint-Jean-Baptiste de Warren, Etat du Rhode Island, 1852-1877* (Montreal: Imprimiries Populaire Limiter, 1952), pp. 18-19, 135-36; *Providence Journal,* January 2, 1879.

[276]*Ibid.,* pp. 20-24.

[277]*Dillon's Catholic Directory of Fall River,* 1894, pp. 73-74.

[278]*Providence Journal,* April 22, 1882.

mately six hundred Irish parishioners of Fr. Bedard in Our Lady of Lourdes in the Flint section had grown increasingly uneasy under their pastor. Early in 1882 they asked to have a parish of their own.[279] Fr. Owen Kiernan, whom the bishop sent to take care of the Irish in Flint village, bought land on the corner of County and Thames streets and broke ground for a church on May 15th. A few weeks later the men of the parish turned out to dig the foundation hole for their new church. Work began on the building itself in April 1883, and on September 14, 1883, Bishop Hendricken dedicated the frame church under the patronage of the Immaculate Conception.[280]

While Fr. Kiernan busied himself with the formation of a new parish in the Flint district, Fr. Patrick F. Doyle received the charge to build a parish in the area of Fall River known as "Rattle Snake Hill." For the first year Fr. Doyle said Mass in a large store at the corner of Eight Rod Way and Snell Street but within a short time the congregation built a frame church called SS. Peter and Paul on Snell Street.[281]

On May 14, 1885, yet another parish, an offshoot of St. Mary's, was organized. Fr. Louis Deady held the new parish's first service in the "Old Thread Mill" on Division Street. Again, land was quickly purchased, and Bishop Hendricken journeyed to Fall River to bless the cornerstone of the church of St. Louis on October 18, 1885. Within a year the basement was finished and used for Mass.[282]

When on June 26, 1882, Bishop Hendricken dedicated the church of St. Joseph in Wood's Hole, the place was still a mission of St. Peter's in Sandwich.[283] However, in July 1883, the bishop appointed Fr. Cornelius McSweeney, until then an assistant at Sandwich, as first pastor of a new parish at Wood's Hole which had missions at Nantucket, Hyannis, Yarmouth and Harwich.[284] For thirty years, Fr. McSweeney would serve this section of the Cape and the islands. Gruff but kindly, he was a man of solid piety who could not be prevented from arriving at one of his missions on the appointed day. He was known to leave for Nantucket in the teeth of a storm so severe that the fishermen took him across only because they would not refuse a priest.[285]

[279]Weekly Visitor, October 13, 1883.
[280]Fall River Evening News, March 28; May 19, 29, 1882; April 9; October 2, 1883.
[281]Dillon's Catholic Directory of Fall River, 1894, pp. 48-49.
[282]Fall River Evening News, October 19, 1885; Dillon's Catholic Directory of Fall River, 1894, p. 52.
[283]Providence Journal, June 30, 1882.
[284]Weekly Visitor, July 14, 1883.
[285]Bradley, Brief History of the Diocese of Fall River, Mass. p. 36.

In November 1882, Bishop Hendricken sent Fr. Napoleon Riviere to establish a parish in the vicinity of the Whittenton Manufacturing Company on the north side of Taunton. Fr. Riviere spent the month of December taking a census among the Irish and French Canadian millworkers who were to form the new congregation.[286] For some reason, Fr. Riviere gave up his assignment and on January 10, 1883, Bishop Hendricken sent Fr. James Roach, a young priest who had studied in Canada and who spoke English and French fluently, to take charge of the parish.[287] Fr. Roach first said Mass in Lovering's Hall but quickly set in motion plans to build a small wooden church that was completed before the end of the year and named in honor of the Immaculate Conception.[288] Fr. Edward Sheridan of St. Mary's vigorously objected to the establishment of the parish since he contended the division removed from his parish those who contributed most generously towards the payment of the heavy debt on St. Mary's. In January 1884, Fr. Sheridan appealed his case to Rome. On July 25, 1884, the Prefect of the Congregation of the Propaganda responded to Fr. Sheridan upholding the bishop's decision.[289]

In Attleboro, the Catholics living in the eastern part of the town found it more difficult to attend Mass after the change of the site of the new church from the Falls to North Attleboro. Their numbers had grown since 1877 and Fr. Mongan, the pastor of St. Mary's, recognizing their need, began in 1880 to come to Attleboro proper to celebrate Mass each Sunday in Dean's Hall and later in Union Hall. In June 1880, Fr. Mongan purchased a site on North Main Street in anticipation of building a church. However, in January 1883, Bishop Hendricken decided to organize a new parish in the eastern part of the town that would include the chapel at Norton. He appointed Fr. John O'Connell as its first pastor. On September 17, 1883, the bishop laid the cornerstone of the church of St. John the Evangelist and dedicated the completed structure on September 27, 1885.[290]

To the south of Attleboro, St. Stephen's mission in Dodgeville had seen the congregation of French Canadians and Irish grow to the point where its 650 people could support a pastor of their own.

---

[286] *Weekly Visitor,* December 9, 1882.

[287] "Funeral of Fr. Roach," *Providence Visitor,* January 13, 1906.

[288] *Taunton Daily Gazette,* July 21, 1960; "Report of the Parish of the Immaculate Conception," January 1, 1884; Byrne, *Catholic Church in the New England States,* I, 447.

[289] Rev. Edward Sheridan to the Congregation of the Propaganda, January 1884, PChA; Congregation of the Propaganda to Rev. Edward Sheridan, July 25, 1884, PChA.

[290] Byrne, *Catholic Church in the New England States,* I, 454; Daggert, *A Sketch of the History of Attleborough,* pp. 308-309.

On February 6, 1885, Bishop Hendricken removed the mission from the jurisdiction of the pastor of St. Joseph's in Pawtucket and sent Fr. Patrick S. McGee to Dodgeville. Fr. McGee's parish included both the Hebronville and Dodgeville sections of Attleboro and parts of Seekonk and Rehoboth.[291]

New Educational and Social Agencies

Among the chief concerns of Hendricken's pastorate in Waterbury had been the education of the young people of his parish, an interest that did not wane when he became bishop. In spite of the renewed hostility that the idea of separate schools provoked in the community at large in the 1870s and 1880s, the number of parochial schools in the diocese increased from nine in 1873 to seventeen in 1886. To support the educational efforts of the priests, Bishop Hendricken invited several orders of sisters to come into the diocese to establish or take over schools. Among the bishop's earliest efforts was his invitation to the religious of the Society of the Sacred Heart to take up residence near Providence.

During the course of diocesan retreats at Holy Cross College in Worcester, Bishop Hendricken became acquainted with Fr. Anthony F. Ciampi, S.J., then rector of the college. In August 1872, Fr. Ciampi accompanied Bishop Hendricken to look at "Elmhurst," the North Providence estate of Dr. William Grosvenor, which was up for sale.[292] Later in August the two men on a trip to New York visited "Kenwood," the novitiate run by the Religious of the Sacred Heart near Albany.[293] Evidently, the bishop discussed with the sisters the possibility of their settling in the Providence diocese, because four days later Mother Hardy, the head of the sisters in the United States, and a companion arrived in Providence to see the Grosvenor estate.[294] The sisters agreed that the property suited their needs, and shortly thereafter Dr. Grosvenor called on the bishop on August 14th and offered to sell the estate for $100,000.[295] When a few weeks later the doctor lowered his price to $75,000, the bishop advised Madam Hardy to accept it.[296] According to a contemporary

---

[291]Byrne, *Catholic Church in the New England States*, I, 450; Daggert, *A Sketch of the History of Attleborough*, p. 309.

[292]Bishop Hendricken, "Diary," August 2, 1872. It would not be until March 1874, that the state legislature would incorporate that section of North Providence within the city limits of Providence.

[293]*Ibid.*, August 8, 1872.

[294]*Ibid.*, August 12, 1872.

[295]*Ibid.*, August 14, 1872.

[296]*Ibid.*, September 10, 1872.

newspaper account, the Religious of the Sacred Heart had been looking for a suitable place to found a school in New England.[297] On November 19, 1872, the sisters purchased the Grosvenor property and on the 20th of November, a group of five or six sisters came to Providence to prepare to open the Academy of the Sacred Heart as a school for young ladies.[298] In 1880 the sisters expanded their endeavors when they erected a one-story wooden building designed to accommodate sixty children of the neighborhood who might be detained at home owing to the distance to the nearest school.[299]

The Religious of the Sacred Heart supplied the staff for another primary school when Fr. Robert J. Sullivan invited them to come to St. Mary's in Providence. After he had taken charge of St. Mary's parish in Olneyville in 1874, Fr. Sullivan, who had been Bishop Hendricken's secretary until he became pastor of St. Mary's, purchased a building adjacent to the church property which he converted into a convent. With the assistance of Bishop Hendricken, the old church on Barton Street would be raised one-story, entirely renovated and fitted up for a Sunday school and day school. The sisters at Elmhurst staffed the schools until 1877 when they withdrew because of other demands on their community.[300]

Fr. Sullivan found new teachers for his parish among the Ursulines who had not served in New England since 1834 when their convent in Boston was burned. Eleven Ursulines came to Providence in August 1877, to continue the boarding school and day academy and to take over the parish schools.[301] Together with the Sisters of Mercy's "Bayview," the academies opened by the Canadian orders of the Sisters of Jesus and Mary and the Sisters of the Holy Cross in Fall River, and the others existing in the diocese, there were ten secondary schools for young ladies by 1886. To provide for the education of young women who were unable to attend school during the day, the Sisters of Mercy opened a night school in the convent in Providence in the 1870s, and similar schools were opened in other cities at about the same time.[302]

There was no increase in the number of academies for young

---

[297]*Providence Morning Herald,* December 12, 1872; *Sadlier's Catholic Directory,* 1874, p. 296.

[298]Bishop Hendricken, "Diary," November 19, 20, 1872; Byrne, *Catholic Church in the New England States,* I, 463. The academy formally opened in February.

[299]*Providence Journal,* October 8, 1881.

[300]Bishop Hendricken, "Diary," July 27, 1874.

[301]Greene, *The Providence Plantations,* p. 160; *Providence Visitor,* August 18, 1882; Bishop Hendricken, "Diary," August 9, 1877.

[302]"Cathedral Announcement Book," September 26, 1874; *Providence Journal,* December 10, 1875.

men in the diocese during Bishop Hendricken's years as bishop. However, there was a significant change in the status of the cathedral parish's Fountain Street academy. In July 1877, following a series of meetings between Bishop Hendricken, the pastors of Providence and the surrounding towns, and Brother Fabrician, the new director of the academy, Brother Fabrician announced that the school was henceforth to assume a diocesan character and a new name—LaSalle Academy. The academy was open to all students and the expenses of the boys were assumed by their pastors.[303]

The same year that Bishop Hendricken took the step of enlarging the scope of the academy, he took another that he hoped would lead to the establishment of a Jesuit college in Providence. On February 19, 1877, Fr. Daniel Kelly, the competent and beloved pastor of St. Joseph's parish in Providence, died after a long illness. Perhaps realizing that his death was near, Fr. Kelly, who had studied with the Jesuits at Holy Cross and at Fordham, had suggested to Bishop Hendricken that perhaps his removal from St. Joseph's would provide the bishop with the opportunity of inviting the Fathers of the Society of Jesus to come to Providence.[304] Years before in Boston, the taking over of St. Mary's parish in 1848 was the first step in the process that led to the founding of Boston College.

Following Fr. Kelly's death, Bishop Hendricken was prepared to act. On April 8, 1877, the bishop went to St. Joseph's to introduce the first Jesuit pastor of the parish, Swiss-born, Fr. John Bapst, S.J., to his new parishioners.[305] Fr. Bapst was already well known because of his faith and courage as a missionary among the Indians of Maine and his success as president of Boston College during its financially troubled years during the Civil War.[306]

In an effort to revive the cause of Catholic journalism and foster the education of the entire Catholic community Bishop Hendricken, in October 1875, began publication of a four-page, four-column Sunday school magazine that he called the *Weekly Visitor*. The *Visitor's* first issue of 1,700 copies, which was distributed on Saturday, October 9th, sold for three cents and its second of 2,000 copies sold for one cent. Since the bishop found that the one cent price did not defray the cost of paper, he decided to enlarge it to a three-column, eight-page format that would sell for two cents. Bishop Hendricken entrusted the editorship of the *Visitor* to a young priest of the cathe-

[303]*Providence Journal,* July 24, 1877; "LaSalle Academy, A History," *Providence Visitor,* September 24, 1971.
[304]"Our Fathers in Providence," *Woodstock Letters,* XXIX (1900), p. 234.
[305]*Providence Journal,* April 9, 1877.
[306]Lord, Sexton and Harrington, *History of the Archdiocese of Boston,* II, 608-11.

dral staff, Fr. William D. Kelly, and he put its publication in the hands of a young book and job printer, Andrew F. Martin, a convert from Maine, who had recently set up a press of his own.[307]

As its full title indicated, *The Weekly Visitor, A Catholic Sunday School Magazine,* the *Visitor* was not intended as a competitor to the established papers of the state. Its first page was taken up by news of church and group activities in the parishes of the diocese, but concentrated mostly on the Providence parishes. Fr. Kelly filled the inside pages with stories and historical articles designed to inform, edify and entertain his readers. The *Visitor* reflected the bishop's own personality and interests, both on its editorial page, to which the bishop himself contributed, and in its interest in temperance affairs and news of Ireland taken from the *Kilkenny Journal.* [308]

After a successful first year, the following announcement appeared on September 16, 1876:

> About Ourselves. On the 30th of the present month, the *Weekly Visitor* will have completed the first year of its publication. Begun to fill a want that had long existed, it has been continued with no small degree of inconvenience to the present managers. Finding that the time devoted to this paper cannot be spared from more important duties, it is deemed advisable to transfer its ownership to other hands whose experience in journalism justifies the hope that an acceptable publication will be presented to the Catholics of the Diocese.

The bishop sold the publication to Michael Walsh who took over as the paper's editor as well as its publisher. On October 7, 1876, the new editor informed his readers that the "change in management of the *Weekly Visitor* in no way affects the character." Under Walsh, the paper was enlarged and its scope broadened to include more current topics and greater news of political and religious doings in Ireland. During the years of his ownership, the style of the *Visitor* evolved in the direction of a regular newspaper but continued to include the "special features" to which Walsh attributed the success of the paper.[309]

In February 1879, the format of the *Visitor* again changed. The publication became larger and it took on an appearance similar to that of other newspapers in the city. Walsh's most significant innovation was to begin publishing two editions, one on Saturday, which went chiefly outside of Providence, and a second on Sunday, which

[307]Bishop Hendricken, "Diary," October 15, 19, 1875; *Providence Journal,* May 15, 1876; *Providence Visitor,* March 10, 1900; August 29, 1913.

[308]*Providence Journal,* January 31, 1876; *Providence Visitor,* June 19, 1886.

[309]*Providence Visitor,* July 25, 1919; *Weekly Visitor,* September 25, 1880.

in September 1877, appeared under the title of the *Sunday Visitor* and was intended for circulation within Providence.

In 1881, wishing to take up the study of medicine, Walsh sold his interest in the paper to the Visitor Printing Company that Bishop Hendricken had formed to continue the work of publishing the *Visitor.* Under the Visitor Company, Walsh's two editions were amalgamated and the Sunday edition was dropped. But by becoming a state-wide weekly, its name conflicted with a paper of the same title published in Central Falls. To avert confusion, the Visitor Printing Company in January 1884, decided to change the name of its publication to the *Providence Visitor.* [310]

Bishop Hendricken also shared his predecessor's concern for the orphans of his diocese and he made frequent visits to the asylum on Prairie Avenue. The bishop's concern was complemented by that of his priests and religious. The Sisters of Jesus and Mary, who had come to Our Lady of Lourdes in Fall River in 1877, opened their convent to the orphaned children of both the Irish and Canadians of the city in 1881.[311] Two years later Fr. Bedard built a separate building to house the orphans.[312] In 1885 the Irish clergy of Fall River purchased "Forest Hill Gardens," a summer resort on Mount Hope Bay near their city as a home for orphaned children of Irish parents in that section of Massachusetts. They gave charge of the home to the Sisters of Mercy who dedicated it to St. Vincent.[313]

The first attempt within the diocese to provide institutional care for the sick came about as a result of the generosity of Mrs. Ada Baker. On February 1, 1873, Mrs. Baker purchased the Russell Homestead at the corner of Pleasant Street and Campbell in New Bedford with the hope that Bishop Hendricken would allow the Sisters of Mercy to establish a hospital there.[314] The bishop assented to Mrs. Baker's wish and put the project in the hands of Fr. McMahon of St. Lawrence's. The Sisters of Mercy, who, as part of their service, visited the homes of the poor to console and minister to the sick, sent three sisters on March 17, 1873, to the homestead to prepare to open the hospital. The sisters later increased the staff to seven when St. Joseph's opened its doors the following June.[315] The financial burden of supporting the hospital proved too great

[310]*Providence Journal,* January 19, 1884.
[311]*Dillon's Catholic Directory of Fall River,* 1894, p. 63.
[312]*Providence Journal,* May 31, 1883.
[313]Carroll, *Annals,* III, 438; Morgan, *Mercy,* pp. 227-30; Byrne, *Catholic Church in the New England States,* I, 462.
[314]Bishop Hendricken, "Diary," February 3, 4, 1873.
[315]Carroll, *Annals,* III, 424; Morgan, *Mercy,* pp. 186-89; Bishop Hendricken, "Diary," February 25; March 19, 1873.

for St. Lawrence parish, especially after 1883, when the parish opened the first of two parochial schools. Gradually, the number of teaching sisters living at the hospital forced the phasing out of its medical mission. In 1884, St. Luke's hospital, a private foundation, had been established in the city and by 1888, St. Joseph's had closed its doors as a hospital and became solely a convent.[316]

By the 1870s the number of elderly Catholics who had no place to go and no one to care for them had become as pressing a cause for concern to the Catholic community as the orphans and the sick. In November 1880, the Mother Provincial of the Little Sisters of the Poor wrote to ask Bishop Hendricken's permission to settle in his diocese.[317] On March 23, 1881, the bishop welcomed three Sisters of the Poor to Providence.

Since their arrival in the United States from France in 1868 the Sisters of the Poor had prospered, and Providence became the twenty-third house of their order. On coming to the city they took up residence in the General James Mansion on Slocum Street in St. Mary's parish. The sisters relied totally on the generosity of the community to support themselves and the elderly poor whom they cared for; generosity that they invited by their example and their door to door visits of homes and businesses in Providence. Within days of their arrival in Providence, the people of the city had contributed food and furnishings for their home so that the sisters were quickly able to welcome the first of their elderly guests.[318]

Although the James Mansion would in time accommodate forty persons, the requests for admittance were such that the need for a larger facility was readily apparent to all. Among those who took an early interest in the work of the Little Sisters were Mr. and Mrs. Joseph Banigan. Mr. Banigan was among the wealthiest members of the Catholic community in the diocese and among the most generous. After purchasing land in 1882 at the junction of Main and Wayland Street in the Woodlawn section of Pawtucket, just over the Providence line, Banigan began construction of a three-story brick building able to accommodate 350 elderly. The building was constructed at a cost of approximately $135,000. On May 29, 1884, clergy and guests celebrated a Mass at the Home of the Aged during which Mr. Banigan formally turned over the keys of the building to the sisters.[319]

[316]Morgan, *Mercy*, pp. 189-205; Albert F. Shovelton, "St. James Parish, 1888-1963" (New Bedford: privately printed, 1963), p. 16.
[317]Bishop Hendricken, "Diary," November 26, 1880.
[318]*Weekly Visitor*, April 2, 9, 1881.
[319]*Providence Visitor*, May 31; June 7, 1884.

Problems Involving Priests
and Pastoral Care

As chief administrator of the diocese, Bishop Hendricken was also the chief arbiter when discord arose within the parishes. As in the days of his predecessors, the bishop dealt with a host of disputes between the people of the diocese and his associates, the pastors. Some were minor and attracted little attention and notice except in the bishop's private letters and diary. Others, such as Fr. Philip Grace's supposed refusal to provide a funeral service in his church for a child whose parents had refused to send her to a Catholic school and had not sent for a priest before she died, created a passing rash of excitement in the press but was quickly forgotten.[320] Disputes involving one of his priests took longer to resolve, especially if the bishop himself was a party to the controversy. Such was the case when Fr. Sheridan objected to the bishop's decision to create a new parish in the Whittendon section of Taunton in the 1880s.

The most difficult and public of the controversies within the diocese during Bishop Hendricken's episcopacy, which was not complicated by ethnic factors, was the question of the ownership of a lot at the corner of High and Barton streets in St. Mary's parish, Providence. When Bishop Hendricken returned on August 23, 1874, from his first trip to Europe, he found waiting for him on his desk a letter from Bishop McFarland in Hartford recounting the substance of a meeting he had a few days earlier with a committee representing some of the parishioners of St. Mary's. A short time after the death of their long time pastor, Fr. John Quinn, on June 8, 1873, the parishioners discovered that the parish did not, in fact, own a lot on Barton Street that Fr. Quinn had led them to believe had been purchased by St. Mary's. Bishop McFarland, who had provided the funds for the purchase of the land from the orphans' and seminarians' funds, held the deed to the property. The property's value had increased over the years and the three-man committee composed of the parish's two lay trustees and one of the chief movers of the affair, Mr. Hugh Falls, called on Bishop McFarland in Hartford to ask him to sell the land to them at a price less than the present value. The bishop, who was in need of funds for his diocese, made a generous offer, lower than the actual value, but higher than what he had originally paid for the land. The committee refused to accept his offer. Suspecting as they did

[320]*Providence Journal,* December 22, 1875; *Rhode Island Country Journal,* December 24, 1875.

that the bishop had somehow swindled them in the first place, the committee left after one of them made the threat that "by next January the church property in Rhode Island will be taken out of the hands of the priests." Bishop McFarland concluded his letter recounting the meeting by promising to abide by Bishop Hendricken's advice in the matter.[321]

Bishop McFarland considered the threat to the administrative position of the bishop and his clergy to be very real. Bishop McFarland wrote a few weeks later reminding Bishop Hendricken of the trouble caused Bishop O'Reilly in 1854 by the men of Norwich and of the difficulties with "Trusteeism" that Bishop Hughes was forced to contend with in New York.[322]

Bishop Hendricken's response to the situation was to go to St. Mary's on Sunday, September 7th and present his understanding of the situation.[323] The dissidents eventually engaged a lawyer to press their case but as the facts of the situation emerged, justice was clearly seen to rest on the side of Bishop McFarland. The chief source of the confusion lay with the impressions Fr. Quinn had conveyed to his parishioners.[324] When faced with the true facts of the situation, the parishioners of St. Mary's, offered in November, a public apology to Bishop McFarland expressing regret for their "imprudent language," and their "fullest confidence in his integrity and those of our ecclesiastical superiors in general."[325]

The dispute at St. Mary's probably served to underline a directive Bishop Hendricken had sent to his pastors the previous December. When Bishop McFarland had come to the diocese in 1858 he toured all the parishes during his first year as bishop collecting statistics on the temporal and spiritual welfare of his See for a report to the Congregation of the Propaganda in Rome. There are in the Providence and Hartford Diocesan Archives only occasional reports from pastors during Bishop McFarland's administration updating the information on their parishes. In December of the year that he became bishop, Bishop Hendricken wrote to his pastors asking them to submit "an exact statement of the condition of their parishes which they were to have audited by their parish committees." He suggested that a clear and certified report of parish ac-

[321]Bishop Francis P. McFarland to Bishop Hendricken, August 19, 1873, PChA; *Providence Journal,* October 1, 1873.

[322]Bishop Francis P. McFarland to Bishop Hendricken, October 12, 1873, PChA.

[323]Bishop Hendricken to Bishop McFarland, September 7, 1873, HChA; *Providence Morning Star,* September 8, 1873.

[324]*Providence Journal,* September 20, 1873.

[325]*Providence Evening Press,* November 7, 1873.

counts, given annually to the people, would remove all "unjust suspicion."[326] The bishop would set the example himself by issuing an annual Treasurer's Report on the condition of the diocese whose affairs were integrally bound up with those of the cathedral parish. From January 1873 on, there are yearly reports from almost all parishes of the diocese.

Dedicated pastor that he was, Bishop Hendricken sincerely tried to provide the Canadians of his diocese with French-speaking clergy. In the main he was successful but they were frequently not the Canadian priests the people hoped for. The difficulty, the bishop would write in 1879, was that "the Canadian Bishops need their priests, and only occasionally do they permit one or another of them to come to us because of their poor health. Few of those who come to us from Canada are willing to bring with them an 'exeat'; they always wish to return to their country whenever they please."[327] The bishop encouraged the Canadians, as he did in speaking to the people of Precious Blood in Woonsocket in 1883, to build their own schools and convents and to cling to their language "as it was in it the principles of religion were furthered." "The English language was necessary," he went on to say, "for the business of life, but the French language was necessary in their homes and in the church."[328]

Although the bishop was, from his first days in Providence, sympathetic to the desire for the Canadians to have a clergy of their own nationality to serve as their pastors, he attempted to maintain the same criteria for accepting Canadian priests into his diocese as he did for all others and expected from the Canadians the same obedience to their pastors and bishop as he did from other groups. For the most part the Canadians appreciated the sincerity of the bishop's efforts and the difficulties under which he labored in securing the priests they desired. However, in the late 1870s, the Canadians had become increasingly sensitive to the prejudice of their neighbors and assertive of their rights both as citizens and as members of the Church. One sign of the growing group consciousness among Canadians was the annual meetings of the Canadians of Rhode Island and Massachusetts which they first called together in 1878.[329]

---

[326]Bishop Thomas F. Hendricken to Pastors of the diocese, December 24, 1872, PChA. The auditing procedure is now required by State incorporation laws.

[327]Bishop Thomas F. Hendricken to Cardinal Simeoni, May 2, 1879, Fall River Diocesan Chancery Archives. Hereafter cited FRChA.

[328]Weekly Visitor, October 6, 1883.

[329]Rumilly, Histoire des Franco-Americains, pp. 96–100; Providence Journal, October 5, 1881.

In February 1877, a group of the Canadians in the mixed Irish-Canadian parish of St. Michael's, Georgiaville, petitioned for the removal of Fr. Berkins from their parish as had their compatriots in Woonsocket in 1875.[330] This time they were unsuccessful. Dissatisfaction also appeared in Central Falls after Fr. Leon Bouland left the parish in May 1880 and was replaced by a young Montreal-trained Irishman, Fr. George Mahoney, who had served the last two years as Fr. Dauray's assistant in Woonsocket. Some of the parishioners complained to the Congregation of the Propaganda that "they did not have a competent pastor because he was not well versed in their tongue." They also claimed that they were unable to secure a priest of their choice when, in danger of death, one of their parish wished to receive the sacrament of Penance.[331]

In Fall River, where the number of Canadians was larger than in Central Falls, a similar controversy developed after June 1878, when Fr. Montaubricq, the pastor of St. Anne's for ten years, resigned his pastorate because of ill health. To fill the vacancy, Bishop Hendricken transferred another young Irish-born priest, Fr. Thomas Briscoe, from his assignment as assistant in the same city in the mixed Irish-Canadian parish of St. Joseph's. Fr. Briscoe had studied in France and spoke French fluently. Yet the Congregation of the Propaganda received another rash of complaints that the congregation's prefect, Cardinal Simeoni, referred to Bishop Hendricken for his response.[332] To strengthen their protest the correspondents included a petition with some five hundred signatures asking for the appointment of a Canadian priest to their parish's "vacant pastorate."[333] Bishop Hendricken responded to Cardinal Simeoni's inquiry by asserting that certain of the Canadians have "persecuted" their former pastor until he resigned and that these same men were now trying to expel Fr. Briscoe. The names on the petition were, he contended, "spurious and false." Since, to his mind, the affairs of St. Anne were in an excellent state and he regarded Fr. Briscoe as one of his finest priests, Bishop Hendricken informed the cardinal he would make no change in the parish.[334]

Although the dissent died down and Fr. Briscoe came to gain the respect and acceptance of most of his parishioners, the Canadians in Fall River continued to be sensitive to any hint of hostility towards them or any disregard of their need for pastoral care. After

[330]Bishop Hendricken, "Diary," February 26, 1877; Fr. James Gibson, "Scrapbook," p. 138.
[331]Cardinal Simeoni, to Bishop Hendricken, September 7, 1880, FRChA.
[332]Ibid., April 3, 1879.
[333]Fall River Evening News, February 8, 1879.
[334]Bishop Thomas F. Hendricken to Cardinal Simeoni, May 2, 1879, FRChA.

returning from a visit to his home in France in 1882, Fr. Montaubricq took up residence in the village of Shove near the Tiverton
line. At the request of the Canadians in his neighborhood, who had
a considerable distance to travel to get to St. Anne's, Fr. Montaubricq asked the bishop for permission to build a small village chapel
at his own expense. The bishop had already refused again to make
him pastor of St. Anne's, and now he refused to grant this second
request. Fr. Montaubricq appealed his case to the Congregation of
the Propaganda in Rome.[335] The bishop, however, changed his
mind and in August 1883, a notice appeared in the papers that the
bishop was establishing a new parish for the French Canadians
living near Tiverton.[336] But when Fr. Briscoe of St. Anne's, whose
parish was in the midst of serious financial difficulties, objected to
the division of his parish, the bishop again withdrew his consent.
The bishop's refusal prompted the priest to abandon the idea of
settling in Massachusetts and instead he returned to live out his life
in France. The incident served to stir up the resentment of those
who already felt the bishop was disregarding their needs.[337] In 1885
the focus of French Canadian discontent shifted to another Fall
River parish, Our Lady of Lourdes.

Fr. Bedard, the pastor of Our Lady of Lourdes or Notre Dame,
as it was most commonly known, had, since coming to Fall River,
built a reputation as a most energetic man, an organizer and a leader
who endeavored to keep alive in his fellow countrymen the national
spirit and religious traditions of their native land.[338] Preservation of
their language and their faith were to him, as to many of the Canadians, one and the same. Fr. Bedard's constant dream was to establish
schools where the young could receive a solid education in their
native tongue. To Fr. Bedard and those leaders of the Canadian
community who shared his convictions, the wish of their neighbors
to see the Canadian children quickly learn English in preference to
French and become culturally integrated was the equivalent of denying the value of French Canadian history and tradition.[339]

Fr. Bedard apparently was the chief instrument in securing the
services of the Sisters of Jesus and Mary who came to teach in the
parish school in May 1877. With the co-operation of the sisters, the
aid of his parishioners, family funds he brought with him from
Canada and his own sharp business sense, Fr. Bedard built, in

[335]Cardinal Simeoni to Bishop Hendricken, February 9, 1882, PChA.
[336]*Fall River Evening News,* August 20, 1883; *Providence Journal,* August 23, 1883.
[337]*Le Rosaire,* June-August, 1969, p. 19.
[338]Byrne, *Catholic Church in the New England States,* I, 441.
[339]Vaillant, "Notes Biographiques," pp. 13-15.

addition to a rectory, convent and orphan's home, a school for boys and a commercial "college" that opened in 1882.[340] College, as used then, referred to the equivalent of a modern high school.

Fr. Bedard's relationship with Bishop Hendricken was initially amicable and while he lived, there was no public expression on the bishop's part of hostility between the two men. However, during the spinners strike in Fall River in 1879, the mostly Irish strikers bitterly protested to Bishop Hendricken against Fr. Bedard's supposed role in procuring French Canadian workers to take their jobs. The bishop wrote Fr. Bedard ordering him not to interfere in the strike. The priest was deeply hurt by the bishop's letter, since, confident of the righteousness of his conduct, he was convinced that the bishop had allowed himself to be taken in. Fr. Bedard's feeling of persecution was further heightened when his church was broken into and the sacramental registers stolen. Suspicious that Fr. Bedard was behind the incident as the register might offer proof of the charges against him, Bishop Hendricken reportedly ordered him to reconstruct the registers or be removed from the parish.[341]

Shortly after, Fr. Bedard giving vent to his sense of humiliation shot back a strangly worded letter to Bishop Hendricken outlining the affairs of his parish. He also outlined his grievances with the bishop in a letter to the Congregation of the Propaganda. In reply to Cardinal Simeoni's letter inquiring into the substance of Fr. Bedard's complaints, Bishop Hendricken sent the cardinal the letter he had received from Bedard. The Providence prelate described Bedard's response as being "full of threats" and asked the cardinal to condemn the priest's irreverent attitude.[342]

The commercial college that Fr. Bedard opened in his parish in 1882 to prepare young men for careers in business and industry was but part of his dream for the Canadians in Fall River. He wished also to open a classical college as the first step towards providing the Canadians in the United States with a national clergy. For reasons of his own, Bishop Hendricken refused him permission to do so. The refusal again served to enhance the sense of persecution Fr. Bedard felt from his bishop.[343]

When Notre Dame was first established, Fr. Bedard ministered to a mixed congregation of Irish and French Canadians. Over the years Bishop Hendricken had assigned several young Irish priests

[340]H. A. Dubuque, *Le Guide Canadien-Francais de Fall River et Notes Historiques sur les Canadiens de Fall River* (Fall River: 1888), pp. 187-89, 199-205.
[341]*Providence Journal*, July 19, 1879; Vaillant, "Notes Biographiques," p. 19.
[342]Bishop Hendricken to Cardinal Simeoni, September 25, 1880, FRChA.
[343]Vaillant, "Notes Biographiques," pp. 16-18.

to assist Fr. Bedard with his Irish parishioners. In April 1882, the Irish of Notre Dame successfully petitioned the bishop for permission to separate from Notre Dame and form a new parish to be called Immaculate Conception. When later that same year Bishop Hendricken reassigned Fr. Bedard's Irish assistant, the stubborn Fall River pastor insisted on having a French Canadian as his new assistant. The pastor's refusal to accept an assistant of the bishop's choice prompted Bishop Hendricken to refuse to grant permission for visiting Canadian clergy to assist in the parish. Bishop Hendricken's action helped further his image in the minds of Fr. Bedard's acquaintances in Canada as a bishop who was anti-French.[344]

While the land on which he built the church was acquired in the name of the bishop, most of the money for the land on which Fr. Bedard would build the rectory, convent and other buildings had come from Fr. Bedard's own family. Fr. Bedard held title to these properties in his own name and paid municipal taxes on them. In 1883 a tax assessor brought to his attention the fact that if a charitable religious corporation held title to his properties, under Massachusetts law, they would be exempt from municipal taxes. Acting on this information, in April 1883, Fr. Bedard formed the Corporation Notre Dame with himself as president and the Sisters of Jesus and Mary as members of the corporation. Wishing to build a new convent, the sisters, in February 1884, withdrew from the corporation and were replaced by Fr. Bedard's two nieces who worked in the rectory, and a group of laymen. Later a large parcel of land was given to the sisters by the corporation as the site for their new convent. The remainder of the property was, according to Fr. Bedard's instructions, to go after his death to the Oblate Fathers whom he hoped would succeed him in the pastorate of Notre Dame.[345]

Fr. Bedard was striken with apoplexy just after spending eight days on retreat with the Jesuits at Sault-au-Recollet, and died on August 24, 1884, at the age of forty-two. His death was mourned not only by his parishioners but by all Canadians of New England to whom he had become a hero in their struggle for recognition and respect.[346] As successor to Fr. Bedard, Bishop Hendricken asked, not the Oblate Fathers as Fr. Bedard had wished, but another Canadian priest of the diocese, Fr. Edouard Nobert, the pastor of Warren, to take charge of the parish. Fr. Nobert served in Notre Dame only a few weeks before he found the financial affairs and other administra-

[344]*Ibid.*, pp. 21-22.
[345]*L'Independant*, April 10, 1885.
[346]Hamon, *Les Canadiens-Francais de la Nouvelle Angleterre*, p. 318; Rumilly, *Histoire des Franco-Americains*, p. 105; D. M. A. Magnon, *Notre Dame de Lourdes de Fall River, Mass.* (Quebec: 1925), pp. 55-59.

tive responsibilities of the parish so complex that he asked the bishop to return him to his post in Warren as he felt his health would not hold up under the strain. Not having another Canadian priest in his diocese who had the experience to take charge of a large parish, Bishop Hendricken, on October 10, 1884, asked Fr. Samuel P. McGee, who was then pastor of the mixed Irish-Canadian parish of St. Joseph's in Natick, Rhode Island, to take temporary charge of the parish as administrator. Born in Canada of Irish and Canadian parents, Fr. McGee had received the bulk of his education there and spoke fluent French but with an accent and anglicisms.[347]

Having Fr. McGee as their pastor was acceptable to a large portion of the parish but not to the trustees of the Notre Dame corporation or to those who put credence in the rumored vow of Fr. Bedard's antagonists among the Irish clergy of the city that Fr. Bedard would be the last French priest of Notre Dame.[348] The trustees appointed a five-man committee to call on Bishop Hendricken during the first week of October to press their demand for a Canadian pastor. According to the report of the meeting found in French Canadian sources, the bishop reminded the delegation that it was not his fault that Fr. Nobert had become so quickly discouraged over the complex financial affairs of the parish. To his mind, the need to have a French priest was at best a temporary measure for he presumed that in ten years everyone in the French Canadian parishes would be speaking English. The delegates on their part reportedly asserted that they felt their language was the guardian of their faith. They noted, too, that their language not only had value in itself but it protected their young people from the dangers present in their Protestant milieu and especially from mixed marriages.[349] During the course of the interview, the bishop allegedly responded to the committee's request to have another priest like Fr. Bedard: "What! Give you another priest like Father Bedard? . . . Father Bedard was a curse to me, curse to you and a curse to everybody!"[350] Even before the visit by the parish delegation, Bishop Hendricken had unleashed his frustration to a Canadian bishop who had some knowledge of the situation in Fall River: "You know how I have tried. The poor unfortunate Bedard of Fall River had bequeathed me a fortune of misery."[351]

[347] *Providence Journal, Fall River Evening News,* October 16, 1884; Rumilly, *Histoire des Franco-Americains,* p. 105.

[348] *Fall River Evening News,* November 5, 1884; Vaillant, "Notes Biographiques," pp. 17-18; Hamon, *Les Canadiens-Francais de la Nouvelle Angleterre,* pp. 317-19.

[349] *L'Independent,* August 28, 1885; Rumilly, *Histoire des Franco-Americains,* p. 106.

[350] Vaillant, "Notes Biographiques," p. 30.

[351] Bishop Thomas F. Hendricken to Bishop L. Z. Moreau, October 7, 1884, St. Hyacinthe Diocesan Chancery Archives. Hereafter cited St HCA.

Bishop Hendricken did not disagree with what the Canadians said and would not have hesitated to send down another Canadian priest as pastor if he had a qualified one to send. He felt, however, that Fr. McGee could at least temporarily provide the pastoral care they desired. When the delegates evidently continued to press their point, they succeeded only in provoking the bishop to say that he knew his business and had appointed a man who could speak better French than themselves.[352] Having determined that the bishop would not immediately replace Fr. McGee with another Canadian priest, the trustees decided to try to force him out. Since the corporation, not the parish, owned the rectory, Fr. McGee was forced to find lodging elsewhere. But in spite of threats against him, he continued on as pastor.

Although faced with the opposition to Fr. McGee, the bishop continued to maintain, in response to reporters questions, that "the appointment of Fr. McGee was a good one and he should not have made it otherwise."[353] At the same time, Bishop Hendricken continued to promise the Canadians "to do the best for them it was possible for him to do."[354] But the bishop was not about to replace Fr. McGee until he had a Canadian priest who had his confidence and one who would not repeat what the bishop considered the mistakes of Fr. Bedard.

Since Bishop Hendricken delayed in sending a French Canadian priest to succeed Fr. Bedard, five of the trustees attempted to take matters into their own hands and wrote to Bishop Charles Fabre of Montreal to inquire whether he would send a Canadian priest to serve Notre Dame. They spoke of their fears that, since Bishop Hendricken had not kept his promise to send a Catholic priest to serve St. Anne's, they would also be similarly deprived.[355] Bishop Fabre informed the trustees that he did not have any priest available nor could he in any way intervene in the matter.[356] The trustees also wrote to Cardinal John McCloskey, who echoed Bishop Fabre's opinion that he could not intervene in the affairs of another diocese.[357]

The cause of the Canadians in Fall River became the rallying point of many nationalists and and provided an opportunity for

---

[352]*Fall River Evening News,* November 5, 1884.

[353]*Ibid.,* December 12, 1884.

[354]*Providence Journal,* December 15, 1884; *Fall River Evening News,* December 16, 1884.

[355]Georges E. Arcand, *et al.,* to Bishop Fabre, December 15, 1885, MChA.

[356]F. Harel, Chancellor, to Georges E. Arcand, *et al.,* December 20, 1884, MChA.

[357]*Fall River Evening News,* January 9, 1885.

manipulation for a few. A Canadian priest, Fr. Alphonse Villeneuve, pastor of St. Paul's in Sandy Hill, New York, who had already established a reputation as a lover of intrigue, offered his services and encouragement to the trustees in appealing their case to the Congregation of the Propaganda in Rome. For the moment, the trustees rejected the idea of sending a delegate to Rome. Instead, at Villeneuve's suggestion, they engaged a canon lawyer in Rome to plead their case before the congregation.[358]

Sometime in early December, Bishop Hendricken assigned a young, newly ordained Canadian priest, Fr. Joseph Bachand, to assist Fr. McGee at Notre Dame. Fr. Bachand's appointment did not satisfy the militants who continued to oppose Fr. McGee's presence. During the next six weeks there were many incidents of disruption of Fr. McGee's Masses which served only to deepen the antagonism. A letter writer to the *Fall River Evening News* who sympathized with the dissidents observed at the end of January that the situation in Fall River "had reached a point where it is almost necessary that something should be done by the most serious and disinterested minds to bring about a cessation of that state of affairs."[359] Evidently Bishop Hendricken was also of the same mind. During the first week of February 1885, the bishop tried to create conditions in which some kind of settlement could be reached by transferring Fr. McGee to the new parish of St. Stephen's in Dodgeville and assigning Fr. Owen Clarke as the new administrator of Notre Dame.[360] Although Fr. Clarke was of Irish background, he had studied philosophy and theology in Canada and had proved a very popular assistant among the Canadians in St. Anne's parish in Fall River.[361] But Fr. Clarke was no better received than Fr. McGee.[362]

The parish's failure to accept Fr. Clarke proved the breaking point for Bishop Hendricken's patience. The bishop ordered Fr. Clarke to strip the altars of the church and remove the vestments and sacred vessels, which he did on Thursday, February 12th. The next day the *Fall River Evening News* printed an official letter from Bishop Hendricken announcing that he had been compelled to close the church "by the insubordination of some of the flock, who, strangely enough, wish to dictate to him on matters which entirely pertain to his authority." The bishop instructed the other clergy-

---

[358]Bishop Charles [Fabre] to Rev. A. Villeneuve, May 18, 1886, MChA; Bishop Elphege [Gravel] to Bishop Hendricken, April 27, 1886, PChA.
[359]*Fall River Evening News*, January 29, 1885.
[360]*Ibid.*, February 7, 1885.
[361]*Ibid.*, February 9, 1885.
[362]*Ibid.*, February 11, 14, 1885.

men of the city to administer the sacraments to any from Notre
Dame who wished to receive them "provided they have not been
participators or abettors in the present controversy," and to attend
any sick calls that may be brought to them.[363] The closure of the
church led the leaders of the movement to confirm what they had
long asserted—Bishop Hendricken was anti-French. A writer in the
city's French language paper, Le Castor, lamented that because of his
refusal to give them a suitable pastor, they were now to be deprived
of the sacraments of salvation, and exposed to excommunication
and damnation.[364]

With the placing of the church of Notre Dame under interdiction, the Providence Visitor editorialized on the situation for the first
time. For the Visitor, the dispute concerned the refusal of the
Canadians to accept episcopal authority. The editor showed little
understanding of why the Canadians persisted in their refusal to
accept an Irish priest. He saw Fr. McGee's reassignment and Fr.
Clarke's appointment as a concession while condemning the obsti-
nancy of the French Canadians as an attempt to dictate the selection
of their priest. For the Visitor writer applying the "test of nationality
to the ministrations of the priesthood was to introduce the Know-
nothing principle."[365]

Buoyed by hope of a positive response from Rome to their plea
for a Canadian pastor, the most active protesters, in March, raised
funds to send a delegate to Rome to personally present their case
before the Propaganda. Their action was spurred by the rumor that
Bishop Hendricken was planning to do the same.[366] The delegate,
Mr. Narcisse R. Martineau, carried with him letters from prominent
members of the parish and clerical supporters in Canada.[367] To
propagate their cause, several of the chief proponents of a Canadian
pastor purchased the presses of Le Castor and began publishing a
weekly called L'Independant that they intended to be the voice of the
Canadians' struggle. L'Independant published its own articles and
reproduced news from other Canadian papers that reflected the
sympathy and attention the cause of the French of Notre Dame
received among Canadians elsewhere.[368] In Worcester, Ferdinand
Gagnon, publisher of the Travailleur, joined the fray by attacking the
priests of the Diocese of Providence who supported assimilation.

---

[363]Ibid., February 13, 1885; Providence Morning Star, February 14, 1885.
[364]Le Castor, February 20, 1885.
[365]Providence Visitor, February 28, 1885.
[366]Le Castor, March 13, 1885.
[367]Fall River Evening News, June 4, 1885.
[368]Le Castor, March 13, 1885; L'Independant, March 27; April 10, 1885.

While the Canadians in Fall River waited for Rome's intervention, a revolt among the French Canadians in Canada led by Louis
Riel was suppressed by the British. Riel's trial was widely publi-
cized and served to quicken the patriotism of the French Canadians and their consciousness of oppression of Canadians everywhere.[369]

In the middle of April, rumors spread among the Canadians in
Fall River that the Prefect of the Propaganda would soon write to
Bishop Hendricken compelling him to hear the grievances of the
parish. At this news, the hopes of the Canadians again soared as they
felt that "their cause was well nigh secure."[370] At the same time
another rumor reportedly circulated in ecclesiastical circles that
Rome would soon move towards a total solution of the problem
created by the demand of the Canadians for French pastors, by
appointing a French bishop to a new diocese to be formed in Massachusetts. Only three years before, a report had begun circulating in
Fall River that a new diocese was to be created embracing Norfolk,
Plymouth, Bristol, Dukes and Nantucket counties in order to avoid
the "annoyance" of having a diocese composed of one state and
part of another. Seemingly, some pinned their hopes of a solution
to the Notre Dame crises in the appointment of a Canadian to the
new diocese.[371]

On May 16, 1885, Cardinal Simeoni wrote to Archbishop John
Williams of Boston detailing reports he had received of parishioners
of Notre Dame being refused absolution and dying without receiving the sacrament. The cardinal referred also to the fact that "many
Bishops" had written the Sacred Congregation "pressing it to apply
a prompt and effective remedy" in order to avert the imminent
danger of defection and apostasy.[372] Simeoni asked Williams, who
as archbishop had pastoral responsibility for the Providence diocese, to assist in bringing about an amicable solution to the controversy. He suggested that "those Canadians who have behaved
wrongly toward the Bishop of Providence make an act of submission
and obedience and humbly ask his pardon for their conduct. After
which, Bishop Hendricken, on his part, would reopen the church
and appoint a French priest as its pastor." The cardinal went on to
suggest that Bishop Goesbriand, the French-born bishop of Bur-
lington, Vermont, might act as a partner in quieting the controversy
and ended with the assurance that Mr. Martineau, who had come to

[369]Rumilly, *Histoire des Franco-Americains,* pp. 107-110.
[370]*Fall River Evening News,* April 20, 1885.
[371]*Ibid.,* June 20; December 30, 1882; February 8; June 15, 1883; April 20, 1885.
[372]Cardinal Simeoni to Archbishop Williams, May 16, 1885, BChA.

Rome as representative of the parish, had promised that he would work for peace among his compatriots.[373]

When Mr. Martineau, who reportedly was twice received by the Holy Father, returned to Fall River on June 3rd, rumors quickly circulated that a cardinal had promised that the church would be opened at once with a French priest and that a French bishop would probably also be appointed. The report suggested that Bishop Hendricken would be simply overruled, an outcome that would have satisfied the leaders as they frequently said they had not wished to see Bishop Hendricken humiliated. However, the same article of the *Fall River Evening News* that reported the rumor, also reported a statement by Bishop Hendricken that there would be no raising of the interdiction until there was entire submission to the authority of the church by the French people of Flint Village.[374]

Even before Archbishop Williams discussed the substance of Cardinal Simeoni's letter with Hendricken and before Mr. Martineau had returned from Rome, Bishop Hendricken had planned to reopen the church. The bishop had scheduled to administer Confirmation at Immaculate Conception in Flint and at Sacred Heart and St. Patrick's in Somerset on June 7th. In reply to the cardinal, Archbishop Williams wrote that Hendricken would reopen the church on the 7th and if this did not take place, he would attend to the business of Simeoni's letter.[375] Apparently, Archbishop Williams decided to postpone intervention to see if Hendricken could work the situation out alone.

On Friday, June 12th, Bishop Hendricken asked Fr. Michael Cassidy, the Irish assistant at St. Anne, to take charge of reopening the parish. The *Fall River Evening News* of June 13th announced the parish's reopening together with the information that Fr. Cassidy would be assisted by Fr. Garin, a French-born Oblate from Lowell, Massachusetts, who was to give a parish mission.[376] Fr. Cassidy was no better received than his two predecessors.[377] When a reporter for the *Providence Journal* interviewed Bishop Hendricken on Monday after Fr. Cassidy's rejection, the bishop recounted for him the understanding on which he acted in reopening the church. The bishop expressed his conviction that "the whole trouble had been brought about by the instrumentality of a few discontented members," a fact that the *L'Independent* later disputed. He stated in the

[373]*Ibid.*
[374]*Fall River Evening News*, April 20, 1885; *Fall River Daily Herald*, June 4, 1885.
[375]Archbishop Williams to Cardinal Simeoni, May 16, 1885, annotation, BChA.
[376]*Fall River Evening News*, June 13, 1885.
[377]*Ibid.*, June 13, 15, 1885.

same interview that to his mind "the trouble involved the mainte-
nance of a principle, which was that the question of nationality
should not enter into the matter of the appointment of priests for
parishes, which principle would be sacrificed if he acceded to their
demands that a Canadian priest be appointed over that parish."[378]

On June 25th, Archbishop Williams wrote to Cardinal Simeoni
giving an account of the situation in Fall River and why the church
had not been reopened.[379] The archbishop's letter was followed by
another rash of complaints and appeals from the Canadians. On
August 29th, Simeoni replied to Archbishop Williams stating that
the demands and complaints of the Canadians seemed endless. The
state of affairs, he said, could not go on any longer and he appealed
to Williams "to endeavor by every means to resolve this controversy." He repeated his previous suggestion for ending the matter,
adding now that Williams himself should select a Canadian priest
"who is prudent and pious to take charge of Notre Dame," but
"only after those who have acted disrespectfully towards the Bishop
of Providence first ask his pardon."[380] Only a few days before Cardinal Simeoni wrote his letter, Bishop Hendricken underscored the
condition given in the cardinal's letter when, on a visit to Fall River,
he was quoted, as saying; "It is very probable that the good people
of Flint Village, the really sensible Catholics, have seen the folly of
their resistance to church authority, but the church will not be
reopened until the congregation of Notre Dame submits to that
authority. The man that went to Rome was going to have the church
reopened immediately on his return, but the church had not been
opened yet."[381]

Within two weeks of Archbishop Williams's receipt of the cardinal's letter, Bishop Hendricken, after discussing the situation with
the archbishop, went down to Fall River himself to reopen the
church. The bishop first wrote to the sisters that he was coming to
reopen the church, retaining for himself the title of pastor. Accompanied by one of his assistants at the cathedral, a Canadian-born
priest, Fr. Peter Feron, the bishop arrived at the sister's convent on
Saturday afternoon and went from there to the church which he
formally opened. Later that evening a committee of four called at
the convent to ask the bishop what his intentions were in coming to
Notre Dame along with Fr. Feron. The bishop replied, as he had

[378]*Providence Journal,* June 16, 1885; *L'Independent,* June 19, 1885.
[379]See notation on Cardinal Simeoni's letter to Archbishop Williams, May 16, 1885, BChA.
[380]Cardinal Simeoni to Archbishop Williams, August 29, 1885, BChA.
[381]*Fall River Evening News,* August 22, 1885.

stated to the sisters, that he had come to reopen the church. The decision as to who was to be pastor had been taken out of his hands by the Propaganda and given over to Archbishop Williams and Bishop Goesbriand.[382]

The news of the bishop's arrival and his plans for the next day prompted a call for a meeting of the parishioners that same evening, at seven for the women of the parish and at eight for the men. The leaders discussed the issues and when a vote was taken, "it was unanimously voted to persist in the demand for a French pastor." Since they still had every hope that Rome would force the bishop's hand, the leaders saw the visit of the bishop as a piece of strategy aimed at inducing the parishioners to give a semblance of submission by attendance at church. To defeat this purpose, those at the meeting voted to stay away from Mass.[383]

The following Sunday, Bishop Hendricken and Fr. Feron again traveled to Fall River to offer Mass. After Mass, the bishop read a letter he had received from Archbishop Williams instructing the parishioners to appoint delegates that would call on the archbishop to discuss the situation.[384] On the Monday, the delegates of the parish were courteously received by Archbishop Williams who informed them that he had received instructions from Rome to provide the parish with a French Canadian priest. There remained, according to the L'Independent's account of the meeting, only formalities to complete. The Canadians took this news as a sign that their struggle was soon to be decided in their favor.[385]

However, at a second meeting between the archbishop and the parish's delegates the following week, the parish learned that before a French Canadian pastor would be appointed, they would have to meet certain conditions. One, already stated by Cardinal Simeoni in his letter, was that the parish apologize to Bishop Hendricken for their treatment of the priests he had sent. This, the parish refused to do. They claimed that they had committed no acts for which they felt bound to apologize; the insults complained of were, in their view, the acts of individuals. The second condition was put to the parish in the form of a question: Did the parish ask to have a French pastor as a right or as a favor? The parish had consistently claimed that it was their right to have a pastor of their own nationality—a sentiment they confirmed in their answer to the archbishop's ques-

[382]Ibid., September 12, 1885; L'Independent, September 11, 18, 1885.
[383]Providence Journal, September 14, 15, 1885.
[384]Fall River Evening News, September 21, 1885; Providence Journal, September 21, 1885.
[385]L'Independent, September 25, 1885.

tion.[386] Only two weeks before, Bishop Hendricken was quoted as saying that the Canadians "are looking for a decision as an act of justice and right, which had they kept quiet, would probably have been granted them long ago as a favor which is the only way it could have been granted."[387]

Bishop Hendricken apparently believed that to concede that the Canadians had an absolute right to a pastor of their own nationality, would have created enormous problems in staffing Canadian parishes with priests who command the respect both of their bishop and their people. Furthermore, if he acknowledged the right of the Canadians to have pastors of their own nationality, the bishop felt that he would be pressed to provide the Portuguese, Italians and Germans of his diocese with pastors of their nationality. When Archbishop Williams, on October 2nd, wrote to Cardinal Simeoni detailing what he had done to resolve the situation in Fall River, he pointed out the difficulties that would ensue if the the assignment of a Canadian pastor to Notre Dame appeared as the consequence of a general principle. There were reports at the time that other bishops had also contacted the Propaganda pointing out the gravity of the situation.[388] In fact, bishops of other dioceses faced with similar problems in relation to their German Catholic populations expressed similar concerns to Cardinal Simeoni.[389]

On October 23, 1885, the cardinal wrote Archbishop Williams giving his decision. While he acknowledged that the Canadians had a right according to Canon Law to have a pastor of their own nationality, Simeoni fully agreed with Williams's judgment that the matter could not be settled in such a way as to become a general principle. He therefore suggested that Williams allow Bishop Hendricken to appoint whomever he wished to head the parish and at the same time to give him a French Canadian assistant with the understanding that he would in time become the pastor.[390] After receiving the cardinal's letter, Archbishop Williams, on November 18th, wrote to Bishop Hendricken informing him of the contents of the letter. On Saturday, both the Fall River and Providence papers printed Williams's letter to Bishop Hendricken.[391]

The publication of the archbishop's letter set the stage for a

[386]*Fall River Evening News; Providence Journal,* September 30, 1885.
[387]*Fall River Evening News,* September 14, 1885.
[388]Archbishop Williams to Cardinal Simeoni, October 2, 1885, BChA; *L 'Independent,* October 16, 1885; February 26, 1886; *Providence Journal,* October 12, 1885.
[389]George Zurcher, "Foreign Ideas in the Catholic Church in America." *The Roycraft Quarterly,* (November 1896), pp. 1-13.
[390]Cardinal Simeoni to Archbishop Williams, October 23, 1885, BChA.
[391]*Providence Journal; Fall River Evening News,* November 21, 1885.

crucial meeting of the boycotters on the evening of November 28th. Convinced by priests sympathetic to their cause and by assurances from the lawyer whom they had hired to pursue their case in Rome that their cause was just, the leaders of the boycott refused to believe that Cardinal Simeoni could now ignore the justice of their claim and ask them to accept an Irishman as their pastor, even if it was only for a short time. To their minds then, Archbishop Williams's letter was not authentic since it empowered Bishop Hendricken to do what the Canadians were convinced he could not canonically do. Dr. John Chagnon, who had previously felt Fr. Bedard's wrath and who was a proponent of compromise, read a letter he had received from a Canadian priest in Rome, which substantially supported his previously expressed views on the need for submission to authority. But Chagnon's advocacy of submission received no support. Fatigue forced an inconclusive end to the meeting at two in the morning. Before they broke up, the protestors voted to continue their boycott of Mass.[392]

Two weeks later, Bishop Hendricken officially appointed Fr. Peter Feron pastor of Notre Dame. On Tuesday, December 8th, the local papers reported the news of his appointment together with a note that the priest had rented a house in the parish belonging to Dr. Chagnon. The boycotters held another meeting that same evening and passed a series of resolutions denying that Bishop Hendricken had the authority to appoint any but a French Canadian pastor. After the vote, a committee visited Fr. Feron to personally protest his appointment.[393] An even larger meeting of the boycotters on Saturday debated the question of accepting Fr. Feron as pastor. The debate ended with a vote against the proposal.[394]

Throughout the dispute Bishop Hendricken maintained the view that a majority of the parishioners would accept whatever priest he assigned. To the bishop's mind, "scarcely more than a half dozen demagogues—all irreligious men, have constituted themselves the people of Flint Village, and brought a bright and good population into every manner of excess against priest and bishop." After publication of Archbishop Williams's letter, and in spite of the declarations of boycotters and their leaders, the bishop wrote to Bishop Moreau of the Diocese of St. Hyacinthe in Canada on December 9th that "the rebellion is breaking up visibly, although much will have to be done before the whole people return to church

[392]*Providence Journal; Fall River Evening News,* November 23, 1885.
[393]*Providence Journal,* December 11, 1885; *Fall River Evening News,* December 10, 11, 1885; *L'Independent,* December 11, 1885.
[394]*Providence Journal,* December 14, 1885.

again." Hendricken's reason for writing to Bishop Moreau was to ask the bishop to allow Fr. Joseph Laflamme to take the important position of assistant pastor at Notre Dame. At the request of his bishop, Fr. Laflamme agreed to go to Fall River.[395]

The choice of Fr. Laflamme proved to be an excellent one. Arriving on December 12, 1885 he soon showed himself to be the "wise, conciliating man" that the situation demanded. His presence helped to assure all but the most extreme that their wish to have a French Canadian priest to attend their needs would be met. During the week of December 20th, Dr. Chagnon took the lead in negotiating some form of settlement with Bishop Hendricken. Neither the bishop's diary nor the newspaper accounts provide any details on the terms of the agreement.[396] The men behind the L'Independent, on their part, saw the Propaganda's decision to allow Bishop Hendricken to appoint Fr. Feron as pastor as a "favor" granted to the bishop.[397]

The fact that Fr. Laflamme gave up an important parish to serve as an assistant in Fall River was evidence enough that he would, after a decent interval, be made pastor. Fr. Laflamme quickly won the acceptance of the parishioners who supported Dr. Chagnon's views. Finally on March 17, 1886, news spread that Fr. Feron had withdrawn and that Fr. Laflamme was to be the new pastor of Notre Dame. The following Sunday, an immense crowd filled the church to hear their new pastor ask their assistance in healing the wounds created by the bitter struggle.[398]

The wounds, however, did not heal easily or quickly. There were those who refused to return to church because of the way the Propaganda had handled the situation or because of personal animosities that had been created during the agitation.[399] But with the help of a majority of his parishioners, Fr. Laflamme quietly began rebuilding the parish, both spiritually and physically. Within a few weeks of his appointment, he secured from Bishop Moreau, with Bishop Hendricken's consent, the assistance of a young Canadian priest, Fr. Joseph Payan, who also was quickly accepted by the people. Together the two men did much to bring peace to the parish.

[395]Bishop Hendricken to Bishop L. Z. Moreau, December 9, 1885, St HChA.

[396]Providence Journal, December 22, 1885.

[397]L'Independent, February 26, 1886.

[398]Dubuque, Le Guide Canadien-Francais de Fall River, pp. 193, 229.

[399]Providence Journal, February 27, 1886; Fall River Evening News, March 18, 1886; Dubuque, Le Guide Canadien-Francais de Fall River, pp. 229-32; Magnon, Notre Dame de Lourdes, pp. 66–67.

Bishop Hendricken and other bishops and priests who became involved in the controversy in Fall River harbored a deep seated fear that the Canadians would express their discontent, especially after the closing of their church, by leaving the Catholic church to join another tradition. A small number of French-speaking residents of Fall River had formed the "Societe evangelique francaise" in May 1882.[400] A larger group of French-speaking Protestants met regularly on Pleasant Street.[401]

The Protestant missionaries expended considerable effort among the French Canadians in Fall River when the boycott of the Irish priests appeared to create a unique opportunity for conversion. To assist in their work, they invited Mr. Charles Chiniquy, an apostate priest, to Fall River. On hearing of his coming, the Canadians of Notre Dame voted to give him no encouragement.[402] In general, the missionary's efforts were expended without success since the Canadians' dispute with Bishop Hendricken was rooted in pride of their heritage, and not in any theological or spiritual antipathy. Their Catholicism was deeply rooted in their Canadian past. Both they and their forefathers had resisted the British pressures on their faith for more than a century and were not about to abandon it over such a cause. If there were some who continued to stay away from Mass, there apparently were none who abandoned the Catholic Church for another.[403]

The Church and Social Concerns

While Bishop Hendricken and his priests and religious devoted the greater part of their efforts to providing for the spiritual needs of their people, the work of the apostolate frequently enough required the teaching church to give witness before the society in which the Church lived and worked. The 1870s were particularly difficult years for workingmen and their families. Even in good years, glutted market conditions, the breakdown or replacement of machinery, or the scarcity of water could lead to plant shutdowns or wage cuts and the creation of resentments and tension between the employer and the employed. In May, 1873, agitation to reduce the work day to ten hours in cotton and worsted mills led the mule spinners to strike in the mills of Pawtucket, Olneyville and Woon-

[400]*Fall River Evening News,* May 10, 1882.
[401]*Ibid.,* July 17, 1882.
[402]*Providence Journal,* November 16, 1885.
[403]Magnan, *Notre Dame de Lourdes,* p. 66.

socket. The effort failed and the strike leaders were blacklisted. The spinners went back to work if they could. The shutdown of mills for those families who lacked savings meant hardships and forced some, especially among the newly arrived French Canadians, to return to Canada until conditions improved, and forced other workers to move on to other areas to secure new jobs.[404]

After the Panic of 1873 hit the state, manufacturers who did not shut down resorted to wage reductions to ease the crunch on their capital. Worker strikes, as in Warwick in 1875, were easily broken because of the surplus of laborers and the anxiousness of many workers to hold onto their jobs, even if wages were lower.[405]

When, in the first half of 1877, the nation sank towards the depths of the depression, wage cuts on the railroads led to strikes and outbreaks of violence and property destruction among workers in various parts of the Country. In July, following a week of reports of riots and bloodshed, Bishop Hendricken offered his views to his congregation at the cathedral. After first expressing his gratitude that Rhode Island had been spared from any outbreaks of violence, the bishop spoke compassionately of the situation of the people of his diocese who were out of work or working at starvation wages, struggling against poverty. He asked his people to remember that conditions in the Country generally were bad. He also cautioned workers not to strike unless they were prepared to lose their jobs and unless they honestly thought they could better their position. The sense of the bishop's message was that it was "unwise" and "injurious" to business and the true interests of the working people to precipitate a conflict between labor and capital until such time as economic conditions improved.[406]

Economic conditions for the millworkers did not improve. On April 1, 1878, the mill operatives in the former Sprague mills in the Pawtuxet Valley villages of Quidnick, Natick and Arctic had their wages cut fifteen percent and in Warren, wages were cut twenty-five percent. The cuts barely left the workers enough to live on. As they had in 1875, some of the operatives walked out, but without prospects of jobs elsewhere, the majority of the workers stayed put, reluctantly taking what they could get.

The situation in the Pawtuxet Valley mills prompted a series of articles in the *Weekly Visitor* on the conditions of laborers in the state in which the paper basically repeated Bishop Hendricken's advice

[404]*Providence Journal,* May 2, 10, 13, 21, 22, 24, 26, 27, 30, 1873; *Woonsocket Patriot,* May 16, 23, 30, 1873.
[405]*Providence Journal,* April 7, 1875; *Rhode Island Country Journal,* April 21, 1875.
[406]*Providence Journal,* July 30, 1877.

and offered as the only remedy for the wage reduction the seeking of "employment with those who will adequately recompense [the working people] for their labor."[407] Although facing difficult times, there were men and women within the community who clung to the American dream—that opportunity existed for financial success for all those who honestly wished to work and sacrifice to get ahead. In reply to a letter writer expressing such an opinion, the *Visitor* advised the correspondent to study the labor question from a Christian standpoint; "Make himself familiar with the sorrows and burdens of the poor; do what he can to relieve their misfortune, to defend them when they are oppressed; to maintain in place and out of place that the laborer should be paid living wages, and not allow himself to be overcome by specious arguments or the meaningless jargon of the counting-house."[408]

In the face of such labor disputes, the Catholic clergy in general appealed to the sense of justice of the employers, counseled the workers against violence in their protests against the prevailing working conditions, and insisted upon the right of each worker to earn a living wage. But they took no other action because they regarded labor disputes as political questions and therefore not a proper matter for the pulpit. Only on occasion, as when the fear that his position on a labor dispute would be thought less than neutral, did a priest like Fr. James L. Smith, the pastor of St. John's, Arctic, speak out. In answer to rumors that he supported the employers, Fr. Smith spoke of his own experience as a mill operative and of the condition of some of the people of the village whom he felt were more unfairly treated than the slaves he had known in Maryland.[409]

A prevailing sense of paternalism prompted a few priests such as Fr. Michael McCabe of St. Charles in Woonsocket to speak out on matters of concern to his people. One such occasion was provided by the labor dispute that arose in the nearby Massachusetts town of Millville. In July 1885, when the effects of the panic had given way to another cycle of prosperity, the Knights of Labor began an extended strike of the Millville Rubber Works, a plant that employed men who attended Mass at St. Charles. When, at a certain point in September, he felt that the strike leaders were being unjust in their charges against the company and the walkout was causing too great a loss among the workers, Fr. McCabe attempted to call the workers together to discuss the situation. Supposing that Fr.

---

[407]*Weekly Visitor,* April 7; May 4, 1878.
[408]*Ibid.,* May 18, 25, 1878.
[409]*Providence Visitor,* April 12, 1884.

McCabe was acting out of sympathy for the company's position, the union's leaders advised the workers against attending the meeting. But Fr. McCabe did have his meeting and his say.[410]

In their struggle to improve their lot, workers had to contend with the reality that their demands for higher wages and shorter hours went contrary to current economic beliefs. In Rhode Island, their efforts were further frustrated by a legislature controlled by rural and conservative interests and by an evolving technology which, especially in the textile industry, gradually reduced the number of jobs requiring unskilled labor. The result was that workers were easy to replace. The working population, made up as it was of British, Irish, French Canadians and Germans, could and did co-operate in political agitation and in strike actions to improve their lot.[411] There were also a number of incidents where the division between strikers and strikebreakers were drawn along ethnic lines. Rhode Island saw the tension between British and Irish and the newly arrived French Canadians millhands flare into violence in Natick in the Pawtuxet Valley in 1875 over the question of strike-breaking.[412] But that incident paled before the more serious confrontation between the older, more established workers and the newcomers in Fall River in 1879. The spinners strike was precipitated again over a cut in wages. The mill operators felt that with the supply of labor available to them, they could get the same work done for less pay.[413]

The leaders of the Spinners Union in Fall River were primarily Irish Catholics who had recently replaced Englishmen who had originally dominated the union. The anger of the strikers was directed not only at the mill managers who cut their wages but also at the French Canadians who were willing to work for the lower wage rates. The union men, however, focused their most severe attack on Fr. Pierre Bedard, the pastor of Notre Dame de Lourdes. On several occasions, newly arrived Canadians had come to his rectory with the Wampanoag Mill superintendent to ask the priest's advice before signing on at the mill, an action in keeping with the place a Canadian pastor played in his community. To the strikers it appeared that Fr. Bedard was actively co-operating with the mill

[410]*Ibid.*, July 11; September 26, 1885.
[411]Italian and Portuguese immigrants were entering the factories in the 1880s, but their numbers were not such at this time to be a factor in labor disputes.
[412]*Providence Journal,* April 7, 1875.
[413]*Providence Visitor,* August 30, 1879; Philip Silvia, "Spindle City: Labor, Politics and Religion in Fall River, Massachusetts, 1870-1905" (Unpublished doctoral dissertation, Fordham University, 1973), pp. 106-20.

owners in securing Canadians as strikebreakers. To the union representatives who called on him to protest against his presumed actions, Fr. Bedard reiterated the conviction he shared with his fellow
clergy, that it was not his business to interfere in the strike. The
union men, not content with his explanation, protested to Bishop
Hendricken. When asked by a reporter for the *Providence Journal*
what advice he would give to any persons seeking counsel on going
to work, Fr. Bedard replied that he "should advise them to go to
work; work was a duty." He repeated to the reporter what he had
said to the delegation of the strikers who had called on him; "If it
was the conviction of the strikers that they would improve their
condition by leaving their work, that was their privilege; but the
civilization of the present day would not sanction any molestation
of those who needed to work, and wished to do so."[414] As the strike
dragged on there was violence and Canadian families were attacked
or harassed.[415] The resentment created on both sides during the
strike would serve to fuel the parish's later dispute with Bishop
Hendricken over the question of Fr. Bedard's successor.

When the effects of the Panic of 1873 began to mitigate at the
end of the 1870s, the working men of Rhode Island and their political allies began, in 1884, a renewed agitation for the passage of an
act to limit the work day for mill employees to ten hours. While the
Visitor lent support in its pages to the effort, the Catholic clergy took
no active role in championing the cause of the working man.[416] The
one exception to this was in the case of the support Bishop Hendricken and his priests gave to the demand made by men and
women who worked as retail clerks in Providence dry goods stores
to close the stores at 6:00 P.M. on Saturday evenings rather than
waiting until the last shopper had gone home. At the beginning of
1886 the clerks formed the Dry Goods Clerks Early Closing Association to push their cause. They requested the support of the clergy
of the city, and on March 10, 1886, Bishop Hendricken responded
with a letter asking his clergy to "beg the ladies of your flock to
abandon henceforth this nightly shopping and thus confer a lasting
favor on the most moral and most generous of the young ladies and
gentlemen of the city."[417]

While the Catholic clergy of the 1870s and 1880s saw labor
disputes as political matters and therefore beyond their compe-
tence, they did readily face the challenge of the misery caused by the

[414]*Providence Journal,* July 19, 1879; *Providence Visitor,* July 26, 1879.
[415]*Providence Journal,* September 18, 1879.
[416]*Providence Visitor,* March 1; May 31, 1884; February 28; March 14, 21, 1885.
[417]*Providence Journal,* March 6, 1886; *Providence Visitor,* March 20; April 3, 1886.

loss of jobs in the depression. Among the first to feel the effects of the panic were the operatives in the Delaine and Riverside Mills in the Olneyville section of Providence. In November 1873, first the Delaine, which alone employed seventeen hundred workers, and then the Riverside Mill shut down. Initially, the men, women and children employed by the mills thought they would reopen in a couple of weeks. But as the weeks dragged on, the small reserves of cash each family had put away to carry them through such difficulties slowly disappeared. The mills held back two weeks pay against the rent of company housing, but since cash was short, the companies could not or would not pay their employees what was their due. Most workers tried to accumulate a cash reserve that might support their families while the men looked elsewhere for work. Many local merchants often risked bankruptcy by extending credit against the hope of renewed employment, but when the reserves were gone and the merchants were no longer able to advance any credit, many workers especially widows with small children, were threatened by starvation during that bleak winter. The plight of the people in Olneyville stirred many individuals and groups in Providence to offer what aid they could. The overseers of the poor in Providence, North Providence and Johnston increased their efforts, while the various relief societies of Providence along with the St. Vincent de Paul Society of St. Mary's raised hundreds of dollars to provide the most destitute with the means of subsistence.[418]

The destitution of the people in Olneyville touched Bishop Hendricken as deeply as anyone in the city. On Sunday, January 4, 1874, the bishop promised to offer Mass for all those who would help the poor with even one cent in the day's collection. With what monies he had available, Bishop Hendricken provided food orders at local merchants for families with nowhere else to turn.[419] Somehow, the people survived the crisis, but the Delaine Mill remained idle until it was finally sold in 1879. Most of its workers moved away.[420]

As the depression deepened in the 1870s, the distress of the working class became more widespread. The St. Vincent de Paul Societies divided their parishes into districts and appointed one of their members to visit those who had requested aid and determine what in the way of food, clothing and shelter would meet their needs. The society also assisted the people by providing for burial

[418]*Providence Journal,* January 2, 1874; *Woonsocket Patriot,* January 30, 1874.
[419]Bishop Hendricken, "Diary," January 2, 3, 4, 5, 1874.
[420]*Weekly Visitor,* March 1, 1879.

expenses and giving assistance in finding jobs. During these years the Vincentians in Providence worked closely with the overseers of the poor who could provide additional relief generally in the form of fuel, shoes or other goods. Given the task the societies faced, the personal dedication of a few could not sustain the organization. For funds the Vincentians relied on the charity of their fellow Catholics, the zeal of their priests in offering lectures and preaching charity sermons, and the regular contributions of their own members.[421]

During 1876 when the depression was at its worst, the needs of the people came perilously close to exhausting the treasuries of the societies. Although economic conditions began to improve after 1876, winter continued to aggravate the sufferings of workers. In January 1879, Bishop Hendricken announced in the cathedral that henceforth all that was derived from the collections above what was needed for the actual running expenses of the church would be devoted to the poor.[422] During that winter, the poor could obtain bread and meat every Monday and Thursday afternoon at the bishop's house.[423] That the bishop and the Vincentians were able to answer the many calls for aid was an impressive tribute to the Catholic people of the diocese who gave what they could even if they themselves had little to spare. In several parishes the pastors organized women into sewing societies that provided both an outlet for the generosity of the parishioners and stretched even further the resources of the parish to aid more people.[424]

Of course the entire Catholic community in Providence and the diocese were not committed in the same way to the relief of the poor. Beginning in 1874 and continuing each year the effects of the depression persisted, the various religious, benevolent and fraternal societies that paraded each March 17th in honor of St. Patrick debated the question of whether or not to celebrate the day or give the money they would spend on the day's festivities to aid the poor. The Ancient Order of Hibernians, which was bound by its charter to celebrate the day, consistently advocated public celebrations while the temperance and benevolent societies generally withdrew or muted their participation.[425] On at least one occasion Bishop

[421]*Ibid.*, December 15, 28, 1878; March 8, 1879; February 7, 1880; McColgan, *A Century of Charity*, II, 234-35.
[422]*Weekly Visitor*, January 19, 1879.
[423]*Ibid.*, March 1, 1879.
[424]*Ibid.*, April 8, 26, 1876; January 27, 1878.
[425]*Providence Evening Press*, January 20; February 6, 1874; *Providence Journal*, January 31, 1876; *Weekly Visitor*, February 3, 1877; January 26; February 5, 1879.

Hendricken stayed out of the city so as to avoid the St. Patrick's day procession.[426]

Since the 1860s many bishops and priests had spoken out against membership in the Hibernian Order because of the violence associated with it, and they refused to allow its members to wear their regalia in church at the funerals of their members. Bishop Hendricken, for one, felt that for a Catholic to be a member of the order was to violate the rules of the Church against secret societies. Sensitive to the bishop's criticism, the Hibernians took pains to point out the benevolent nature of their order and the difference between themselves and other associations condemned by the Church that cloaked their activities in secrecy. They were at pains also to disassociate themselves from the violence that some Hibernians had reputedly been guilty of in the past.[427] While Bishop Hendricken refrained from an outright ban on membership in the order, the depression effected a sharp decrease in its membership because many working men lacked the ability to pay dues.[428]

While the Catholic church throughout most of the nineteenth century consistently required its clergy to refrain from making public statements on political affairs, the clergy and laity did challenge the Catholic community itself to a life of self-discipline and personal morality. Many within the Catholic community, including Bishop Hendricken, saw the abuse of drink as a major cause of poverty and immorality. The Catholic temperance movement, which had regained strength after 1869, continued into the early 1870s as an important part of parish life. The societies held rallies and regular business meetings to stir up and sustain dedication to the cause of temperance. They also served to meet social and recreational needs that their members might have ordinarily sought in the local taverns or rum shops. Many temperance societies formed military companies of temperance cadets for the young men of the parish.

In 1874 the Rhode Island General Assembly, in response to the pressure of individuals and temperance societies within the entire state, passed a law prohibiting the sale of liquor as a beverage and providing for a force of state constables to enforce the ban. Bishop Hendricken felt such a law was necessary, at least for a time, so that a habit of temperance might develop within the state and especially among the young.[429] When, in the fall of the same year, the bishop

[426]Bishop Hendricken, "Diary," March 17, 1875.
[427]*Ibid.*, October 12, 1873; *Providence Evening Press*, April 14, 1874; *Rhode Island Country Journal*, April 24, 1874; *Weekly Visitor*, June 14, 1879.
[428]*Weekly Visitor*, June 3, 1883.
[429]*Providence Evening Press*, February 23, 1874.

traveled to the Pawtuxet Valley parishes to confirm, the topic of temperance was chosen as the theme of the bishop's address to the people of the three parishes. The cause of temperance had always had a warm friend in Fr. James Gibson of St. Mary's. The bishop spoke of the "folly and wickedness of spending their money for rum, thereby keeping themselves and their families poor and destitute, and often times, criminal before the law, to their own, their families, and their churches' disgrace, as well as the distress of their neighbors and friends." During each of the ceremonies the bishop asked the young children to pledge themselves to abstain from the use of intoxicating liquors until they were twenty-one.[430]

The prohibition law passed in 1874 proved impossible to enforce. Governor Howard reported to the legislature in 1875 that the state constables charged with enforcing the law were ineffective because "of the powerful organized opposition, the apathy of one portion of the public, the antipathy of another and the lack of cooperation on the part of the peace officers of the state generally." At its May session in 1875, the assembly repealed the 1874 law and enacted a local option law for towns and created for Providence a license commission to be elected by the Board of Aldermen.[431]

The appeal of the Catholic temperance organizations waned for a time after 1876. Perhaps the cause of the decline lay with the fiasco of the 1874 law; perhaps with the depression that made parish life less stable as men moved about seeking work. Some of the priests interested in the temperance movement continued to actively support the organizations. Sacred Heart's Fr. James Brennan in East Providence, who was a former President of the State Catholic Temperance Union, frequently used the pulpit to foster temperance. In July 1877, he informed his people that he was going to ascertain who among their number was guilty of selling liquors on Sunday and threatened to expose such persons from the pulpit.[432] However, by February 1881, a temperance man wrote to the *Visitor* asserting that for two years no priest could be found to accept an office on the Board of Government of the State Union. During those years the union's state conventions were not well attended and membership generally had declined.[433] After the winter of 1881 the temperance men exerted themselves once more and the cause revived. In the early 1880s membership rolls again began to grow.[434]

---

[430]*Providence Journal,* October 23, 1874.
[431]*Acts and Resolves,* January Session, 1875; Carroll, *Rhode Island,* II, 648-50.
[432]*Providence Journal,* July 25, 1877.
[433]*Weekly Visitor,* February 5, 1881.
[434]*Ibid.,* July 2, 1881; *Providence Journal,* November 29, 1884.

The revival of the temperance cause within the Catholic community paralleled a similar revival of influence in other groups in the state. On March 17, 1885, the general assembly approved a resolution proposing an amendment to the State Constitution that read; "The manufacture and sale of intoxicating liquor to be used as a beverage shall be prohibited." Approved by the following assembly, the amendment was adopted by the state's voters on April 7, 1886, by a total of five hundred votes over the necessary sixty percent. Because the law could not be effectively enforced any more than the previous state attempt at prohibition, the provision was repealed in June 1889. Throughout the period the Church as a whole continued to favor moral persuasion as a remedy to the problems caused by drinking over any sort of legislation.[435]

Except for the increasing number of French Canadian clergy, the majority of the priests of the Diocese of Providence acquired the values they taught through the medium of Irish traditions and the virtuous example of the Sulpician Fathers in whose seminaries most of the younger clergy and many of the older had studied their moral theology. One cause for concern among both clergy and laity was the nature of the obligation the people had to financially support the work of the church. Pew rent was the ordinary source of the bulk of a parish's funds. In the cathedral the pew rents were collected quarterly by men appointed to the task. The rental prices were graded so that no one would be deprived of a place. In some parishes, such as the cathedral, St. Patrick's, Providence and St. Mary's, Newport, the clergy would take up a yearly collection in their parish by going door to door. Fr. Grace in Newport published not only the amounts each of his parishioners contributed but the reason why some failed to contribute. On other occasions during the year, special collections were taken up at Mass for the orphans, the education of seminarians or for the Pope. These ordinary sources of revenue were from the very beginning of the Church in Rhode Island supplemented by such extraordinary means of fund-raising as fairs and bazaars. The clergy resorted to them reluctantly as they felt uneasy in associating spiritual ends with a means that they felt might compromise the virtue of their people.

In the minds of the parishioners, additional collections that were taken up at the door of the church for a variety of civil and religious causes merely added to their burden. In considering the question of proper administration of the property of the Church, the bishops at the Third Plenary Council of Baltimore decided to

---

[435]Carroll, *Rhode Island*, II, 649-52; *Providence Visitor*, October 2, 1886.

ban all such collections at church doors.[436] To compensate for the loss of revenue involved in such a ban, the priests of the cathedral urged their people to greater care in the rental of pews. As the council also stressed the need to make sure the poor were not embarrassed because they lacked the means to rent a pew, the priests suggested a scale of prices that the people could choose as they were inclined. At the same time, they provided seats in the church for those who did not wish to rent a seat, and free seats for the poor who could not pay. Some, however, were less sympathetic. The pastor at St. John's in Providence in 1885 removed the last six rows of pews to provide standing room for those who did not wish to pay to sit down.[437]

The bishops of the council also banned the practice of church sponsored picnics, excursions and fairs that were intended to raise money for religious purposes. Picnics and excursions were times of relaxation and often enough occasions for drinking, sometimes to excess. Where the bishops felt exceptions should be made, wines and liquors were not to be permitted. Church sponsored fairs were also banned both for the prevalence of "gambling" and dancing that seemed to accompany these events.

The Catholic community was not alone in seeing the contradiction of games of chance being a means for raising funds for religious purposes; there was a considerable agitation in the public press against such practices.[438] Bishop Hendricken's own feelings on the appropriateness of the Church's role in sponsoring such activities can clearly be seen in the regulations of the Diocesan Synod of 1878 which allowed such activities in country parishes at the discretion of the pastor and in city parishes, only with the bishop's explicit permission.[439]

In May 1884, Bishop Hendricken decided that church fairs, excursions and picnics for the purpose of raising money for religious use were no longer to be permitted.[440] The bishop's ban included the traditional Orphan's Fair. Funds for the support of the orphans would come henceforth from a tax per child from a city parish and a yearly tax leveled on the country parishes.[441]

Although the cathedral fairs never allowed dancing, dances

---

[436]Acts of the Third Plenary Council of Baltimore, 1884, Chapter IX.

[437]*Providence Visitor*, February 14, 1885; *Providence Journal*, April 15, 1885; *Providence Morning Star*, March 9; April 27, 1885.

[438]*Providence Journal*, January 2, 1885.

[439]"Constitutiones Diocesanae," 1878, Title III.

[440]*Providence Visitor*, May 31, 1884.

[441]Sister M. Cecilia to P. A. Baach, February 28, 1885, UNDA.

other than round dances had been allowed at fairs in other parishes. Bishop Hendricken was not alone in his opposition to dancing. The *Visitor* reported that in June 1878, the pastor of the Immaculate Conception parish in North Easton, Massachusetts, Fr. Thomas Carroll, "on hearing of the plans of a party of young people to have a dance in a certain house in the town, visited the place, doffed his hat and coat and prepared to spend the evening whereupon the young people all left."[442]

In November 1883, the bishop wrote a letter to his pastors which they read from their pulpits. In the letter the bishop noted that his judgment and personal observations as well as the testimony of his clergy had convinced him that dancing at church fairs and bazaars "is not calculated to elevate the moral character of the Catholics of this diocese."[443] The ban had the support of most priests but it caused a stir among the laity and in the local press. In response to a reporter's question, the bishop pointed out that his stand on dancing at church fairs did not touch the right or wrong of dancing as an amusement but rather that "it did not elevate the standard of morality to be observed."[444] Among the prohibitions of the Third Plenary Council issued a year later was one that forbade balls for pious purposes.

Bishop Hendricken as well as his priests often spoke of the possible evil influence that some of the popular literature of the day might have on the minds of the young.[445] That this was a concern of the Church as a whole is evident from the pastoral letter that the bishops addressed to the Catholics of the United States at the end of the Plenary Council in 1884. In the letter the bishops called particular attention to the importance of the Christian home in preaching the gospel and supervising the recreational and informational needs of children. In April 1885, Bishop Hendricken pointed out that there was a definite danger in the amusements one found in the so-called dime museums and the possible evil associations one might form in frequenting skating rinks.[446]

Among men and boys, swearing and immodest language has traditionally been a supposed mark of manhood. In 1877, a Dominican preacher, Fr. Charles McKenna, at the close of a very successful mission at St. John's, Providence, suggested to the men of the parish the idea of forming a Holy Name Society devoted "to the prevention

[442] *Weekly Visitor*, June 1, 1878.
[443] *Providence Visitor*, November 24, 1883; Fr. James Gibson, "Scrapbook," p. 138.
[444] *Providence Morning Star*, November 20, 1883.
[445] *Weekly Visitor*, April 20, 1878.
[446] *Ibid.*, April 18, 1885.

of blasphemy and immodest language." Over three hundred names were taken that day.[447] The assistant at St. John's, Fr. James C. Walsh, over the years would be particularly active in promoting the cause. Within a few years other Providence city parishes organized their own Holy Name Societies.

Not only did the concerns of the Church regarding the dangers to the morals of its people crystallize in the form of admonitions to the laity, but the Third Plenary Council also attempted to formulate guidelines for priests that sought to define priestly conduct and quality of life. Bishop Hendricken's "Diary" reveals that the bishop had already anticipated much of what the Third Plenary Council would mandate. In February 1879, Fr. Christopher Hughes had taken the initiative among pastors of the diocese, probably as Bishop Hendricken himself had done in similar situations at the bequest of Bishop McFarland, in setting up a fund to care for sick and infirm priests.[448] Up to this time, such priests had to rely on the help of their families or on the generosity of their bishops. Under the guidance of a committee of pastors of the diocese, Fr. Hughes set up the Clerical Fund Society to which each priest contributed and from which those in need were provided for.[449]

In 1878 Bishop Hendricken had gathered the pastors of his diocese together to consult with them on the canonical procedures they would follow in the administration of their parishes and in the pastoral ministries. The "Constitutions of the Diocese," which the bishop published that same year, basically reiterated the decrees of the Second Plenary Council of Baltimore. Priests were reminded in the diocesan document, as they would be in the decrees of the Third Plenary Council, of the need to give good example in carrying out their ministry. Bishop Hendricken demanded a high level of character from his priests and would release those priests from diocesan service who failed to respond to his paternal admonitions.

Anti-Catholicism in the 1870s and 1880s

The Country as a whole in the late 1860s saw a revival of anti-Catholic sentiments and organizations. Seeking to exploit the situation, "escaped nuns" and "converted" priests detailed their experience before audiences who wished to hear their latent suspi-

[447]*Ibid.*, October 27, 1877.
[448]*Providence Journal*, February 22, 1879.
[449]*Weekly Visitor*, June 17, 1882.

cions confirmed. A Rhode Island girl, Edith O'Gorman, delivered a lecture in Providence in 1871 on "Convent Life."[450] Her lecture prompted the *Providence Journal* to wonder about the intelligence of the people who went to hear her.[451]

The deep-rooted bigotry that triggered this revival of anti-Catholic and anti-foreign sentiment, while surfacing at times in the popularity of lectures like that of Miss O'Gorman, often was more subtle, more personal. A millworker wrote to the *Visitor* in 1880 complaining of the arbitrariness of the superintendent of the Wanskuck Mills in refusing the use of the company's hall for Catholic socials while allowing its use to a Protestant group. What particularly incensed the writer was his conviction that the superintendent assigned work to favored laborers who shared his own religious beliefs—work that could determine the size of a man's pay.[452]

The "No Popery" excitement of the 1870s was in many ways a revival of the nativist agitation that had been shunted aside as the nation tumbled into Civil War.[453] As Robert H. Lord has already pointed out in his study of the neighboring Archdiocese of Boston, no other question of the day agitated such religious sentiment or occasioned so much friction and ill feeling as the "School Question."[454] The Catholics continued to hold in the 1870s that only education that dealt with spiritual and moral as well as material knowledge was adequate. Since they were taxed for the support of public education, many felt that the state should provide Catholic children with funds for an education that did not do violence to their conscience.

That religion was an important part of education commanded the assent of a large segment of the population of New England, but none of the sects wanted their children educated in a school which taught the beliefs of a particular sect. In the face of this divergence there was a growing party in the state as elsewhere, a party for whom the *Journal* would be willing a spokesman. They argued that religious instruction is "far better provided for by other agencies than the public schools."[455] Although in many public schools, explicit instruction in religion or even reading of the Bible had been discontinued in the face of parental protests, from the Catholic point of

---

[450]*Boston Pilot*, February 18, 1871; *Weekly Review*, March 4, 1871.
[451]*Providence Journal*, February 25, 1871.
[452]*Weekly Visitor*, April 17; May 15, 1880.
[453]John Higham, *Strangers in the Land: Patterns of American Nativism, 1860-1925* (New York: Atheneum, 1965), pp. 28-30.
[454]Lord, Sexton and Harrington, *History of the Archdiocese of Boston*, III, 75-79.
[455]*Providence Journal*, March 18, 1871.

view, the schools were still Protestant in spirit. As Bishop McQuaid of Rochester noted in an address in Providence in February of 1874, the public school teacher, "be he Catholic, Infidel or Protestant could not help impressing his religious convictions on the minds of his pupils."[456]

Bishop Hendricken, a former member of the Waterbury Public School Board, agreed with Bishop McQuaid. The Providence prelate pointed out in an address in the cathedral the following April that because of the Protestant nature of the public schools, Catholics, which then made up, by his estimate, one-third of the state's population and fully one-half of the city of Providence, were practically debarred from schools that they supported by their taxes.[457] The bishop's remarks provoked a reply from a *Journal* letter writer who signed himself Roger Williams. The writer denied that the state had an obligation to provide schools acceptable to the religious convictions of any sect.[458] The exchange prompted a series of letters and articles in the *Journal* which rehearsed both sides of the question.[459]

The defenders of the public school system were convinced that the schools were the bulwark of American democracy and interpreted Catholic objections as an attempt to demolish the system. The same concern for integrity of American democracy appeared also in another issue that roused considerable feeling in many states—that of the legitimacy of tax exemptions of churches, private schools and charitable institutions. In 1870 the Rhode Island legislature limited the exemption of property held for religious purposes to $20,000.[460] The following year the legislature passed but the people rejected a proposed amendment to the state constitution that provided "that no sectarian or denominational school or institution shall receive any aid or support from the revenues of the state, nor shall any tax be imposed upon the people or property of the state in aid of such schools or institutions."[461] The question of state aid to private charitable institutions was one that received considerable attention in neighboring Massachusetts and elsewhere at that time.[462]

In January 1875, in response to charges that exempted institutions in the state were abusing their preferred tax status, a joint

[456]*Ibid.*, February 26, 1874.
[457]*Ibid.*, April 29, 1874.
[458]*Ibid.*, April 30, 1874.
[459]*Ibid.*, May 6, 11, 19, 1874.
[460]*Acts and Resolves,* January Session, 1870.
[461]*Acts and Resolves,* January Session, 1871; Carroll, *Rhode Island,* II, 1001-1002.
[462]Lord, Sexton and Harrington, *History of the Archdiocese of Boston,* III, 68-69.

special committee of the Rhode Island legislature held a series of four hearings at which the pros and cons of the question were aired. Bishop Hendricken appeared along with Bishop Thomas M. Clarke of the Episcopal diocese of Rhode Island, President E. G. Robinson of Brown University and other churchmen to argue the legitimacy of the existing exemptions.[463] The majority of those who expressed their views before the committee spoke of the valuable contributions made by the exempted institutions. However, many on the committee were swayed by the argument that since all benefit from the protection of the state, all are liable for the taxes which finance that protection. Exemptions, it was further argued, placed a heavier burden on the taxpayers. But forcing religious institutions to pay for their own protection conflicted with the constitutional provision against taxation for sectarian purposes. In the end, the committee recommended a compromise proposal reducing the exemptions. The general assembly, however, rejected the committee's recommendation. At its January 1876 session the assembly voted to continue tax exemptions but to limit exemption of educational institutions to free public schools and of churches, to buildings and land surrounding the same but not exceeding one acre.

The *Journal* and the *Visitor* joined in their criticism of the assembly's action.[464] As in the past, debates over the philosophical and political merits of a legislative action broke down to reveal the underlying anti-Catholic bias that prompted some members of the legislature to vote in favor of the act. A Warwick representative, convinced that the tax exemptions were in actuality an aid to religion and particularly to the Catholic religion, regaled his fellow legislators with his reasons why the Catholic church was unworthy of such aid.[465] To the minds of many, including Bishop Hendricken, the act in removing the tax exemption from Catholic schools was aimed at halting the growth of Catholicism in the state and forcing Catholics to accept the public school system.

While Bishop Hendricken and others in the Catholic community saw underlying motives in the assembly's action, there was some doubt as to the meaning of the act's provision for the exemption of free public schools. To test the meaning of the act, St. Joseph's church, in 1878, brought suit against the assessors of taxes in Providence on the grounds that in taxing St. Joseph's school, the city had taxed lots and buildings exempt according to the law be-

[463]*Providence Journal,* February 17, 1875.
[464]*Ibid.,* February 7, 1876; *Weekly Visitor,* February 12, 1876.
[465]*Weekly Visitor,* April 1, 1876.

cause they were in fact free public schools. The parish also claimed exemption for the rectory because it contained a chapel used for religious purposes. The Rhode Island Supreme Court ruled against the parish holding that the meaning of the act in reference to schools covered only those schools that were "established, maintained and regulated under the statute laws of the State." As to the legitimacy of an exemption for the rectory, the court ruled that using a part of the building for religious purposes does not exempt the entire structure from taxation.[466]

Four years later, in 1883, a second challenge to the act came before the Supreme Court when the City Treasurer of Providence denied a tax exemption to St. Mary's church on the grounds that while the act exempted schools and church buildings used exclusively for education and religion, St. Mary's, in using its church for the educational purpose of a Sunday school, therefore did not qualify for an exemption under a strict reading of the law. The court did not agree. It held that use of the church for educational purposes was allowable under the statute so long as the use was merely occasional or so long as the use, if habitual, was purely permissive and voluntary and did not interfere with the use for religious purpose.[467] It would not be until 1894 that the state would reinstate the tax exemption of private schools. In the interval the Catholics would have to bear what the *Visitor* referred to as a triple taxation; tax for the support of the public schools, taxing themselves for the support of Catholic schools and now a tax upon Catholic schools.[468]

Although the Roger Williams doctrine of equal treatment by the state of all religions continued to be publicly espoused, Catholics and others in the 1870s and 1880s continued to point the difference between the theory and the practice. Bishop McFarland had played a significant role on the committee that raised the funds for the founding of Rhode Island Hospital and a collection was taken up each year in Providence's Catholic churches for the benefit of the hospital, yet Catholic priests initially found considerable difficulty in obtaining permission to visit a Catholic patient there. By 1880 the situation had considerably improved.[469]

The most glaring contradiction of Rhode Island's claimed tolerance remained the state's continued refusal to allow Catholics

---

[466]"St. Joseph's Church *vs* the Assessors of Taxes of Providence," in *Reports of Cases Argued and Determined in the Supreme Court of Rhode Island* (Boston: Houghton, Mifflin and Co., 1880), XII, 19–20. Hereafter cited as *Rhode Island Reports.*

[467]"St. Mary's Church *vs* Benjamin Tripp, City Treasurer of the City of Providence," *Rhode Island Reports, XIV,* 307-309; *Weekly Visitor,* December 29, 1883.

[468]*Weekly Visitor,* January 28, 1878.

[469]*Ibid.,* July 30, 1881.

confined in the state penal or mental institutions the free exercise
of their religion. A priest could enter the institutions to anoint a
dying inmate if he was called in time, but in general Catholics and
other inmates or prisoners were forced to attend the services provided by the state-appointed chaplains who were exclusively Protestant ministers.[470] The practice of requiring all prisoners to attend
the same service on Sunday was defended on the grounds that
prison discipline required it. It was also maintained that the religious instruction was non-sectarian and confined to truths which all
Christians shared, an argument Catholics found no more convincing than when it was used in reference to the public schools.[471]

The argument that discipline required that all attend the same
service could not apply to the mentally and physically ill at the State
Farm which the state had set up at the village of Howard in Cranston
in 1868. By the 1870s a large percentage of the inmates were Catholic. After June 1875, Fr. Rivier of Natick paid a weekly visit to the
farm to administer the sacraments and offered Mass at Christmas
and Easter. According to a contemporary account, the priest was
"ever a welcome visitor among its unfortunate inmates and is loud
in praise of its officers for their kindness and courtesy to him."[472]

Control of the state institutions rested with the Board of State
Charities and Corrections which was appointed by the legislature. In
February 1884, Bishop Hendricken asked the board to accord Catho-
lic clergy the same privileges of ministering to the spiritual needs of
Catholics in the penal and reformatory institutions of the state as
Protestant clergy were accorded. When the board refused to grant
the request the bishop prepared a petition to the state legislature
which was also signed by Bishop Clarke, Rev. Augustus Woodbury,
President Robinson of Brown and other Protestant and Catholic
clergy. The petition was referred to the Joint Committee on State
Charities and Corrections which gave a public hearing to those
interested on April 10th. Charles E. Gorman, Bishop Hendricken
and Fr. Joseph McDonough presented the case of the petitioners.
The three stated that they wished to have ministration of religion
allowed as a matter of right and justice and not as a concession,
dependent upon the good will of the members of the state board.
They referred to Massachusetts, Connecticut and other states as
examples of legislative precedent for the privileges they asked.[473]

The Board of State Charities was represented at the hearing by
Thomas Coggeshall, the postmaster of Newport, who produced a

[470]*Ibid.*, April 15; June 17, 1876.
[471]Lord, Sexton and Harrington, *History of the Archdiocese of Boston*, III, 69-71.
[472]*Weekly Visitor*, January 20, 1877; January 19, 1879.
[473]*Ibid.*, April 26, 1884.

resolution passed by the board that same day granting the same privileges as granted by Massachusetts. In 1875, the Massachusetts legislature had explicitly stated that no inmate should be denied the free exercise of his religion, a right that was extended also to inmates of that state's charitable and reformatory institutions in 1879.[474] However, while the Massachusetts statutes acknowledged the right of all to freely exercise their religion, both measures stipulated that nothing in the acts should be construed to impair the discipline of any person so far as may be needful for the good government and safe custody of its inmates.[475] This meant that the inmates could still be required to attend the official religious services provided by the state's chaplains. While recognizing that such a guarantee as proposed by the board rested only on its word, Coggeshall, who was sympathetic to the cause of the petitioners, warned the petitioners they might imperil their chances of obtaining their ends by asking for action by the legislature.

Coggeshall evidently read the situation well. In the midst of a flurry of adverse opinion expressed in the local press, the petition passed the house, but the state senate referred the bill to its committee on judiciary where it died.[476] A month later Coggeshall introduced a motion at a meeting of the state board that it fulfill the promise made before the legislative committee, but the board tabled the resolution.[477]

The following November, the state board finally reached a decision on the matter and voted to adopt the Massachusetts law granting the clergy of all denominations the right to visit all state institutions except the reform school once a month. On February 1, 1885, Mass was said for the first time at the workhouse and house of correction and at the state prison.[478]

However, since the boys and girls at the reform schools were not included in the board action, the agitation continued. The *Visitor* challenged the conscience of Rhode Island by its assertion that, in spite of its professed traditions, the state still continued to deny religious liberty.[479] Bishop Hendricken also continued to focus attention on the issue.[480]

---

[474]The legislation did not of course end discrimination. See "Agitation of St. Vincent de Paul Society in Fall River," *Weekly Visitor,* December 3, 1881; "Protest of treatment of Catholic inmates in Alms House," *Weekly Visitor,* April 1, 1882.

[475]Lord, Sexton and Harrington, *History of the Archdiocese of Boston,* III, 72.

[476]*Providence Visitor,* May 17, 1884.

[477]*Ibid.,* October 25, 1884; April 25, 1887.

[478]*Providence Journal,* November 22, 1884.

[479]*Providence Visitor,* January 17; April 18, 1885.

[480]*Providence Journal,* March 15, 1886.

When the legislature met at the beginning of 1886, the struggle
for the passage of a bill similar to that enacted in Massachusetts was
renewed by Catholics and others. Since the Massachusetts bill allowed services held by other than the chaplains to be held only once
a month and accorded great latitude to officials of the institutions
to frustrate the intent of the act, the partisans of Bishop Hendricken's position submitted an act drawn up by a cathedral assistant, Fr. Charles J. Burns, who had a law degree from Boston Law
School. Fr. Burns's bill provided for complete religious freedom for
all inmates of the institutions and forbade any compulsion that
would violate their religious beliefs. Although the legislature held
hearings on Fr. Burns's bill, no action was taken on it for several
years. Although opponents of Bishop Hendricken's bill effectively
controlled the legislature, public sentiment in the state was such
that the State Board of Charities, on April 15, 1887, formally passed
a resolution allowing Catholic and Protestant clergy to hold services
every Sunday in all state institutions provided that the religious
services should not impair the discipline of the institutions.[481]

The Struggle for Political Rights

Originally attracted to the state by the wages offered in its mills,
factories and railways, the Catholics of Rhode Island had by the
1880s become an important part of the state's economic life, not
only as workers but also increasingly as merchants and professional
men. Some indication of the economic status of the Catholic community can be garnered from the published list of individual contributors to a great variety of religious and Irish national causes.
There were relatively few great contributors but a number of substantial givers.[482]

The state census taken in 1875 gave ample evidence to all
concerned that the birth rate of the state's foreign-born population
was significantly higher than that of the state's native-born population. Governor Van Zandt alluded to the political implications of
these statistics and exposed nativist fears in his 1877 message to the
general assembly. Emphasizing the need for education, the Rhode
Island chief executive warned that "the lesson of our late census
teaches us only too plainly that the balance of political power is

---

[481]*Providence Visitor,* April 25, 1887.

[482]See the yearly reports of the Cathedral parish, Providence; St. Patrick's, Providence; St. Mary's, Newport as published in the *Visitor.*

passing into the hands of our illiterate class, who will become by
force of circumstances a caste by themselves through whose barriers
it will be found well nigh impossible to break."[483]

In the urban and industrial areas of the state, the impact of
foreign and Catholic immigration was even greater. The census of
1885 listed Providence's population at 118,070. In June 1886,
Bishop Hendricken estimated that there were fifty thousand Catholics in the city who attended Mass at thirteen churches, sent their
children to five parochial schools and six academies and were served
by twenty-seven priests.[484] Such numbers reawakened fears in many
hearts and resentment in others.

The importance of the foreign-born population was also being
felt in the area of politics. Except for two short intervals, the mayor
of Providence, from 1864 to his death in office in 1886, was a
native-born Irish American, Thomas A. Doyle. Most of the citizens
of Providence might well have disagreed with the mayor at some
point in his career but he was universally liked and respected. As he
had with Bishop McFarland, the Irish Protestant mayor formed a
warm friendship with Bishop Hendricken.[485] It was during Mayor
Doyle's extended service to the city that its population and wealth
doubled and Providence became the second largest city in New
England. While never laying himself open to a charge of partiality,
Doyle was the first executive to appoint Irish Americans to the
police force—a step that did not go unnoticed by his critics.[486]

While their numbers grew, the naturalized citizens who wished
to vote continued to be deprived of the opportunity to make their
influence felt because of the property qualification. Attempts to
redeem the promise of full citizenship made by the state to the
foreign-born volunteers who served in the Civil War was rejected
for a third time in November 1876. Efforts designed at having
Rhode Island's suffrage restriction declared in violation of the new
fourteenth and fifteenth amendments to the United States Constitution succeeded in bringing a subcommittee of the United States
Senate headed by Senator William Wallace to Rhode Island in August 1879, but even their presence accomplished little more than
publicizing the injustice.[487]

In January 1881, the Rhode Island Suffrage Reform Association, which had sponsored so many efforts at reform, gave way to

[483]Acts and Resolves, January Session, 1877.
[484]Greene, The Providence Plantations, p. 157.
[485]Providence Visitor, August 7, 1886.
[486]Ibid., June 19, 1886.
[487]Weekly Visitor, August 10, 17, 1879.

a new group, the Equal Rights Association, headed by Dr. Lucius F. C. Garvin of Cumberland.[488] Dr. Garvin, a native of Tennessee and a veteran of the Union Army, had come to Rhode Island to work at the Lonsdale Company in Lincoln as a mill doctor. The association set as its purpose the elimination of suffrage restrictions through a constitutional convention. Soon after its formation, supporters of equal rights petitioned the general assembly to issue a call for a convention. In February 1881, the committee on the judiciary held a public hearing on the petition. Dr. Garvin and a number of others argued their case on the need for a variety of constitutional reforms.[489] So many, in fact, appeared to testify that the committee was forced to hold a second hearing a week later. In the interval Senator Henry B. Anthony, attempting to justify Rhode Island's suffrage restrictions in an address in the United States Senate, described naturalized citizens as belonging "to a class . . . composed of men who came upon us uninvited and on whose departure there is no restraint."[490]

Senator Anthony's remarks were severely criticized by several speakers who addressed the judiciary committee at its second hearing.[491] A third hearing was necessary before all who wished to address the committee were heard.[492] Although the committee recommended calling for an election of delegates to a constitutional convention, there were enough in the house who shared Senator Anthony's sentiments or who had doubts as to whether the assembly had the right to convene a constitutional convention to reject the committee proposal.

The leaders of the Equal Rights Association organized Equal Rights Clubs in most of the urban areas of the state and held monthly meetings to discuss methods of gaining electoral reform. The association was the catalyst for the submission of a second series of petitions, signed by over two thousand people, to the general assembly in January 1882. The leadership of the assembly referred the petitions to a joint special committee which held a series of five hearings.[493] A majority of the committee rejected all the petitions and issued a report in which they contended that the assembly lacked the authority to call a convention. However, the committee's report did

---

[488]*Providence Journal,* January 26, 1881; Carroll, *Rhode Island,* II, 647-48, 655-57; Nelson, "The Influence of Immigration on Rhode Island Politics," pp. 62-89.
[489]*Weekly Visitor,* February 12, 1881.
[490]H. B. Anthony, "Defense of Rhode Island," *Congressional Record,* 46th Congress, 3rd Session, February 12, 1881, XI, 1490-91.
[491]*Weekly Visitor,* February 19, 1881.
[492]*Ibid.,* February 26, 1881.
[493]*Ibid.,* March 4, 1881; *Providence Journal,* March 1, 8, 9, 1881.

recommend that the legislature submit to the electorate an amendment to the state constitution specifically authorizing the general
assembly to call a convention.[494] As prohibition advocates also saw a
convention as the most convenient way to bring about the changes in
the law they wished to accomplish, the assembly adopted the committee's proposal.[495] After being approved by the next general assembly at its May 1882 session, the proposed amendment was submitted to the voters on November 17, 1882. In rejecting the
amendment, the majority of the native-born citizens showed that
they shared the conviction of the majority of the joint committee that
foreign-born citizens could not be trusted to use the right to vote in
the best interests of the state.[496] The equal rights advocates were not
disappointed at the result of the vote. To them it was anti-climactic.
They were convinced that the general assembly had the right to call a
convention and had already refused to do so.

Although the conservatives were successful in their refusal to
share political prerogatives on an equal basis with foreign-born
citizens, the state election in April 1883, showed that the tide was
definitely beginning to turn against those who wished to maintain
the status quo. The Republican candidate for governor, Augustus
O. Bourn, defeated two Democratic rivals, former governor and
senator William Sprague, who had the support of liberal Democrats
and of the Equal Rights Association, and Charles R. Curtis, who had
the support of conservative Democrats. Sprague's candidacy in
splitting the Democratic party, provided the opportunity for the
Irishmen among the Democrats to secure leadership positions in
the party since many of the older leaders chose to support Curtis
rather than accept Sprague. The split was widened by the refusal of
some Irish Democratic leaders to support Grover Cleveland for
president because Cleveland had voted for the Know Nothing ticket
in 1860. However, in spite of the division within the party, Democratic voting strength remained strong.[497]

In these years the Republicans were also experiencing tension
within the ranks of their party. The demand of working men for a
ten-hour law and for the removal of property qualifications for
voting crossed party lines and advocates were found among Republicans as well. More troublesome to the Republican leadership were

[494]*Report of the Joint Select Committee on Changes in the Constitution Made to the General Assembly at Its January Session* (Providence, 1882).

[495]*Weekly Visitor,* March 25, 1881.

[496]*Ibid.,* April 1, 8; November 11, 1882.

[497]Carroll, *Rhode Island,* II, 654-55; Nelson, "The Influence of Immigration on Rhode Island Politics," pp. 75-83.

demands for a constitutional prohibition on the sale of liquor. Advocates of prohibition were a strong element within the party. Their threat to bolt the party if their demands were not met compelled the Republicans to allow an amendment to prohibit the manufacture and sale of liquor to go before the voters. At the same time advocates of an amendment to extend suffrage to foreign-born veterans of the Civil War, also were successful in putting that question on the ballot. The voters gave both amendments the necessary three-fifths vote.[498] But carrying out the will of the people was another matter.

When in 1886 the Republican controlled legislature proceeded to enact legislation to provide for the enforcement of prohibition, the Republican leadership scandalized the state by a series of laws that advanced party interest over the wishes of the people who had adopted the amendment. When party interest again dominated legislation to reform the state's judicial system, the sense of resentment only grew. The outcry that followed the so called "May Deal" brought many independent voters and some of the more principled Republicans to support Democratic candidates for Congress in November 1886 and for state offices the following April. Their efforts were partially successful in both elections.[499]

In an attempt to undo the damage done by the "May Deal," the Republican convention in March 1887, endorsed the principle of suffrage extension. The success of the Democrats in winning control of the House of Representatives in the state election the following April, and a desire to sway into party ranks French Canadian voters who were among those petitioning for the right to vote, prompted the Republicans to allow a suffrage amendment to appear on the ballot in April 1888. The amendment, as proposed by Augustus Bourn, then a member of the senate, would remove the real estate requirement and allow foreign-born citizens to vote on the same terms as natives except on questions related to taxes and expenditure and for city councilmen who controlled financial matters in the cities. In both these cases, the real estate qualification would remain as the criteria for voting. On April 4, 1888, the voters approved the amendment. The Bourn amendment did not end conservative control of Rhode Island politics. But it was a sign that the foreign-born citizens and their descendents had become an important part of the fabric of the state.[500]

---

[498]Carroll, *Rhode Island*, II, 655; Nelson, "The Influence of Immigration on Rhode Island Politics," pp. 90-92.

[499]Nelson, "The Influence of Immigration on Rhode Island Politics," pp. 92-106.

[500]*Ibid.*, pp. 106-21; Matthew J. Smith, "The History of a Reform: The Bourn Amendment" (unpublished master's thesis, Providence College, 1966), pp. 25-46.

The growing importance of the foreign-born citizens and their descendents in the political life of the state was acknowledged by the nominations of Catholics in increasing numbers for political office in the 1870s and 1880s. Several Irish Catholics won election to the office of alderman from the Irish wards of Providence in the 1870s. In 1873 Joseph Osfield became the first Catholic to sit in the general assembly when his neighbors in Cumberland elected him as their representative. In 1887 a Providence lawyer, Edwin D. McGuinness, whose father had been one of the men who gathered to defend the convent of the Sisters of Mercy back in the Know Nothing days, was the first Irish-Catholic nominated for statewide office and the first elected as a Democrat to the office of Secretary of State. Another Providence lawyer, George J. West, who had left the Democratic party as a protest against the nomination of Cleveland, was elected to the house in 1884 by the Republicans as part of their plan to court the Irish vote. In 1887 the first Catholic of French Canadian background, Aram J. Pothier, was elected to serve in the general assembly by the Republicans of Woonsocket.

Catholic Awareness of A Unique Heritage

Although acquisition of their full rights as citizens remained a goal of many Catholics in Rhode Island, the clergy and people of the Diocese of Providence had by 1886 a growing sense of accomplishment. Fr. James Fitton's *Sketches of the Establishment of the Church in New England* appeared in print in 1872, as a testimony to the struggle of the first Catholics. Bishop Hendricken, who had a personal interest in history, shared in the sense of adventure and importance of the times. He loved to reminisce of the days when he first came to Providence as a young priest. He once appointed one of his priests "to gather up facts regarding the different churches and parishes in the diocese, their history and foundations; but this fell through." The bishop wrote these lines to James M. Smyth, a Woonsocket newpaperman, who had sent him a pamphlet history of the Catholic church in Woonsocket, which Smyth published at the end of 1878.[501]

In the *Visitor,* the Catholics of the diocese had a vehicle in which to record some of their memories, a task which took on greater importance as death relentlessly claimed the oldest members of the Catholic communities. In April 1885, for example, the *Visitor* re-

---

[501]Thomas F. Hendricken to James M. Smyth, February 2, 1879, printed in Smyth, *Catholic Church in Woonsocket,* pp. 6–7.

called the first St. Patrick's Day banquet held by the Catholic Irish in Providence at the city hotel. Only John Devlin, who had presided at the banquet and who then lived in Pawtucket, and Mr. Bernard Hagney of Providence were still alive.[502]

A New Cathedral

Shortly after coming to Providence, Bishop Hendricken announced his intention to erect a suitable cathedral for the new diocese.[503] Bishop McFarland had initially proposed replacing the increasingly decrepit and inadequate cathedral church, but the ambitious plans of both bishops did not meet with general favor. Even some of the bishop's closest friends endeavored to divert him from the attempt.[504]

Before any new building could be constructed, the cathedral parish's existing debt of about $16,000 had to be paid. From the very beginning of the project, Bishop Hendricken, experienced collector and builder that he was, determined that the parish was to incur no debt in the course of the erection of the new church. The work proceeded no faster than there was money on hand to pay for it. As a first step, the bishop persuaded many prominent laymen and priests to accept "notes" or pledges payable in five years in equal yearly payments. The method was so successful that in the initial burst of enthusiasm, about $80,000 was pledged.[505] Among the largest contributors were the pastors of the diocese. A list of clergy contributors published in the *Boston Pilot* in January 1873, noted twenty-one subscriptions to the cathedral fund in excess of $1,-000.[506] Other funds came in from fairs held in the parishes of the diocese for the new cathedral.

At the end of 1873 and every year thereafter, Bishop Hendricken provided his people with a clear and detailed statement of monies he had received and how they were expended. These statements were not only read from the pulpit of the cathedral, but printed in circular form, and after 1876, also published regularly in the *Visitor*. Everyone who contributed a single dollar or dime to the new cathedral knew how their money was spent and how much the work cost. Bishop Hendricken was very conscious of his stewardship in all his financial transactions. The practice he adopted regarding

[502]*Providence Visitor*, April 25, 1885.
[503]*Woonsocket Patriot*, May 31, 1872.
[504]*Providence Visitor*, June 19, 1886.
[505]*Ibid.*
[506]*Boston Pilot*, January 11, 1873.

the cathedral fund was intended as a model for the clergy of the diocese who were also expected to provide their parishioners an annual accounting of church monies received and expended.[507]

As funds accumulated, the bishop was able to begin the slow step-by-step process needed to accomplish his project. The first task was to acquire the Truman lot on the corner of High and Fenner streets, which Bishop Tyler had attempted to purchase but had found the price too high. In July 1872, after some negotiations and consultation, the bishop agreed to pay $33,000 for the last parcel of land necessary to round out the site for the new construction.[508]

Once the dimensions of the site were settled, Bishop Hendricken proceeded to engage an architect for the project. In the Country at that time, there was only one man who possessed an unrivaled reputation as a church builder—Patrick C. Keely of Brooklyn.[509] On August 22nd Mr. Keely called on the Bishop of Providence to discuss the bishop's wishes.[510] The architect returned to Providence the following March to make specific arrangements for the building.[511] As Bishop Hendricken conceived the new cathedral, it was to be one of the finest churches in the Country. Keely was free to draw up plans unhampered by excessive financial restrictions.[512] The two men agreed in the March meeting on a schedule for delivery of plans and specifications for the structure's basement and for its front elevation.

Before any construction could take place, a temporary wooden church had to be constructed to provide a place for the cathedral congregation to worship while the old cathedral was torn down. The choice of a site for the pro-cathedral and its design waited until August 1873, when Bishop Hendricken returned from his first visit to Rome. Land was available for the purpose on the garden lot adjoining the convent of the Sisters of Mercy at the corner of Broad and Claverick streets. Since the initial collection was expended in paying past debts of the cathedral parish, additional funds were needed. During the first weeks of September, the bishop wrote the pastors asking them to take up a collection for the new cathedral among their people as the priests of the cathedral were doing in their own parish.

---

[507]*Providence Visitor,* June 16, 1886.
[508]Bishop Hendricken, "Diary," June 7, 11, 13; July 20, 1872.
[509]Kervick, "Patrick C. Keely," pp. 12–17.
[510]Bishop Hendricken, "Diary," August 22, 1872.
[511]*Ibid.,* March 27, 1873.
[512]Kervick, "Patrick C. Keely," p. 14; James L. Meagher, *The Great Cathedrals and the Most Celebrated Churches of the World* (New York: The Christian Press Association, 1883), pp. 429-37.

As the new funds came in, the bishop announced in October that he would soon begin construction of the pro-cathedral.[513] The bishop's announcement, however, was premature. Work did not begin on the foundation until February 16, 1874. On March 12th, the bishop signed a contract for $18,950 for a building which James Murphy of Providence designed with an eye more to seating capacity than to harmony of line. The contract stated the work would be finished by September 15th.[514] To cover the construction bills as they came due, the bishop announced that the Easter collection, which was taken up each year for the general needs of the diocese would go towards the cathedral fund. In 1875, the collection amounted to over $10,000.[515] Apparently the bishop did not succeed in raising sufficient funds to complete the building that year because it was not completed until February 1876. Bishop Hendricken said the first Mass there on February 6th, when he offered Mass for the children of the Sunday school whose classes were then being held in the building.[516]

The old episcopal residence that Bishop Tyler had purchased was also on the proposed site for the new church. It, too, had to be removed and a new one built. On May 16, 1874, the priests of the cathedral informed their parishioners that they had purchased the lot adjoining the cathedral property as the site for the new residence and asked their help in paying for it. The collection realized $941.00 which was, as Bishop Hendricken noted hopefully in his diary, "a small beginning."[517]

The bishop and the cathedral priests moved out of the old residence on May 19th and took up temporary quarters in the Truman House on the corner of Fenner and High streets. By June, the bishop had arrived at terms with a contractor to build a three-story brick building at the corner of Fenner and Pond streets for $31,-675.[518] The new home was completed by the following August, although it was not until the end of 1877 that the joint efforts of the diocesan clergy and the people of the cathedral parish succeeded in paying off its cost.[519]

---

[513]*Providence Journal,* October 6, 1873; *Providence Evening Press,* October 6, 1873.

[514]Bishop Hendricken, "Diary," February 16; March 12, 1874; *Providence Journal,* March 16; December 10, 1875.

[515]Bishop Thomas F. Hendricken to clergy of the diocese, May 18, 1875, PChA.

[516]Bishop Hendricken, "Diary," February 6, 1876; *Providence Journal,* February 9, 1876.

[517]Bishop Hendricken, "Diary," May 20, 1874; SS. Peter and Paul, "Announcement Book," May 16, 1874.

[518]Bishop Hendricken, "Diary," June 26, 1874.

[519]SS. Peter and Paul, "Announcement Book," August 29, 1875; Bishop Thomas F. Hendricken to clergy of the diocese, May 30, 1876; June 29, 1877, PChA.

Bishop Hendricken was over optimistic about the progress of his church, an optimism that was fueled by the generosity of the people. In spite of the economic difficulties that followed the Panic of 1873 and the subsequent strain on the church's resources, the bishop managed to set aside $20,000 each year for the project. Keely had nearly finished the blueprints for the church by the spring of 1877. The bishop first hoped to begin construction of the new cathedral that summer, but since the costs of the new episcopal residence were still outstanding, he had to wait another year.[520]

In early spring 1878, the bishop was prostrated for six weeks and his friends again feared for his life. When he showed signs of recovery, his doctors advised him to leave the city for a time to recuperate. He accepted this advice and made plans to visit Rome in May. Hardly had he recovered from his illness when he began to talk again about the consummation of his fondest hope—the erection of the cathedral. His Vicar General, Fr. Lawrence McMahon, later recalled how, at the urging of many of the clergy and people, he tried to persuade the bishop not to go on with the task as it would prove his destruction. But the bishop would not be dissuaded.[521] Before leaving for Rome, Bishop Hendricken, on April 5, 1878, signed the initial contract for the construction of the basement story of the new church.[522] The following Sunday, in making the announcement of the prospective start of construction, the bishop told the cathedral congregation that he expected the construction of the church structure itself to take two years. The first year would be spent on the basement that he anticipated would cost $41,000. To emphasize his own personal commitment to the work, the bishop announced that he had given his year's salary to aid the project and called on his people to be generous in their own way.[523] The bishop left the details of the construction of the basement in Fr. McMahon's hands. Such was his interest that he had Fr. O'Reilly, the rector of the cathedral, send him weekly reports on its progress while he was in Europe.[524]

The *Visitor* shared the bishop's optimism, observing that "no better times could be selected for the work, for materials and labor are probably cheaper than they have been for thirty years." The writer added, to reassure those still dubious as to the demands that would be made on them; "there are no calls to be made for very

[520]*Providence Journal,* March 12; December 4, 1877; *Weekly Visitor,* December 8, 1877.
[521]*Providence Visitor,* July 24, 1886.
[522]Bishop Hendricken, "Diary," April 5, 1878.
[523]*Providence Journal,* April 8, 1878; *Weekly Visitor,* April 14, 1878.
[524]Clarke, *Lives of the Catholic Bishops,* III, 159.

extraordinary sums of money. It is expected that generous people in and out of the church will aid in its erection, but no one must imagine that the new cathedral will accept from any man a dollar beyond what he wishes to contribute freely, and what he considers himself able to give. Just now good will is as necessary as money."[525]

During the first week of May 1878, following the celebration of Holy Week, the last services were celebrated in the old cathedral. Workmen then began demolishing the building. The passing of the "old church" brought tears to the eyes of many who remembered the difficult struggle with which it was built and the pride the parish took in its humble, but now decrepit presence.[526] By the middle of June, the walls of the church had been torn down and excavation for the new building was well underway, so that on August 24th, construction of the basement itself began.[527]

As the end of November approached, the Catholic community of Providence proposed to celebrate Thanksgiving day by laying the cornerstone of the new cathedral. The stone itself, of black, Irish marble from the quarries near the bishop's home in Kilkenny, was a gift of the quarry owner and was intended as a memorial to the Catholics of the diocese who claimed Ireland as their homeland.[528] The Catholic societies planned the day's celebration to be an elaborate and joyous affair, and so it was. Mr. Thomas Cosgrove, one of the oldest Catholics of the city and a parishioner of the cathedral for forty years, was given the honor of being the chief marshal of the day. Dignitaries of church and state attended the ceremonies and listened to the Passionist, Fr. Fidelis, compare the Irish in America with the people of Israel whom the Lord led out of a land of bondage into a good land. The day's celebration also had a serious purpose. Bishop Hendricken hoped to realize, in the collection taken up among the crowd who came to witness the ceremony, enough money to pay off the cost of the basement's construction.[529]

Although generous, the collection at the ceremony did not wipe out the debt. Hoping to push the work forward the next spring and not wishing to burden the people with another collection in that difficult winter, the bishop decided to give a series of lectures in every parish of the diocese through which he hoped to raise the needed funds. He began in January at the pro-cathedral taking "Reminiscences of Ireland" as his topic.[530] By Easter, a debt of

[525] *Weekly Visitor,* April 7, 1878.
[526] *Ibid.,* April 28; May 5, 13, 1878.
[527] *Ibid.,* June 9; November 24, 1878.
[528] *Ibid.,* October 28; November 24, 1878.
[529] *Ibid.,* December 1, 1878.
[530] *Ibid.,* January 26, 1879.

$9,000 still remained, but the traditional Easter collection for the general needs of the diocese that year yielded $9,128, enough to allow the bishop to proceed with construction of the superstructure of the building.[531] A high board fence was erected around the site "to protect the workmen from the inquisitiveness of outsiders" and a steam engine erected to assist in moving stone.[532]

That May when he visited Woonsocket to confirm at St. Charles and Precious Blood, the men of the St. Jean Baptiste Society presented him with a contribution of $100 towards the new cathedral.[533] After that, the bishop began to mention how much he received in each parish in order to prompt the pastor to outdo his neighbor. The next fall, with the rising walls to inspire him, Bishop Hendricken set out on a five-year personal quest to raise the funds necessary to see the building through to completion. He would make a tour of the parishes of the diocese that year and every year until his death, confirming the children and taking up a collection for the cathedral. His personal diary reveals the single-mindedness of the bishop's efforts. While his spirit remained as alive and vigorous as ever, his already weak health forced him to take extended vacations in warmer climates. In spite of occasional disappointments and at least one extended argument with one of his pastors over priorities, the bishop's fund-raising efforts met with success. In the first year he toured the diocese, the bishop was able to report to the congregation at the cathedral on October 5th that "the work so far had been paid for and there is enough money on hand to meet the cost of about a foot or more of the walls of the edifice."[534]

Although the winter of 1879–1880 was again a difficult time for both the working men and the cathedral parish, with the coming of spring the bishop began another tour of the parishes.[535] Again the people responded and the bishop was able to pay his debts as they came due. By October 1880, the cathedral's roof was on and slated.[536] Tired by his labors, the bishop was struck that November with an attack of asthma so severe that he was kept at home until coming of milder weather in the spring.[537]

By December 1881, the exterior of the church was all but

---

[531]Bishop Thomas F. Hendricken to clergy of the diocese, April 21, 1879, PChA; Bishop Hendricken, "Diary," Easter Collection, April 13, 1879; *Providence Journal,* April 7; May 24, 1879.
[532]*Weekly Visitor,* June 8, 15, 22, 1879.
[533]*Ibid.,* May 24, 1879; October 6, 1883.
[534]*Providence Journal,* October 6, 1879.
[535]*Ibid.,* May 1, 1880; *Weekly Visitor,* June 26, 1880.
[536]*Sunday Visitor,* October 3, 1880.
[537]*Weekly Visitor,* April 16, 27, 1881.

finished and work had already begun on the interior furnishings and decoration.[538] In October 1882, at the end of his fourth tour of the parishes, the bishop reported to the people of the cathedral that the most difficult part of construction was finished.[539] The work of interior decoration took at least a year longer than the bishop had estimated. He set the feast of SS. Peter and Paul in 1885 as the date for the dedication and consecration of the church, only to be forced to delay that longed-for date a full year.[540]

In March 1886, Bishop Hendricken appealed to his flock to make one final effort in behalf of the church. Although his health had grown increasingly worse so that during the last four years of his life he did not have a whole night's sleep, yet, with the goal so near, he would not relax his efforts. In the spring of 1886 he set out on his final tour of the parishes. On May 16th, the bishop spent a long and exhausting day visiting the five parishes in the Pawtuxet Valley. He caught a cold that day and still had it a week later when he visited Holy Name parish in Providence. Realizing his weakness, the bishop spoke of his probable death adding the hope that the Lord would spare him to see his cathedral consecrated.[541]

On his return home that day he went to bed, seriously ill. As his condition grew worse, his priests administered the sacrament of the sick. But he rallied and for awhile his doctors had some hope that he might recover. On June 9th, a relapse set in but again the bishop rallied. His weakened body, however, could not sustain the effort. On Friday, June 11, 1886, Bishop Thomas F. Hendricken died at the age of fifty-nine, after fourteen years service as bishop. His funeral was the first Mass celebrated in the new cathedral.

Bishop Hendricken in Retrospect

The news of the bishop's death spread quickly and brought forth an impressive demonstration of affection and respect from his people and priests, his neighbors and fellow citizens. Bishop Hendricken was first and foremost a pastor, who saw as his first duty, the sharing of the sacraments with his people. To accomplish this, he had increased the number of priests who served the diocese from 53 to 104 and added new churches and mission chapels in addition to schools, orphanages, a hospital and additional orders of nuns and

[538]*Ibid.,* December 17, 1881.
[539]*Providence Journal,* October 9, 1882.
[540]*Providence Visitor,* April 4, 1885; March 13, 1886.
[541]*Ibid.,* June 19, 1886.

a society of priests to assist him in his ministry. As a priest and a bishop, he took great delight in all his work, especially those duties that brought him in contact with the young. All who wrote of the bishop before and after his death spoke of his accomplishments as an administrator. But the reasons for the sorrow at his death lay more in what he was as a Christian. "No man," the *Visitor* would write, "was more approachable. He received rich and poor alike with an easy grace. . . . He would never say No when it was possible to say Yes; but when circumstances demanded prompt decision no one could display more firmness of character."[542]

At his death, the local papers were warm in his praise as a citizen who spoke out on the practical and moral questions that concerned all citizens of Providence. When the new Providence City Hall was dedicated, Bishop Hendricken had offered the closing prayer. To the *Journal's* recollection, this was the first time "a Roman Catholic prelate figured in like capacity anywhere in New England."[543] Active citizen that he was, Thomas Hendricken yet retained a warm love of Ireland throughout his life and gladly lent a hand in any worthy cause to aid the people of his native land.

When the Third Plenary Council gathered at Baltimore in 1884, the bishop's illness allowed him to play only a minor role in the deliberations. Since most of the council's sessions were held in private, a newspaper writer from New York, to fill out his copy, produced a series of biographical sketches of the prelates. The *Visitor* reprinted the one of Bishop Hendricken with the comment that it well summed up the man:

> While all the Bishops are distinguished for their learning, prudence and wisdom, some excel in these great gifts. Bishop Hendricken of Providence, R. I., in spite of a delicate frame, exemplifies in his private and public life the qualities one associates with the idea of patriot-prelate. He is intensely American, intensely Irish and intensely Catholic, and yet he is beloved by men of all nationalities and all creeds. He has modeled his life on that of St. Paul, and like the Apostle of the Gentiles, is 'all things to all men,' and so successfully that he had quietly gained for his flock rights that are denied Catholics in other dioceses.[544]

To the minds of his own priests and people, Bishop Hendricken needed no other testimony to his service to them than the cathedral he gave so much of himself to build. The dream of building the church sustained him and according to his Vicar General, Fr. McMa-

[542] *Ibid.*
[543] *Providence Journal; Providence Evening Telegram,* June 12, 1886.
[544] *Providence Visitor,* December 20, 1884.

hon, the dream gave the bishop the strength to struggle on against the illness that so sapped his strength.[545] Among the last citizens of Providence to call at the cathedral rectory to see Bishop Hendricken was the mayor of Providence, Thomas Doyle, who, a few days before the bishop's death, was himself fatally stricken. The bishop was not conscious when the mayor called. Later when Hendricken had rallied for what was to be the final time, he learned of the mayor's death and sent one of his priests to convey his personal sympathy to the mayor's family. It is perhaps fitting that the monuments of each man, one a statue, the other, a cathedral church, would for so many years stand side by side in the city each had served.

As the bells of Providence tolled for the mayor and the bishop that June in 1886, the citizens of Providence were preparing to celebrate the 250th anniversary of Roger Williams's settlement of their city. Williams had come to the shores of Narragansett Bay in search of a place to worship God, to settle with his family and to earn his living in peace. The Catholic immigrants who came to the city he founded and to the state he helped weld together sought the same for themselves and for their families. By 1886 the Catholic immigrant had become an integral part of the economic, political and social fabric of Rhode Island and Massachusetts. To that fact, the cathedral Bishop Hendricken had labored to build over the foundation of Fr. Corry's church gave eloquent witness.

---

[545] *Ibid.*, July 24, 1886.

Bibliography

Primary Materials

Providence Diocesan Chancery Archives (PChA)
    Diaries of Bishop Hendricken for 1872-81
    Occasional Official Correspondence
    Yearly Reports of Pastors
    Diocesan Circulars, 1872-86
    Cathedral of SS. Peter and Paul Announcement Books
    Records of the Minutes of the Young Catholic's Friend
    Society and Records of the Minutes of the Roman
    Catholic Orphans Asylum and School Society
Hartford Archdiocesan Chancery Archives (HChA)
    Vertical files of the correspondence of Bishop Francis P. McFarland
    Reports of the Priests of the Diocese
    Letters between individual Clergymen
    Diaries kept by Bishop McFarland
    Letterbook of Bishop William Tyler
    Diary of Bishop William Tyler
    Diocesan Circulars, 1850–72
    Partial list of priests ordained for the diocese between 1852 and 1872
Boston Archdiocesan Chancery Archives (BChA)
    Bishop Benedict J.B. Fenwick's "Memoranda," three volumes, November 1, 1825—December 31, 1844
University of Notre Dame Archives (UNDA)
    Archives of the Society for the Propagation of the Faith, Paris (SPFP)
    The Ludvig Mission Society Papers, Munich (LMS)

The Leopoldine Mission Society of Vienna Correspondence(LMSV)

All Hallows College, Dublin, Missionary Correspondence (AHMC).

Montreal Archdiocesan Chancery Archives (MChA)

Correspondence Register

Rhode Island State Archives

Legislation files; Petitions Not Granted

Rhode Island Historical Society Library

Rhode Island Manuscripts; Census Manuscripts

Providence Public Library

Miscellaneous uncatalogued papers of George Potter

Newspapers

Rhode Island

Central Falls
Central Falls Weekly Visitor, 1869-87.
East Greenwich
Rhode Island Pendulum, 1857.
Newport
Newport Daily News 1886-87.
Newport Mercury, 1780-1822, 1842, 1847-50.
Pawtucket
Pawtucket Gazette and Chronicle, 1838-87.
Providence
Morning Star, 1869-72.
Providence Daily Journal, 1830-87.
Providence Daily Post, 1850-67.
Providence Daily Transcript, 1856-57.
Providence Daily Tribune, 1853-59.
Providence Evening Press, 1859-84.
Providence Gazette, 1795-1811, 1820-25.
Providence Morning Herald, 1867-70.
Providence Morning Star, 1869-86.
Providence Patriot, 1819-35.
Providence Sunday Journal, 1885-87.
Providence Visitor, 1884-87.
Republican Herald, 1828-52.
Rose and Lily, 1844-45.

Weekly Review, 1870-71.
Weekly Visitor, 1875-84.
Wakefield
   Narragansett Times, 1855-87.
Warren
   Northern Star & Warren & Bristol Gazette, 1826-55.
Warwick
   Kent County Atlas, 1850-52.
   Pawtuxet Valley Gleanor, 1878-87.
Westerly
   Narragansett Weekly, 1869-70.
Woonsocket
   Woonsocket Patriot and Rhode Island State Register, 1856-87.

Massachusetts

Boston
   Boston Pilot, 1836-87.
Fall River
   Fall River Evening News, 1869-87.
   L'Independent, 1885-88.

New York

New York City
   Freeman's Journal and Catholic Register, 1864-70.
   New York Tablet, 1857-66.

Secondary Materials
Parish Histories

Rhode Island

St. Bernard's, Wickford:
   "St. Bernard's Church, Wickford, Rhode Island: A Century of
   Change and Growth." Hackensack, N.J.: Custombook, 1975.
St. Charles, Woonsocket:
   "St. Charles'—Old and New: Being a brief record of the
   origin and development of Catholic life in Woonsocket in so
   far as that life was affected by the origin and development
   of St. Charles' Parish." Privately printed, 1928.

St. Edward's, Providence:
Walsh, Richard A. *The Centennial History of Saint Edward
Church, Providence, Rhode Island, 1875-1974.* Privately printed,
1974.
St. James, Manville:
"St. James Church, Manville: Joy, Thanksgiving, Hope."
Hackensack, N.J.: Custombook, 1974.
St. John the Baptist, Warren:
Forget, Ulysse. *La Paroisse Saint-Jean-Baptiste De Warren, Etat
Du Rhode Island, 1877-1952.* Montreal: Imprimeries
Populaire Limitee, 1952.
St. John the Baptist, West Warwick:
"St. John the Baptist Church, West Warwick, Rhode Island:
Faith and Sacrifice Build a Parish," Hackensack, N.J.:
Custombook, 1974.
St. John the Evangelist, Slatersville:
"St. John's Centennial, 1872-1972." Privately printed, 1972.
St. Joseph's, Newport:
Greene, John H., Jr. "The Story of Early Catholicism in
Newport and History of Saint Joseph's Parish." St. Joseph's
Church, Reference Book, Newport, Rhode Island, 1935.
St. Joseph's, Providence:
[Reilly, James F. and F. J.]. "Souvenir Booklet
Commemorating the One Hundredth Anniversary of the
Founding of St. Joseph's Parish, Hope Street, Providence,
Rhode Island, 1851-1951." Privately printed, 1951.
St. Joseph's, West Warwick:
"St. Joseph's Church, West Warwick, R. I.: 100th
Anniversary, 1873–1973." Privately printed, 1973.
St. Mary's, Bristol:
Goff, Frederick T. "St. Mary's Church, Bristol, Rhode
Island, May 11, 1869—May 11, 1969: The First One
Hundred Years." Privately printed, 1969.
St. Mary's, Carolina:
"St. Mary's, Carolina: A Heritage of Holiness." Hackensack,
N. J.: Custombook, 1972.
St. Mary's, Newport:
"Golden Jubilee of the Church of the Holy Name of Mary,
Our Lady of the Isle, Newport, R. I., 1852-1902." Privately
printed, 1902.
St. Mary's, Pawtucket:
Cassidy, Thomas V. *Saint Mary Church of Pawtucket, Rhode*

Island: A Sesquicentenial Story, 1829–1979. Privately printed,
1979.

McKenna, John H. *The Centenary Story of Old St. Mary's,
Pawtucket, R. I., 1829–1929.* Providence: Providence Visitor
Press, 1929.

St. Mary's, Providence:
Streker, Joseph A. "Centennial Commemoration, St. Mary's
Parish, Broadway, Providence, Rhode Island, 1853-1953."
Privately printed, 1953.

St. Mary's, Warren:
"St. Mary of the Bay, Warren, R. I. July 19, 1970,
Dedication Day." Privately printed, 1970.

St. Michael's, Georgiaville:
Campbell, Paul, *et al.* "St. Michael's Church, Georgiaville,
Rhode Island: A Century of Faith and Sacrifice, 1875-1975."
Privately printed, 1975.

St. Michael's, Providence:
Ferland, Oscar R. "One Hundred Years, St. Michael's
Parish, Providence, Rhode Island, 1859–1959." Privately
printed, 1959.

Notre Dame, Central Falls:
"Notre Dame Church, Central Falls, Rhode Island: The
Seed Has Grown to Harvest." Hackensack, N. J.:
Custombook, 1974.

Our Lady of Mercy, East Greenwich:
"Our Lady of Mercy Parish Celebrates One Hundred and
Five Years of Growth in Christ's Love and Truth,
1867-1972." Privately printed, 1972.

Sacred Heart, East Providence:
Sullivan, Hazel, *et al.* "In the Hand of the Lord: Sacred
Heart Parish Centennial, 1876–1976." Privately printed,
1976.

St. Patrick's, Providence:
McGeough, Jude. "St. Patrick's Parish, 1841-1973: A Brief
History." Privately printed, 1973.

SS. Peter and Paul Cathedral, Providence:
Campbell, Annie E. "The Souvenir of the Consecration: SS.
Peter and Paul's Cathedral." Providence: J. A. & R. A. Reid,
1889.

SS. Peter and Paul, West Warwick:
"SS. Peter and Paul, Phenix, Rhode Island, 1974: Parish
Directory." Privately printed, 1974.

322 Catholicism in Rhode Island

Precious Blood, Woonsocket:
> [Cichon, Joseph A., Jr.]. "Church of the Precious Blood: A
> Century of Change and Growth." Hackensack, N. J.:
> Custombook, Inc., 1975.

Massachusetts

St. Anne's, Fall River:
> Lachance, Pierre. "St. Anne's Centennial, 1869-1969."
> Privately printed, 1969.

St. John the Baptist, New Bedford:
> "St. John the Baptist Church: The First Portuguese Church
> in the United States, 1871-1971." Privately printed, 1971.

St. Lawrence, New Bedford:
> "Consecration of St. Lawrence Church, 1953." Privately
> printed, 1953.

St. Mary's Cathedral, Fall River:
> "St. Mary's Cathedral, Fall River, Massachusetts: Centennial
> Observance, 1838-1938." Privately printed, 1938.

St. Mary's, Taunton:
> Murphy, Maydell. "All in the Family: An Informal Sketch of
> St. Mary's Parish, 1828-1958." Privately printed, 1959.

Notre Dame, Fall River:
> Magnan, D. M. A. *Notre-Dame de Lourdes De Fall River, Mass.*
> Quebec, 1925.

SS. Peter and Paul, Fall River:
> "SS. Peter & Paul Parish, Fall River, Massachusetts, On the
> Occasion of the Dedication of the New Church and Parish
> Center, April 27, 1975." Privately printed, 1975.

St. Peter's (later Corpus Christi), Sandwich:
> Bourgoin, Raymond B. *The Catholic Church in Sandwich, 1830-
> 1930.* Boston: E. L. Grimes Publishing Co., 1930.

St. Peter's, Provincetown:
> "Church of St. Peter the Apostle, Provincetown,
> Massachusetts: The First Hundred Years, 1874-1974."
> Privately printed, 1974.

Selected Works

Adams, William F. *Ireland and Irish Immigration to the New World
from 1815 to the Famine.* New Haven: Yale University Press,
1932.

Arnold, Samuel Greene. *History of the State of Rhode Island and Providence Plantations.* 2 vols. 2nd ed. New York: D. Appleton & Co., 1874.

Bartlett, John Russell, ed. *Records of the Colony of Rhode Island and Providence Plantations in New England.* 10 vols. Providence, R. I. 1856-1865. Reprinted by A M S Press, New York, 1968.

Bayles, Richard M., ed. *History of Providence County, Rhode Island.* 2 vols. New York: W. W. Preston & Co., 1891.

Billington, Ray Allen. *The Protestant Crusade, 1800–1860: A Study of Origins of American Nativism.* New York: The Macmillan Co., 1938.

Biographical Cyclopedia of Representative Men of Rhode Island. Providence: National Biographical Publishing Co. 1881.

Bonier, Marie Louise. *Débuts de la Colonie Franco-Américaine de Woonsocket, Rhode Island.* Framingham, MA: Lakeview Press, 1920.

Bonsal, Stephen. *When the French were Here: A Narrative of the Sojourn of the French Forces in America and Their Contributions to the Yorktown Campaign, Drawn from Unpublished Reports and Letters of Participants in the National Archives of France and the M. S. Division of the Library of Congress.* New York: Doubleday, Doran & Co., 1945.

Bradley, Francis J. *A Brief History of the Diocese of Fall River, Mass.* Privately printed, 1931.

Brennan, Joseph. *Social Conditions in Industrial Rhode Island, 1820-1860.* Washington: Catholic University of America Press, 1940.

Byrne, Stephen. *Irish Emigration to the United States.* New York: The Catholic Publication Society, 1873.

Byrne, William, *et al. History of the Catholic Church in the New England States.* 2 vols. Boston: Hurd and Everts Co., 1899.

Carroll, Charles. *Public Education in Rhode Island.* Providence, R. I.: E. L. Freeman Co., 1918.

————. *Rhode Island: Three Centuries of Democracy.* 4 vols. New York: Lewis Historical Publishing Co., Inc., 1932.

[Carroll, Mary Theresa Austin]. *Leaves from the Annals of the Sisters of Mercy.* Vol. III. New York: The Catholic Publishing Society Co., 1889.

Chaffin, William L. *History of the Town of Easton, Massachusetts.* Cambridge: John Wilson & Son, 1886.

Chandonnet, T. A. *Notre Dame des Canadiens et les Canadiens aux Etats Unis.* Montreal, P.Q.: Desbarats, 1872.

Chastellux, Marquis de. *Travels in North America in the Years 1780, 1781 and 1782.* A revised translation with introduction and notes by Howard C. Rice, Jr. 2 vols. Chapel Hill: University of North Carolina Press, 1963.

Chyet, Stanley F. *Lopez of Newport.* Detroit: Wayne State University Press, 1970.

Clarke, Richard H. *Lives of the Deceased Bishops of the Catholic Church in the United States.* 4 vols. Published by the author, 1887-1889.

Clarkin, Harold E. "Pioneer Catholicism: The Life and Time of Father Edward Murphy, 1840-1877." A paper read before the Fall River Historical Society, May 16, 1949.

Cole, J. R. *History of Washington and Kent Counties.* New York: W. W. Preston & Co., 1889.

Coleman, Peter J. *The Transformation of Rhode Island, 1790–1860.* Providence: Brown University Press, 1969.

Conley, Patrick T. "Rhode Island Constitutional Development, 1636–1841: Prologue to the Dorr Rebellion." Unpublished doctural dissertation, University of Notre Dame, 1970.

Conley, Patrick T. and Matthew J. Smith. *Catholicism in Rhode Island: The Formative Era.* Providence: Diocese of Providence, 1976.

Craig, Wheelock, *et al. History of the Churches of New Bedford.* New Bedford: E. Anthony and Sons, 1869.

Cullen, Thomas F. *The Catholic Church in Rhode Island.* Providence: The Fransican Missionaries of Mary, 1936.

————. "William Barber Tyler, 1806-1849, First Bishop of Hartford, Connecticut." Paper read at the Seventeenth Annual Meeting of the American Catholic Historical Association. December 29, 1936. Providence, Rhode Island. *Catholic Historical Review,* XXIII (April 1937), 17-30.

D'Amato, Donald A. "William Sprague, Rhode Island's Enigmatic Governor and Senator." Unpublished masters thesis, University of Rhode Island, 1956.

D'Arcy, William. *The Fenian Movement in the United States, 1858–1886.* Washington: Catholic University of America Press, 1947.

Denison, Frederick. *Shot and Shell: The Third Rhode Island Heavy Artillery Regiment in the Rebellion, 1861-1865.* Providence, 1879.

Dillon, James F., comp. *Dillon's Catholic Directory of Fall River and Vicinity Including a History of the Church in Fall River and Vicinity up to the Time of Publication.* Fall River, MA., 1894.

Dubuque, H. A. *Le Guide Canadien-Francais de Fall River et Notes Historiques sur les Canadiens de Fall River.* Fall River, MA., 1888.

Duggan, Thomas S. *The Catholic Church in Connecticut.* New York: The States History Co., 1930.

Fenner, Henry M. *History of Fall River.* New York: F. T. Smiley Publishing Co., 1906.

Field, Edward, ed. *State of Rhode Island and Providence Plantations at the End of the Century: A History.* 3 vols. Boston & Syracuse: The Mason Publishing Co., 1902.

Fitton, James. *Sketches of the Establishment of the Catholic Church in New England.* Boston: Patrick Donahue, 1877.

Fitzgerald, Albeus John. "A History of the Christian Brothers' Schools in Rhode Island." Unpublished masters thesis, Manhattan College, N. Y., 1954.

Fowler, Orin. *History of Fall River with Notices of Freetown and Tiverton.* Fall River: Almy & Milne, 1862.

Fuller, Oliver Payson. *The History of Warwick.* Providence: Angell, Burlingame & Co., 1875.

Goldstein, Sidney and Kurt Meyer. *The People of Rhode Island.* Providence, R. I.: Planning Division, Rhode Island Development Council, 1963.

Goodrich, Massena. *Historical Sketch of the Town of Pawtucket.* Pawtucket: Nickerson, Sibley & Co., 1876.

Greene, Welcome Arnold, *et al. The Providence Plantations for Two Hundred and Fifty Years.* Providence: J. A. & R. A. Reid, Publishers and Printers, 1886.

Grieve, Robert. *An Illustrated History of Pawtucket, Central Falls and Vicinity.* Pawtucket: Pawtucket Gazette and Chronicle, 1897.

Guilday, Peter. *A History of the Councils of Baltimore, 1791-1884.* New York: The Macmillan Co., 1932.

Hadcock, Editha. "Labor Problems in Rhode Island Cotton Mills." Unpublished doctoral dissertation, Brown University, 1945.

Hamon, E. *Les Canadiens-Francais de la Nouvelle Angleterre.* Quebec: N. S. Hardy, 1891.

Handlin, Oscar. *Boston's Immigrants: A Study in Acculturation.* Revised and enlarged edition. New York: Atheneum, 1968.

Harpin, Mathias. *Trumpets in Jericho.* West Warwick, R. I.: Commercial Printing and Publishing Co., 1961.

Harvey, George. *North Smithfield Centennial, 1666-1971.* Privately printed, 1971.

Healy, Kathleen. *Frances Warde: American Founder of the Sisters of Mercy.* New York: The Seabury Press, 1973.

Herron, Eulalia. "The Work of the Sisters of Mercy in the United States." *Records of the American Catholic Historical Society of Philadelphia.* XXXIII (1922), 144-92.

Keehan, Martha Julie. "The Irish Catholic Beneficial Societies Founded Between 1818-1869." Unpublished masters thesis. Catholic University of America, 1953.

Keim, DeB. Randolph. *Rochambeau: A Commemoration by the Congress of the United States of America of the Services of the French Auxiliary Forces in the War of Independence.* Washington: Government Printing Office, 1907.

Kelly, Raymond M. "The Pastoral and Circular Letters of the Diocese of Providence, 1872-1958: A Bibliographical Index with Annotations." Unpublished masters thesis. Catholic University of America, 1963.

Kenneally, Finbar. *United States Documents in the Propaganda Fide Archives: A Calender.* First Series. 6 vols. Washington, D. C.: Academy of American Franciscan History, 1966–1975.

Kennedy, Ambrose. *Quebec to New England: The Life of Monsignor Charles Dauray.* Boston: Bruce Humphries, Inc., 1948.

Kervick, Francis W. "Patrick Charles Keely, Architect: A Record of His Life and Work." South Bend, Indiana: Privately printed, 1953.

Kirk, William. *A Modern City: Providence, Rhode Island and Its Activities.* Chicago: The University of Chicago Press, 1909.

Lapati, Americo D. "A History of Catholic Education in Rhode Island." Unpublished doctoral dissertation, Boston College, 1958.

Lemieux, Lucien. *L'Establissement de la Premiere Province Ecclesiastique au Canada, 1783-1844.* Montreal: Fides, 1968.

Le Prohon, Edward P. "Memorial to the Rt. Rev. William Tyler, First Bishop of Hartford, Connecticut." Translated by Rev. J. M. Toohey from the original French. *American Catholic Historical Researches,* Vol. 12, 1895.

Lord, Robert H., John E. Sexton and Edward T. Harrington. *History of the Archdiocese of Boston in the Various States of Its Development, 1604 to 1943.* 3 vols. New York: Sheed & Ward, 1944.

Loughran, Mary Christopher. "The Development of the Church in the City of Fall River from the Beginning until 1904." Unpublished masters thesis, Catholic University of America, 1932.

McColgan, Daniel T. *A Century of Charity: The First One Hundred Years of the Society of St. Vincent de Paul in the United States.* 2 vols. Milwaukee: The Bruce Publishing Co., 1951.

McPartland, Martha R. *The History of East Greenwich, Rhode Island, 1677–1960, with Related Genealogy.* East Greenwich, R. I.: East Greenwich Free Library Association, 1960.

Maroney, M. Josephine. "Catholic Church History: A Story of Faith." *The Pawtucket Times Historical Magazine,* October 8, 1921.

Mason, George Champlin. *Reminiscences of Newport.* Newport: Charles E. Hammett, Jr., 1884.

Mayer, Kurt B. *Economic Development and Population Growth in Rhode Island.* Providence: Brown University Press, 1953.

Mayer, Kurt B. and Sidney Goldstein. *Migration and Economic Development in Rhode Island.* Providence: Brown University Press, 1958.

Melville, Annabelle M. *Jean Lefebvre Cheverus, 1768-1836.* Milwaukee: The Bruce Publishing Co., 1958.

Metropolitan Catholic Almanac and Laity's Directory. Baltimore, 1839-1857.

Metropolitan Catholic Almanac and Laity's Directory for the United States. Baltimore, 1860-1861.

[Morgan, Catherine]. *Mercy, A Little Sketch of the Work of the Sisters of Mercy in Providence, Rhode Island, from 1851-1893.* Providence: F. A. & R. A. Reid, 1893.

Nelson, Mary Cobb. "The Influence of Immigration on Rhode Island Politics, 1865-1910." Unpublished doctoral dissertation, Harvard University, 1954.

Newman, Sylvanus Chase. *A Numbering of the Inhabitants: Together with Statistical and Other Information, Relative to Woonsocket, R. I.* Woonsocket: Printed by S. S. Foss, 1846.

O'Donnell, James H. *History of the Diocese of Hartford.* Boston: The D. H. Hurd Co., 1900.

Payne, Abraham. *Reminiscences of the Rhode Island Bar.* Providence: Tibbets & Preston, 1885.

Pease, John C. and John M. Niles. *A Gazetteer of the States of Connecticut and Rhode Island.* Hartford: William S. Marsh, 1819.

Pease, Zepaniah W., ed. *History of New Bedford.* 2 vols. New Bedford, 1906.

Peck, Henry J. *200th Anniversary of Warren, Rhode Island.* The Town of Warren, 1947.

Pesaturo, Ubaldo U. M. *The Italo-Americans in Rhode Island: Their Contributions and Achievements.* Privately printed by the author, 1936. Revised edition, 1940.

Podea, Iris S. "Quebec to 'Little Canada:' The Coming of the French Canadians to New England." *New England Quarterly,* XXIII (1950), 365-380.

Potter, George. *To the Golden Door: The Story of the Irish in Ireland and America.* Boston: Little, Brown and Co., 1960.

Preston, Howard W. *Rhode Island's Historic Background.* Providence: Rhode Island Tercentenary Commission, 1936.

Providence Directory Containing the Names of the Inhabitants, Their Occupations, Places of Business and of Residence . . . Providence: H. H. Brown, 1850.

Raber, Lawrence Bruce. "The Formation and Early Development

of the Republican Party in Rhode Island, 1850–1865." Unpublished masters thesis, University of Rhode Island, 1965.

Rand, Larry Anthony. "The Know-Nothing Party in Rhode Island: Religious Bigotry and Political Success." *Rhode Island History,* XXIII (July 1964), 102-116.

Ray, John M. "Anti-Catholicism and Know-Nothingism in Rhode Island." *American Ecclesiastical Review,* CXLVIII (January 1963), 27-36.

Reuss, Francis X. *Biographical Cyclopedia of the Catholic Hierarchy of the United States, 1784-1898.* Milwaukee: M. H. Wiltzius & Co., 1898.

Rice, Howard C., Jr. and Anne S. K. Brown, ed. *The American Campaigns of Rochambeau's Army, 1780, 1781, 1782, 1783.* Vol. I: *The Journals of Clermont-Crevecoeur, Verger and Berthier.* Jointly printed. Providence: Brown University Press and Princeton: Princeton University Press, 1972.

Riley, Arthur J. *Catholicism in New England to 1788.* Washington: Catholic University of America Press, 1936.

Robitaille, Georges. "L'Expansion religieuse des Canadiens Francais aux Etats-Unis." in G. Lanctot *Les Canadiens Francais et leurs Voisins du Sud,* Montreal, 1941.

Roemer, Theodore. *Ten Decades of Alms.* St. Louis and London: B. Herder Book Co., 1942.

Rooney, James A. "Early Times in the Diocese of Hartford, Conn., 1829-1874." *The Catholic Historical Review,* I (April 1915—January 1916).

Rothan, Emmet H. *The German Catholic Immigrant in the United States, 1830-1860.* Washington: Catholic University of America, 1946.

Rumilly, Robert. *Histoire des Franco-Americains.* Published by L'Union Saint-Jean-Baptiste D'Amerique, 1958.

Rushowski, Leo F. *French Emigré Priests in the United States, 1791–1815.* Washington: Catholic University of America Press, 1940.

Ryan, T. E. *Burrillville, R. I. and the Catholic Church.* Providence: By the author, n.d., *ca.* 1925.

Sadlier's Catholic Almanac and Ordo. New York. 1864-1886.

Shannon, William V. *The American Irish.* Macmillan Company, 1969.

Shearer, Donald S. *Pontificia Americana: A Documentary History of the Catholic Church in the United States, 1794–1884.* Washington: Catholic University of America Press, 1933.

Silvia, Philip T. "The Spindle City: Labor, Politics and Religion in Fall River, Massachusetts, 1870-1905." Unpublished doctoral dissertation, Fordham University, 1973.

Smyth, James W. *History of the Catholic Church in Woonsocket and Vicinity from the Celebration of the First Mass in 1828 to the Present Time.* Woonsocket: Charles E. Cook, Printer, 1903.

Snow, Edwin M. *Report Upon the Census of Rhode Island.* Providence: Providence Press Co., 1877.

————, comp. *Census of the City of Providence Taken in July, 1855 . . . and an Appendix Giving an Account of Previous Enumerations of the Population of Providence.* 2nd ed. Providence: Knowles, Anthony & Co., 1856.

Staples, William R. *Annals of the Town of Providence.* Providence: Knowles and Vose, 1843.

Stone, Edwin M. *Our French Allies.* Providence: The Providence Press Company, 1884.

Vaillant, P. U. "Notes Biographiques sur l'Abbe P. J. B. Bedard, Le Pretre Patriote, Fondateur de la Paroisse Notre Dame de Lourdes a Fall River." Fall River, MA, 1886.

Wade, Mason, "The French Parish and *Survivance* in Nineteenth Century New England." *Catholic Historical Review,* XXXVII (July 1950), 163-69.

Ware, Caroline F. *Early New England Cotton Manufacture.* Boston and New York: Houghton Mifflin, 1931.

Wellen, Jean-Edmond. *Rochambeau, Father and Son: A Life of the Marechal de Rochambeau and The Journal of the Vicomte de Rochambeau.* Translated by Lawrence Lee. New York: Henry Holt and Co., 1936.

Wheeler, Robert A. "Fifth Ward Irish: Immigrant Mobility in Providence 1850-1870." *Rhode Island History,* XXXII (May 1973), 53–61.

Williams, Alfred M. and William F. Blanding, ed. *Men of Progress: Biographical Sketches and Portraits of Leaders in Business and Professional Life in the State of Rhode Island and Providence Plantations.* Boston: New England Magazine, 1896.

Wilson, Arthur E. *Paddy Wilson's Meeting-House in Providence Plantations, 1791-1839.* Boston: The Pilgrim Press, 1950.

Index

Hendricken *(cont.)*
263–81, 284–87, 290–93, 295,
297–300, 304, 306–13
Hendricken family, 197
Henniss, Rev. Henry E. S., 215,
218
Herald, 78
Hibernian Hall (Westerly), 249
Hibernian Orphans Society, 39,
102
Hibernian Relief Society, 39
High Street (Providence), 27,
33, 114, 262, 306–307
Highland Street (Warwick), 170
Holme's Hole (Martha's Vine-
yard), 218
Holy Cross Church, 14
Holy Cross College, 70, 92, 205,
256, 258
Holy Family Church (Taunton,
Mass), 225
Holy Name of Jesus (East
Greenwich), 114, 171
Holy Name Parish (Providence)
249, 311
Holy Name Society, 249, 291–92
Holy Trinity Church (Harwich,
Mass.), 228–29
Home of the Aged (Pawtucket),
261
Hope Street (Bristol), 253
Hope Street (Providence), 16,
104–106
Hoppin, William, 131
Hornsby, Thomas, 5
House of Mercy (Newport), 101,
108
Howard (Cranston), 236, 297
Howard Hall (Providence), 84
Hughes, Archbishop John, 46,
47, 141, 146–47, 178, 263
Hughes, Rev. Christopher, 174,
246–47, 292

Hughes, Rev. Henry, B. M.,
243
Hughes, Rev. James, 106, 127,
139, 160, 162–63, 171, 192,
250
Hunter Street (Fall River), 221
Hye, Francis, 27–29

I

Immaculate Conception Church
(Fall River), 254, 268, 274
Immaculate Conception Church
(North Easton, Mass.), 226,
291
Immaculate Conception Church
(North Providence), 158–59,
166, 211
Immaculate Conception Church
(Pawtucket), 109
Immaculate Conception Church
(Providence), 249, 251
Immaculate Conception Church
(Taunton), 255
Immaculate Conception Church
(Westerly), 249
Independence Hall (Warren),
253
India Point (Providence), 32,
118, 207
Infant Asylum (Providence),
128–30
Insane Hospital, 63
Irish, 9, 12–14, 17–19, 24, 26–
27, 29, 32, 36, 39–40, 46, 77,
79–82, 92–93, 95, 97, 101,
105–106, 115, 120, 122–24,
139, 141, 146, 148, 153, 155,
169, 179, 182–83, 188, 203,
211, 214, 222–23, 228, 233,
235–36, 246, 255, 265, 267,